EARLY EGYPTIAN
CHRISTIANITY

COPTIC STUDIES

EDITED BY

MARTIN KRAUSE

IN CONJUNCTION WITH

Antoine Guillaumont - Rodolphe Kasser - Pahor Labib
Hans-Jakob Polotsky - Torgny Säve-Söderbergh
Robert McL. Wilson - Dwight W. Young

VOLUME 2

EARLY EGYPTIAN CHRISTIANITY

FROM ITS ORIGINS TO 451 C.E.

BY

C. WILFRED GRIGGS

SECOND EDITION

E.J. BRILL

LEIDEN · NEW YORK · KØBENHAVN · KÖLN
1991

The paper in this book meets the guidelines for permanence and durability of the Committee on Production Guidelines for Book Longevity of the Council on Library Resources.

First edition 1990 (cloth)

Illustration on cover from P. van Moorsel et al., *The central church of Abdallah Nirqi*, Leiden, Brill, 1975.

Library of Congress Cataloging-in-Publication Data

Griggs, C. Wilfred
    Early Egyptian Christianity: from its origins to 451 C.E. / by C.
Wilfred Griggs.
        p.   cm.—(Coptic studies, ISSN 0167-5818; v. 2)
    Bibliography: p.
    Includes index.
    ISBN 90-04-09159-9
    ISBN 90-04-09407-5 (pbk).
    1. Egypt—Church history. 2. Church history—Primitive and early
church. ca. 30-600. I. Title. II. Series
BR190.G75   1989
276.2'01—dc20   89-9723
                                                               CIP

                            ISSN   0167-5818
                            ISBN   90 04 09407 5

TABLE OF CONTENTS

Preface..*vi*

Introduction..1

   I. The Diffusion of Early Christianity: An Appraisal...........3

  II. Early Christianity in Egypt...............................13

 III. The Emergence of Orthodoxy and Heresy in Egyptian
      Christianity..45

 IV. Egyptian Christianity in the Third Century: The Development
      of Local Christianity.................................79

  V. The Fourth Century: Schisms and Consolidation..........117

 VI. Autocracy in Christian Egypt and the Separation from
      Catholicism 171

Epilogue 229

Bibliography..233

Indices 251

Maps...275

PREFACE

Discoveries of manuscripts in Egypt during the past century, especially those directly related to the establishment and development of the Christian religion in that country, coupled with the continual advance of archaeological discoveries, necessitate an evaluation of Early Egyptian Christianity. The evidence now available to the investigator not only suggests the time and manner by which Christianity was introduced along the Nile, but also indicates that early Egyptian Christians were not bound by a centralized ecclesiastical organization nor did they have a stringent and well-defined doctrinal tradition.

Biblical and non-biblical manuscripts signify an early arrival of Christians in Egypt, perhaps as early as the middle of the first century. Traditional Christian historical sources, beginning with Eusebius, are shown to describe the introduction of nascent Catholic Christianity into Egypt near the end of the second century, which resulted in an increasingly tense struggle between the two types of Christianity during the succeeding centuries. Part of the tension was overcome by the gradual absorption of local Christian groups and institutions into the Catholic organization in the third and early fourth centuries. Although monasticism arose as a fresh expression of Egyptian Christianity during the third century, the effort of strong Catholic bishops in Alexandria resulted in keeping monasticism from becoming entirely separated from Catholic Ecclesiasticism. Athanasius, Theophilus, and Cyril are especially noteworthy as examples of those who struggled to maintain an alliance between the monks and the bishops. The emergence of strong personalities both in the bishops of Alexandria and the monastic leaders during the fourth and fifth centuries led to an alliance of those two organizations, and this unity provided a strong organizational base upon which a national Christian church could be built.

The fourth century not only marked the generally successful efforts of the Alexandrian bishops to bring all Egyptian Christianity effectively, not just theoretically, under their control, but also signalled the growing influence of the see of Constantinople, the new Eastern capital city of the Empire, at the expense of the prestige which Alexandria customarily enjoyed in the East. The competition between the two cities over leadership of the Eastern Christian churches was exacerbated by Canon III of the Council of

Constantinople in 381, which established Constantinople as second only to Rome in ecclesiastical affairs. Alexandria had also experienced lengthy doctrinal disputes with Antioch, and the appointments of Antiochenes to the bishopric of Constantinople during the late fourth and early fifth centuries were added blows to the Egyptian archbishop's influence and authority outside Egypt. Theophilus' overthrow of Origenist theology in favor of the anti-Origenist position taken by the majority of the monastic communities in the late fourth century further alienated Alexandria from other Eastern sees.

The majority of the Egyptian Christian leaders and their followers were increasingly separated from Christianity elsewhere in the Mediterranean region and, coupled with the increasingly unified organization of Christians within Egypt, this led naturally, if not inevitably, to the reshaping of Egyptian Christianity into a national Egyptian church as a result of the Council of Chalcedon in 451 C.E. Intransigent leaders were unable to modify or compromise their political and religious differences at that Council, and the separation which was already a reality by that time was formalized then and led to the development of the Egyptian Christian Church during the next century.

INTRODUCTION

The history of the introduction and early development of Christianity in Egypt has not been maligned so much as ignored. This neglect might not be unexpected or unjustified were it not for the two following observations. First, the history of Early Christianity is of continuing significance and interest to a sizable portion of the world's population, both to those who profess attachment to some manner and measure of Christian beliefs, and to those in the occident who are interested in the development of the Western religious and philosophical traditions. Second, during the last century Egypt has been a major site for discovering thousands of manuscripts which were written or copied during the first few centuries of the Christian era, and those which relate to Christianity would be expected to provide a substantial documentary basis from which to study Early Egyptian Christianity. Despite these considerations, to the present time the study of the arrival of Christians and the subsequent development of their faith along the Nile has dealt with the manuscript discoveries only in haphazard fashion, and with Early Egyptian Christianity only as being in the periphery of Christian history before the time of Clement of Alexandria.

The present study focuses on the history of Christianity in Egypt from its earliest recorded origins to the Council of Chalcedon in 451 C.E., when the Egyptian Coptic Church became a national religion because of its separation from Catholic Christianity. Within this time period one can observe the development of features unique to Egyptian Christianity, the imposition of Catholic ecclesiasticism in Alexandria and southward, and the presence of forces which would lead to the establishment of a national religion. Increased understanding of Early Egyptian Christian history will enhance one's ability to assess the manner in which that religion was dispersed in other countries where documentation is presently much more scanty and less satisfactory. This study also will contribute to a greater comprehension of the general history of Early Christianity.

Special thanks are due to Professor Dr. Dr. Martin Krause, editor of the series in which this volume appears, for patience and encouragement while the text underwent revisions and, hopefully, improvements in the decade since its first appearance. Cecelia Mahoney also read the penultimate copy and made many helpful observations and suggestions for improvement. Mrs. Connie Gaither typed the manuscript, preventing many errors and mistakes from continuing into the final copy. Mrs. Patricia Ward also assisted in the preparation of the final copy of the text and the production of the indices. Mrs. Lucinda Smith gave detailed and devoted attention to the typesetting of the manuscript at the Brigham Young University Press. Stephen Griggs produced the maps of Christian Egypt which occurs at the end of the book, and Kent Griggs assisted with the indices and proofreading.

The author's debts to those whose works and ideas provided the background and evidence used in this study are immense. Gratitude is cheerfully given, with the attendant recognition that responsibility for the errors which remain, as well as for the views and opinions expressed, belongs to the author.

C. Wilfred Griggs
Thanksgiving, 1988

CHAPTER I

THE DIFFUSION OF EARLY CHRISTIANITY: AN APPRAISAL

Christianity was a proselytizing religion from the time of John the Baptist, who preached and challenged the Jews to repent and be baptized in preparation for the imminently expected Messiah.[1] The Gospels recount the calling of disciples by Jesus relatively soon after His baptism,[2] and they were sent as His emmissaries to the various regions of Palestine (except Samaria) to announce His arrival and proclaim the requirements for the Jews to enter the Kingdom of God.[3] Although some proselytes were made from among the Samaritans and Gentiles,[4] and notwithstanding the enlarged scope of missionary endeavors among non-Jews indicated at the close of the Synoptic Gospels,[5] missionary journeys by the Christian Apostles to countries beyond Palestine do not appear to have been undertaken for more than a decade after Jesus' death.

At the beginning of the book of Acts, Jesus commanded the Apostles to remain in Jerusalem until they received a spiritual endowment of power, which is recorded as taking place some two months after the crucifixion.[6] This experience was to signal the commencement of a ministry which would begin in Jerusalem and move outward ἐν πάσῃ τῇ Ἰουδαίᾳ καὶ Σαμαρείᾳ καὶ ἕως ἐσχάτου τῆς γῆς [7] (throughout Judea and Samaria and to the end of the earth). While some disciples were scattered to Samaria and Damascus during the next three years or so because of persecution,[8] there is no extant record historically acceptable to modern scholars which chronicles any early missionary journeys of apostles to lands outside Palestine, with the notable exception of Saul of Tarsus, recorded in the book of Acts.[9] After his own remarkable conversion experience just outside Damascus,[10] Saul began preaching his newly found faith in Jewish synagogues until his erstwhile associates plotted his death.[11] His subsequent three-year flight to Arabia had long been thought by later biographers to encompass a period of meditation portending the future monastic movement in Christianity, even as was supposedly the case earlier with both John the Baptist and Jesus being in the desert for extended periods of time. Nevertheless, F. F. Bruce suggests that the three years in Arabia were likely years of missionary or proselyting activity, and that Saul's well-known capacity for wearing out his welcome may have led to his falling into disfavor with the Nabataean authorities (esp. the ethnarch of the Nabataean king, Aretas).[12]

The so-called First Missionary Journey of Saul (who is henceforth designated as Paul as soon as he embarks on the gentile-oriented aspect of his life[13]) did not occur until nearly a decade after his departure from Damascus to Jerusalem three years after his conversion. Thus the injunction of Jesus "to go to all the world" was not immediately fulfilled, especially in the limited account contained in the New Testament.

The book of Acts, the only extant attempt at historical narrative during the Apostolic period, continues to outline the major missionary activities of Paul as he journeyed through the Roman provinces, especially Cilicia, Galatia, Asia, Macedonia, and Achaea. Acts ends with Paul's journey to Rome, where the Apostle was to present his appeal before the tribunal of Nero. The title of the book, "Acts of the Apostles," is thus only symbolically represented in the contents, for the opening Apostolic ministry is epitomized in the deeds of Peter and John, and the later missionary activity in the travels of Paul.

> "Rome is the goal toward which the whole of Acts tends. The Gospel spread out from Palestine in every direction, but the direction in which Luke is interested is the road that leads to Rome. Hence he emphasizes the rise of Gentile evangelization, the Holy Spirit's choice of Paul and Barnabas for this work, the spread of the Gospel through Asia Minor to Europe, and at last the chain of events by which Paul achieves his long-conceived desire to see Rome. As Rome draws near, the interest quickens, and the climax is reached when Paul is established at the heart of the Empire . . ."[14]

While no evidence can be cited to prove that this symbolic representation of Acts for all the Apostolic ministry was followed by a similar symbolic representation of the Apostolic writings by those collecting and defining the New Testament canon, one may note that the epistles and the Apocalypse fit within the same geographical and, for the most part, historical limitations observed in Acts. All the epistles associated with Paul, including Hebrews and the Pastorals, which are not generally thought to be Pauline, must be placed somewhere along "the road that leads to Rome" from Jerusalem. The Epistles of James and Jude are the most difficult among the so-called General Epistles to place in a geographical context, but Palestine and Syria are re-garded as likely possibilities.[15] The origin of the two Petrine and three Johannine epistles is somewhat more securely placed in Asia Minor, and the Apocalypse, with its brief addresses to seven churches of Asia Minor in chapters two and three, certainly belongs to this region. Goodspeed suggested that the publication of Luke's works influenced an Ephesian Christian to undertake a collection of Paul's letters from the Pauline churches mentioned in Acts, and he is followed more recently by others.[16] Harnack[17] preferred Corinth as the city where the collection was first made, and that position has also been taken more recently by Schmithals.[18] Not only is the Pauline collection often thought to have influenced the collection of the other New Testament writings, but Goodspeed argued that the Pauline corpus established the letter as the "favorite form of Christian literary expression" from Rome to Syria.[19] Evidence cited in favor of this position includes the seven letters of Ignatius of Antioch, the letters of Polycarp and Barnabas, and the Epistle of the Apostles. The writings in the New Testament, therefore, are not only limited in their geographical origin and scope, but also tend to define a limited literary tradition followed by later Christian writers from the same area. This observa-tion does not compel one to conclude that these writings were not known elsewhere in the Christian world by the second century (for indeed they were), nor that different genres of Christian literature were unknown to the churches from Asia Minor to Rome during the same period (many are in fact mentioned), but the acceptance of or preference for writings in the epistolary tradition in a developing canon would be naturally expected. The evidence of Eusebius is significant on this point, for the only books even considered in his categories of τὰ ὁμολογούμενα, τὰ ἀντιλεγόμενα, and τὰ νόθα (the accepted, the disputed, and the spurious), are those associated with the authors of New Testament writings or the geography of the book of Acts.[20] Even among these, Eusebius is quite willing to place the Apoca-lypse among the spurious books as well as in the recognized group. This is likely because of an antipathy toward the apocalyptic genre of writings in the fourth century, which can be observed easily through a brief survey of its history in early Christianity.

Apocalypticism is well attested in the first-century Christian Church. Some have gone so far as to argue the importance of apoca-lypticism in early Chiristianity by claiming "that apocalyptic Judaism was the mother of all Christian theology."[21] The so-called Synoptic Apocalypse, found in various settings in Mark 13, Matthew 24, and Luke 21, is Apocalyptic in content, though the explicit visionary aspect is lacking. The transfiguration account in the Synoptic Gospels[22] can be interpreted as an Apocalyptic incident especially if seen against stock motives of recently-recovered Jewish and Christian Apocalypses and similar accounts of divine revelation. The transfiguration took place on a high mountain, the face of Jesus was changed and shone like the sun, a voice spoke from the cloud which overshadowed those present, Moses and Elijah appeared in glory (as interpreting angels, a common feature of such accounts), and the disciples were so frightened that they fell upon their faces.

The continuation and development of the Christian Apocalyptic tradition was well known among all sects of Christianity, especially the Gnostics who highly esteemed Paul not because he *followed* Christ, but because Christ *revealed* Himself to Paul. A number of references to Pauline visions exist in the New Testament,[23] some containing more details than others within the Apocalyptic genre. Although most of these accounts are very brief, often containing only a laconic Apocalyptic setting within which God's command to Paul is given, the visionary tradition is fully accepted and established in the Apostolic era.

Christian Apocalypticism is best seen in the Revelation of John, a fully-developed Apocalypse embodying many Jewish elements and some Christian adaptations. While one cannot argue with certainty that John borrowed from any one of the Jewish Apocalypses extant at the time, it is quite certain that he was well acquainted with the elements of visionary literature. John was caught up to heaven,[24] beheld the throne of God,[25] and while there saw the history of God's cosmos in true Apocalyptic fashion.[26] An *angelus interpres* gives the bulk of the revelation to John although Christ is obviously the central figure of the book.[27] Angelology is quite developed,[28] and the symbols of eschatology are found in abundance.[29]

The *Didache* and *The Shepherd of Hermas* deserve to be considered in a discussion of early Christian Apocalypticism, although the former exhibits Apocalyptic eschatology only in the closing chapter, similar in nature to the Synoptic Apocalypse mentioned above. *The Shepherd of Hermas* is more Apocalyptic in form than is the *Didache*, being a compilation of visions followed by a number of Mandates and Similitudes which are all given to Hermas through an *angelus interpres*, but the normal Apocalyptic content is absent. Both works date from the early second century, but for Christianity of the later second century and following (at least Christianity from Syria to Rome), the Apocalyptic tradition established by Christ and carried on by the Apostles was acknowledged to be past history.[30]

That Apocalyptic literature did not simply atrophy as a literary genre but suffered antagonism in the Graeco-Roman segment of Christianity can be ascertained in the case of *I Enoch* (Ethiopic). This work, accepted as inspired and canonical in many Jewish and Christian circles from the second century B.C.E., was quoted as scripture in Jude[31] and, according to Charles, "has had more influence on the New Testament than has any other apocryphal or pseudepigraphic work."[32] *I Enoch*, because of its Apocalyptic form and content, fell into disrepute through its rejection and ban by such Christian authorities as Hilary,[33] Jerome,[34] and Augustine.[35] From the fourth century onward, the Book of Enoch "passed out of circulation, and became lost to the knowledge of Western Christendom" until its rediscovery in the last century.[36]

Additional support for the observation made above that Western Christianity (defined here as Christianity in the Asia Minor-Greece-Rome sphere of influence) had not only a narrow geographical outlook, but also a limited literary tradition can be drawn from Eusebius. Beyond his categories of Recognized, Disputed, and Spurious works, the fourth century historian makes mention of other writings associated with the names of Apostles which he claims

> ὅθεν οὐδ' ἐν νόθοις αὐτὰ κατατακτέον, ἀλλ' ὡς ἄτοπα πάντῃ καὶ δυσσεβῆ παραιτητέον.[37]
>
> *Wherefore, one ought not even to classify them among the spurious (writings), but should reject them as entirely wicked and impious.*

Although a *Gospel of Peter* and an *Acts of John* are mentioned in a brief reference by Eusebius to heretical works, neither seems to be well known before Eusebius' time within the geographical range of the book of Acts. The *Gospel of Peter* was first found in modern times at Akhmim in upper Egypt with fragments of an *Apocalypse of Peter* and a Greek *Book of Enoch* (*I Enoch*), and some have suggested that the *Gospel* and the *Apocalypse of Peter* were originally part of the same work.[38] The first direct attestation of the *Acts of John* is the one in

Eusebius, but earlier indirect references are claimed by Schäferdiek to be found in Manichaean sources.[39] Ephraim, Patriarch of Antioch from 527 to 545, is quoted by Photius[40] as referring to "the Acts of the Beloved John and the Life which is used by not a few." This work also then appears to have found acceptance outside Western Christianity, but was rejected within it. The other writings mentioned by Eusebius in this context are associated with Apostles whose travels (according to apocryphal texts) took them to lands not associated with the New Testament's limited portrayal of the growth and spread of Christianity. Tradition had it that Thomas went to India,[41] Matthias to Ethiopia,[42] and Andrew to Scythia.[43] Although some of these works (and others doubtless implied but not specified by Eusebius—"and others also") were popular in diverse regions and were accepted as authoritative, Eusebius tells his audience

ὧν οὐδὲν οὐδαμῶς ἐν συγγράμματι τῶν κατὰ τὰς διαδοχὰς ἐκκλησιαστικῶν τις ἀνὴρ εἰς μνήμην ἀγαγεῖν ἠξίωσεν . . .[44]

of which not one did any man of those who succeeded in the orthodox church tradition think it proper to refer in his writings.

One might suggest that while some writings were rejected primarily because of teachings which were regarded to be heterodox, yet the wholesale rejection as heretical of those works which originated from or related to lands outside a limited geographical area indicates an early tendency toward geographical eclecticism. It is possible, even likely, that a careful examination of Early Christianity in other geographical areas will disclose similar tendencies based on different traditions and a modified literary development in history. Walter Bauer gives both a warning and a methodological challenge to anyone making such an examination:

1. The warning is that "even today the overwhelming dominant view still is that for the period of Christian origins, ecclesiastical doctrine (of course, only as this pertains to a certain stage in its development) already represents what is primary, while heresies, on the other hand, somehow are a deviation from the genuine. I do not mean to say that this point of view must be false, but neither can I regard it as self-evident, or even as demonstrated and clearly established."[45]

2. The challenge is to make the examination of early Christianity elsewhere in the same way that has been developed for Western Christianity. "We need to understand them also in terms of their own time, and not to evaluate them by means of ecclesiastical doctrine which was developing, or which later became a ready-made norm."[46]

ENDNOTES

[1] Mark 1:2–5; Matthew 3:1–3. In the latter reference, the Greek, Μετανοεῖτε, ἤγγικεν γὰρ ἡ βασιλεία τῶν οὐρανῶν, should be translated: "Be converted, for the Kingdom of the heavens has arrived."

[2] Mark 1:16ff.; Matthew 4:18ff.; Luke 5:4ff.; John 1:35ff. No attempt will be made here, to harmonize the chronology of the accounts, for recent scholarship has generally confirmed the position that the Gospels were not written as biographies in the traditional sense; rather, the authors selected and ordered their material according to their theological purposes. It is significant that modern scholars tend to regard the historicity of John's Gospel in a more favorable light than before. See e.g. R.E. Brown, "The Problem of Historicity in John," *New Testament Essays* (New York: Bruce Pub. Co., 1965), pp. 187–217, and Leon Morris, *Comment. on the Gospel of John* (Grand Rapids: Eerdmans Pub. Co., 1971), pp. 40–49.

[3] Matthew 10:5–6; 15:24.

[4] Luke 17:11–16; John 4:3–42; Mark 7:24–30; Matthew 8:5–13 (Cp. Luke 7:1–10 and John 4:46–54).

[5] Mark 16:15–18; Matthew 28:18–20; Luke 24:46–48. Although Mark's πορευθέντες εἰς τὸν κόσμον ἅπαντα emphasizes geography while Matthew and Luke use πάντα τὰ ἔθνη with its corresponding emphasis on people, there can be no question that this charge of Jesus to His disciples is meant to include the Gentiles as well as the Jews.

[6] Acts 1:6–8; 2:1–4. The modern trend in scholarship is away from accepting the historicity of Acts. See E.R. Goodenough, "The Perspective of Acts," *Studies in Luke-Acts* (Nashville: Abingdon Press, 1966), pp. 51–59, and Ernst Haenchen, "The Book of Acts as Source Material for the History of Early Christianity," *Studies, op. cit.*, pp. 258–278. While the non-historical view of Acts would strengthen the position taken in this study, even the acceptance of an historical origin for the episodes relating to the early history of the Christian Church emphasizes the lack of material relating to early Egyptian Christianity.

[7] Acts 1:8.

[8] Acts 8. The presence of Christians in Damascus is evident from Saul's journey to that city to arrest and punish members of that faith (Acts 9).

[9] This is not to say that no such literature exists, however, since much apocryphal literature associated with the names of the Apostles has been recovered during the past century, and many texts purport to give accounts of the missionary journeys of the Apostles to different lands. See in this regard *Acts of Thomas*, *Acts of John*, *Acts of Peter*, *Acts of Andrew*, etc. (R.A. Lipsius, *Acta Apostolorum Apocrypha*, 3 vols. Darmstadt: Wissenschaftliche Buchgesellschaft, 1959). These 'Acts' usually contain an account of a journey and the martyrdom of the Apostle, and they encompass a widespread geography as, for example, Thomas going to India. See also Hennecke and Schneemelcher, *New Testament Apocrypha* (Philadelphia: Westminster Press, (1964) vol. 2.

[10] Galatians 1:15–17; Acts 9:1–9. Cp. Acts 22:5–11 and 26:12–20.

[11] Acts 9:19–24.

[12] F.F. Bruce, *New Testament History* (New York: Doubleday and Co., Inc., 1972), pp. 242–243. On the problem of the relationship of Damascus to the Nabataean Kingdom, see A. Plummer, *Commentary on The Second Epistle of St. Paul to The Corinthians* (Edinburgh: T.& T. Clark, 1975 reprint of earlier edition), pp. 332–333 and refs. See also F.F. Bruce, *The Acts of The Apostles* (Grand Rapids: Eerdmans Pub. Co., 1968), p. 205.

[13] Acts 13:9ff.

¹⁴ Bruce, *Acts*, p. 31.

¹⁵ W. G. Kümmel, *Introduction to The New Testament* (London, SCM Press, Ltd., 1970), pp. 289–291, 300–302.

¹⁶ Edgar J. Goodspeed, *Paul* (New York: Abingdon Press, 1947), pp. 214–216. See Ackroyd and Evans, *The Cambridge History of the Bible* (Cambridge Univ. Press, 1975), I, p. 241.

¹⁷ Adolph Harnack, *Die Briefsammlung des Apostels Paulus* (Leipzig: J.C. Hinrichs, 1926), pp. 8–9. Harnack argues against J. Knox and C.L. Mitton, who had earlier posited an Ephesian origin for the Pauline collection.

¹⁸ Walter Schmithals, *Paul and The Gnostics* (New York: Abingdon Press, 1972), pp. 239–274.

¹⁹ Goodspeed, *op. cit.*, pp. 216–219.

²⁰ Eusebius, *H.E.* III.25. Eusebius is clearly following an old tradition, as is typified in his statement concerning the Gospels: καὶ δὴ τακτέον ἐν πρώτοις τὴν ἁγίαν εὐαγγελίων τετρακτύν . . . Although the so-called Muratorian Canon mentions Luke as the "third book of the Gospel" and John as the author of "The fourth of the Gospels," in the text published by F.W. Grosheide, *Some Early Lists of the Books of the New Testament*, Textus Minores, Vol. 1 (Leiden, 1948), Eusebius' language is more reminiscent of that of Irenaeus (*Adv. Haer*. III.8): Neque autem plura numero quam haec sunt, neque rursus pauciora capit esse Evangelia Ἐπειδὴ . . . τέσσαρα κλίματα τοῦ κόσμου, ἐν ᾧ ἐσμὲν, καὶ τέσσαρα καθολικὰ πνεύματα κατέσπαρται δὲ ἡ Ἐκκλησία ἐπὶ πάσης τῆς γῆς . . . ἔδωκεν ἡμῖν τετράμορφον τὸ Εὐαγγέλιον . . . There is no reason to assume that Irenaeus is the founder of such a tradition in his polemic, but he appears to be using arguments probably familiar to Christian apologists in his day.

²¹ J.H. Charlesworth, "Introduction to Apocalyptic Literature and Related Works," in J.H. Charlesworth, ed., *The Old Testament Pseudepigrapha, Vol. 1: Apocalyptic Literature and Testaments*. New York: Doubleday and Co., 1983, p. 3.

²² Mark 9:2–13; Matthew 17:1–13; Luke 9:28–37335. Cf. Also the reference to the Transfiguration or perhaps a similar Apocalyptic experience in II Peter 1:16–18. The wording at the end of verse 16 is more in keeping with a Resurrection Apocalypse than the transfiguration experience: ". . . ἀλλ' ἐπόπται γενηθέντες τῆς ἐκείνου μεγαλειότητος."

²³ Acts 9:3–8; 22:5–11; 26:12–19 (Conversion); Acts 16:9–10 (Macedonian vision); Acts 18:9–11; 22:17–19; 23:11 (visions of God); Acts 27:21–26 (angelic vision). II Corinthians 12:1–4 and Galatians 1:12 are also Apocalyptic references which may or may not coincide with the preceding references.

²⁴ Revelation 4:1–2.

²⁵ Revelation 4:2f.

²⁶ This history is introduced by the statement, Ἀνάβα ὧδε, καὶ δείξω σοι ἃ δεῖ γενέσθαι μετὰ ταῦτα.

²⁷ Visions are commonly presented in dialogue form with some heavenly being. In the *Epistle of Peter to Philip* and the *Apocryphon of John*, as examples, Jesus fulfills the role of *angelus interpres* in imparting knowledge and comfort to his troubled disciples. See also Robinson and Koester, *Trajectories Through Early Christianity* (Philadelphia: Fortress Press, 1971), p. 197. In a note comparing the dialogue passages in John's Gospel to later Gnostic revelation discourses, Koester says: "See the casting of the discourses into the pattern of the disciples' questions and Jesus' answers. The corresponding pattern of Apocalypses is well known: The seer asks and an *angelus interpres* answers and gives explanations and revelations." P. Vielhauer takes an opposite position (Hennecke-Schneemelcher, *N.T. Apoc. II*, 623), stating that only rarely is an *angelus interpres* the

mediator of the N.T. Apocalypse, while Christ is the major interpreter. Nevertheless, apart from the dialogue in chapter 1 (and even there the being is ὅμοιον υἱὸν ἀνθρώπου), the warnings in the 7 letters (chps. 2–3) which were likely given by Christ to John, and three brief passages elsewhere (16:15; 21:5–8; 22:6-end), the bulk of the revelation is presented by angels and not by Christ. It could be argued that some unidentified voices are really the Christ speaking (4:1;14:13; 16:1; 18:4ff.), but not argued with certainty, for an angel just as easily might have been speaking.

[28] In addition to the various functions the angels perform throughout the Revelation, chapter 12 gives a good description of the heavenly war fought between Michael and his angels against Satan and his angels.

[29] Chps. 6–17 recount the history of the last days, 18–20 give the account of the end of the earth, and 21–22 prophesy the establishment of the new heaven and earth.

[30] Justin Martyr, *Exh. to Greeks*, chp. 8; *Dial. with Trypho*, chp. 82; Origen, *Contra Celsum* II.8; Eusebius, *H.E.* III.32,7–8 (quoting Hegesippus).

[31] Jude 14.

[32] R.H. Charles, *Apoc. and Pseudepig. of the Old Testament*, 2 Vols. (Oxford: Clarendon Press, 1913), II, p. 180.

[33] Hilary, *Comment. in Ps.*, 132:3.

[34] Jerome, *De Viris Illustr*. 4; *Comment. in Epist. ad Titum* 1:12.

[35] Augustine, *De Civ. Dei* 15:23.4 and 18:38. The work was also rejected in the *Constit. Apost.*, 6:16.

[36] R.H. Charles, *op. cit.*, II, p. 163. See E. Isaac, "1 Enoch", *The Old Testament Pseudepigrapha, Vol. 1* (ed. Charlesworth). New York: Doubleday and Co., 1983, p. 8. Apparently following Charles, Isaac states: "1 Enoch played a significant role in the early Church; it was used by the authors of the Epistle of Barnabas, the Apocalypse of Peter, and a number of apologetic works. Many either knew 1 Enoch or were inspired by it. Among those who were familiar with 1 Enoch, Tertullian had an exceptionally high regard for it. But, beginning in the fourth century, the book came to be regarded with disfavor and received negative reviews from Augustine, Hilary, and Jerome. Thereafter, with the exception of a few extracts made by Georgius Syncellus, a learned monk of the eighth century, and the Greek fragments found in a Christian grave (c. A.D. 800), 1 Enoch ceased to be appreciated except in Ethiopia. The relegation of 1 Enoch to virtual oblivion by medieval minds should not diminish its significance for Christian origins; few other apocryphal books so indelibly marked the religious history and thought of the time of Jesus."

[37] Eusebius, *H.E.* III.25.7.

[38] Hennecke-Schneemelcher, *op.cit.*, I, p. 179.

[39] *Ibid.*, II, pp. 188–190.

[40] Photius, *Patrol. Graec*. 103, 985–988, and cited in *N.T. Apoc.* II, p. 192.

[41] *The Acts of Thomas* relates the account of his missionary travels to India, but many think that the account originated in Edessa. Greek, Syriac, Ethiopic, and Armenian versions survive, demonstrating the popularity of this work in the Eastern Mediterranean world. Eusebius, *H.E.* III.1, notes that when the world was divided by lot among the Apostles for missionary work, Parthia fell to Thomas.

[42] In the Πράξεις ᾿Ανδρείου καὶ Ματθεία εἰς τὴν πόλιν τῶν ἀνθρωποφάγων (*Acta Apost. Apoc.* II, *1*, pp. 65ff.), this land is described as the land of the cannibals, where men οὔτε ἄρτον ἤσθιον οὔτε οἶνον ἔπινον, ἀλλ᾿ ἦσαν ἐσθίοντες σάρκας ἀνθρώπων καὶ πίνοντες αὐτῶν τὸ αἷμα (chp.1). Another work, the *Gospel of Matthias*, was rejected with the *Gospel of Thomas* by Origen (*in Luc. hom*, I, p. 5.14 Rauer, cited in *N.T. Apoc.* I, p. 308). While Basilides is said to have traced some of his teachings back to Matthias,

Puech notes that the fragments of Matthias' gospel quoted by Clement "have manifestly no marked Gnostic character" (*N.T. Apoc.* I, p. 309).

[43] Eusebius, *H.E.* III.1.

[44] *Ibid.*, III.25.6.

[45] Walter Bauer, *Orthodoxy and Heresy in Earliest Christianity*, R. Kraft and G. Krodel, eds. (Philadelphia: Fortress Press, 1971), p. xxiv.

[46] *Ibid.*, p. xxii.

CHAPTER II

EARLY CHRISTIANITY IN EGYPT

The founding of the Christian movement in Egypt is obscured by legends which are difficult to evaluate for historical accuracy. The problem does not arise from a lack of materials, for Egypt has been the site for discovering many thousands of manuscripts and fragments of texts during the past century, and of those found many were seen to relate to the early Christian movement in that country. Nevertheless, no manuscript has yet been discovered which defines the time when Egyptian Christianity was founded or chronicles the religion's earliest development along the Nile. Before turning to the materials from Egypt which relate directly to the early period of Christian origins, some attention will be given to the sources of early Christianity for which Egypt is at best of secondary interest.

The birth account of Matthew contains the earliest chronological reference connecting Egypt with Jesus, and numerous legends sprang up amplifying the Matthaean narrative. (The chronological sequence of the events is treated here, not the chronological order of the composition of the writings). In an account strikingly similar in many respects to the Old Testament account of Moses' early life,[1] the author tells of the flight to Egypt of Joseph, Mary, and Jesus in order to save the child from Herod's edict to kill the children in and about Bethlehem.[2] The length of the family's stay in Egypt is not given in Matthew's account, and any attempt to link this experience to the founding of Christianity in Egypt is at best fanciful and imaginative. Such attempts were made, however, and are quite similar to the fabulous accounts of the miracle-working child in other later so-called Infancy Gospels. Jesus is portrayed in the *Arabic Infancy Gospel*, for example, as a miracle worker and a prophet even during the flight to Egypt.[3] The *Gospel of Pseudo-Matthew* contains not only stories of miracles performed by the child, but also an account of the conversion of an entire city (Sotinen, in the region of Hermopolis?) to Christianity because of a miracle performed in an Egyptian temple.[4] Present-day visitors to Egypt also encounter legends associated with the visit of this Jewish family, but they have no more foundation in historical evidence than the Infancy Narratives which were invented-from the second century onward.[5]

The next reference to Egypt in a Christian context occurs in Acts 2, where the author relates that the Christian disciples miraculously spoke in foreign tongues to men who gathered from all nations to Jerusalem for the Passover Feast and who remained through Pentecost. Two points of special emphasis are found in this narrative, and the first concerns the makeup of the audience:

> Ἦσαν δὲ εἰς Ἰερουσαλὴμ κατοικοῦντες Ἰουδαῖοι, ἄνδρες εὐλαβεῖς ἀπὸ παντὸς ἔθνους τῶν ὑπὸ τὸν οὐρανόν
>
> *And there were living in Jerusalem Jews, devout men from every nation beneath heaven.*

In verses 9–11 this statement is expanded to a list of nations inhabited by Jews, including Egypt. Some theories have been advanced concerning the nature of the list itself, and it is sometimes argued that the countries subordinated to and associated with the twelve signs of the zodiac correspond to Luke's catalogue,[7] but there is no doubt that Jews did dwell in the countries listed. Concerning the Nile Valley, Bruce notes that "Jews had lived continuously in Egypt from the time of Psammetichus II (c. 590 B.C.E.), receiving fresh accessions from time to time."[8] Both Philo and Josephus attest to the great numbers of Jews in Egypt, the former stating that no fewer than a million lived from Alexandria to Ethiopia:

> καὶ ὅτι οὐκ ἀποδέουσι μυριάδων ἑκατὸν οἱ τὴν Ἀλεξάνδρειαν καὶ τὴν χώραν Ἰουδαῖοι κατοικοῦντες ἀπὸ τοῦ πρὸς Λιβύην καταβαθμοῦ μέχρι τῶν ὁρίων Αἰθιοπίας.[9]
>
> *. . . and that there are no fewer than one million Jews dwelling in Alexandria and the land from the steep slope toward Libya to the boundaries of Ethiopia.*

If Josephus' estimate of the total Egyptian population is credible (7,500,000, exclusive of Alexandria),[10] the Jewish Egyptians then comprised approximately an eighth of the entire provincial population. Even if the accuracy of the figures is questionable, these authors elsewhere give ample evidence that numerous Jews were to be found in all countries of the Mediterranean,[11] and particularly in Egypt and Alexandria.[12] Josephus gives the unbelievably high figure of 2,500,000 for the number of Jews who would be present at Jerusalem during the Passover Feast (he states that his figure is based on a census taken by Cestius for Nero).[13] Despite this exaggeration, many Jews from the Dispersion, and particularly from the large Egyptian Jewish population, would have been in Jerusalem for the Passover and

Pentecost feasts related in Acts 2. As they came in contact with Christianity through the Pentecost speech of the disciples (and probably in earlier years by direct or indirect contact with Jesus and the disciples), these Jews would have returned to their homes with varying degrees of information and conviction concerning the Christian faith.

The second point of emphasis in the Acts narrative concerns the speaking in tongues:

ἐξίσταντο δὲ καὶ ἐθαύμαζον λέγοντες, οὐχ ἰδοὺ ἅπαντες οὗτοί εἰσιν οἱ λαλοῦντες Γαλιλαῖοι; καὶ πῶς ἡμεῖς ἀκούομεν ἕκαστος τῇ ἰδίᾳ διαλέκτῳ ἡμῶν ἐν ᾗ ἐγεννήθημεν;[14]

They were both astonished and amazed as they said, "Consider, are not all these who are speaking Galilaeans? Yet how are we hearing, each one in our own native language?"

The significance of this experience is related to the meaning assigned to διάλεκτος (*Dialectos*), for the possibilities range from regional differences within the same language[15] to the various languages of different countries.[16] If the latter possibility is chosen, the pilgrims in the audience not only took some form of Christian belief back to their homeland, but might have been expected to proselytize subsequently in their native language. In the case of Egypt, the traditional position taken by commentators is that Christianity spread first to Alexandria as a 'Greek-speaking' religion and only considerably later was taken to the native population in their local languages. Greek was the scriptural language of Jews in Egypt, and although there is some evidence that they had utilized Aramaic centuries before Greek became a predominant language in Egypt (at Elephantine, for example), it is certain that the Jews did not use Egyptian as their spoken language. Thus, even if the Acts 2 account refers to many languages as opposed to local dialects of the Aramaic language, this is not by itself compelling evidence to argue for a proselyting effort among Egyptian natives shortly afterward. The best evidences currently available which are germane to the question of Christian origins are the Biblical texts and Christian writings found in Egypt, and these will be treated below.

In summary of the Pentecost narrative, one can suggest that Christianity would likely have spread to various countries through reports of pilgrims and travelers to Jerusalem. Nevertheless, two problems arise concerning the dissemination of the apostolic Kerygma and the relationship of converts in other countries to the Christians in Palestine. The difficulty in arriving at a solution is compounded by a lack of suitable criteria with which an assessment can be made.

The first of these, concerning how much of the apostolic Kerygma would be passed on effectively and accurately by such informal and unofficial means, is well illustrated by the incident of Apollos of Alexandria,[17] as will be seen shortly. The second, that of the relationship of converts made indirectly (i.e. taught and converted by disciples other than the apostles or missionaries commissioned by them) can be answered partially by an appeal to Acts 11. When persecution caused a dispersion of Christians from Jerusalem, some disciples from Cyprus and Cyrene went to Syrian Antioch and taught the Christian message to Gentiles (vss. 20ff.). The success which attended this effort came to the notice of the Jerusalem authorities, who sent Barnabas to establish a bond between the Gentile converts in Antioch and the central congregation in Jerusalem.[18] Although similar attempts to unite or to reunite disparate Christian groups can be observed in the Pauline corpus,[19] no meaningful estimate can be made concerning the number of Christians in the Mediterranean world who remained independent of Jerusalem or other major Christian centers. One may assume that Christian groups sprang up in many lands which were not united, either ecclesiastically or doctrinally, with the Jerusalem church or its satellites. Egypt, with its large Jewish population, may well have been a spawning ground for a number of such groups along the length of the Nile.[20] The episode of Apollos presents some evidence that Christianity had arrived in Alexandria, at least, by the middle of the first century.

> Ἰουδαῖος δέ τις Ἀπολλῶς ὀνόματι, Ἀλεξανδρεὺς τῷ γένει, ἀνὴρ λόγιος, κατήντησεν εἰς Ἔφεσον, δυνατὸς ὢν ἐν ταῖς γραφαῖς. οὗτος ἦν κατηχημένος τὴν ὁδὸν τοῦ κυρίου, καὶ ζέων τῷ πνεύματι ἐλάλει καὶ ἐδίδασκεν ἀκριβῶς τὰ περὶ τοῦ Ἰησοῦ, ἐπιστάμενος μόνον τὸ βάπτισμα Ἰωάννου.[21]

> *A certain Jew named Apollos, a native Alexandrian who was eloquent and well-versed in the scriptures, arrived at Ephesus. This man had been instructed in the way of the Lord and, burning with zeal, he was speaking and teaching accurately the things concerning Jesus, although he knew only the baptism of John.*

To this text the bilingual Western text, Codex Bezae (D) adds the following after κατηχημένος: ἐν τῇ πατρίδι.[22] (*He had been instructed in his homeland*). The reactions to this passage in general, and to the addition that Apollos had been instructed in *his own country*,[23] have been varied, but there is general consensus that Christianity had to be taken to Egypt by approximately 50 C.E., and most commentators accept that interpretation.[24] However much agreement can be found concerning the *date* that Christianity arrived in Egypt, some difficulty persists in determining the *kind* of Christianity first attested there. The text of Acts cited above states not only that Apollos was "burning with zeal" but also that he "was teaching accurately concerning Jesus, although he knew only the baptism of John." The point of the Acts narrative in recounting the Apollos episode appears to be twofold: (1) Paul's earlier associates, Aquila and Priscilla, had to take him aside and teach him ἀκριβέστερον (*more accurately*) the ways of God, and (2) Paul, in Chapter 19:1–7, had to rebaptize some who had been taught by Apollos because they had not been correctly taught. The general explanation given regarding one who taught "accurately" yet had to be taught "more accurately" is that Apollos taught correctly, but inadequately. Bruce suggests that he knew only a Galilean gospel or a 'Sayings' Gospel,[25] while Käsemann believes that Apollos is a Christian teacher who is independent of the ecclesiastical, or 'apostolic' Christianity.[26] Bauer takes a position similar to Käsemann, arguing:

> "Surely no one would care to label as in any sense 'ecclesiastically oriented faith' that mixture made up of Alexandrian Judaism and scriptural learning, of discipleship to John which knows only the baptism of the Baptist and of Christian ingredients—Apollos himself does not at first proclaim more than this at Ephesus."[27]

In summary of this passage from Acts, then, one can support the position that Christianity reached Egypt (at least Alexandria) at quite an early date,[28] but no details of its transmission or its content can be deduced from the account. The value of Apollos for the Lukan narrative is the role he plays in the Ephesian ministry of Paul and his associates, and any ancillary material relating to Egypt would have been omitted for its relative unimportance.

The only other passage of the New Testament which has been understood by some as a direct reference linking Christianity to Egypt is I Peter 5:13 Ἀσπάζεται ὑμᾶς ἡ ἐν Βαβυλῶνι συνεκλεκτὴ καὶ Μάρκος ὁ υἱός μου· (*the congregation at Babylon, chosen together with you, and my son, Mark, send you greetings*). Because there existed a fortress or castle in the Nile delta near modern Cairo which was named Babylon,[29] some few modern commentators have thought Peter was writing from there (the association of Peter with Mark, the traditional founder of Christianity in Egypt—to be discussed below—is a major consideration in opting for the Egyptian site). A recent version of this argument is put forth by Altheim and Stiehl, who dismiss Rome and Mesopotamian Babylon as candidates for the site from which Peter was writing, since neither is adequately identified or well-founded in legend as the origin of Peter's letter. Unfortunately for the choice of Egyptian Babylon as the site, the evidence is not compelling. A later bishop from a neighboring region identifies a bridge at Taposiris (some 25 miles west of Alexandria) which was named for the Apostle Peter. The modern authors suggest that perhaps the Apostle crossed over the bridge or preached there, but one observes against such a theory that no church is named after the Apostle in the neighborhood (the usual method of commemorating sites made holy by visits of religious leaders). Even less convincing evidence is brought into the picture, such as the now discredited identification by Jose O'Callaghan of Mark's Gospel among the Dead Sea Scrolls, or some inscriptional material from the Sudan which contains Peter's name.[30] Apart from such evidence, one must repeat that there is still some attractiveness to the Egyptian Babylon, both because of Peter's association with Mark and the tradition of Mark preaching in Alexandria. The entire argument identifying Egyptian Babylon with I Peter is a weak one, however, and a telling response notes that "The Alexandrian Church laid no claim to it and this Babylon was so small a district that it seems highly improbable that Peter made his headquarters there without such a fact leaving any trace in early tradition."[31] Furthermore, as in Bell, "it is doubtful whether as early as this it was more than a military centre, and whether we take ἡ συνεκλεκτή (that [female] which has been chosen with [you]) as the Church or St. Peter's wife it is unexpected to find either in a military camp."[32] Most of those commenting on this passage prefer to understand 'Babylon' as symbolic of evil, and a common pseudonym for Rome in Jewish and Christian Apocalyptic literature of the first century C.E.[33]

Another disputed text thought by some to contain an early reference to Christianity in Egypt is a well-known letter of the Emperor Claudius, discovered in 1920.[34] The emperor was answering complaints brought to him by two delegations (whether both were sent by Jews or one Alexandrian and the other Jewish is disputed[35]) which were also delivering greetings and congratulations for Claudius' accession. The emperor censures the Alexandrians and then warns the

Jews "not to strive for more privileges than they possessed earlier," but rather exhorts them

> "to profit by what they possess, and enjoy in a city not their own an abundance of all good things; and not to introduce or invite Jews who sail down from Syria or Egypt, thus compelling me to conceive the greater suspicion; otherwise I shall by all means take vengeance on them as fomenting a general plague for the whole world."[36]

Salomon Reinach was the first and most dedicated proponent of the "Christian interpretation" of this document,[37] and he has had some following, including M. Cumont.[38] The latter believed there was some connection between the language of *P. Lond.* 1912 and Acts 24:5, where Paul is described as a pestilent fellow who was causing a social revolution among Jews throughout the world, extending Reinach's earlier theory that Christianity caused social unrest because of its hope for an expected return of the Messiah. The probability of the text referring to Christians is weakened considerably by the observation that Jewish-Greek tensions and conflicts were not new with Christianity, and Jewish Christians were not the only Jews with active Messianic expectations.[39] Further, the belief of Reinach and Cumont that Christian proselyting activity was responsible for social unrest between Jews and Gentiles cannot be defended until considerably later in the reign of Claudius, especially outside Palestine. The narrative of Acts mentions that a famine occurred during the reign of Claudius,[40] and that event is portrayed as preceding the formal spread of the Christian faith beyond Judea and Syria. That Claudius had fears of a social revolution caused by the Christian movement soon after his accession seems quite impossible in the face of present evidence. *P.Lond.* 1912, as is generally agreed, likely has to do with limiting the influx of Jewish immigrants to Egypt, and thus attempting to control the riots which often took place between the Greeks and Jews.[41]

The well-known tradition that Mark was the official founder of Egyptian Christianity is first recorded by Eusebius:

> τοῦτον δὲ Μάρκον πρῶτόν φασιν ἐπὶ τῆς Αἰγύπτου στειλάμενον, τὸ εὐαγγέλιον, ὃ δὴ καὶ συνεγράψατο, κηρῦξαι, ἐκκλησίας τε πρῶτον ἐπ᾽ αὐτῆς Ἀλεξανδρείας συστήσασθαι.[42]

> *Now this Mark is the one whom they say to have been the first sent to Egypt to preach the Gospel, which he had also written down, and the first to establish churches in Alexandria itself.*

Eusebius gives no evidence from early sources for this tradition, which continued in Egyptian sources and legends from the time of Eusebius to the present,[43] and the account appears all the more desperate in its claim for authenticity due to Eusebius' attempt to make Philo's Jewish Therapeutae the first converts of Mark in and about Alexandria.[44] Even Eusebius understands that his connecting the Therapeutae to Christianity is based only on similarities rather than explicit references to Christianity by the Philonic group, for he concedes that many who are not Christian may doubt the strength of the parallels which he cites:

εἰ δέ τῳ μὴ δοκεῖ τὰ εἰρημένα ἴδια εἶναι τῆς κατὰ τὸ εὐαγγέλιον πολιτείας, δύνασθαι δὲ καὶ ἄλλοις παρὰ τοὺς δεδηλωμένους ἁρμόττειν . . .[45]

If someone does not think that the things which have been spoken are peculiar to the Gospel way of life, but that they can be applied also to others besides those already indicated . . .

ταύτας τοῦ Φίλωνος σαφεῖς καὶ ἀναντιρρήτους περὶ τῶν καθ' ἡμᾶς ὑπάρχειν ἡγούμεθα λέξεις.[46]

These statements of Philo we think to be clearly and undeniably relating to our religion.

The assertion that Mark was the first missionary to Egypt is also couched in somewhat ambiguous terms, for Eusebius apparently had no document or authority beyond the local tradition suggested by φασίν (*they say*). Morton Smith wrote that φασίν, "If not used impersonally, should refer to Clement and Papias, who were named as the sources of information in the preceding sentence."[47] Smith noted that there is no mention of Mark journeying to Alexandria in the preserved works of Clement, but in 1958 he discovered a lost letter of Clement to Theodore, in which Clement states that Mark traveled from Rome to Alexandria after Peter's death. Mark is further stated in the letter to have composed a "more spiritual gospel" in Alexandria to use for the initiation of worthy Christians into secret mysteries. Within the letter Clement both admits the existence of the secret gospel and supports the implication that at least in Alexandria there was a dimension of Christianity not generally known in the world.[48] The value of this evidence relating to Christian origins in Egypt will depend upon the degree of one's acceptance of the letter as actually originating with Clement. A decade after publishing his *Clement of Alexandria and a Secret Gospel of Mark*, Smith published an article in which he summarized responses of scholars to the new discovery.[49]

The overwhelming majority of those who had written on the subject believe that the letter of Clement is genuine, but virtually nobody was willing to accept the authenticity of the Gospel fragments as originating with Mark.[50] Apart from a strange inconsistency in judging historical authenticity on the basis of literary evidence, the summary given by Smith shows a continued scholarly bias against the traditional role of Mark in Egyptian Christian history.

Bauer, for reasons which will be discussed at length in another context below, believes that the problems associated with the origins of Egyptian Christianity are accentuated by the account of the succession of Alexandrian bishops traced in Eusebius.[51] One cannot fault Eusebius for omitting biographical information on all the Christian bishops in the various churches and cities he treats, even if such information were available to him,[52] but the stark recital of names associated with the Alexandrian succession and interspersed through the Eusebeian account[53] is devoid of *any* life-giving detail for Christianity in that region down to the episcopate of Julian, in whose reign Pantaenus is described as a learned teacher presiding over ecclesiastical education:

> Ἡγεῖτο δὲ τηνικαῦτα τῆς τῶν πιστῶν αὐτόθι διατριβῆς ἀνὴρ κατὰ παιδείαν ἐπιδοξότατος, ὄνομα αὐτῷ Πάνταινος, ἐξ ἀρχαίου ἔθους διδασκαλείου τῶν ἱερῶν λόγων παρ' αὐτοῖς συνεστῶτος.[54]

> *At that time a man named Pantaenus having a great reputation for his education was directing the way of life of the believers in Alexandria, for from ancient custom a school of sacred teachings had existed among them.*

That much detail concerning Pantaenus already distinguishes him from all that had been said previously by Eusebius about Christians or Christianity in Egypt, but the historian continues to develop a portrait of Pantaenus, while admitting his dependence upon tradition (in V. 10.1 he uses λόγος ἔχει [*there is an account*], and in 10.2 φασίν [*they say*]). Pantaenus was influenced by Stoicism, was appointed to preach in the East, and traveled among the Indians where he found converts from an earlier evangelistic mission by Bartholomew. His reputation as a scholar and teacher are further enlogized by Eusebius, who even suggests that Pantaenus also may have left writings:

> ζώσῃ φωνῇ καὶ διὰ συγγραμμάτων τοὺς τῶν θείων δογμάτων θησαυροὺς ὑπομνηματιζόμενος.[55]

> . . . *orally and through writings he interpreted the treasures of the divine doctrines.*

This remarkable and historically plausible description of Pantaenus strengthens Bauer's point that the first ten Alexandrian bishops named in Eusebius "are and remain for us a mere echo and a puff of smoke; and they scarcely could ever have been anything but that."[56] If, as has been mentioned above, Christianity was taken to Egypt by the middle of the first century, an inexplicable silence in Christian sources concerning the leaders of the movement and the development of the church over the next 125–150 years is probably unique in the history of Christianity.

One non-Christian source which has been thought by a few scholars to shed light on second-century Christianity in Egypt is a letter written to the Consul Servianus[57] and attributed to the Emperor Hadrian.[58] Were the letter authentic it would say little about the nature of the Christians, for the intent of the author is to depict the fickleness and capriciousness of the Egyptians rather than comment on the Christian religion. The uncomplimentary tone of the letter toward Christians refutes the possibility stated by Harnack that it could be a Christian fabrication,[59] and there is no clear indication within the text identifying who might have written it or what motive lay behind it. Johannes Leipoldt admitted that the text does reflect a knowledge of conditions in Egypt, and further stated that perhaps the authenticity of the letter had been wrongfully denied.[60] One must conclude that its value in the history of Egyptian Christianity is limited to giving a *terminus a quo* for the arrival of that religion in Egypt, but even that value is compromised or discounted by the uncertainty of the date of the letter. The possibility of using the text as a commentary on the nature of Christian orthodoxy or practice must also be discounted because of the sarcastic tone and non-specific identity of the Christians in question. The terms used, if not meant to be seen as pejorative, are too general to be of descriptive or analytical value (although terms such as *archisynagogus Judaeorum* and *Christianorum presbyter* do show at least superficial awareness of the organization of the groups mentioned). For these reasons the letter cannot be pressed into service as evidence for the introduction of Christianity into Egypt.

Although repeated assertions have been made above concerning the early advent of Christianity in Egypt, it is clear that an appeal to traditional literary sources which could be expected to shed light on the subject cannot yield conclusive evidence for a first century arrival, with the possible exception of the Apollos episode recounted in Acts.

Even Bell's hypothesis that the existence of the Catechetical School of Alexandria in the second century was evidence of a substantial and earlier Christian community is not compelling,[61] for no figures are available concerning the size of the school, the date of its origin, or the stimuli responsible for its beginning.[62] Similar schools are not associated with other major Christian centers in the early centuries, suggesting that the intellectual climate of Alexandria rather than the size of the Christian community was responsible for the rise of the School.

There remain two areas, however, in which archaeological discoveries of recent years have produced sufficient evidence on the question of Early Egyptian Christianity to be useful in this study. The first of these has to do with the Biblical and non-Biblical Christian manuscripts found at many sites along the Nile, both of Old and New Testament texts. The second is the vexing question of Gnosticism and Gnostic sources relating to the first two centuries. This latter question deals not only with the approximate time when Christianity was brought to Egypt, but also with the nature of that religion as it was introduced to Alexandria, the Delta, and the Nile valley, or as it was modified soon after its arrival.

The science of papyrology has been developed from meager beginnings about a century ago, so that H. I. Bell in his inaugural lecture as a Reader at Oxford, could say of Grenfell and Hunt: "When they began their careers papyrology was still so young that a man might almost carry the whole of it in his head, and specialization had not yet become necessary."[63] Discoveries of thousands of papyrus manuscripts from Egypt alone span the millenium from the establishment of the Ptolemaic dynasty in Egypt in the late fourth century B.C.E. to (and even beyond) the Arab invasion in the seventh century C.E., and the manuscripts include every kind of literary and non-literary text.[64] This remarkable wealth of materials recently recovered has caused an emergent awareness of the degree of literacy in the Hellenistic world. C. H. Roberts declares that in the first century C.E., writing was pervasive through all levels of society, "to an extent without parallel in living memory."[65] The same author observes that reading (and writing, by implication) is not an unusual accomplishment among Christians in the New Testament. Jesus is pictured as closing arguments against His Jewish opponents with the challenge "Have you not read . . . ?" (Matt. 12:3; 19:4 of. 21:42), and, Roberts asserts, one may then suppose that literacy was likely as common in

Palestine and among Christians generally as the vast quantity of papyri argues to be the case in Middle and Upper Egypt.[66] So that one should not understand that Christians were limited to literacy within their own religious tradition, Roberts elsewhere presents a selection of authors and works from the Classical tradition found in Christian libraries, from which he concludes: "What impresses most is the range of reading among educated Christians in provincial Egypt . . ."[67]

The problem of determining the date of the establishment of Christianity in Egypt from evidences in non-biblical papyri is difficult to evaluate, for the use of specific Christian formulae in contracts, wills, or other official documents would not be expected in the first two centuries, and the absence of specific Christian phrases in private letters may be due either to the lack of their development and usage in this early period or simply to the accident of preservation. Whatever the reasons, "when we turn to the papyrus documents in search of evidence for the results of such missionary effort we find, in the first two centuries of our era, next to no traces of Christianity."[68]

Against the paucity of Christian evidences in non-literary papyri can be placed an impressive array of Biblical texts from Egypt, including the oldest known fragment of the New Testament.[69] This papyrus text, (Papyrus Rylands Greek 457, or P 52), measuring 3.5 by 2.3 inches and containing John 18:31–33 on the *recto* and 18:37–38 on the *verso*, was obtained by B. P. Grenfell in Egypt in 1920, and is thought to have been recovered from Oxyrhynchus or perhaps the Fayum. As in the case of a great number of Egyptian manuscripts, the precise provenance is elusive because native discoverers are not likely to divulge readily the source of their treasures and undermine a lucrative business. Because the text continues from *recto to verso* (when giving allowance for the gap created by the missing part of the page), it is clear that the fragment belongs to a codex rather than a scroll. Much has been written concerning the significance of the codex as a Christian departure from traditional Jewish practice,[70] and one study provides evidence not only to show Christian preference for the codex, but also to suggest "that its use (by Christians) was all but invariable from the earliest times."[71] The Rylands fragment has been dated no later than the middle of the second century,[72] and Roberts, who made a careful comparison of the text with non-Christian papyri from the end of the first and early second centuries, noted special similarities in letter forms to texts bearing dates corresponding to 94 C.E. and 127 C.E.[73] This Egyptian copy of the gospel of John, then, can be dated to the first quarter of the second century, and perhaps as early as the end of the first century. If, as is generally assumed, John's Gospel was composed originally in or about Ephesus, this text is precious evidence that Christianity not only arrived at an early date (at least the latter part of the first century), but that Christian literature was being produced and circulated by early in the second century in Middle or Upper Egypt. The early dating of this manuscript also argues for a more rapid reproduction of Christian texts as authoritative records for disciples than is usually presumed, for the final editing of the Gospel of John is commonly dated to the end of the first century. The possibility therefore exists, as Bell notes, "that this scrap may take us back within twenty years of the original composition."[74]

Other notable manuscript discoveries from Middle or Upper Egypt, such as the Bodmer Papyri, the Chester Beatty Papyri (guesses on the provenance of these two collections range from as far north as the Fayum to Panopolis, or Akhmim, in the south), or the Oxyrhynchus Papyri, also contain Christian Biblical texts dating from the second century C.E. onward and representing an early proliferation of Christian writings throughout Egypt.

In a remarkable study analyzing the Greek Biblical papyri discovered in Egypt and dated through the fourth century (when the author of the study considers the value of the papyrological evidence to become outweighed by the "major manuscripts"), C. H. Roberts could catalogue no fewer than 116 Greek fragments of the Bible which can be dated conservatively in the second, third, and fourth centuries.[75] Of the 116 texts or fragments, 8 (all codices) are assigned to the second century, although three of those are called "border-line" cases, possibly belonging to the third century.[76] Other Biblical texts besides these mentioned by Roberts in his study have also been assigned to the second century, including the P. Rylands 457 mentioned above.[77] The weight of this evidence is great in favor of the early diffusion of Christianity throughout Egypt, but some apparently prefer to ignore such evidence, as W. Telfer, who argued in 1952, on the basis of a Palestinian letter concerning the date of the Passover, that "Egyptian Christianity in A.D. 190 was thus confined to the city (Alexandria) and its environs."[78] Roberts replied in 1954 that Telfer's "astonishing statement" had the effect of denying the papyrological evidence which has come forth from Egypt.[79] Telfer admitted that Christianity probably arrived in Alexandria quite early, perhaps by the middle of the first century, but he offers no explanation as to how or why it was confined there, and his omission of the Biblical textual evidence weakens his argument considerably. Perhaps he would not have considered the owners of the Biblical texts to be Christian, however, since he calls Demetrius, the bishop in Alexandria from 189 C.E., the "Second Founder of the Church of Alexandria."[80] All who preceded Demetrius in Alexandria are thus categorized as harboring "provincialisms that had been characteristic of local Christianity" and out of harmony with the 'catholocism' established in other Mediterranean countries. The question of orthodoxy will be treated shortly, but here one should note that Telfer appears willing to include the idiosyncratic Alexandrian Christians (and those elsewhere in Egypt?) as non-Christians rather than identify them as heterodox Christians.

In addition to the canonical Biblical papyri, a significant Christian text dating no later than the middle of the second century, and perhaps closer to the beginning of the century, was published in 1935 as *Fragments of an Unknown Gospel* (P. Egerton 2).[81] Far from being an heretical composition, the three extant fragments from this codex show close affinities with all four canonical gospels, especially John, and at the same time are not simply a harmony or series of quotations from them. The text is not a collection of logia as those recovered in the *Gospel According to Thomas*,[82] but rather contains parts of four pericopes within the life of Jesus, including a denunciation of lawyers by Jesus, a healing of a leper, a discourse on tribute-money, and a miracle of sowing grain on the bank of the Jordan river and then causing the grain to grow and ripen immediately afterward. The first of the pericopes is rather Johannine in style, dealing with the confrontation between Jesus and the lawyers,[83] and the most striking parallels from the Gospel fragment and John are as follows:

ἐραυνᾶτε τὰς γραφάς, ἐν αἷς ὑμεῖς δοκεῖτε ζωὴν ἔχειν· ἐκεῖναί εἰσιν αἱ μαρτυροῦσαι περὶ ἐμοῦ. μὴ δοκεῖτε ὅτι ἐγὼ ἦλθον κατηγορῆσαι ὑμῶν πρὸς τὸν πατέρα μου· ἔστιν ὁ κατηγορῶν ὑμῶν Μωϋσῆς, εἰς ὃν ὑμεῖς ἠλπίκατε. αὐτῶν δὲ λεγόντων· εὖ οἴδαμεν ὅτι Μωϋσεῖ ἐλάλησεν ὁ θεός, σὲ δὲ οὐκ οἴδαμεν πόθεν εἶ, ἀποκριθεὶς ὁ Ἰησοῦς εἶπεν αὐτοῖς· νῦν κατηγορεῖται ὑμῶν ἡ ἀπιστία . . . (fragment 1v, ℓℓ. 7–19). ἐραυνᾶτε τὰς γραφάς, ὅτι ὑμεῖς δοκεῖτε ἐν αὐτοῖς ζωὴν αἰώνιον ἔχειν· καὶ ἐκεῖναί εἰσιν αἱ μαρτυροῦσαι περὶ ἐμοῦ (John 5:39). μὴ δοκεῖτε ὅτι ἐγὼ κατηγορήσω ὑμῶν πρὸς τὸν πατέρα· ἔστιν ὁ κατηγορῶν ὑμῶν Μωϋσῆς, εἰς ὃν ὑμεῖς ἠλπίκατε (John 5:45). ἡμεῖς οἴδαμεν ὅτι Μωϋσεῖ λελάληκεν ὁ θεός, τοῦτον δὲ οὐκ οἴδαμεν πόθεν ἐστίν (John 9:29).

You search the scriptures, in which you think you have life; they are witnesses of me. Do not suppose that I came to accuse you before my father; there is one who accuses you, Moses, in whom you have placed your hope. And when they said, "We know well that God spoke to Moses, but we do not know from where you come," Jesus answered and said to them, "Now your lack of faith is accused . . ." (fragment 1v, ℓℓ.7–19).

"You search the scriptures because you think you have eternal life in them; even they are witnesses of me" (John 5:39). "Do not suppose that I will accuse you before my father; there is one who accuses you, Moses, in whom you have placed your hope" (John 5:45).

"We know that God spoke to Moses, but as for this man, we do not know from where he comes" (John 9:29).

These passages are certain evidence that the author of the *Unknown Gospel* knew John's Gospel, but it appears that he took passages from John and reworked them into a new and equally coherent narrative, rather than to be a slave to the text. It may also be true that the author simply had the same material independently in a context different from John's Gospel. Parallels to the other canonical gospels are given by Bell and Skeat,[84] and though they are not exactly parallel to the Egerton fragments, scholars agree that the compiler knew some form of all the gospels, even if he did not have a copy before him as he wrote.[85] While the miracle beside the Jordan river is not found in the canonical gospels, it is not inharmonious with some miracles described in them, such as the withering of the fig-tree,[86] finding tribute money in a fish,[87] or the calming of a storm.[88] The *Unknown Gospel* is thus closer to the canonical tradition which is thought to have preceded it than to the apocryphal works believed to have been composed in the second and third centuries. The provenance of *P. Egerton* 2 is uncertain, but the fact that a number of papyri acquired with the fragments came from Oxyrhynchus makes that location a natural possibility.[89] Where the gospel originated is also unknown, but because of its ties with John (thought to have originated in Asia near the end of the first century), and because it was likely composed before the end of the first century, Bell and Skeat consider Asia and Egypt to be possible sites of composition.[90] Its discovery in Egypt with papyri of Egyptian origin weigh heavily in favor of an Egyptian origin over an Asian one, however, especially since the papyrological evidence shows that the Gospel of John was known in Egypt by the end of the first century.

One may summarize that the evidence of the Christian Biblical papyri found in Egypt (including the quasi-canonical *Unknown Gospel*) argues strongly for the arrival of the Christian religion in Egypt before the end of the first century, and further that Christianity was not confined geographically to the Alexandrian region. This supposition is in accord with the picture of the spread of Christianity drawn from other sources, and also meets expectations caused by the presence of a large Jewish population in Egypt and the Christian proselyting done among the Jews according to the well-known pattern of missionary efforts elsewhere. To these factors must be added also the degree to which literacy pervaded society during the first centuries C.E., the early production of Christian writings, and the leading role which Egypt (especially Alexandria) played in perpetuating the cultural and educational heritage of the Hellenistic world.

It is from Egypt that one would expect to obtain the most detailed picture of the growth and development of the new religion, and consequently it is the unexpected and enigmatic silence of traditional literary sources that is most disappointing. One must conclude either that no evidence survived for chroniclers and historians to utilize (most unlikely, since similar materials survived elsewhere) or that such materials and traditions as did survive were purposely overlooked or omitted by such writers as Clement, Origen, or Eusebius, who would be expected to draw on previous traditions and sources in their own works. An explanation for such attitudes and behavior can perhaps be inferred from two separate, but related, observations.

The first was developed in the previous chapter, where Roman or later Catholic Christianity was seen to have developed within a narrowly defined geographical and literary tradition, which tradition it later imposed throughout the Mediterranean world where it became established. The second observation takes into account the material developed in this chapter. If, as Telfer suggested above,[91] Demetrius should be characterized as the "Second Founder of the Church of Alexandria" to correspond with the arrival of the 'catholicism' established elsewhere, one might then account for the silence among his successors concerning the previous 'Christianity' in Egypt on the grounds that they did not consider it Christianity at all. The history of an established church would be covered by the invention of a list of bishops succeeding from a traditional founder, Mark (who may or may not be connected historically with the first mission to Egypt), but no details were attempted, except Eusebius' awkward association of the Therapeutae with Christianity.

The second observation suggested above is less easily documented than the first, but is supported by the scanty sources available at the present time, namely that the earliest Christian congregations in Egypt likewise developed eclectic tendencies. The word "developed" could be misleading here, for it is possible that Egyptian Christianity in its early period may have resembled the original movement in Palestine more closely than the Asia Minor version of Christianity in the early second century, and may thus be seen as a *continuation* rather than a *development* of the religious movement. There remains too much uncertainty at present concerning the church in the middle of the first century to make a final decision, however, and "developed" is a less controversial choice.

Some important non-Biblical textual fragments might well be considered here as they relate to the question of early Egyptian Christianity. In 1897, Grenfell and Hunt began excavating at Oxyrhynchus, and the first year they discovered a large collection of Greek papyri dating from the first to the seventh centuries C.E., including one page from a book of *Sayings of Jesus*.[92] They returned for further excavation in 1903 after a six-year hiatus, and found another Sayings fragment, this one written on the back of a survey-list of various pieces of land which was written at the end of the second century or beginning of the third.[93] Some eight fragments of a papyrus roll found at Oxyrhynchus were also published in 1904 and identified as a second or third century compilation of Jesus' sayings[94] and bearing considerable resemblance to the Synoptic Gospels. Since the discovery of the Coptic *Gospel of Thomas* in the Nag Hammadi Library found in c. 1945, the sayings in that gospel which were common to these fragments have led many to conclude that the Oxyrhynchus fragments represented a Greek original of the later Coptic translation of a *Gospel of Thomas*. Schneemelcher notes that since the three papyri did not derive from the same book, their homogeneity could be maintained only with great caution before the discovery of the Coptic text. Even since that discovery it is apparent that the Logia of *P. Oxy.* 1 are not simply the Greek original for the Coptic, as can be seen in the following example:

λέγει Ἰησοῦς, ὅπου ἐὰν ὦσιν β̄ οὔκ εἰσιν ἄθεοι, καὶ ὅπου εἷς ἐστιν μόνος, λέγω ἐγώ εἰμι μετ' αὐτοῦ· ἔγειρον τὸν λίθον κἀκεῖ εὑρήσεις με, σχίσον τὸ ξύλον κἀγὼ ἐκεῖ εἰμι.[95]

Jesus said, "where there might be two, they are not without God, and where there is one man alone, I say that I am with him; Raise the stone and there you will find me; split the wood (cross) and there I am."

This logion is found in two passages in the *Gospel of Thomas*, logion 30 and logion 77:

ⲠⲈϪⲈ ⲓ̅ⲥ̅ ϪⲈ ⲠⲘⲀ ⲈⲨⲚ̅ ϢⲞⲘⲦ Ⲛ̅ⲚⲞⲨⲦⲈ Ⲙ̅ⲘⲀⲨ ⲌⲚ̅ ⲚⲞⲨⲦⲈ ⲚⲈ ⲠⲘⲀ ⲈⲨⲚ̅ ⲤⲚⲀⲨ
Ⲏ ⲞⲨⲀ ⲀⲚⲞⲔ ⲦϢⲞⲞⲠ · ⲚⲘⲘⲀϤ ·
ⲠⲰⲌ Ⲛ̅ⲚⲞⲨϢⲈ ⲀⲚⲞⲔ' ⲦⲘ̅ⲘⲀⲨ ϤⲒ Ⲙ̅ⲠⲰⲚⲈ ⲈⲌⲢⲀⲒ̈ ⲀⲨⲰ ⲦⲈⲦⲚⲀⲌⲈ ⲈⲢⲞⲈⲒ Ⲙ̅ⲘⲀⲨ

Jesus said, "where there are three Gods, they are gods; where there are two or one, I am with him."
"Split a piece of wood and I am there. Lift up the stone and you will find me there."

It is obvious that the Coptic Gospel represents a new ordering of the sayings, or perhaps that both texts were derived from a common or similar source. In any case, the second century date for the Oxyrhynchus text and the conjectured second or third century Coptic translation both represent texts "of very great age."[96] The other sayings of *P. Oxy.* 1 bear resemblance both to the Synoptics and to the Coptic *Gospel of Thomas*, again suggesting a common or similar source for both.[97] The relationship between *P. Oxy.* 1 and the related texts (*Gospel of Thomas* and the Synoptics) is quite similar to that between the Egerton Papyrus Gospel fragments and the New Testament Gospels mentioned above. In each instance the texts involved are dated earlier than would be expected if established sources were being transported to Egypt and there radically recast into new compositions.

P. Oxy. 654 bears a closer resemblance to the text of the *Gospel of Thomas* than does *P. Oxy.* 1, but the Greek text is so fragmentary that many gaps can be restored only hypothetically. Both texts clearly purport to present the ministry of the Living Jesus (i.e. after the resurrection),[98] and this theme is common to many Christian texts found in Egypt.[99] The extremely fragmentary state of *P. Oxy.* 655 makes extensive parallel analysis impossible, but the text of fragment no. 2 also shows some contact with the *Gospel of Thomas* or its sources:

τὶς ἂν προσθ⟨εί⟩η ἐπὶ τὴν ἡλικίαν ὑμῶν; αὐτὸ[ς δ]ώσει ὑμῖν τὸ ἔνδυμα ὑμῶν. λέγουσιν αὐτῷ οἱ μαθηταὶ αὐτοῦ· πότε ἡμῖν ἐμφανὴς ἔσει καὶ πότε σε ὀψόμεθα; λέγει ὅταν ἐκδύσησθε καὶ μὴ αἰσχυνθῆτε.[100]

Who could add to your stature? He himself will give to you your clothing. His disciples say to him, "when will you be revealed to us and when will we see you?" He said, "when you shall be undressed and not be ashamed . . .".[101]

*His disciples said, "when will you be revealed to us and when will we see you?"
Jesus said, "when you take off your clothing without being ashamed and take up
your clothes and place them under your feet like little children and tread on them.
Then you will see the Son of the Living One and you will not be afraid."*

The preceding examples indicate a relationship does exist between
the Oxyrhynchus papyri fragments and the *Gospel of Thomas*, even if
the precise nature of that relationship cannot be established with
certainty. Further complicating the origin of these early Christian
sources are some statements of Clement of Alexandria in his work,
Stromateis. The *Gospel of the Hebrews*[102] is lost, but fragments known
primarily through secondary sources have given it a generally orthodox reputation among modern scholars,[103] and in the first quotation
given below, Clement compares a quotation from a *Gospel of the
Hebrews* to Plato's *Theaetetus* and also to the *Traditions of Matthias*:

ἢ κἂν τῷ καθ᾽ Ἑβραίους εὐαγγελίῳ ὁ θαυμάσας βασιλεύσει γέγραπται καὶ
ὁ βασιλεύσας ἀναπαυθήσεται.[104]

*And also in the Gospel According to the Hebrews it is written, "He who has
marveled shall reign, and he who has reigned shall be refreshed."*

Clement later gives an expanded version of the same saying although he does not cite his source in this later case:

οὐ παύσεται ὁ ζητῶν, ἕως ἂν εὕρῃ, εὑρὼν δὲ θαμβηθήσεται, θαμβηθεὶς δὲ
βασιλεύσει, βασιλεύσας δὲ ἐπαναπαύσεται[105]

*He who seeks will not cease until he should find, and when he finds he will be
astonished, and when he is astounded he will obtain royal power, and after he has
gained power he will find rest.*

In the second usage of the *Gospel of The Hebrews*, without formally
naming his source, Clement appears to regard the text as authoritative. Nevertheless, the four canonical gospels apparently had *more
authority* for Clement, for elsewhere he refers to an apocryphal *Gospel
of the Egyptians*:

Πρῶτον μὲν οὖν ἐν τοῖς παραδεδομένοις ἡμῖν τέταρσιν εὐαγγελίοις οὐκ
ἔχομεν τὸ ῥητὸν ἀλλ᾽ ἐν τῷ κατ᾽ Αἰγυπτίους.[106]

*In the first place, among the four gospels which have been handed down to us, we
do not have the saying, but in the Gospel According to the Egyptians.*

Until the discovery of the Coptic *Gospel of Thomas*, the Oxyrhynchus
papyri fragments were widely thought to be part of the *Gospel of the
Hebrews*, based primarily on the following saying from *P. Oxy.* 654:

λέγει Ἰησους· μὴ παυσάσθω ὁ ζητῶν . . . ἕως ἂν εὕρῃ καὶ ὅταν εὕρῃ
θαμβηθήσεται καὶ θαμβηθεὶς βασιλεύσει καὶ βασιλεύσας ἀναπαήσεται.[107]

*Jesus said, "He who seeks, let him not cease until he finds, and when he finds he
shall be astonished, and when he is astounded he will obtain royal power, and after
he has gained power he will find rest."*

Comparison with the earlier quotations from Clement demonstrates
clearly that the texts are related, just as earlier comparison between
the *P. Oxy.* fragments and the *Gospel of Thomas* showed them to be
related. The key which would open modern understanding to that
relationship has not yet been found, but all three extant texts clearly
depend upon one or more earlier sources whose time and place of
origin can only be conjectured. The time of origin must be at least
early in the second century, if not earlier, allowing the development
of different names and textual traditions to develop by the end of the
same century, and the fact that all three sources known today came
from Egypt argues strongly for that country as the place of origin.
Although Bauer is certainly mistaken when he argues that the *Gospel
of the Egyptians* was the heretical "life of Jesus" used in Egypt as the *only*
life of Jesus,[108] and that the *Gospel of the Hebrews* was the same kind of
work used by Jewish Christians in Alexandria,[109] it is not possible to
determine how Christians in Egypt viewed these works as compared
to the four canonical gospels. It is certain that both the canonical and
the non-canonical writings enjoyed widespread usage and popularity,
as is evidenced by the gospel fragments and texts found among early
Biblical papyri on the one hand, and the use of the early so-called
apocryphal texts and titles in the later literary development of Egyptian Christian literature on the other hand.

Instead of pursuing the somewhat fruitless arguments (made fruitless by the fragmentary nature of the evidence) of Bauer, Telfer, and
others about the orthodoxy or heresy of earliest Egyptian Christianity, the archaeological evidence rather seems to point toward an
undifferentiated Christianity based on a literary tradition encom-
passing both canonical and non-canonical works (both categories
being named as such here in light of their *later* status as defined by the
Catholic tradition). The forces which caused the narrow geographical
and literary outlook of the Western Church, as defined in the previous chapter, do not appear to have been felt strongly in Egypt during
the first two centuries of the Christian era. Bauer may be correct in
asserting that what later heresiologists attacked as "gnosticism" in

Egypt at first may have been simply "Christianity" to Egyptian Christians, but he does not pay sufficient heed to the evidence of so-called "orthodox Christianity" existing alongside it. Egyptian Christians did accept the Apocalyptic literary tradition so notably rejected by the Western Church, especially as reflected in the Resurrection Ministry texts,[110] but not at the expense of the gospel or epistolary tradition of the emerging Catholic Church.

The process of differentiation in Egyptian Christianity may have begun, as Telfer suggests, during the time of Demetrius' episcopate,[111] but perhaps for quite a different reason from the one given by him. While Demetrius may have been responsible for purging "Alexandrine Christianity of its idiosyncrasies," and may "have begun a new age for it,"[112] the impetus behind such action may have been provided by a work written a short time earlier in the West. *P. Oxy.* 405 was dated by H. I. Bell to "a date around about A.D. 200,"[113] and by Grenfell and Hunt "not later than the first half of the third century and (it) might be as old as the latter part of the second."[114] Although the latter believed the text to be the oldest Christian fragment then published, its date is not more significant than its identification as part of the Greek text of Irenaeus' *Adversus Haereses*.[115] C. H. Roberts makes a telling observation on the importance of this text for the early period of Christianity in Egypt:

> "Irenaeus' work was written at Lyons about A.D. 180 and in this scrap we should recognize not only the first fragment of a manuscript of Christian literature contemporary with its author but evidence of the immediate circulation of this powerful attack on Gnosticism among the Egyptian churches and yet another witness to the close relationship subsisting between the church of Alexandria and the West."[116]

The close relationship between Alexandria and the West may have begun, rather than continued, with the heresy hunting inaugurated by the appearance of Irenaeus' work in Alexandria, and one may then account for the distinction being drawn during the next century between orthodoxy and heresy in Egypt. The same narrow approach to literature earlier established in the West would then be imposed upon Egypt, and the result would be a modification, or polarization, of Christianity in Egypt from that time forward. This proposed reconstruction of the history of Egyptian Christianity during the first two centuries would account for the strange silence of Eusebius concerning Egypt for most of that period, since his sources would naturally date from the imposition of a "Western Christianity" along the Nile. The early written texts relating to Christianity would also be accounted for, since Christianity is presumed to have made its arrival by the middle of the first century or soon afterward, and texts later deemed heretical would, during the first two centuries, exist alongside Biblical texts and would also have authority equal or nearly equal to them.

Such a tantalizing historical reconstruction must remain conjectural, however, for there is not sufficient corroborative evidence to sustain certainty of the hypothesis. It is possible that Irenaeus was a leading representative in the attempt to define orthodoxy and heresy which was occurring in many parts of the Christian Church toward the end of the second century, rather than that Western Father being the cause of such a movement. A Gnostic type of Christianity was apparently more prevalent in Egypt than in the West, however, as attested by extant evidence. One must emphasize that this is not to argue that Gnosticism was predominant in Egypt, as some have done, or that Catholicism was absent. Rather, Egyptian Christianity was founded on a more broadly-based literary tradition and a less defined ecclesiastical tradition than was the same religion in the region from Syria to Rome, and it was only when that more stringently defined Christianity made its appearance near the end of the second century along with the *Adversus Haereses* of Irenaeus, that "orthodoxy" and "heresy" began to be defined along lines now familiar to Christian historians.

ENDNOTES

[1] Matthew 2. Cp. Exodus 1–4. Raymond Brown gives a list of significant parallels in *The Birth of the Messiah* (New York: Doubleday and Co., 1977), p. 113. Brown further notes that the non-Biblical traditions (in the midrashic writings) concerning the infancy of Moses provide even more parallels between Jesus and Moses (pp. 114ff.); and he suggests that such "parallels between the Moses legend and the pre-Matthaean Jesus infancy narrative may have been more obvious than we can now perceive" (p. 115). Development of Old Testament themes in The New Testament has been long observed by scholars, generally resulting in a lack of belief in the historical accuracy of the New Testament narrative.

[2] The problems of the historicity of this account and its reconciliation with contemporary evidence (e.g. the rather detailed account of Herod The Great's last days in Josephus, yet without mention there of such a notorious act present problems for the commentator) are well outlined by Brown, *Birth*, pp. 225-228. One should note that lack of evidence supporting this narrative in contemporary sources does not by itself invalidate Matthew's historical credibility.

[3] *N.T. Apoc.* I, pp. 408–409.

[4] *Ibid.*, I, pp. 410–413.

[5] Brown, *Birth*, pp. 203f., lists some of the better known sites associated with the family's Egyptian sojourn. Such places in Egypt, as elsewhere, are primarily visited by believers on pilgrimages, and have little, if any, bearing on the reconstruction of the early historical period. Otto Meinardus, *Christian Egypt: Ancient and Modern* (Cairo: American University Press, 1977), pp.1–2, comments briefly on the many legends surrounding the Holy Family's visit to Egypt, including the unprovable assertion that their stay lasted three years. He also notes that many modern Copts believe that many in Egypt accepted the infant Jesus as divine and became converts to Him at that time.

[6] Acts 2:5. The textual variants for this passage present numerous difficulties. Metzger (*Text. Comment.* pp. 290f.) gives a summary of some of the problems: "Why should Luke think it necessary to mention that Jews were dwelling in Jerusalem? Likewise, why should it be said that they were devout men; would not this be taken for granted from the fact that they were Jews? Most amazing of all is the statement that these Jews were persons from every nation under heaven. Out of all *lands* under heaven could be understood—but since Jews were already an ἔθνος, to say that these were from another ἔθνος is tantamount to a contradiction of terms." Further, κατοικοῦντες generally means permanent residence, as differing from ἐπιδημοῦντες, which signifies visiting on a journey (both are found in Luke's writings). The narrative infers the audience is composed of visitors, but the text is not consistent; in vss. 9 and 10 both words are used to describe this same group: καὶ οἱ κατοικοῦντες τὴν Μεσοποταμίαν, and καὶ οἱ ἐπιδημοῦντες Ῥωμαῖοι.

[7] Ernst Haenchen in *The Acts of the Apostles* (Philadelphia: Westminster Press, 1971), pp. 169–170, note, gives a good summary of the argument. Studies done by F. Cumont and F. C. Burkitt have shown the extent of astrological lore in the Old Testament, and S. Weinstock tried to show that Acts 2:9–11 was an astrological list. Other commentators followed the argument, including B. Reicke, who suggested that the Christian missionaries were dispersed from Antioch on the basis of this astrological list. Deviations from the correct order and selection of countries in an astrological catalogue lead Haenchen to conclude: "We do not know where Luke found this list; presumably his source contained names only of countries, not of signs of the Zodiac." He does not deny a possible "zodiac-origin" for Acts, but argues that alterations were made to suit the purpose of the author.

⁸ F. F. Bruce, *Acts*, *op, cit.*, p. 85.

⁹ Philo, *Flaccus*, 43. For Jews living outside Alexandria in Egypt see below n.34.

¹⁰ Josephus, *B. J.* II.385. The accuracy of Josephus' figures may be enhanced by the observation that a regular census was taken in Egypt (every 14 yrs. beginning in 9 B.C.E. Cf. W. M. Ramsay, *The Bearing of Recent Discoveries on The Trustworthiness of the N.T.*, 4th Ed. London, 1920, pp. 255–274), and Josephus likely would have had access to imperial census records in Rome through his patrons in the Flavian dynasty toward the end of the first century A.D.

¹¹ Josephus, *B. J.* VII. 43: τὸ γὰρ Ἰουδαίων γένος πολὺ μὲν κατὰ πᾶσαν τὴν οἰκουμένην παρέσπαρται τοῖς ἐπιχωρίοις, πλεῖστον δὲ τῇ Συρίᾳ, passim.

¹² Philo, *Flaccus* 55. Philo states that two of the five quarters of Alexandria were primarily Jewish, although Jews were to be found also in numbers elsewhere in the city: πέντε μοῖραι τῆς πόλεώς εἰσιν, ἐπώνυμοι τῶν πρώτων στοιχείων τῆς ἐγγραμμάτου φωνῆς· τούτων δύο Ἰουδαϊκαὶ λέγονται διὰ τὸ πλείστους Ἰουδαίους ἐν ταύταις κατοικεῖν· οἰκοῦσι δὲ καὶ ἐν ταῖς ἄλλαις οὐκ ὀλίγοι σποράδες. Harnack (*The Mission and Expansion of Christianity in the First Three Centuries*, J. Moffatt, trans. and ed. New York: Harper and Bros., 1961), p. 8, argues that such a large percentage of Jews in the Empire could be realized only through widespread proselyting of Gentiles and non-Jewish Semites, with the result that "The Jews of the Diaspora were genuine Jews only to a certain extent."

¹³ Josephus, *B.J.* VI.422–427.

¹⁴ Acts 2:7–8.

¹⁵ Bruce, *Acts, op. cit.*, p. 83 says "While διάλεκπος does not exactly correspond to the modern sense of 'dialect', having the wider meaning 'manner of speech', yet 'dialect' is pretty much what is meant here: cf. The variant expression ταῖς ἡμετέραις γλώσσαις in ver. 11." The latter reference tends to weaken this position, for γλῶσσα is more commonly found in Christian and Jewish (LXX) literature as 'language' than 'dialect' (cf. Arndt and Gingrich, *Greek-English Lexicon of the N.T. etc.* Chicago: U. of Chicago Press, 1957, p. 161). Yet the fact that the people are portrayed as sharing the knowledge with each other might suggest a common language with minor variants.

¹⁶ Haenchen, *op. cit.*, pp. 168f: "The equation of 'tongue' (vs. 4) and διάλεκτος in verse 8 shows that speech in different languages is meant ... At all events, the assembled pious Jews of the diaspora are thunderstruck, since each hears Christians speaking in his own native tongue. Luke expresses this in few words, as verse 4 has made it clear that the Christians are speaking several different languages; it is of little consequence how many Christians speak Parthian etc."

¹⁷ Acts 18:24–19:6; cp. 1 Cor. 1:12; 3:4–23; 4:6; 16:12; Titus 3:13. One cannot prove that all the references are to the same Apollos, but most commentators assume that to be the case.

¹⁸ Some differences may be seen in the reporting of events after Paul's conversion in Gal. 1:21 and Acts 9:23–30; 11:25–30. The accounts are not irreconcilable, however, and Paul's association with Barnabas is assumed in Galatians 2:1 (indirectly agreeing with the Acts narrative).

¹⁹ Paul had not visited Rome when he wrote to the Romans, but he hoped to do so (15:28f.) for the purpose of uniting them to his other branches (1:9–13; 15:19–25). The Galatians are chided for removing their allegiance from Paul to another faction (1:6–10), and the divisiveness of the Corinthians is denounced in favor of unity based on the earlier preachings of Paul (1 Cor. 1:10–3:23).

²⁰ Bauer, *op. cit.*, p. 46 n.6, asks "Is it possible to demonstrate not as an occasional occurrence, but as a general rule, that a large population of Jews should immediately attract Christianity?" As for Jews living south of the delta, see notes 9 and 10.

[21] Acts 18:24f.

[22] B. Metzger, *Text. Comment. on the Greek N.T.* (New York: United Bible Societies, 1971), p. 466. See also J. Finegan, *Encountering New Testament Manuscripts* (Grand Rapids: Eerdmans Pub., 1974), p. 64 for a brief statement of the nature of the codex.

[23] πατρίς is given in A&G as meaning both homeland or country and hometown or one's own part of the country. For present purposes it makes little difference where in Egypt Apollos would have received his Christian training, although most would assume his native Alexandria.

[24] F. F. Bruce, *The New International Commentary*, Acts (Grand Rapids: Eerdmans, 1954), p. 381: "It is not explicitly stated (except in the Western Text) that Apollos received his accurate instruction 'in the way of the Lord' in his native Alexandria, but he may well have done so. The origins of Alexandrian Christianity are lost in obscurity, but the gospel certainly reached the Egyptian capital at a very early date." Cp. Bruce, *Acts, op. cit.*, p. 351, and Haenchen, *op. cit.*, p. 550, who cites as "unlikely" an argument by Zahn that some pilgrims had taken a vague report concerning John the Baptist and Jesus back to Alexandria. Johannes Munck gives one of the most sceptical positions (*Acts of the Apostles*, New York: Doubleday & Co., 1967), pp. 182–183, when he states that "Apollos may well have grown up and been educated in places other than the city where his family had originally resided." Bauer, *op. cit.*, p. 46 sees it as "no accident" that "an amplification of the original text insists on knowing something about the most primitive period of Christian Egypt."

[25] Bruce, *Acts, op. cit.*, p. 351.

[26] E. Käsemann, "Die Johannesjunger von Ephesus," *Zeitscrhift für Theologie und Kirche* (1952), p. 153.

[27] Bauer, *op. cit.*, p. 46.

[28] H. I. Bell is a notable exception to the preceding argument. Commenting on Acts 18:24ff., Bell says: (*Evidences of Christ. in Egypt etc.*) "This also has been taken as evidence for the early presence of Christianity at Alexandria, but if it has any relevance at all it seems to me to make in the opposite direction. We do not know at what age Apollos left Alexandria . . . It is true that D adds after κατηχημένος the words ἐν τῇ πατρίδι, but this is one of those Western variants which look very much like interpolations." Bell's argument is possibly correct but it is also unnecessarily destructive of the evidence, since no reason compels the reader to doubt Apollos could have received Christianity in Egypt or that the Western text editor had some ulterior motive for adding the variant in question. Bell's argument is the more curious on this point, since he concludes his article with the following observation (p. 204): "This evidence seems to justify the inference that even in the second century the number of Christians in Middle Egypt was considerable." He had argued earlier (p. 190) that although he discounted the value of Acts in determining the existence of a Christian community in Alexandria during the first century C.E., he still believed that such a community did exist. Cp. Bell, *Cults and Creeds in Graeco-Roman Egypt* (New York: Philosophical Library, 1953), p. 79.

[29] Josephus, *Antiq.* II.315; Strabo XVII.30; Diod. I.56. Smith (*Dict. of Greek and Roman Geog.* London: John Murray, 1873), p. 360 describes the Egyptian fortress (modern *Baboul*) as the border town "between Lower and Middle Egypt, where the river craft paid toll ascending or descending the Nile . . . In the age of Augustus the Deltaic Babylon became a town of some importance, and was the headquarters of the three legions which ensured the obedience of Egypt."

[30] Franz Altheim and Ruth Stiehl, *Christentum am Roten Meer, Zweiter Band.* Berlin: Walter de Gruyter & Co., 1973, pp.297–299.

[31] Donald Guthrie, *N.T. Intro.*, vol 3: *Hebrews to Revelation* (Chicago: Inter-Varsity Press, 1964), p. 126.

[32] H. I. Bell, *Evidences*, *op. cit.*, p. 187.

[33] See esp. Rev. 14:8; 16:19; 17:5; 18:2,10,21. Cp. *Sibylline Books V.* 143; *II Baruch* 11:1, passim.

[34] The papyrus text was designated London Papyrus 1912, published by H. I. Bell in *Jews and Christians in Egypt* (London: Oxford Univ. Press, 1924).

[35] Bell, *Evidences*, *op. cit.*, p. 188. Cp. K. Baus, *From The Apostolic Community to Constantine* (London: Burns & Oates, 1965), p. 128.

[36] *P. Lond*. 1912, *ℓℓ.*98–100, transl. by Bell, *Jews and Christ.*, *op. cit.*, and *Evidences*, *op. cit.*, pp. 188–189.

[37] Salomon Reinach, "La première allusion au christianisme dans l' histoire," *Revue de l'histoire des religions* 90 (1924), pp. 108–122.

[38] M. Cumont, "La Lettre de Claude aux Alexandrins," *Revue de l'histoire des religions* 91 (1925), pp. 3–6.

[39] See Bell, *Evidences*, *op. cit.*, p. 189. The recently-discovered Dead Sea Scrolls and much Pseudepigraphic literature recovered during the past century are replete with references to an expected Messiah. Some works (e.g. *I Enoch*, *III Baruch*, and the *Testaments of the Twelve Patriarchs*) contain such specific references to the messianic age that scholars generally argue for Christian interpolations and editing of those texts.

[40] Acts 11:26–28.

[41] Bell, *Evidences*, *op. cit.*, pp. 189–190. Cp. Baus. *op. cit.*, p. 128, who says "its wording can without difficulty be understood as referring to the continual quarrels of the Jewish inhabitants of Alexandria among themselves and with the Greek population, which repeatedly led to bloodshed."

[42] Eusebius, *H.E.* II.16:1. A. Harnack (*Mission, op. cit.*), II, p. 159 claims that "Eusebius found nothing in his sources bearing on the primitive history of Christianity at Alexandria . . ." Bauer, *op. cit.*, p. 45, responds that Eusebius was diligent in *trying* to find Christian evidences in his sources even citing unnamed Greek authors for material relating to the Jewish revolt under Trajan: ταῦτα καὶ Ἑλλήνων οἱ τὰ κατὰ τοὺς αὐτοὺς χρόνους· γραφῇ παραδόντες αὐτοῖς ἱστόρησαν ῥήμασιν. (*H.E. IV* 2.5).

[43] See e.g. Gregory Nazianz, *On Athanasius* (XXI.7), where the author speaks of Athanasius being led up to the throne of St. Mark to become Patriarch of Alexandria; Jerome, *Commen. in Matt.*, Prooem.6, and *De Vir. Illustr.* 8 (both probably derived from Eusebius) and John Cassian, *Institutes* (11.5), who claims that the monks "received that mode of life from the Evangelist Mark of blessed memory, the first to preside over the Church of Alexandria as Bishop . . ." A. S. Atiya, *Hist. of Eastern Christianity* (Notre Dame: U. of Notre Dame Press, 1968), p. 25f. gives a bibliography for the earliest patriarchs of Alexandria, but the Markan tradition cannot be pressed beyond Arabic sources to Coptic or Greek originals, thus weakening its claim to be early or authentic. C. H. Roberts, "Books in the Graeco-Roman World and in the New Testament," *The Cambridge History of The Bible* (Ackroyd and Evans, eds. Cambridge: Cambridge U. Press, 1970) I, p. 59, makes the interesting observation that Mark is "a minor founder figure for a major church."

[44] Philo describes the Therapeutae in his *De Vita Contemplativa*, and he compares them to the Essenes, who are more active and less severe in asceticism. Eusebius is anachronistic in reading Christian monastic practices back to this group who lived in isolation near Alexandria and also near Lake Mareotis. The Christian monastic movement began considerably later and had Egyptian, rather than Jewish, origins. One might note in this regard, that although Sozomen used Eusebius as a source for his work (*H.E.* I.1). and despite the exaggerated value he puts upon monastic discipline as

the true Christian philosophy (I.12,13; III.14, passim), this historian does not stress the Christianity of Philo's Therapeutae (I,12): "In this narrative, Philo appears to describe certain Jews who accepted Christianity, and yet retained the customs of their nation; for no remains of this way of life can be found elsewhere."

⁴⁵ Eusebius, *H.E.* II. 17.15.

⁴⁶ *Ibid.*, II.17.18.

⁴⁷ Morton Smith, *Clement of Alexandria and a Secret Gospel of Mark* (Cambridge: Harvard U. Press, 1973), p. 27.

⁴⁸ *Ibid.*, p. 446.

⁴⁹ Morton Smith, "Clement of Alexandria and Secret Mark: The Score at the End of the First Decade," *Harvard Theological Review* 75:4 (1982), pp.449–461.

⁵⁰ *Ibid.*, p.457: "In sum, 'the state of the question' would seem to be about as follows: Attribution of the letter to Clement is commonly accepted and no strong argument against it has appeared, but Clement's attribution of the gospel to 'Mark' is universally rejected."

⁵¹ Bauer, *op. cit.*, p. 45.

⁵² Eusebius emphasizes the uniqueness of his work in *H.E.* I.1.3: ἐπεὶ καὶ πρῶτοι νῦν τῆς ὑποθέσεως ἐπιβάντες οἷά τινα ἐρήμην καὶ ἀτριβῆ ἰέναι ὁδὸν ἐγχειροῦμεν . . . Eusebius declares that not even the bare footsteps of earlier writers can be seen, except in a few instances of contemporary records left for the future. Even allowing for literary exaggeration, one has no reason to doubt the difficulty Eusebius had in obtaining suitable sources concerning the churches and their leaders. The selective nature of his work is also stressed by Eusebius:

ὅσα τοίνυν εἰς τὴν προκειμένην ὑπόθεσιν λυσιτελεῖν ἡγούμεθα τῶν αὐτοῖς ἐκείνοις σποράδην μνημονευθέντων, ἀναλεξάμενοι καὶ ὡς ἂν ἐκ λογικῶν λειμώνων τὰς ἐπιτηδείους αὐτῶν τῶν πάλαι συγγραφέων ἀπανθισάμενοι φωνάς, δι' ὑφηγήσεως ἱστορικῆς πειρασόμεθα σωματοποιῆσαι, ἀγαπῶντες, εἰ καὶ μὴ ἁπάντων, τῶν δ' οὖν μάλιστα διαφανεστάτων τοῦ σωτῆρος ἡμῶν ἀποστόλων τὰς διαδοχὰς κατὰ τὰς διαπρεπούσας ἔτι καὶ νῦν μνημονευομένας ἐκκλησίας ἀνασωσαίμεθα. (I.1.4).

⁵³ The Eusebeian catalogue of the accession of the first twelve Alexandrian bishops is as follows: Mark (II.16); Annianus (II.24); Abilius (III.14); Cerdon (III.21); Primus (IV.1); Justus (IV.4); Eumenes (IV.5.5); Marcus (IV.11.6); Celadion (IV.11.6); Agrippinus (IV.19–20); Julian (V. 9); Demetrius (V. 22). Eusebius uses a combination of emperor year-rules and episcopal year-rules ("after so many years," etc.) to establish chronology, but with the sole exception of Pantaenus' rule of the catechetical school at Alexandria no event or personal description serves to suggest this list is more than a fabrication by Eusebius or perhaps someone else in the third century.

⁵⁴ Eusebius, *H.E.* V.10.1.

⁵⁵ Euseb., *H.E.* V.10.4 H. J. Lawlor and J. E. L. Oulton, Eusebius (London: SPCK Press, 1954) II, p. 165, dispute this point, saying Eusebius "nowhere mentions any written work of Pantaenus, and there is no good evidence from any other source that Pantaenus was a writer." They continue that Clement can be used as evidence against Pantaenus writing, for in Euseb. *H.E.* V.11.3, where the *Stromateis* are quoted, Clement says he is writing to preserve what he heard from Pantaenus and other teachers. Later, in VI.13.9, Clement is quoted in his *De Pascha* as saying that he ἐκβιασθῆναι ὁμολογεῖ πρὸς τῶν ἑταίρων ἃς ἔτυχεν παρὰ τῶν ἀρχαίων πρεσβυτέρων ἀκηκοὼς παραδόσεις γραφῇ τοῖς μετὰ ταῦτα παραδοῦναι . . . The fact that Clement was compelled to write what he had heard from his teachers hardly seems to justify the assumption that the tradition of Egypt, and especially of Alexandria, would suggest otherwise. As papyrus collections

found in Egypt during the past century show that writing was common among poorly-educated people, who would argue that a religion so tied to books and written traditions as was Christianity would not produce some writing within the Alexandrian school before Clement? On the other hand, with all the texts now known, some written record might have been expected to survive, and one might question how well established the school was before the time of Clement.

⁵⁶ Bauer, *op. cit.*, p. 45.

⁵⁷ On the relationship of Servianus to Hadrian see Dio's *Roman History* LXIX.17.

⁵⁸ The letter is quoted by Flavius Vopiscus, *Vita Saturnini* 8. See Ernst Hohl, ed., *Scriptores Historiae Augustae*, 2 vols. (Leipzig: Teubner, 1927, reprinted 1971, Vol. 2, pp. 227–228). Bauer, *op. cit.*, p. 47, considers the document spurious, but admits it is significant that a great historian (H. Gelzer) regarded it as authentic. Harnack, *Mission, op. cit.*, I, pp. 250, 275, and II, p. 160, admits the letter is controversial and should be used cautiously except as a third century witness. The relevant portion of the text is as follows: "Aegyptum, quam mihi laudabas, Serviane carissime, totam didici levem pendulam et ad omnia famae momenta volitantem. Illic qui Serapem colunt, Christiani sunt et devoti sunt Serapi, qui se Christi episcopos dicunt; nemo illic archisynagogus Judaeorum, nemo Samarites, nemo Christianorum presbyter, non mathematicus, non haruspex, non aliptes. Ipse ille patriarcha cum Aegyptum venerit, ab aliis Serapidem adorare, ab aliis cogitur Christum . . . unus illis deus nummus est; hunc Christiani, hunc Judaei, hunc omnes venerantur et gentes."

⁵⁹ A. Harnack, *op. cit.*, I. p. 250.

⁶⁰ Johannes Leipoldt, *Das Evangelium Nach Thomas*. Berlin: Akademie Verlag, 1967, p.3.

⁶¹ Bell, *Cults and Creeds, op. cit.*, p. 80.

⁶² Atiya, *op. cit.*, p. 33 gives the following description of the school, although he does not cite references or sources: "The Catechetical School of Alexandria was undoubtedly the earliest important institution of theological learning in antiquity. . . . Yet it would be an error to limit its curriculum to theology. It was a college in which many other disciplines were included from the humanities, science and mathematics, although its chief function in the age of faith was religion." Bell (*Cults and Creeds, op. cit.*, p. 96) is not so specific in spelling out the curriculum, but he is in general agreement with the description of Atiya: ". . . The principal motive was no doubt to provide for Christians a means of higher education other than that of the pagan university in the Museum."

⁶³ H. I. Bell, *Recent Discoveries of Biblical Papyri*. (Oxford: Clarendon Press, 1937), p. 3. Hunt and Edgar, *Select Papyri* (Cambridge: Harvard U. Press, 1959, 1963) I, p. IX suggest a more recent date for the beginning of papyrology: "A scientific pursuit of Greek papyri has been in progress for little longer than a generation."

⁶⁴ *Ibid*. Bell lists the following as illustrative of the subjects in the papyri: ". . . from the Paeans of Pindar or an Ode of Sappho to the popular literature of Graeco-Roman Egypt or late rhetorical exercises, Biblical fragments and works of Christian theology, documentary papyri of every category . . ." The table of contents for Vol. 1 of the Hunt and Edgar collection extends the list to include agreements, receipts, wills, letters, invitations, orders for payments, prayers, horoscopes, etc. This list implies that the modern reader can glimpse the gamut of the common man's activities, habits, religious ideas, and culture by studying this written legacy from the past.

⁶⁵ C. H. Roberts, "Books in the Gr.-Rom. World," *op. cit.*, I, p. 48.

⁶⁶ *Ibid*.

⁶⁷ C. H. Roberts, *Manuscript, Society, and Belief in Early Christian Egypt*. London: Oxford Univ. Press for the British Academy, 1979, p.63.

[68] Bell, *Evidences*, *op. cit.*, p. 191. In his *Recent Discoveries*, *op. cit.*, p. 29, Bell indicates the relative insignificance of the lack of evidence for Christianity in the legal documents of the first two centuries: "legal and official documents cannot in any case be expected to indicate the religion of the persons mentioned in them."

[69] C. H. Roberts, *An Unpublished Fragment of the Fourth Gospel* (Manchester: The Manchester University Press, 1935).

[70] Jack Finegan, *Encountering New Testament Manuscripts* (Grand Rapids: Eerdmans Pub. Co., 1974), pp. 27–29. See also L. D. Reynolds and N. G. Wilson, *Scribes and Scholars, A Guide to the Transmission of Greek and Latin Literature*, 2nd Ed., Revised (Oxford: Clarendon Press, 1975), pp. 30–32. C. H. Roberts, "Books" *op. cit.*, p. 58, emphasizes the point, "as it marks the independence of the Church from Jewish traditions and practices and points the way to the formation of the Christian Canon."

[71] C. H. Roberts, "The Christian Book and the Greek Papyri," *Journal of Theological Studies* 50 (1949) p. 158. F.G. Kenyon, *The Text of the Greek Bible*, 3rd Ed., Rev. by A. W. Adams (London: Duckworth, 1975), p. 8, says of the Christian use of the codex: "But discoveries in Egypt, especially some of quite recent date, have shown that not later than the early years of the second century the experiment was tried of utilizing the codex form for papyrus. It seems that this was almost certainly the invention of the Christian community and is closely associated with the Bible itself." Bell, *Recent Discoveries*, *op. cit.*, p. 25, says ". . . and the fact is the more remarkable because second century papyri of pagan literature are almost, perhaps entirely, without exception in roll form."

[72] Bell, *Evidences*, *op. cit.*, pp. 199–200.

[73] Roberts, *Unpublished Fragment*, *op. cit.*, pp. 13–16.

[74] Bell, *Evidences*, *op. cit.*, p. 200.

[75] Roberts, "The Christian Book . . .," *op. cit.*, pp. 155ff. It is well known that although papyrus rolls were commonly used in the Graeco-Roman world, most climates are not hospitable to the preservation of papyrus (dryness makes it brittle and dampness makes it rot). The Egyptian climate south of the Delta is sufficiently dry that if the papyrus were above the Nile flood level, it would be preserved indefinitely, even if becoming brittle with age. The climate of Khirbet Qumran near the Dead Sea and a very few other locations are also capable of preserving texts, and recent discoveries in these areas suggest a widespread interest in books and texts throughout the Mediterranean Hellenistic world.

[76] The eight listed are (and the last three are the questionable ones); P. Baden 4, P. Oxy. IV.656, P.Ryl. i.5, The Chester Beatty Numbers and Deuteronomy, P. Lips. 170, The Chester Beatty Ezekiel, Daniel, and Esther, the Jeremiah from the same collection, and P. Antinoopolis inedit. (Psalms). The codex form in all cases of the Old Testament texts mentioned, and the Christian contractions, the *nomina sacra* in some of them (e.g. $\overline{\text{ic}}$, $\overline{\text{kc}}$, and $\overline{\text{kv}}$ in P. Beatty 6 and P. Baden IV,56), are considered sufficiently strong reasons for assigning them a Christian, rather than a Jewish, origin. On *nomina sacra* in The Old Testament, see Roberts, "Books in The Graeco-Roman World . . .," *op. cit.*, pp. 60–61.

[77] P.S.I. VIII, 921, a fragment of a Psalter of Florence which was written on the *verso* of a document dated in 142–143 C.E., was rejected as a second century text by Roberts for "palaeographical similarities with the next century," but Bell (*Evidences*, *op. cit.*, p. 201) argues that "it is most unusual in a roll used again in this way to find a longer interval between *recto* and *verso* than about fifty years." He thus prefers a second century date. A fragment of a codex containing Exodus and Deuteronomy, P. Baden IV.56, was assigned to the second century by the editor Bilabel, who was followed by Bell (*Recent Discoveries*, *op. cit.*, p. 15).

[78] W. Telfer, "Episcopal Succession in Egypt," *JEH* 3 (1952), p. 2. The letter is quoted in part in Eusebius, *H.E.* V.25, and was written during the time of Victor, who became bishop of Rome in 189, the same year that Demetrius became bishop of Alexandria.

[79] C. H. Roberts, "Early Christianity in Egypt: Three Notes," *JEA* 40 (1954), p. 92.

[80] Telfer, *loc. cit.*

[81] H. I. Bell and T. C. Skeat, *Fragments of an Unknown Gospel and Other Early Christian Papyri* (London: British Museum Pub., 1935). The dating to the early second century is based on comparison with P. Berol. ined. 6854, written in the reign of Trajan, P. Lond. 130, a horoscope calculated from 1 April A.D. 81, and P. Fay. 110, dated to A.D. 94 (See pp. 1–2).

[82] Guillaumont, *et al.*, *The Gospel According to Thomas* (New York: Harper and Row, 1959). The Coptic text was one of 52 tractates associated with the Nag Hammadi Library, purportedly found near the city of the same name in 1945. More of its significance in the history of Egyptian Christianity will be mentioned later.

[83] J. Jeremias, in *N.T. Apoc.*, *op. cit.*, I, pp. 94–95, understands the passage to be the conclusion of a trial in which Jesus had been accused of breaking the law, perhaps a violation of the sabbath.

[84] Bell and Skeat, *op. cit.*, pp.27–35.

[85] Jeremias, *loc. cit.*: "There are contacts with all four Gospels. The juxtaposition of Johannine (I) and Synoptic material (II and III) and the fact that the Johannine material is shot through with Synoptic phrases and the Synoptic with Johannine usage, permits the conjecture that the author knew all and every one of the canonical Gospels. Only he had no one of them before him as a written text."

[86] Mark 11:12–21; Matt. 21:18–21.

[87] Matthew 17:24–27.

[88] Mark 4:35–41; Matt. 8:23–27; Luke 8:22–25. These miracle-accounts were selected because they exhibit characteristics similar to the miracle in P. Egerton 2, namely Jesus' miraculous control over the elements. Miracles of catching many fish, causing the destruction of many pigs, providing food to feed thousands, and others also fit the same general pattern.

[89] Bell and Skeat, *op. cit.*, p. 7.

[90] *Ibid.*, p. 39.

[91] See above, note 78.

[92] B. P. Grenfell and A. S. Hunt, *New Sayings of Jesus and Fragment of a Lost Gospel from Oxyrhynchus* (New York: Oxford Univ. Press, American Branch, 1904), p. 9. This fragment is now known as *P. Oxy.* 1.

[93] *Ibid.*, pp. 9–10. The dating is moved back from late third century in Grenfell-Hunt to late second or early third century by W. Schneemelcher, *N.T. Apoc.* I, pp. 98–99. This fragment is now known as *P. Oxy.* 654.

[94] *Ibid.*, pp. 39–47, for the text and commentary of these fragments, known as *P. Oxy.* 655.

[95] *P. Oxy.* 1, logion 5.

[96] Schneemelcher, *N.T. Apoc.* I, p. 98.

[97] *Ibid.*, pp. 105–110 for the parallels and references.

[98] *P. Oxy.* 654, 11.1–5: {οἱ}τοῖοι οἱ λόγοι οἱ[. . . οὓς ἐλά]λησεν Ἰησοῦς ὁ ζῶν κ[ύριος . . .] καὶ θωμᾷ καὶ ἔιπεν [αὐτοῖς· πᾶς ὅστις] ἂν τῶν λόγων τούτ[ων ἀκούσῃ θανάτου] οὐ μὴ γεύσηται. *Gosp. Thomas*, *N.H.* II. 32:10–14:

ⲚⲀⲈⲒ ⲚⲈ Ⲛ̄ϢⲀϪⲈ ⲈⲐⲎⲠ' ⲈⲚⲦⲀⲒ̅Ⲥ̅ ⲈⲦⲞⲚϨ· ϪⲞⲞⲨ ⲀⲨⲰ ⲀϤⲤϨⲀЇⲤⲞⲨ Ⲛ̄ϬⲒ ⲆⲒⲆⲨⲘⲞⲤ ЇⲞⲨⲆⲀⲤ ⲐⲰⲘⲀⲤ ⲀⲨⲰ ⲠⲈϪⲀϤ ϪⲈ ⲠⲈⲦⲀϨⲈ ⲈⲐⲈⲢⲘⲎⲚⲈⲒⲀ Ⲛ̄ⲚⲈⲈⲒϢⲀϪⲈ ϤⲚⲀϪⲒ ϮⲠⲈ ⲀⲚ Ⲙ̄ⲠⲘⲞⲨ·

[99] Examples include the *Apocryphon of John, Gospel of Thomas, Sophia Jesu Christi, Second Jeu, Pistis Sophia, The Epistle of Peter to Philip* and *Dialogue of The Redeemer*. Schneemelcher (*op. cit.*, I, p. 82f.) informs the reader that "In these revelation writings we are for the most part concerned with works in which visions and dialogues of Jesus with His disciples are reported. In them Jesus is on most occasions the risen Lord, the exalted Revealer, that is to say these writings are interested primarily not in the historical Jesus but in the heavenly Redeemer." The phrases ʼΙησοῦς ὁ ζῶν and ⲒⲤ ⲈⲦⲞⲚⲎ are generally agreed to refer to the Resurrected Christ in such literature. For a sound treatment of the question of the resurrection ministry, see H. Nibley, "Evangelium Quadraginta Dierum," *Vigiliae Christianae* 20 (1966), pp. 1–24, reprinted as "The Forty-day Mission of Christ—the Forgotten Heritage," in *When The Lights Went Out* (Salt Lake: Deseret Book, 1970), pp. 33–54.

[100] *P. Oxy.* 655, 11. 13–23.

[101] *Gospel of Thomas*, N.H.II, 39:27–40:2.

[102] Jerome's comments (*in Matt.* 12:13) that he had translated the Gospel of the Nazarenes and Ebionites into Greek, and (*de Vir. Illust.* 2) that he had "translated into Greek and Latin" The Gospel of the Hebrews "which Origen often uses" have caused some to believe that the two gospels are really one and the same. Until the texts of both can be recovered, an attempt to argue for one or for two must remain open-ended, and for present purposes the one title "The Hebrews" will be used as found in Clement.

[103] F. L. Cross, *Oxford Dict. of the Christ. Church* (London: Oxford Univ. Press, 1974), p. 626.

[104] Clement, *Stromateis* II.9.45.

[105] *Ibid.*, V.14.96.

[106] *Ibid.*, III.13.93. This apocryphal gospel, known today only through a few surviving quotations, is *not* related to the two versions of the *Coptic Gospel of The Egyptians* found in the Nag Hammadi Codices.

[107] *P. Oxy.* 654:5–9. The text is given in Grenfell and Hunt, *Oxyrhynchus Papyri* IV (London: Egyptian Exploration Fund, 1904), p. 4.

[108] Bauer, *op. cit.*, p. 50. So little is known of the contents of the *G. Egypt.* mentioned by Clement and others that one cannot speak with certainty of its contents, and the Coptic version is a cosmogonical and cosmological gospel in the tradition of the Resurrection Ministry writings. The early datings of the Biblical papyri refute Bauer's contention that the *G. Egypt.* was the only gospel used in early Egyptian Christianity.

[109] *Ibid.*, p. 52. Bauer's attempt to place an heretical stamp on almost all non-canonical writings appears to have blinded him to the rather favorable impression most scholars have of the few fragments known today.

[110] The Western Church did not reject the reality of the 40-day Ministry, as seen in Euseb., *H.E.* II. 1. 3f.; III.32.8. As Nibley notes in "The Forty-day Mission," *op. cit.*, p. 43 n.61, "The charge of Irenaeus against the Gnostics is not that they invent new absurdities, but that they misrepresent true and familiar doctrines, so also Polycarp, *Ep. Phil.*, c.7; P. Bodmer X:52:3, etc." this acceptance of the reality of that ministry makes the rejection of the literature associated with it all the more curious, and reinforces the conclusion reached earlier that it was essentially the self-imposed eclecticism of the Western Church which caused rejection of everything outside of itself.

[111] Telfer, *op. cit.*, p. 2.

[112] *Ibid.*

[113] Bell, *Evidences*, *op. cit.*, p. 202.

[114] Grenfell and Hunt, *Oxyrh. Pap.*, *op. cit.*, III 405.

[115] *Ibid.*, Appendix to Part IV, p. 264.

[116] C. H. Roberts, "Early Christianity in Egypt: Three Notes," *JEA* 40 (1954), p. 94.

CHAPTER III

THE EMERGENCE OF ORTHODOXY AND
HERESY IN EGYPTIAN CHRISTIANITY

The suggestion was made at the close of the previous chapter that an infusion of a stringently defined Christianity into Egypt occurred near the end of the second century. This suggestion is supported both by the beginning of a conventional Christian historical tradition at that time and by the discovery in Egypt of a fragment of Irenaeus' *Against the Heresies* dated to the late second century, the latter portending a new and defined awareness of the distinction between "orthodoxy" and "heresy." Although many Biblical and non-Biblical Christian texts dating from the late first or early second century demonstrate the presence of Christians in Egypt by the end of the first century, it is to such early heresiologists as Irenaeus, Hippolytus, and Tertullian that one must turn for information concerning the nature of second century Egyptian Christianity. The heresiologists believed that those against whom their volleys were fired were at best Christians gone astray, and usually worse, that the heretics were not really Christians but men who simply paraded under the banner of Christ while continuing in paganism.[1] It has been shown above that a radical bifurcation of Christianity into orthodoxy and heresy cannot be shown to have existed in Egypt during the first two centuries, and this agrees with Bauer's hypothesis that:

> ... perhaps certain manifestations of Christian life that the authors of the church renounce as 'heresies' originally had not been such at all, but at least here and there, were the only form of the new religion—that is, for those regions they were simply 'Christianity.'[2]

The barren picture found in traditional literary sources concerning Christian history in Egypt before the episcopacy of Demetrius (the barrenness is made all more obvious through the discoveries of early Christian manuscripts) is thus viewed from a later and narrower perspective of Christian understanding and may be filled in somewhat if the broader horizons of "heresy" are taken into consideration. It is noteworthy that even by the standards of the ancient heresiologists, who argued that heresy is a deviation from the right path, the presence of heretics in the early second century in Egypt would presume the earlier presence of more "orthodox" Christians—of whom no mention is found in their works (the shadowy bishops in Eusebius excepted). That no battle for hegemony of the church in Egypt can be found in the evidence for this early period, when the heterodox are supposed to be so well known and identifiable as heretics, is all the more reason to doubt that such a battle took place or that the heresiologists' division of Christianity into sects can be defended. No argument can be presented and defended which shows that doctrinal or ecclesiastical unity in the Christian church definitely was of great concern in the first and early second century Egypt. This argument is usually assumed, but its presence in Egypt cannot be established earlier than Irenaeus, who stated that a heretic is defined as one who teaches doctrines different from

τῆς οὔσης Ἐκκλησίας πάσης μίαν καὶ τὴν αὐτὴν πίστιν ἐχούσης εἰς πάντα τὸν κόσμον.[3]

the entire existing church which possesses one and the same faith throughout the world.

Irenaeus includes Egypt in his geographical catalogue of churches,[4] but such a portrayal of unity as the test for correctness is clearly idealistic rather than realistic.

The following examination of the so-called heretics in second century Egypt and their relationship to their more "orthodox" successors will illustrate how fluid and undefined are their theological differences. One *caveat* to be observed is that most of the information presently available on the heretics comes from Western sources who are removed both in geography and in sympathy from their subjects, rendering them at least suspect as to their accuracy in understanding and explaining the authors and movements they oppose. Discoveries of manuscripts acceptable to and possessed by these so-called heretical groups in Egypt, even if not always composed by them, makes possible for the first time in centuries an examination of the heretics from sources sympathetic to their beliefs. Some of the early heretical leaders and movements denounced by the Church Fathers are illuminated by the manuscripts, while others remain relatively obscure due to lack of evidence originating with those so-called heretics. Some texts do not seem to fit any known groups, causing some scholars to desire a new nomenclature for early Egyptian Christian heretical movements.[5] There is no such purpose in this study, which will be confined to analysis of the charges of heterodoxy leveled at specific Egyptian Christians by the Church Fathers, notably against Cerinthus, Carpocrates, Basilides, and Valentinus.

In 1895, Carl Schmidt discovered 15 leaves of a Coptic text of an *Epistula Apostolorum*,[6] of which a complete text in Ethiopic was edited and published in 1913.[7] This work, otherwise unknown in the literature of early Christianity, is said by Schmidt to have originated in Egypt between 160 and 170 C.E., a date slightly later than that suggested by other commentators. The beginning of the text is preserved only in Ethiopic, and contains a warning about two false teachers:

> What Jesus Christ revealed to his disciples as a letter, and how Jesus Christ revealed the letter of the council of the apostles, the disciples of Jesus Christ, to the Catholics; which was written because of the false apostles Simon and Cerinthus, that no one should follow them . . .[8]

Somewhat later in the text, where the Ethiopic is joined by the Coptic, another reference is made to these two teachers: "Cerinthus and Simon have come to go through the world. But they are the enemies of our Lord Jesus Christ . . ."[9] The post-resurrection dialogue is a typical setting for a gnostic document,[10] but the emphasis on the physical resurrection of Jesus and the free and literal use of the New Testament throughout the work show that it is not a typical representative of gnostic thought.[11] Although the association with Simon (Magus) might suggest a Samaritan origin for Cerinthus, Irenaeus says "Et Cerinthus autem quidam in Asia,"[12] (*And Cerinthus, a certain man in Asia*) and Hippolytus, perhaps a student of Irenaeus,[13] states that Cerinthus was educated in the wisdom of the Egyptians.[14] Irenaeus is more probably correct in the matter, for he is likely Hippolytus' source. He also records a story of John confronting Cerinthus at a bath in Ephesus,[15] and there is nothing beyond the *Epistula Apostolorum* reference to place Cerinthus in Egypt. Even in that text one notes that the rejection of the supposedly gnostic Cerinthus is contained in a literary setting usually associated with gnostic writings.

The scanty evidence relating to Cerinthus is scarcely better when one turns to Carpocrates, said by Theodoret to be a successor of Cerinthus and to have lived during the time of Hadrian.[16] If the reports concerning Carpocrates can be believed, that man and his followers were condemned more on account of immoral practices than because of doctrinal error.[17] Beyond a general charge concerning the nature of Christ and the identity of the creators of the world, Irenaeus dwells on the licentious practices of the Carpocratian cult, especially rejecting their opinion-based justification for such activities.[18] Most of the later writers who attack heresies depend upon Irenaeus' account for their material concerning Carpocrates,[19] but Clement adds information which indicates a knowledge of the sect based on other sources.[20] From Clement one learns that Carpocrates was an Alexandrian[21] and, in his only statement concerning the metaphysics of the sect, that Carpocrates "was instructed in the Monadic Gnosis."[22] Clement is not supported by other sources. Chadwick believes, however, that this reference to Monadism is reflected in two Latin Christian writers thought to have used a lost work of Hippolytus as their source.[23] Many have argued against the accuracy of Clement's description of the Carpocratians, especially concerning the cult which sprang up after the death of Carpocrates' son, Epiphanes.[24] The ritual of branding an ear with a hot iron is not included in Clement as in the other accounts, and some have tried to discredit his description for that reason, but an *argumentum e silentio* from some authors is hardly a solid basis for rejecting what *is* stated in Clement. A greater difficulty is involved when one tries to establish what effect Carpocrates and his followers had on the majority of the Christians in Egypt. Extremely immoral practices would guarantee headlines in the accounts of their more pious opponents, but no evidence exists to suggest that they offered a religious philosophy which was very popular and threatening to a more normative and continent Christianity. The Carpocratians did not all remain in Egypt, however, for a woman, Marcellina, is reported by Irenaeus to have gone to Rome and there seduced others to the licentious practices of the sect.[25] Irenaeus says that Carpocratians called themselves gnostics,[26] but the term cannot in this instance be subjected to systematic or theological analysis. In a fragment of a letter from Clement to Theodore, which Morton Smith discovered in 1958 and believes to be genuine (see above, p. 20), the worst thing Clement can say against the Carpocratians is that Carpocrates illegally obtained a copy of Mark's secret Gospel, corrupted the text with additions, and misinterpreted it in public.[27] This is perhaps the best reference available linking Carpocrates with Gnostic thinking, but Clement appears in the letter to Theodore to be the real Gnostic and Carpocrates only a thief and an imitator. The lack of evidence except from their avowed enemies makes what has been said about the Carpocratians somewhat tenuous and precludes further speculation on the historical impact of this movement (if indeed, it can be called properly a movement).[28]

One is on scarcely firmer ground when turning to evaluate the evidence concerning Basilides. Conflicting accounts of his thought are found in Irenaeus,[29] Hippolytus,[30] and Clement of Alexandria.[31] According to the account in Irenaeus, which is followed by Epiphanius, Pseudo-Tertullian, Philaster, and others,[32] Basilides posited a first heaven comprised of the first six begotten powers from an Unbegotten Father, and their generated powers, and angels. By successive emanations other heavens with other powers came into being, comprising a total of 365 heavens. Those in the last heaven are the creators of the world, and they allotted to themselves the lands and peoples of the earth, and the head of these creators is supposed to be the God of the Jews. When opposed by the other powers of the same heaven, the God of the Jews was aided by the Unbegotten Father of the first heaven, who sent the first emanation from himself as Christ to the earth. Docetic theology then enters the system, since Christ could not suffer (being Himself incorporeal and a power of the first heaven), and Simon of Cyrene is said to have suffered in His place. If that were not sufficiently revolting to his audience, Irenaeus adds that the Basilidians also practiced *every* kind of immorality (nobody's sensibilities could remain untouched by that) and all kinds of magical arts. In true gnostic fashion, those who have obtained all this knowledge are not to make any of it known to others, but are to keep everything secret and be inconspicuous in the world:

> Et sicut Filium incognitum omnibus esse, sic et ipsos a nemine oportere cognosci; sed cum sciant ipsi omnes, et per omnes transeant ipsos omnibus invisibiles et incognitos esse . . . et non oportere omnino ipsorum mysteria effari, sed in abscondito continere per silentium.[33]

> *And as the Son is unknown to all, so likewise must they be known by no one; but while they know all and they pass through all, they remain invisible and unknown to all . . . and (they) must not at all declare openly their mysteries, but they are to keep them secret through silence.*

Hippolytus, who might have been expected to follow Irenaeus if he were his student, nevertheless gives quite a different account of Basilides and his system. In his description, a completely ineffable god puts forth a seed, from which all things in the world were produced. Within the seed were all the powers of the world, including a threefold Sonship, each one corresponding, respectively, to God's realm, the heavens, and the earth. The advent of the Gospel and the mediation of the Holy Spirit combine to accomplish the salvation of the souls of men according to the 'kind' of soul in each man. Hippolytus states that Basilides is simply advancing for his own doctrines the clever musings of Aristotle,[34] which he is further stated to have learned in Egypt.[35] About the only things agreed upon by the commentators are that Basilides lived in Egypt or learned his philosophy there,[36] and also that they disagreed with his way of thinking.

One should not conclude that the differences of opinion regarding Basilides are due to lack of materials, for the available evidence indicates that Basilides was a very productive writer. At the close of the Muratorian Canon he is credited with writing a book of Psalms (there he is identified as the Asian Basilides, possibly a different person), and elsewhere he is said to have written many books, all of which contain difficult and vague doctrines.[37] Some aspects of Basilidian thought as portrayed in the various fathers correspond to tenets associated with Gnosticism, such as the emanations of the heavens, secrecy of the doctrines, the docetic tendencies, and the teachings on salvation. The dualism usually expected in such systems is lacking, however, and the conflicting evidence does not permit one to categorize Basilides with confidence into any system or well-defined heretical movement. Clement quotes rather freely from his writings,[38] but rather than help define Basilidian Christianity, the diversity of thought pushes one toward the following conclusion: "... his own teaching may perhaps have been typical of an ill-defined and speculative theology prevalent at Alexandria in his day."[39] Put an alternate way, he may not have been considered so heretical among his contemporaries as he was by some of his successors. Futhermore, some of the charges leveled against the Carpocratians and the Basilidians are perhaps applicable to some who, in the following generations, distorted or modified the teachings of the noted teachers. In Book III of the *Stromateis*, for example, Clement quotes from a work supposedly written by Carpocrates' son, Epiphanes, entitled Περὶ Δικαιοσύνης (*On Righteousness*).[40] Chadwick observes that "this work merely consists of the scribblings of an intelligent but nasty-minded adolescent of somewhat pornographic tendencies."[41] The same inclination of some followers to move toward licentiousness is also observed in the case of Basilides, for Clement states: ἐπεὶ μηδὲ ταῦτα αὐτοῖς πράττειν συγχωροῦσιν οἱ προπάτορες τῶν δογμάτων.[42] (*For the founding teachers of their doctrines did not permit them to do these things*). Although Irenaeus accuses Basilides himself of immorality, Chadwick says that "The charge is evidently not true of the master himself . . . Irenaeus is not well informed about the teachings of the historical Basilides."[43]

If immoral practices were or became a feature of the two systems of Christian interpretation associated with Carpocrates and Basilides, the same certainly was not the case with the most famous of the so-called Egyptian Gnostic sects, the Valentinians.[44] The followers of Valentinus not only espoused monogamous marriage but, according to Tertullian, considered that those who were unmarried would not achieve as great a salvation as those who were.[45] The Valentinians, characterized as being between the extremes of asceticism and licentiousness,[46] are better known to modern commentators than any other Christian sect in second century Egypt. Despite all the documentation relating to this school, including the recently-found *Gospel of Truth* which many believe comes from Valentinus, little of the known material relates directly to the founder himself, "and it is only with difficulty that we can form a picture of him."[47]

Irenaeus claims to have received his information concerning the Valentinians from a personal examination of some of their works and also by becoming acquainted with some disciples of Valentinus.[48] Although the Greek text of Irenaeus does not give credit to any one source for his material, Epiphanius, who quotes Irenaeus' account in his own treatise against the heresies, closes his lengthy citation with, "And this is the account of Ptolemaeus."[49] This ending corresponds with the Latin ending of Irenaeus' *Adv. Haer*. I.8, "Et Ptolemaeus quidem ita" (*And this is according to Ptolemaeus*), which may have been added by an editor after the time of Epiphanius, or perhaps was simply omitted in the Greek text. In either instance, both Irenaeus' claim to have learned from a disciple of Valentinus and the occurrence of the name 'Ptolemaeus' correspond with Tertullian's statement that Valentinus was followed by Ptolemaeus, "who afterwards entered on the same path."[50] Tertullian lists his own sources for his refutation of Valentinianism, including Justin, Miltiades, Irenaeus, and Proculus,[51] and it is certainly suggestive of the popularity of the cult to have attracted so many antagonists within the second century. Tertullian admits as much in the beginning of his work, when he describes the Valentinians as "frequentissimum collegium inter haereticos" (*a very numerous society among the heretics*) and says they are comprised of so many apostates from the truth who have no spiritual discipline to protect them from a propensity for fables.[52] Yet even in this sect, as in the instances of the Carpocratians and Basilidians above, Tertullian distinguishes between the more moral (if misguided) Valentinians of the first generation and the more spiritually and doctrinally promiscuous followers in succeeding generations.[53] Two warnings concerning the accuracy of these reports can be observed in Tertullian and should underline the difficulty in describing the Valentinians:

(1) "Not even to their own disciples do they commit a secret before they have made sure of them."[54] Any system based on secret and esoteric teachings is subject to the *caveat* that what is divulged by apostates or excommunicants is liable to be distorted, and if the person giving the information is still faithful to his oath of secrecy, his version may be intentionally misleading. Even the texts from Nag Hammadi which are thought to be Valentinian have not brought modern commentators to a unity of belief regarding the Valentinian system of thought.

(2) ". . . we are quite aware why we call them Valentinians, although they affect to disavow their name."[55] The problem of identifying a Valentinian in Tertullian's day or a Valentinian writing found today is compounded by this admission that the members or adherents of the cult did not advertize themselves under that heading. The heresiologists of that time obviously exaggerated the differences between the groups they attacked and their own version of Christianity, and they minimized the similarities. In the case of the newly-found texts, identifications with any given heretical movement tend to be self-confirming, and the difficulty in establishing the cult in history is increased.[56]

In addition to the stress placed on monogamous marriage and on ethical purity and integrity generally, the Valentinian version of Christianity included an involved cosmological speculation consisting of a heavenly realm, the Pleroma, which was comprised of thirty or more worlds or aeons. Emanations within the aeons correspond to number systems, which Irenaeus claims originated with Pythagoras,[57] including tetrads, the first two of which form the first-begotten Ogdoad, the ῥίζαν καὶ ὑπόστασιν τῶν πάντων[58] (*root and foundation of all things*). In the thirty aeons the emanations were considered triadic, or tripartite, being divided into an Ogdoad, a Decad, and a Duodecad.[59]

One emanation within the Pleroma, Sophia, brought about the Fall and, eventually, the creation of the world. Although Sophia is purified and restored to the Pleroma, her abortive thought must remain outside,[60] and the thought of Sophia (Enthymesis, Achamoth, etc.) was later given form by Christ and brought forth all things outside the Pleroma.[61] A triadic way of thinking is applied also to man, for Valentinians perceive men either as ὑλικοί, ψυχικοί, or πνευματικοί (*material ones, natural [animate] ones, or spiritual ones*). The first category cannot be saved, μὴ γὰρ εἶναι τὴν ὕλην δεκτικὴν σωτηρίας.[62] (*for matter is not capable of receiving salvation*). The second group can be partially saved, but cannot be received into the Pleroma, because they do not possess τὴν τελείαν γνῶσιν[63] (*the perfect knowledge, or the gnosis accompanied by ritual*). Of course the Valentinians are the πνευματικοί (*the spiritual ones*) who shall be fully saved by having gnosis, and that because they are spiritual in nature.[64]

This involved cosmological system, which for that very reason differs somewhat in the accounts of the heresiologists and even among texts assumed to be Valentinian, must be understood as supplementing, rather than replacing, the scriptures of the Christian religion. Irenaeus charges them with misusing the scriptures, not with rejecting them.[65] Tertullian infers the same by suggesting that the Valentinians were not satisfied with the traditional customs, but were always seeking to add innovations under the guise of "new revelations."[66] General charges are hurled against the gnostic heretics for erroneous doctrines based on misunderstanding of the scriptures, but the specific accusations are laid against the additional doctrines which the heretics claimed to have. Within the context established in an earlier chapter, this is to be expected. The Christianity which was defined more stringently both doctrinally and ecclesiastically could not accommodate the more liberal and inclusive doctrines and rituals of the Christian sects found in Egypt without attempting to pare them to acceptable dimensions.

Concerning Valentinus himself, Epiphanius was the first to state that he was born in Egypt, received his education in Alexandria, and spread his doctrines in Egypt before he went to Rome.[67] This is also the first explicit chronological reference to the spreading of Christianity in Egypt outside of Alexandria, although the Biblical and non-Biblical Christian texts discussed earlier give ample testimony supporting that assertion. Irenaeus gives a brief account of Valentinus coming to Rome during the episcopate of Hyginus (ca. 136–140 C.E.), flourishing under Pius (ca. 150–155) and remaining until Anicetus' time (ca. 155 to 160).[68] While in Rome, Valentinus had some expectation of being made bishop in that city "on account of his intellectual force and eloquence,"[69] but he was disappointed in his hopes when another was appointed. Tertullian remarks that because of his failure to become bishop "he broke with the church of the true faith,"[70] while Epiphanius said that it was toward the end of his life, while living at Cyprus, that Valentinus separated himself entirely from the church.[71]

By all accounts it should be obvious that Valentinus was not considered heretical during the period of his life in Egypt, and while a faint possibility exists that he *and* his disciples turned toward heretical doctrines during or after his stay in Rome, it would seem quite unlikely that a movement which was by then so widespread and popular could have been uniformly altered in doctrine.[72] Even those who attack Valentinus grudgingly admire his abilities, for Irenaeus interrupts his attack to state that no *ruler* in the church, however gifted he may be, would alter the doctrine, paying indirect homage to the intelligence of Valentinus (and perhaps others):

> καὶ οὔτε ὁ πάνυ δυνατὸς ἐν λόγῳ τῶν ἐν ταῖς Ἐκκλησίαις προεστώτων, ἕτερα τούτων ἐρεῖ . . .[73]
>
> *Yet not even one of the leaders of the churches who is very powerful in speech will teach doctrines different from these . . .*

(Meaning, of course, doctrines he considers to be orthodox.)
And a sentence later, he adds:

> τὸ δὲ πλεῖον, ἢ ἔλαττον κατὰ σύνεσιν εἰδέναι τινάς, οὐκ ἐν τῷ τὴν ὑπόθεσιν αὐτὴν ἀλλάσσειν γίνεται . . .[74]
>
> *The greater or lesser degree of intelligence which men have does not permit them to change the subject-matter itself . . .*

Irenaeus also suggests obliquely that Valentinus was orthodox before he adapted the gnostic theology to his own doctrines:

> ὁ μὲν γὰρ πρῶτος, ἀπὸ τῆς λεγομένης Γνωστικῆς αἱρέσεως τὰς ἀρχὰς εἰς ἴδιον χαρακτῆρα διδασκαλείου μεθαρμόσας Οὐαλεντῖνος.[75]
>
> *For the first one who transposed the principles of the so-called Gnostic heresy into the peculiar character of his school was Valentinus.*

Hippolytus may contain the key to Valentinus' unpopularity among church authorities and authors after he arrived in the west, for he says that Valentinus alleged to have received his doctrine through an Apocalyptic experience, and his disciple, Marcus, is depicted as one "imitating his teacher" by his claims to have visions also.[76] The unpopularity in the Western Church of a growing body of esoteric Apocalypses in non-Catholic Christianity during the first two centuries may well account for the spawning of heresiologists in the latter half of the second century and later, whose primary targets would be the so-called Gnostics who claimed to receive their doctrine in revelation from heaven rather than by reasoning through the scriptures.

Far from being a local sect with limited appeal, Valentinian adherents appear to have permeated Christianity. The Marcosians, an offshoot of Valentinianism named after a certain Marcus, were found thriving near the Rhone in the time of Irenaeus.[77] That the sect was using an Apocryphal work, *The Infancy Gospel of Thomas*, can be observed in Irenaeus, who records a strange incident from that work concerning the boy Jesus learning the alphabet.[78] F.M. Cross observed that there are more famous disciples of Valentinus who began schools in the West than in the East, all which indicates the acceptance this type of Christianity enjoyed among the lay members, if not always with the leaders.[79]

In summary of the preceding examination of the three well-known heresies associated with second century Egypt, one notes that information on the Carpocratians and the Basilidians is too scanty to provide an adequate opportunity to evaluate their beliefs in terms of orthodoxy or heresy. Their opponents are primarily engaged in hurling ethical charges rather than outlining heretical beliefs, and at that, the charges appear to fit the later followers of those for whom the movements are named, rather than Carpocrates or Basilides. Still, it must be admitted that these figures have only slightly more historical 'flesh' than the Egyptian bishops listed by Eusebius for the same period. Valentinus is the first 'real' Egyptian Christian encountered in this study (excepting Apollos a century earlier, whose Christian understanding was rather defective), and even he becomes tangible only after his arrival in Rome. His earlier shadowy existence in Egypt appears to be associated rather with a type of Christianity still acceptable throughout the Mediterranean region than with an heretical offshoot from an established orthodoxy. This seems so especially since he was able to travel to Rome and, after some years there, entertain some real hope of becoming bishop in that city. Therefore, although the heresiologists' search for targets for their venomous darts has long been thought successful, a closer examination in the case of Egypt has revealed less than satisfying results. One cannot argue that heretical figures and movements did not arise, but the application of that charge to the earliest teachers mentioned in this chapter will not stand examination, and it cannot even be shown that most of the later followers of these groups turned to the more licentious and libertine forms of the movements in the last half of the second century. The problem of defining heresy in Egypt becomes more, not less, complex when one turns from the so-called gnostic heretics to the earliest representatives of "orthodoxy" for whom any real historical information exists.

The relative obscurity which darkens modern understanding of early Egyptian Christianity is only slightly diminished by the historical information concerning Pantaenus during the early period of Demetrius' episcopate, but when Clement is introduced, the contrast at first makes the observer feel that the shroud of darkness is gone. This illusion is enhanced by the relative abundance of Clement's works extant today (compared to those who preceded him), but the scene is still rather opaque for one who tries to write about Clement's life or specify his relationship to the nascent gnostic systems just discussed.

Clement's birthdate and birthplace are both uncertain, although Epiphanius records two traditions known in his day concerning the possible place of his birth: Κλήμης τε, ὅν φασί τινες ᾿Αλεξανδρέα, ἕτεροι δὲ ᾿Αθηναῖον⁸⁰ (... And Clement, who some say is an Alexandrian, but others say is an Athenian). Most modern writers select Athens and date his birth to about the middle of the second century.[81] The same commentators generally assume that, as was customary at the time, Clement traveled widely to receive instruction from various teachers and philosophers, and the supposition is supported by Clement's own statement concerning his education:

> ἀλλά μοι ὑπομνήματα εἰς γῆρας θησαυρίζεται λήθης φάρμακον, εἴδωλον ἀτεχνῶς καὶ σκιογραφία τῶν ἐναργῶν καὶ ἐμψύχων ἐκείνων, ὧν κατηξιώθην ἐπακοῦσαι, λόγων τε καὶ ἀνδρῶν μακαρίων καὶ τῷ ὄντι ἀξιολόγων. τούτων ὁ μὲν ἐπὶ τῆς ῾Ελλάδος ὁ ᾿Ιωνικός, οἱ δὲ ἐπὶ τῆς μεγάλης ῾Ελλάδος· τῆς κοίλης θάτερος αὐτῶν Συρίας ἦν· ὁ δὲ ἀπ᾿ Αἰγύπτου· ἄλλοι δὲ ἀνὰ τὴν ἀνατολήν· καὶ ταύτης ὁ μὲν τῆς τῶν ᾿Ασσυρίων, ὁ δὲ ἐν Παλαιστίνῃ ῾Εβραῖος ἀνέκαθεν. ὑστάτῳ δὲ περιτυχὼν

(δυνάμει δὲ οὗτος πρῶτος ἦν) ἀνεπαυσάμην ἐν Αἰγύπτῳ θηράσας λεληθότα. Σικελικὴ τῷ ὄντι ἡ μέλιττα· προφητικοῦ τε καὶ ἀποστολικοῦ λειμῶνος τὰ ἄνθη δρεπόμενος, ἀκήρατόν τι γνώσεως χρῆμα ταῖς τῶν ἀκροωμένων ἐνεγέννησε ψυχαῖς.[82]

    ... but my memoranda are treasured up for my old age as a remedy against forgetfulness, simply an image and a scene-painting of those clear and animated speeches which I was honored to hear, and of blessed and truly noteworthy men. Of these, one was in Greece, the Ionian, and others were in Magna Graccia (southern Italy); another one was from Coele-Syria, one was from Egypt, and others were in the East; one was from the land of the Assyrians, and another was a Hebrew by origin in Palestine. But when I met with the last one (though in power this one was the first), having hunted him out from his concealment in Egypt, I rested. The Sicilian, in reality the bee, having plucked for himself the flowers from the prophetic and apostolic meadow, engendered in the souls of those who listened an undefiled measure of knowledge.

The identity of the first teachers is not known, but there is no doubt that the last mentioned is Pantaenus, the head of the Catechetical school in Alexandria whom Clement succeeded. Whether the reference to Sicily really denotes Pantaenus' home[83] or is simply a metaphorical reference to the quality of his instruction[84] is disputed. So far as this study is concerned, if one believes that Pantaenus really was from Sicily, the case for an imposition of a Western or Roman-dominated Catholic Christianity upon Egypt in the time of Demetrius would be strengthened considerably, especially since his successor is also a man thought to have been born in Athens. The first head of the school to come from Egypt, then, would be Origen, and he had difficulties with the bishop Demetrius. As tantalizing as this line of conjecture is, lack of evidence makes it impossible to argue strongly in its favor.

How early in his life Clement was converted to Christianity is unknown (he is assumed to be pagan for much of his early life, an assumption supposedly borne out by his knowledge of Greek philosophy), but Clement likely met Pantaenus in c. 180, the time when Eusebius states that the latter was in charge of the Alexandrian School.[85] The content of Pantaenus' teaching is not known, but his influence on Clement was great, both by Clement's own admission and by the statement in Eusebius that "Clement was famous in Alexandria for his study of the Holy Scriptures with Pantaenus."[86] Sometime afterwards Clement succeeded Pantaenus as the director of the school, "and proceeded to give lectures and to write works intended to win over to the Church the educated classes of Alexandria."[87] Clement was also made a presbyter in the church, either when he took over the school or a short time later.[88] Although the nature of the school and the succession from Pantaenus to Clement and later to Origen as given here is found in Eusebius and related sources, some dispute the claimed relationship of the Teachers and also of the curriculum and status of the school in Alexandria. Perhaps the best recent essay on this issue was written by Manfred Hornschuh, who gives an overall history of the Catechetical school from Pantaenus to Origen.[89]

In 202 C.E., during the persecution of Severus, Clement was compelled to leave Alexandria,[90] and in the beginning of Caracalla's reign he was at Jerusalem.[91] There is even record of his traveling to Antioch, and having a letter of recommendation from Alexander, the bishop of Jerusalem.[92] The date of Clement's death is not known certainly, but Quasten states that "he died shortly before 215 A.D. without having seen Egypt again."[93]

Of Clement's numerous works only a few survive at present, although fragments of others can be recovered from quotations in later authors. The most important of those that remain are *Protrepticus* (*The Exhortation to the Greeks*), *Paedagogus* (*The Instructor*), *Stromateis* (*The Miscellanies*), and a less significant work, *Quis Dives Salvetur?* (*The Rich Man's Salvation*). In the instance of Clement, therefore, unlike that of his predecessors, any difficulty in understanding and evaluating his role in the development of Christian thought in Egypt would not be due so much to lack of materials as to dealing properly with those which are available. The problem does in fact exist, and Chadwick notes that "It has even been suggested that only this obscurity of his style prevented Clement from suffering condemnation like Origen in later centuries."[94] Cross observes that Clement's name occurred on early lists of martyrologies on the date of 4 Dec., but it was removed on the advice of C. Baronius because of questions concerning Clement's orthodoxy.[95] Photius gave rather sharp criticism concerning a lost work, *The Hypotyposeis* (The Outlines) of Clement:

Αἱ μὲν οὖν Ὑποτυπώσεις διαλαμβάνουσι περὶ ῥητῶν τινων τῆς τε παλαιᾶς καὶ νέας γραφῆς, ὧν καὶ κεφαλαιωδῶς δῆθεν ἐξήγησίν τε καὶ ἑρμηνείαν ποιεῖται. καὶ ἐν τισὶ μὲν αὐτῶν ὀρθῶς δοκεῖ λέγειν, ἐν τισὶ δὲ παντελῶς εἰς ἀσεβεῖς καὶ μυθώδεις λόγους ἐκφέρεται.[96]

The Hypotyposeis thus treats some passages of both the Old and New Testaments, concerning which, in fact, he primarily produces an explanation and interpretation. And in some of them he seems to speak correctly, but in others he is entirely carried away into unholy and legendary stories.

A most significant part of this last denunciation is Photius' observation that Clement believed he could support his doctrines from the scriptures. In the work which was before Photius, Clement did not turn to the classical authors whom he knew well,[97] but understood that he was writing his doctrines in light of the Christian scriptures and must have considered it consistent with his Christian beliefs to do so.

Clement anticipated the difficulty his writings would face, and he intentionally cloaks his meaning on occasion in order to forestall possible criticism:

> The Stromateis will contain the truth mixed up with the opinions of philosophy, or rather covered over and hidden, as the edible part of the nut in the shell. For, in my opinion, it is proper that the seeds of truth be kept for the husbandmen of faith, and nobody else.[98]

Avoiding criticism for his teachings was not sufficient reason for Clement to write enigmatically, however, and a more significant reason for doing so is found in Eusebius' quotation from *The Hypotyposeis*:

> ὁ δ᾽ αὐτὸς ἐν ἑβδόμῳ τῆς αὐτῆς ὑποθέσεως ἔτι καὶ ταῦτα περὶ αὐτοῦ φησιν Ἰακώβῳ τῷ δικαίῳ καὶ Ἰωάννῃ καὶ Πέτρῳ μετὰ τὴν ἀνάστασιν παρέδωκεν τὴν γνῶσιν ὁ κύριος, οὗτοι τοῖς λοιποῖς ἀποστόλοις παρέδωκαν, οἱ δὲ λοιποὶ ἀπόστολοι τοῖς ἑβδομήκοντα· ὧν εἷς ἦν καὶ Βαρναβᾶς.[99]
>
> *The same author in the seventh book of the same work (Hypotyposeis) further says concerning him (James the Just): To James the Just and to John and to Peter the Lord transmitted the knowledge (gnosis) after his Resurrection. These transmitted it to the other Apostles, and the other Apostles to the Seventy, of whom Barnabas also was one.*

Clement is thus placed in the midst of the gnostic milieu by accepting the tradition of a secret gnosis, and in Book VII of the *Stromateis* he defines in the most positive terms what a true Gnostic is to be.[100] The difficulty in defining a gnostic has caused many commentators to despair of arriving at a consensus. After giving a lengthy attempt to define the essence of gnosis as religious knowledge imparted spiritually with saving power, Werner Foerster then admits that there are a great many gnostic systems.[101] Not all gnostics or gnostic systems use every element associated with gnosticism, and the problem of determining what proportion of the gnostic ingredients to "orthodox" theology is in an author or movement is a vexing one at the present time. Wilson focuses on the difficulty by asking how one is "to distinguish between the Christian Gnosticism which is orthodox, or comparatively orthodox, in Clement of Alexandria and Origen, and the Christian Gnosticism which is heretical in Basilides or in Valentinus?"[102] Gnostic elements found both in Clement and in famous gnostic leaders led Chadwick to voice a commonly held opinion when he says that, "With the teachings of Basilides and more especially of Valentine, Clement found himself in a fair degree of sympathy."[103] It is not impossible that he avoided rejection by the Church as a gnostic primarily because Irenaeus wrote his polemic against the gnostics before Clement's time.

Clement is the best evidence available on the question of orthodoxy and heresy in Egyptian Christianity at the end of the second century, and he treats the question of heresy along rather different lines from those established by other heresiologists. Where they speak of ecclesiastical unity and doctrinal harmony within the boundaries of their own traditions, Clement divides the heretics into two camps:

> Φέρε, εἰς δύο διελόντες πράγματα ἁπάσας τὰς αἱρέσεις, ἀποκρινώμεθα αὐτοῖς· ἢ γάρ τοι ἀδιαφόρως ζῆν διδάσκουσιν, ἢ τὸ ὑπέρτονον ἄγουσαι, ἐγκράτειαν διὰ δυσσεβείας καὶ φιλαπεχθημοσύνης καταγγέλλουσι.[104]

> *Now, after having divided all the heresies into two groups, let us give an answer to them; for either they teach one to live indiscriminately or to observe excessive asceticism, and they proclaim a self-control which is based on ungodliness and quarrelsomeness.*

One observes with Morton Smith that of all the sects which Clement attacks in *Stromateis III*, he is more concerned with the Carpocratians than with any other, while for Irenaeus and the other heresiologists the Valentinians are the most significant.[105] The explanation for this must certainly be due to the different reasons given for considering a group heretical, and the conclusion is inescapable that not even by the time of Clement had the presence of Western Christianity been felt strongly enough to establish its criteria for determining what was orthodox or heretical. The syncretism with which the Gnostics are accused by modern commentators is a major aspect of Clement's writings. Throughout his works one finds encouragement to study philosophy, which he felt was capable of protecting and adding to faith. Rather than attempting to define and restrict the concept of the Christian dogma, Clement searched even among heretical literature for material he could utilize,[106] and as Quasten puts it: ". . . it is not exaggeration to praise him as the founder of speculative theology."[107] The later orthodox church would certainly question whether he ought to be praised for that accomplishment.

Clement's famous successor, and perhaps student as well, was Origen.[108] The date and place of his birth are not known for certain, but scholarly consensus places it in Alexandria in c. 185 C.E. From his early youth Origen exhibited a zeal which often outstripped his judgment[109] and, in the persecution of Severus in 202 (if one can trust Eusebius on the matter), he avoided fulfilling his desire to follow his father, Leonides, into martyrdom only because his mother prevented his going outside by hiding his clothes.[110] Despite his youth, Origen's precociousness, coupled with the apparent lack of other qualified teachers after Clement's departure during the persecution, caused him to succeed as head of the catechetical school at age 17.[111] On another occasion the usually allegorical Origen took Matthew 19:12 literally in the message of some men making themselves eunuchs for the kingdom, and shortly afterward emasculated himself.[112] Eusebius reports that although Demetrius was shocked at the act,

> τὴν δέ γε προθυμίαν καὶ τὸ γνήσιον αὐτοῦ τῆς πίστεως ἀποδεξάμενος, θαρρεῖν παρακελεύεται, καὶ νῦν μᾶλλον ἔχεσθαι αὐτὸν τοῦ τῆς κατηχήσεως ἔργου παρορμᾷ.[113]
>
> *he approved both his zeal and the genuineness of his faith, he encouraged him to have confidence, and he urged him now even more to hold fast to the work of instruction.*

Some years later, Demetrius had a change of heart (out of envy because of Origen's popularity, according to Eusebius[114]) and attempted to use the deed as the basis for repudiating Origen, who by then had been invited to lecture in Arabia and Palestine and had been ordained to the presbyterate by Palestinian bishops.[115] In Rufinus' translation-paraphrase of Eusebius, the bishops of Palestine were reported to be on the verge of making Origen a bishop,[116] so that Demetrius wrote both to prevent that consecration and to censure the bishops for making him a presbyter. The obvious tension between Demetrius and Origen which this extraordinary event underlines can be explained, perhaps, in one of the following ways.

Earlier invitations to lecture before bishops and in church assemblies (as a teacher, but one without priesthood[117]) in Arabia and Palestine were repudiated by Demetrius as being irregular, but the underlying problem may have been Demetrius' attempt to control Origen and the school to a greater extent than was the case in the time of Pantaenus or Clement. Jerome stated that down to the episcopacy of Dionysius, the presbyters of Alexandria selected one of their num-

ber to be bishop, and he served without being consecrated.[118] If such
were the case, Chadwick observes that perhaps "during the long term
of office of Demetrius (190–233), things at Alexandria were already
moving towards such a system of monarchical episcopacy as encouraged Demetrius to emphasize his authority."[119] An ordained and
consecrated Origen, who was more popular in Egypt than Demetrius,
and who enjoyed a growing international reputation besides, could
have been no inconsiderable threat to his episcopally unconsecrated
presbyter-bishop in Alexandria if he had been made a bishop.[120]

It is difficult to assess the true significance of the "irregular ordination" of Origen, for evidence is lacking which would lead to a definite
conclusion concerning its legality in the church. Baus refers to the
ordination of foreign bishops without permission from Demetrius
only as an "ostensible cause," stating that the real reason "was the
bishop's inability to have a man of such high reputation and intellectual quality by his side."[121] Bigg had earlier noted that the ordination
by foreign bishops was not considered improper in Palestine (obviously), and he questioned whether it was really unlawful in Alexandria or simply considered inadmissable to Demetrius.[122] Butterworth
must have chosen the latter alternative, for he notes that the ordination caused the final break with the bishop, "who strongly disap-
proved of it."[123] Danielou further observed that the synod convened
by Demetrius did not go so far as to declare Origen's ordination
invalid, although it did "pronounce Origen unfit for catechizing and
expel him from the Church of Alexandria."[124] Disagreement persists
over the matter, for Cross states that Demetrius "deposed him from
the priesthood, and sent him into exile . . . for the irregularity of his
ordination."[125] M. Cadiou took the same position, arguing that the
ordination was irregular for two reasons: Origen had received the
priesthood without permission from his own bishop, and he had
deliberately mutilated himself.[126] From the foregoing one observes
that attempts to settle the question of the validity of Origen's ordination have not resulted in agreement among the commentators.

Another approach to the difficulty between Demetrius and Origen
is suggested by Eusebius in his statements concerning Origen writing
letters to bishops of other churches:

γράφει δὲ καὶ Φαβιανῷ τῷ κατὰ Ῥώμην ἐπισκόπῳ ἑτέροις τε πλείστοις
ἄρχουσιν ἐκκλησιῶν περὶ τῆς κατ᾽ αὐτὸν ὀρθοδοξίας.[127]

And he also wrote to Fabian, the Bishop of Rome, and to very many other rulers of churches concerning his orthodoxy.

Chadwick's note on this passage deserves quotation:

> It is scarcely sufficient to suppose, as deFaye does, that this was merely to repudiate falsifications of what he had actually said in public discussions. That he was sometimes misrepresented is undoubtedly true. But the phrase 'very many other rulers of Churches' suggests, on the evidence of his warm admirer, that Origen's teachings had, even in his own lifetime, given rise to widespread questioning.[128]

Eusebius states that Origen studied under Ammonius, a Platonist philosopher of the first half of the third century who taught Plotinus, the famous Neoplatonist.[129] Eusebius further attempts to protect Origen's orthodoxy by refuting Porphyry's statement: τὸν δ' Ἀμμώνιον ἐκ βίου τοῦ κατὰ θεοσέβειαν ἐπὶ τὸν ἐθνικὸν τρόπον ἐκπεσεῖν[130] (*and that Ammonius fell from a life of fearing God into paganism*). The historian is clearly mistaken, however, for Ammonius was not a Christian toward the end of his life, and may never have been a Christian.[131] Eusebius' greatest error in this instance, however, is confusing Ammonius Saccas with another Ammonius, who was a Christian author of the same age as Origen.[132] Hornschuh gives the argument against the identification in Eusebius, concluding that one cannot have confidence in the historian's knowledge of Origen's youth or in the Alexandrian school.[133] The confusion of identities, however, is not uncommon in similar circumstances where two persons with the same name and similar occupations (author and philosopher here) lived at nearly the same time. Dillon mentions two Origens (distinguished as the *Platonist* and the *Christian*) who studied under Ammonius, and further states that if Origen the *Christian* studied with Ammonius, he did so two or three decades before Plotinus began his decade of study with the philosopher (from 231–242).[134] In light of such confusion, one may be more sympathetic with Eusebius than Hornschuh recommends.

Origen's training in Greek literature is also noted in many instances, especially in the account relating to his father's death[135] and in one of his letters preserved in Eusebius.[136] In a reference to heretics (which here denotes pagans rather than Christian dissenters), Eusebius states that although Origen met often with heretics, he "could never be persuaded to join with (them) in prayer," so great was his loathing for heresies.[137] His disdain for these pagan heretics or philosophers apparently was not reciprocated, for:

μυρίοι δὲ τῶν αἱρετικῶν φιλοσόφων τε τῶν μάλιστα ἐπιφανῶν οὐκ ὀλίγοι διὰ σπουδῆς αὐτῷ προσεῖχον, μόνον οὐχὶ πρὸς τοῖς θείοις καὶ τὰ τῆς ἔξωθεν φιλοσοφίας πρὸς αὐτοῦ παιδευόμενοι.[138]

And countless numbers of the heretics and not a few of the most renowned philosophers listened to him very carefully, being instructed by him not only in divine matters, but also somewhat in secular philosophy.

Far from any indication that Origen spurned such attention from those whom he "loathed," Eusebius notes with pride that many philosophers mentioned him in their writings, dedicated books to him, and even submitted literary works to him to seek his evaluation and approval.[139] Origen did not follow his teacher, Clement, in sympathizing with the non-extreme Christian Gnostics, such as the Valentinians, at least according to Eusebius.

ἐν τούτῳ καὶ Ἀμβρόσιος τὰ Οὐαλεντίνου φρονῶν αἱρέσεως, πρὸς τῆς ὑπὸ Ὠριγένους πρεσβευομένης ἀληθείας ἐλεγθείς . . .[140]

At this time, Ambrose, who shared the views of the heresy of Valentinus, was refuted by the truth which Origen represented . . .

It has been argued by Quispel, however, that the distance between Origen and Valentinian gnosticism has been narrowed considerably by the discovery of the Valentinian writings in the Jung Codex of the Nag Hammadi Library.[141] More of his argument will be considered below.

One should observe that while Clement considered asceticism one of the major indicators of Christian gnostic heresy, Eusebius (certainly looking back through the perspective of a developing ascetic tradition within the monastic movement—and looking favorably at that) mentions in positive terms Origen's own tendency toward asceticism. Pursuing a manner of life very similar to that of the later Egyptian monks, Origen would labor through the day and devote most of the night to reading the scriptures. He would sleep on the floor rather than on a bed, and Eusebius portrays him as "going to the extreme limit of poverty," so that he did not even wear shoes for a number of years. He omitted wine and all unnecessary foods from his diet: ὥστε ἤδη εἰς κίνδυνον ἀνατροπῆς καὶ διαφθορᾶς τοῦ θώρακος περιπεσεῖν (. . . *so that he ran the risk of upsetting and ruining his stomach*).[142] Thus it appears that while Clement eschewed asceticism as one of the extremes of Gnosticism in favor of a more moderate position, his successor turned to that way of life.

Origen was a prolific writer, but an evaluation of his theology with respect to gnostics, for example, is nevertheless quite difficult because many of his writings have perished, and of those which remain most are fragmentary or exist only in Latin translation. While still in Alexandria Origen wrote a major theological work, *On First Principles*, which treats the subjects of God and heavenly beings, man and the material world, free will, and Holy Scripture. One observes that gnostic writings deal with precisely the same topics, even if not precisely in the same way as does Origen. The teacher also wrote five books of his *Commentary on John*, two volumes on *The Resurrection*, a *Commentary on Psalms* 1–25, eight volumes on *Genesis*, five on *Lamentations*, and ten volumes of *Miscellanies* (*Stromateis*). His productivity continued at Caesarea, where he composed *Commentaries* on nearly every book of the Bible, sermons on scriptural passages (*Homilies*), a *Discussion with Heraclides*, numerous *scholia*, a treatise on *Prayer*, an *Exhortation* to *Martyrdom*, wrote numerous *Letters* and composed a defense of Christianity, *Against Celsus*, in response to an attack against Christianity by a Greek of that name about a half century earlier.

While Origen was more closely aligned with the ecclesiastical tradition than was Clement, he still maintained a considerable degree of separation from the earthly church organization in his writings. He maintained that there are two congregations present for worship, one of men and one of the angels,[143] a belief commonly found in later Byzantine orthodoxy. The church is even compared to parts of the temple, the earthly corresponding to the Holy Place, and the heavenly to the Holy of Holies.[144] Even the Gospel is divided in like fashion, and it is to the Spiritual Church, not the one on earth, that the Eternal Gospel belongs, for the Eternal Gospel is to the Gospel in the New Testament as the New Testament is to the Torah.[145] The priesthood is also spiritualized, for in the heavenly church every true Christian is a priest.[146] Origen also taught that the earthly church had been corrupted by prosperity, stating that only a few of those professing godliness would attain to the election of God and blessedness.[147] Men are accused of conspiring to be bishops, deacons, and priests,[148] and Origen argues that anyone can celebrate solemn liturgical functions before the people, but not many lead holy lives and know much about Christian doctrine.[149] Not only are unworthy clergy chastised, but Origen berates those who are monks and teachers and yet only *profess* to be religious.[150] Thus, he argues, only the form of the church is given to the priests.[151] It is small wonder that he had difficulty getting along with such an increasingly autocratic bishop as

Demetrius, and that he was finally expelled from the church in Alexandria. His foreign ordination, legal or illegal, would have been a threat to local priesthood leaders when coupled with such censures of *their* authority.

If Origen does not appear to be in agreement with gnostic thinking (which is itself increasingly hard to define due to the numerous and doctrinally diverse texts being discovered and ascribed to gnostics), he is certainly at home with gnostic syncretism. One of his students, Gregory Thaumaturgos, said of Origen that he taught his students to collect all the writings of the ancient philosophers and poets when studying philosophy. They were not to reject anything except the words of Epicureans, who denied the existence of a Providence. All others were to be studied for the truth which could be found in them.[152] Even in the writing of scriptural Commentaries, Origen followed the pattern of the gnostic Heracleon, the first commentator on John (whom Origen attacks[153]). Some claim that Origen is more Platonic and philosophical than the gnostics, but that argument becomes less tenable with the discovery of a fragmentary text from Plato's *Republic* as part of the gnostic library from Nag Hammadi. Origen speaks of mysteries which may not be entrusted even to paper, including secrets of the Eternal Gospel, doctrines of angels and demons, and the history of the soul after death.[154] These subjects happen to be foci of recently found gnostic texts which claim to contain secret doctrines or mysteries.

It is within the context of new light being cast on gnosticism that Quispel says "a new stage (of research on Origen) has already begun, which pays full attention to Origen in so far as he is a Gnostic."[155] Quispel is guilty of assuming the fact of the non-Christian origin of gnosticism when he states that "Heracleon christianised Valentinus and Origen in his turn Heracleon,"[156] but his observation that Origen comes close to some aspects of Valentinian theology suggests more accord with gnosticism than has been thought previously. Danielou speaks of Origen's methods, if not his system, as gnostic,[157] and Butterworth concurs with deFaye, whom he quotes as rightly observing "that Origen's system is in the same class with the Gnostic speculations of his time."[158] Origen sometimes appears consciously to retreat from gnostic ways of thinking, perhaps to avoid offending Christians who cannot accept "more profound and abstruse explanations."[159] Even so, "it is scarcely surprising that Origen's bold and original speculations excited a sharply critical reaction"[160] in more orthodox circles. Although Origen is not so explicitly gnostic in his way of thinking or manner of expression as was Clement, his closer doctrinal and ecclesiastical alignment with the bishop was not sufficient to overcome the ecclesiastical tension between them.

In 231–232 Origen left Alexandria permanently and traveled to Caesarea, making his home there by 240.[161] In the sixth book of his commentary on John, Origen speaks of his departure from Egypt:

> We proceeded as far as the fifth volume in spite of the obstacles presented by the storm in Alexandria, and spoke what was given us to speak, for Jesus rebuked the winds and the waves of the sea. We emerged from the storm, we were brought out of Egypt, that God delivering us who led His people forth from there.[162]

The theologian was imprisoned and tortured during the Decian persecution, but survived for some years, dying in c. 255 in broken health.[163]

Heraclas succeeded Origen as head of the catechetical school in Alexandria,[164] but he had one decided advantage over his predecessor in terms of his relationship with Demetrius: he had been ordained a presbyter in Alexandria.[165] The school thus came under tighter control of the bishop, and the relationship between the two organizations is best illustrated by the fact that when Demetrius died in 233 after serving as bishop for 43 years, Heraclas succeeded him in that office. Although a student of Origen, Heraclas did not invite his former mentor to return to Egypt, possibly indicating that the student had turned toward the ecclesiastical position in Egypt against his teacher. Information concerning Heraclas' role in defining Christian orthodoxy is lacking, but his successor, Dionysius, leaves a path more easily followed.

Dionysius acceded to the bishopric in 247 after Heraclas' death,[166] and he held that position for 17 years to his death in 264–265.[167] Born of pagan parents who were quite wealthy,[168] he enjoyed a liberal education and by his own admission had broad exposure with secular and heretical literature.[169] He was a prolific writer, but most of his works have been lost, and most of that which remains has been preserved by Eusebius. A few references to his letters occur in Book VI of the history, and Eusebius derived most of the material for Book VII from his collection of Dionysius' works.[170] With Dionysius, ecclesiastical unity between Egypt and the Western Church can be observed for the first time, for his letters are written to bishops in other cities and are concerned with the same issues faced elsewhere.

The Alexandrian bishop was forced to flee during the Decian persecution, and after his return wrote a defense against one Germanus in order to justify his forced exile.[171] He also wrote a letter to Fabius, bishop of Antioch, in which he chronicles the persecutions in Alexandria, but at the close of that letter Dionysius asked for advice from Fabius concerning those who had lapsed during the persecutions:

τί οὖν ἡμῖν, ἀδελφοί, περὶ τούτων συμβουλεύετε; τί ἡμῖν πρακτέον; . . . ταῦτα δ᾽ εἰκότως ὁ Διονύσιος παρατέθειται, τὸν περὶ τῶν ἐξησθενηκότων κατὰ τὸν τοῦ διωγμοῦ καιρὸν ἀνακινῶν λόγον . . .[172]

What, then, do you recommend to us concerning these matters, brethren? What ought we to do? . . . Dionysius mentioned this matter quite reasonably, raising the question concerning those who had shown utter weakness at the time of the persecution . . .

Not content to ask for advice from fellow bishops, Dionysius also wrote a letter to Novatian, founder of the rigorist schism in Rome, and exhorted him to repent and return to the church. The letter is strongly worded, and Dionysius is definitely in the role of arbiter of the faith and unifier of the church:

ἔδει μὲν γὰρ καὶ πᾶν ὅτι οὖν παθεῖν ὑπὲρ τοῦ μὴ διακόψαι τὴν ἐκκλησίαν τοῦ θεοῦ, καὶ ἦν οὐκ ἀδοξοτέρα τῆς ἕνεκεν τοῦ μὴ εἰδωλολατρῆσαι γινομένης ἢ ἕνεκεν τοῦ μὴ σχίσαι μαρτυρία, κατ᾽ ἐμὲ δὲ καὶ μείζων. ἐκεῖ μὲν γὰρ ὑπὲρ μιᾶς τις τῆς ἑαυτοῦ ψυχῆς, ἐνταῦθα δὲ ὑπὲρ ὅλης τῆς ἐκκλησίας μαρτυρεῖ.

For one ought thus to suffer anything rather than to break in two the Church of God, and martyrdom in order to avoid schism would not be less noble than martyrdom which occurred to avoid idolatry, but even more noble in my opinion. For in the latter instance a man is martyred on behalf of his own single soul, but in the former on behalf of the whole Church.

Dionysius also wrote letters to bishops elsewhere in Egypt (to be considered later), as well as to Laodicea, Armenia, and Rome.[174] He reportedly received an invitation to attend a bishops' synod in Antioch,[175] indicating that orthodoxy had become firmly established in Alexandria. His letter to Cyprian in Africa is especially clear on this point:

ἴσθι δὲ νῦν, ἀδελφέ, ὅτι ἥνωνται πᾶσαι αἱ πρότερον διεσχισμέναι κατά τε τὴν ἀνατολὴν ἐκκλησίαι καὶ ἔτι προσωτέρω, καὶ πάντες εἰσὶν ὁμόφρονες οἱ πανταχοῦ προεστῶτες.[176]

But know now, Brother, that all of the churches in the East and yet farther away which formerly were divided have been united, and all of their leaders in every place are of one mind . . .

Other letters to Xystus in Rome and to a Roman presbyter, Philemon, attack the Sabellian schism raging there,[177] and in the last-mentioned epistle goes so far as to refer to his predecessor, Heraclas, as "our blessed pope":

τοῦτον ἐγὼ τὸν κανόνα καὶ τὸν τύπον παρὰ τοῦ μακαρίου πάπα ἡμῶν Ἡρακλᾶ παρέλαβον.

This rule and model I received from our blessed pope, Heraclas.

This is the first known instance of this term being used of an Alexandrian bishop, but the practice continued later. Dionysius composed festal letters, in some of which he attempted to settle the date of the feast of the Pascha,[178] and in others gives advice and commands as he sees fit.

Not all the correspondence of Dionysius to bishops outside Egypt resulted in increased harmony with western bishops, especially his namesake in Rome. Around 260 C.E., the Alexandrian bishop wrote a number of letters directed against some professing Sabellianism (a belief that in the Godhead the only differentiation between the Members was a mere succession of modes or operations[179]) in Libyan Pentapolis (an area under his jurisdiction).[180] For reasons not stated (Eusebius omits the resulting dispute from his account), the Sabellians appealed the matter to Dionysius, the Roman bishop, rather than making an appeal to a council of bishops. The rash language of the Alexandrian bishop's letters made him susceptible to attack, and Dionysius of Rome criticized the tritheistic language in the letters, which he felt undermined the unity of the Godhead.[181] In rejoinder, Dionysius of Alexandria was somewhat conciliatory in tone, while defending the reality of the three persons in the Godhead. His agreement that the three persons were not to be separated apparently defused the tension, for there is no indication that the disagreement persisted. The constant contact and relatively close relationship which the Roman and Alexandrian bishops maintained through the episode overshadows the specific difference of theology which each represents. Later the theological problem would erupt in a more serious way, but the Origen-trained bishop could not afford a rupture with the Western church while he was attempting to consolidate his own position in Egypt. Despite his being a student of Origen in his early life, there is no indication during his episcopacy of an attempt to heal the break with his former teacher. Even if the two were now incompatible in thought, Dionysius' continued unwillingness to be reconciled to Origen may be attributed to ecclesiastical politics, for the bishop would not want any difficulty with one who might undermine his position or strength.

The establishment of catholicism in Alexandria should not be understood, however, as reflecting ecclesiastical unity throughout the region, for in a letter to Hierax, a bishop in Egypt, Dionysius admits that factions still exist in the church.[182] He goes so far as to say that foreign travel is easier than to traverse the schisms that still exist in Alexandria. The distinction between the church in Alexandria and that in Egypt is emphasized when Eusebius relates how Dionysius, after peace was established in Alexandria, sent a festal letter to the brethren in Egypt.[183] The division between Alexandria and Egypt is further noted when Dionysius opposes Nepos, "a bishop over those in Egypt."[184] Perhaps Dionysius' reluctance to pursue his doctrinal dispute with Dionysius of Rome (unlike later successors, who were more assertive) is due to his lack of real authority and control over the Egyptian churches which he only claimed to represent. One notes in this respect that when he writes letters to the bishops in Egypt, the address is as if to a foreign country rather than to some of his own flock.[185]

To the middle of the third century, therefore, one notes at least in Alexandria a developing awareness of doctrinal unity and ecclesiastical authority. The catechetical school, which was relatively independent of the bishop in the days of Pantaenus and Clement, became increasingly tied to the authority of the bishop in the episcopacy of Demetrius and afterward. The undifferentiated Christianity of the first two centuries was being officially, if not completely, replaced by the more severe Christianity which existed in Rome and her allies and satellites.

ENDNOTES

[1] Origen, *Comment. on the Song of Songs*, 3, speaks of heretics as deviating from the rule of faith: "omnes enim haeretici primo ad credulitatem veniunt, et post haec ab itinere fidei et dogmatum veritate declinant." Irenaeus, *Adv. Haer.* I, 1, begins his attack on heretics by denouncing them for replacing the truth with false ideologies: ἐπὶ τὴν ἀλήθειαν παραπεμπόμενοί τινες, ἐπεισάγουσι λόγους ψευδεῖς . . . Later in I.28.2: ". . . non est numerum dicere eorum, qui secundum alterum et alterum modum exciderunt a veritate." Tertullian, in *Prescript. against Heretics* 36, compares heretical movements to a wild olive tree which grows from a tame or cultivated seed. Hippolytus, *Refutatio* I, preamble 11,: "Let us inquire to begin with as to what men first taught natural philosophy among the Greeks. The founders of sects on the whole appropriated their doctrines from these men, as we shall prove from comparisons, in what follows." The unanimous opinion of ancient commentators is summarized in A. von Harnack's famous definition of Gnosticism as "the radical Hellinization of Christianity." Most follow Irenaeus, who claims that the pre-Socratics and Plato provided the heretics with most of their ideas (II.14).

[2] Bauer, *op. cit.*, p. xxii.

[3] Irenaeus, *Adv. Haer.* I.10.3.

[4] *Ibid.*, I.10.2.

[5] See, for example, Bentley Layton, ed. *The Rediscovery of Gnosticism, Proceedings of the Conference at Yale*. 2 Vols. (I: *The School of Valentinus*; II: *Sethian Gnosticism*). Leiden: E.J. Brill, 1980, 1981.

[6] Carl Schmidt, *Gespräche Jesu mit seinen Jüngern nach der Auferstehung* (Texte und Untersuchungen 43. Leipzig, 1919).

[7] Louis Guerrier, *Le Testament en Galilée (Patrologia Orientalis)* IX, 3. (Paris, 1913).

[8] *Epistula Apostolorum* 1, H. Duensing, ed. *N.T. Apoc.*, *op. cit.*, I, p. 191.

[9] *Ibid.*, 7.

[10] Manfred Hornschuh, *Studien zur Epistula Apostolorum*. Berlin: Walter de Gruyter & Co., 1965, pp.6–7, passim.

[11] J. Quasten, *Patrology* (Utrecht: Spectrum Publishers, 1966) I, p. 151, notes that in addition to the New Testament, "The author has used the apocryphal *Apocalypse of Peter*, the *Epistle of Barnabas*, and the *Shepherd of Hermas*." He also observes (p. 152) that "Although there are some Gnostic ways of thought, there is a definite anti-Gnostic tendency in this writing."

[12] Irenaeus, *adv. Haer.* I.26. This is the reading of the Latin text, not preserved in the reading preserved by Hippolytus. For a discussion of Cerinthus in Asia, see Hornschuh, *op. cit.*, pp.99ff.

[13] Photius, *Bibl. Cod.* 121, states that Hippolytus, in a writing no longer extant, claimed to be a disciple of Irenaeus.

[14] Hippolytus, *Refutatio* VII.7.33 and 10.21.

[15] Irenaeus, *Adv. Haer.* III.3.4. The account is repeated in Eusebius, *Hist. Eccles.*, III.14.6.

[16] Theodoret, *Haer. Fab.* I.5.

[17] W. Foerster, *Gnosis* (Oxford: Oxford Univ. Press, 1972) I, p. 34, goes so far as to state that one cannot speak of a doctrinal system "even with Carpocrates, concerning whom Irenaeus presents a relatively detailed report . . . since the Church Father occupies himself principally with ethics."

[18] Irenaeus *Adv. Haer.* I.25.4. "Et in tantam insaniam effrenati sunt, uti et omnia quaecumque sunt irreligiosa et impia, in potestate habere, et operari se dicant. Sola enim humana opinione negotia mala et bona dicunt."

[19] Hippolytus, *Refutatio* VII.32; Tertullian, *de Anima* 23 and 35; Pseudo-Tertullian, *Adv. Omnes Haereses* 3; Eusebius, *Hist. Eccl.* IV.7.9; Augustine, *de Haer.* 7; etc.

[20] Clement, *Stromateis* III.2–6.

[21] *Ibid.*, III.2. Speaking of Epiphanes, Carpocrates' son, Clement says: τὰ μὲν πρὸς πατρὸς Ἀλεξανδρεύς, ἀπὸ δὲ μητρὸς Κεφαλληνεύς.

[22] *Ibid* . . . καθηγήσατο δὲ τῆς μοναδικῆς γνώσεως.

[23] Pseudo-Tertullian, *Adv. Omnes Haereses* 3 and Filastrius 35. See Chadwick's argument in *Alexandrian Christianity* (Philadelphia: Westminster Press, 1954), p. 27.

[24] See Chadwick, *op. cit.*, pp. 27ff. for a summary of the arguments. The major issue has revolved around the monthly celebration of Epiphanes' birthday after his death, but the details in Clement are too intricate to deny the plausibility of his account.

[25] Irenaeus, *Adv. Haer.* I.25.6.

[26] *Ibid.* "Gnosticos se autem vocant . . ."

[27] Letter of Clement to Theodore, Plate II:folio 1 verso,11.3–10. For the text, see Morton Smith, *Clement of Alexandria and a Secret Gospel of Mark* (Cambridge: Harvard Univ. Press, 1973), pp. 450ff.

[28] Morton Smith, *op. cit.*, pp. 266–278, gives a lengthy digression on Carpocrates and his followers, but is unable to do more than raise questions about earlier conclusions. For Smith, "The best evaluation of Carpocrates" was given by Danielou (*Theologie*, 1958, pp. 97f.), who identified Carpocrates with Jewish Gnosticism. Smith tries to make Carpocrates more orthodox as a Christian by insinuation: "This lacks only the realization that Jesus also was a heterodox Jew" (p. 278).

[29] Irenaeus, *Adv. Haer* I.24.

[30] Hippolytus, *Refutatio* VII.1–15 and X.10 (for a summary of his doctrines).

[31] Clement, *Stromateis*, passim.

[32] See W. Foerster, *op. cit.*, I, p. 59.

[33] Irenaeus, *Adv. Haer*. I.24.6.

[34] Hippolytus, *Refutatio* VII.2.

[35] *Ibid.*, VII.15.

[36] Irenaeus, *Adv. Haer*, I.24.1; Hippolytus, *Refutatio* VII.15; Euseb., *Hist. Eccl.* IV.7.

[37] Hegemonius, *Acta Archelai* 67:4–6,12. Cp. Clement, *Stromateis* IV.12.

[38] Clement, *Stromateis* I.21; II.3,8,20; III.1; IV.12,24,25; passim.

[39] Cross, *Ox. Dict.*, *op. cit.*, p. 141.

[40] Clement, *Stromateis* III.2, passim.

[41] Chadwick, *op. cit.*, p. 25.

[42] Clement, *Stromateis* III.1.

[43] Chadwick, *op. cit.*, p. 30.

[44] Bentley Layton (*The Gnostic Scriptures*. New York: Doubleday, 1987, pp.215–353), devotes a portion of his book to the Valentinians, beginning with an historical introduction and continuing with translations of Valentinian writings. There is also a section on the School of Valentinus, which shows the spreading influence of this sect in the following centuries.

[45] Tertullian, *Adv. Valent*. 30. Irenaeus, *Adv. Haer*. I.6.4, says that the Valentinians taught that marriage was the mark of a pneumatic. Clement, *Stromateis* III.29, notes that for Valentinians the sacred marriages among the gods are a pattern for earthly marriages.

[46] Chadwick, *op. cit.*, p. 30.

[47] Foerster, *op. cit.*, p. 121. For an argument that Valentinian gnosticism took over theological elements from earlier sources (gnostic and non-gnostic), see Josef Frickel, *Hellenistiche Erlösung in Christlicher Deutung*. Leiden: E.J. Brill, 1984, pp.160–171.

[48] Irenaeus, *Adv. Haer.*, Pref.2: ἀναγκαῖον ἡγησάμην ἐντυχὼν τοῖς ὑπομνήμασι τῶν, ὡς αὐτοὶ λέγουσιν, Οὐαλεντίνου μαθητῶν, ἐνίοις δὲ αὐτῶν καὶ συμβαλὼν, καὶ καταλαβόμενος τὴν γνώμην αὐτῶν, μηνῦσαί σοι, ἀγαπητέ, τὰ τερατώδη καὶ βαθέα μυστήρια.

[49] Epiphanius, *Panarion* 31.27.16.

[50] Tertullian, *Adv. Valent*.4.

[51] *Ibid*.,5.

[52] *Ibid*.,1.

[53] *Ibid*., 5. In chp. 4, Tertullian states: "Solus ad hodiernum Antiochiae Axionicus memoriam Valentini integra custodia regularum eius consolatur. Alioquin tantum se huic haeresi suadere permissum est, quantum lupae feminae formam quotidie supparare solemne est."

[54] *Ibid*.,1.

[55] *Ibid*.,4.

[56] Illustrative of the difficulty of identifying and defining the Valentinians in Egypt is a statement given by G.C. Stead at the 1978 Yale Conference on Gnosticism: "Any effort to give a credible picture of Valentinus encounters an immediate difficulty: as de Faye noted, there is a sharp contrast between the fragments from his own writings preserved by Clement and the complex cosmic myth known from the heresiologists' accounts of the Valentinians. Even the discovery of the new Valentinian texts from Nag Hammadi has not made clear how we are to understand the fragments, which could have been written simply by a Biblical Platonist not far from Christian orthodoxy." (G.C. Stead, "In search of Valentinus," *Rediscovery of Gnosticism, Vol. 1: The School of Valentinus*, ed. by B. Layton. Leiden: E.J. Brill, 1980, p.95). Other participants at the conference disputed Stead and each other concerning various aspects of Valentinianism, esp. the essays by R. McL. Wilson, "Valentinianism and the Gospel of Truth," pp.133–145, and R.A. Greer, "The Dog and the Mushrooms: Irenaeus's View of the Valentinians Assessed," pp.146–175. The expectation that the discovery of the Nag Hammadi Codices would help solve the problem of the identification and development of such early Christian groups has not been realized. Opinions have multiplied, and questions are often raised asking whether earlier attempts at solutions were even approaching the problems correctly.

[57] Irenaeus, *Adv. Haer.* I.1.1.

[58] *Ibid*.

[59] *Ibid*., I.1.3.

[60] *Ibid*., I.2.3–5.

[61] *Ibid*., I.4–5.

[62] *Ibid*., I.6.1.

[63] *Ibid*., I.6.2. It becomes at least partially obvious why Irenaeus did not agree with such a system when one reads that the Valentinians put churchmen into this category: Εἶναι δὲ τούτους ἀπὸ τῆς Ἐκκλησίας ἡμᾶς λέγουσι.

[64] *Ibid*. See summary in I.7. This version of the tripartite nature of being is not found in all sources or agreed upon by all commentators. G.C. Stead, "In Search of Valentinus," *op. cit.*, p.81, notes: "For what it is worth, then, Hippolytus does claim that Valentinus distinguished three levels of reality; and not, in this case, the usual triad of spirit, soul, and matter. I think that in 6.37.5 the emendation Σιγήν (for MS πᾶσι γῆν) must be wrong, since it leaves the following genitive unexplained; I prefer Hilgenfeld's πηγήν; we then have a triad of the Father, the Aeons, and the cosmos, which is roughly comparable to the familiar middle-Platonic triad of God, the Ideas, and matter."

[65] *Ibid*., I.8. See also similar inference I.1.3; III.14; passim.

[66] Tertullian, *Adv. Valent*. 39. Tertullian does not appear to consider the Valentinians entirely Gnostic rather than Christian, for he concludes his treatise: "And it thus happens that the doctrines which have begun with the Valentinians have already extended their rank growth to the woods of the Gnostics."

[67] Epiphanius, *Panarion* 31.7–12.

[68] Irenaeus, *Adv. Haer*. III.4. He is quoted by Eusebius, *Hist. Eccl*. (IV.11.1) Just what he did "to ripen" (ἀκμάζω) during the rule of Pius is not at all clear, especially if Epiphanius was right concerning the period of his doctrinal development in Egypt years earlier. Perhaps this text simply refers to the amount of influence he enjoyed in Rome.

[69] Tertullian, *Adv. Valent*. 4: "quia et ingenio poterat et eloquio."

[70] *Ibid*.

[71] Epiphanius, *Panarion* 31.

[72] One should note that Hippolytus, *Refutatio* VI.15 claims that Valentinus came to Rome and got his system from the Simonians, but there are at least two reasons to discount his report in this study. First, Hippolytus is not internally consistant on this point, for a chapter later he modifies his claim to state that Valentinus really borrowed his system from Plato and Pythagoras, thus exchanging a more magical origin for a more philosophical one. Hippolytus concludes VI.16 by stating that the Valentinian system is not connected with Christ, but is really a Hellenic heresy. Second, the oriental successors of Valentinus are charged with having the same heretical views as the western successors, which would not be the case if the teacher had not acquired his own misunderstanding until he arrived in Rome. Furthermore, the discovery of "Valentinian" texts in Egypt would be harder to explain if Hippolytus were correct.

[73] Irenaeus, *Adv. Haer*. I.10.2. Jerome is illustrative of the regard which the Fathers had for Valentinus' mental abilities: "No one can bring a heresy into being unless he is possessed, by nature, of an outstanding intellect and has gifts provided by God. Such a person was Valentinus" (*In Hos*. 11.10).

[74] *Ibid*.,I.10.3.

[75] *Ibid*.,I.11.1.

[76] Hippolytus, *Refutatio* VI.37.

[77] Irenaeus, *Adv. Haer*.I.13.7.

[78] *Ibid*., I.20.1. Cp. "Evangelium Thomae Graece A.," *Evangelia Apocrypha*, K. von Tischendorf, ed. (Hildesheim: Georg Olms, 1966), VI.2–3 (pp. 145f.).

[79] Cross, *op. cit*., p. 1423.

[80] Epiphanius, *Panarion* 32.6.

[81] So Chadwick, *op. cit*., p. 16; Butterworth, *Clement of Alexandria* (Cambridge: Harvard Univ. Press, 1968), Intro., p.Xl; Cross, *op. cit*., p. 303; etc.

[82] Clement, *Stromateis* I.1.31–38. The passage is repeated in Euseb., *Hist. Eccl*. V.11.3ff., but Eusebius makes no mention of the last teacher being a Sicilian bee. Perhaps the historian had no taste for honey.

[83] Lawlor and Oulton, *op. cit*. II,pp. 166–167. "The turn of the Greek, in fact, seems to indicate that 'Sicilian' is not metaphorical, but a statement of fact, namely that Pantaenus was native of Sicily. . ." Other considerations are adduced to support this interpretation, as, for example, Sophocles being known as the "Attic Bee" and Clement mentioning both the home of the teacher and the place where they met.

[84] Chadwick, *op. cit*., p. 16. "The best honey came from Sicily, so that this is Clement's way of complimenting him upon the brilliance of his lectures."

[85] Euseb., *Hist. Eccl*. V.9–10.

[86] *Ibid*. V.11.1.

[87] Chadwick, *op. cit.*, p.17.

[88] Jerome, *De Viris Illustr*. 38; Photius, *Bibl. Cod.* 111.

[89] Manfred Hornschuh, "Das Leben des Origenes und die Entstehung der alexandrinischen Schule," *Zeitschrift für Kirchengeschichte* 71 (1960), pp. 1–25, 193–214.

[90] Fabricius, *Bibl. Gr.* (in Migne, *Patrol., Graec.* 8, col.11) Cp. Cross, *op. cit.*, p. 303.

[91] A.C. Coxe, *Fathers of The Second Century* (Grand Rapids: Eerdmans Pub. Co., 1971), p.169.

[92] Eusebius, *Hist. Eccl.* VI.11.6.

[93] J. Quasten, *op. cit.*, II, pp. 5–6.

[94] Chadwick, *op. cit.*, p. 19, citing A. Jülicher, "Clemens Alexandrinus," in Pauly-Wissowa, *Real-Encyclopaedie*. Stuttgart, 1901. Vol. 4, col.13.

[95] Cross, *op. cit.*, p. 303.

[96] Photius, *Bibl. Cod.* 109. The text continues with some specific indictments, especially noting that Clement taught that there were numerous worlds before Adam, transmigrations of souls, a dual system of Logoi (only the lesser appeared to man), that matter is eternal, etc.

[97] There is consensus among scholars that Clement knew Greek literature very well. Chadwick's summary is typical: "He knew well Homer and Euripides, Plato and the Stoics. Platonic allusions are particularly frequent and probably even now not all of them have been noticed and identified. Equally familiar to him were the writings of Philo of Alexandria, from whom he quotes almost as often as Plato" (*op. cit.*, p.21).

[98] Clement, *Stromateis* I.20–21. See also I.56; IV.4; VI.2; VII.110–111.

[99] Eusebius, *Hist. Eccl.* II.1.4.

[100] Esp. chps. 1–3 and 10–13. C. Bigg, *The Christian Platonists of Alexandria* (Oxford: Clarendon Press, 1968, Reprint of 1913 edition), p. 151, states that Gnosticism was Clement's difficulty. One must remember that until the mid-twentieth century gnostic sources were nearly unknown, and all earlier judgments about what was gnostic were subject to major revision and possible rejection in light of newly-found texts.

[101] Foerster, *op. cit.*, Vol. 1, pp. 1–9.

[102] R. McL. Wilson, *Gnosis and The New Testament*: Philadelphia: Fortress Press, 1968, pp. 11–12. C.H. Dodd (*Interpretation of the Fourth Gospel*, p. 97) makes the statement more positively: "there is a sense in which orthodox Christian theologians like Clement of Alexandria and Origen, on the one hand, and Hellenistic Jews like Philo, and pagan writers like the Hermetists, on the other, should be called gnostics . . ."

[103] Chadwick, *op. cit.*, p. 31.

[104] Clement, *Stromateis* III.5.

[105] Smith, *op. cit.*, p. 82.

[106] He even quotes from Tatian's *On Perfection According to the Savior* in *Stromateis* III.12, although Tatian had been excommunicated in 172 C.E.

[107] Quasten, *op. cit.*, II, p.20.

[108] Eusebius, *Hist. Eccl.* VI.6. Πάνταινον δὲ Κλήμης διαδεξάμενος, τῆς κατ' Ἀλεξάνδρειαν κατηχήσεως εἰς ἐκεῖνο τοῦ καιροῦ καθηγεῖτο, ὡς καὶ τὸν Ὠριγένην τῶν φοιτητῶν γενέσθαι αὐτοῦ. Despite this affirmation by Eusebius that Origen was a student of Clement, the relationship of Clement and his successor is disputed by modern commentators. Chadwick (*op. cit.*, p. 173), speaks of Origen as "Clement's most brilliant pupil, although apparently only his pupil for a short time." Danielou, *Origen* (New York: Sheed and Ward, 1955, pp. 9ff.), skirts the question of the relationship of these two men by turning to a discussion of the nature of the school, concluding (with meager evidence indeed) that its main function was to prepare candidates for baptism rather than educate them in science and philosophy. Danielou infers that Origen was prepared for baptism by his Christian father rather than by Clement, although he

asserts that Origen was acquainted with Pantaenus, Clement's predecessor (p. 14). The implicit assumption surely must be that Origen also knew Clement, even if a formal student-teacher relationship were not established.

[109] *Ibid.*, VI.2.6. Eusebius diplomatically says having "a zeal, intense beyond his years": τῆς προθυμίας ὑπὲρ τὴν ἡλικίαν ἐπιτεινομένης.

[110] *Ibid.*, VI.2.1–5. The reason for the persecution, according to Spartian (*Severus* 16f.), was to prevent Jews and Christians from making proselytes, rather than being an attempt to destroy them. It will be remembered that it was during this persecution that Clement had to leave Alexandria, never to return. Taking into account the later attitude held toward those fleeing martyrdom, Clement's flight on that account without subsequent censure is difficult to understand, although others associated with the school also left at that time.

[111] *Ibid.*, VI.3.3. See Hornschuh, *op. cit.*, pp.2–3 for a discussion of whether the teachers were really acquainted with each other.

[112] *Ibid.*, VI.8.1–3.

[113] *Ibid.*

[114] *Ibid.*, VI.8.4.

[115] *Ibid.*, VI.8.5. Cf. VI.23.4 for the account of his ordination at Caesarea while on his way to Greece. This was obviously an improper or forbidden ordination (outside his home region), and Eusebius assisted in writing a defence of the action nearly a century later.

[116] Rufinus, *Transl. of Eusebius, Eccl. Hist.*, VI.8.4: "summo eum sacerdotio iam iamque dignum probarent."

[117] Danielou, *op. cit.*, p. 20.

[118] Jerome, *Epistle* CXLVI.1 This passage has been much disputed as to its accuracy, but recent opinion seems to be more in its favor. There is no evidence available for conjectured alternatives.

[119] Chadwick, *op. cit.*, p. 175.

[120] See above, note 115. See Hornschuh, *op. cit.*, pp.210–212. He earlier argued (p.12) that Bardy was in error when he stated that Origen got authority to teach from the bishop. This study is in agreement with Hornschuh on the matter.

[121] Baus, *op. cit.*, p. 235.

[122] Bigg, *op. cit.*, p. 155.

[123] G. W. Butterworth, ed. Origen, *On First Principles* (New York: Harper and Row, 1966), p. xxiv.

[124] Danielou, *op. cit.*, p. 23. Jerome, *Ep.* XXXIII, declares that jealousy was the primary reason for Origen's condemnation, not heretical doctrines. He further specifies that Demetrius, (not the church) condemned him.

[125] Cross, *op. cit.*, p. 1008.

[126] R. Cadiou, *La jeunesse d'Origène; histoire de l'École d'Alexandrie au début du IIIe siècle*. Paris: G. Beauchesne et ses fils, 1935, p. 99.

[127] Eusebius, *Hist. Eccl.* VI.36.4. The reader should note well that it is the *Roman* bishop who is specified, and likely that most of the other bishops were Western as well. With the invitations Origen received to speak in various regions of the East, it is virtually certain that he would not have to defend his positions to those who continued extending such opportunities.

[128] Chadwick, *op. cit.*, p.178.

[129] This nearly unknown Alexandrian philosopher was also the teacher of Longinus. His death is estimated to have occurred in c. 243 C.E. J. M. Dillon, *The Middle Platonists* (Ithaca: Cornell Univ. Press, 1977), p. 380, says ". . . we know almost nothing of him . . ."

[130] Eusebius, *Hist. Eccl.* VI.19.9.

[131] Dillon, *op. cit.*, pp. 381–382 does not take a position regarding Ammonius' Christianity, but there is nothing in the philosopher's life besides the statement of Porphyry (quoted in Eusebius, *Hist. Eccl.* VI.19.7) that links him to that religion.

[132] A. Jülicher, "Ammonios", in Pauly-Wissowa, *Real-Encyclopaedie*. Stuttgart, 1894, Vol. 1, part 2, col. 1867. Virtually nothing is known of this Christian exegete.

[133] M. Hornschuh, *op. cit.*, p.14. One need not go so far as Hornschuh, since a mistaken identity made over a century later, and that in the context of a religious argument, does not necessarily negate every other historical point in Eusebius' narrative.

[134] Dillon, *op. cit.*, pp.381–2.

[135] Eusebius, *Hist. Eccl.* VI.2.15.

[136] *Ibid.*, VI 19.11–14.

[137] *Ibid.*, VI.2.14.

[138] *Ibid.*, VI.18.2.

[139] *Ibid.*, VI.19.1.

[140] *Ibid.*, VI.18.1.

[141] Gilles Quispel, "Origen and the Valentinian Gnosis," *Vigiliae Christianae* 28 (1974), pp. 29–42.

[142] Eusebius, *Hist. Eccl.* VI.3.9–13.

[143] *In Lucam Hom.* xxiii "Duplex hic adest ecclesia, una hominum, altera angelorum."

[144] *In Lev. Hom.* ix.9.

[145] See *De Princ.* iv.25; *in Joan.* i.9.10; *In Rom.* i.4,ii.5; *In Lev. Hom.* xiii.2.

[146] *In Lev. Hom.* iv.6, vi.5, ix.1.8, xiii.5. Note the difference in *In Num. Hom.* ii.1, where priests are said to be *in professione religionis*.

[147] *In Jer. Hom.* iv.3.

[148] *In Matt. Comment. Ser.* 12.

[149] *In Lev. Hom.* vi.6.

[150] *In Num. Hom.* ii.1.

[151] *In Num. Hom.* ix.1.

[152] Gregory Thaumaturgos, *Panegyric to Origen* 13, *Patrol. Gr.* 18.740.

[153] *In Joan. Comment.* ii.8.15, passim.

[154] *In Rom.* ii.4.

[155] Quispel, *op. cit.*, p. 29.

[156] *Ibid.*, p. 37.

[157] Danielou, *op. cit.*, p. 194.

[158] Butterworth, *op. cit.*, p. liv.

[159] *In Matt. Comment.* xv.37.

[160] J.N.D. Kelly, *Early Christian Doctrines* (London: Adam and Charles Black, 1968), p. 182.

[161] Chadwick, *op. cit.*, p. 177.

[162] Origen, *In Joan. Comment.* vi.1.

[163] Eusebius, *Hist. Eccl.* VI.39.5; VII.1.

[164] *Ibid.*, VI.26.

[165] *Ibid.*, VI.19.13.

[166] *Ibid.*, VI.35.

[167] *Ibid.*, VII.28.3.

[168] Quasten, *op. cit.*, II,p. 101.

[169] Eusebius, *Hist. Eccl.* VII.7.1–3.

[170] *Ibid.*, VII. Intro.

[171] *Ibid.*, VI.40.

[172] *Ibid.*, VI.42.5f.

[173] *Ibid.*, VI.45.

[174] *Ibid.*, VI.46.

[175] *Ibid.*

[176] *Ibid.*, VII.5.1.

[177] *Ibid.*, VII.6–7.

[178] *Ibid.*, VII.20.

[179] Cross, *op. cit.*, p.929 ("Monarchianism").

[180] Eusebius, *Hist. Eccl.*, VII.26. Cp. Athanasius, *De Sent. Dionys.*, where Athanasius attempts to defend the Alexandrian bishop's orthodoxy in the matter.

[181] Baus, *op. cit.*, pp. 259f. An unmistakable reference of Dionysius of Rome to the Alexandrian bishop is contained in Athanasius, *De decr. Nic. Syn.* 26.

[182] Eusebius, *Hist. Eccl.* VII.21.

[183] *Ibid.*, VII.22.11. See also VII.22.12.

[184] *Ibid.*, VII.24.1.

[185] Compare Eusebius, VII.20, where Dionysius writes to his fellow- presbyters at Alexandria, and VII.22, where he writes again to *the brethren*, with VII.21 where the letter is to "Hierax, bishop of those in Egypt," and VII.24, where the same phrasing occurs with Nepos.

CHAPTER IV

EGYPTIAN CHRISTIANITY IN THE THIRD CENTURY:
THE DEVELOPMENT OF LOCAL CHRISTIANITY

The time span from Demetrius to Dionysius in Egyptian Christianity can be characterized as the period when Alexandria begins to emerge as an important center of the church in the Mediterranean world and when the Alexandrian bishop acquired an authoritative position equalling and sometimes rivalling that of other bishops in the major cities such as Rome, Antioch, and Jerusalem. The primary reason for this development occurring in Alexandria, as has been shown earlier, was the imposition into Egypt of an ecclesiastically and doctrinally well-defined Christianity in the person and bishopric of Demetrius near the end of the second century. The institution in Alexandria which at that time offered the greatest competition to the office of bishop was the catechetical school, directed in turn by Pantaenus, Clement, Origen, Heraclas, and Dionysius. Under the direction of the first three men, the school was relatively independent in its operations and activities, and to it were drawn students of virtually every philosophical and religious persuasion, both inside and outside of Christianity. The tension between Origen and Demetrius, essentially ecclesiastical in nature, led to the exile of the former and the subsequent binding of the school to close episcopal supervision under Heraclas and his successors. Dionysius was sufficiently secure in his episcopacy to write letters to bishops, presbyters, and heretics throughout the Mediterranean world, exhorting and advising on diverse matters as an authority representing a major geographical segment of Christianity. It is incumbent upon the historian to look carefully at the nature of the Egyptian Church outside Alexandria during the third century and determine whether Dionysius reflected an accurate state of affairs for the entire country or if his inference of an Egyptian monarchical episcopacy was simply wishful thinking.

The attempt to examine Christianity in Egypt outside of Alexandria is especially difficult due to the relative paucity of source materials, and those which do remain often emphasize the obscurity which exists rather than give clarification. For the earliest indisputable evidence that Christianity penetrated to Upper Egypt by the end of the

first century, one must turn to the Christian texts discovered along
the Nile Valley, and it has been shown that the evidence confirmed
not only the presence of Christians as far south as the Thebaid but
also that the apocryphal texts found with Biblical texts indicated a
Christianity with more extensive literary tradition and broader theological tendencies than those found in the nascent Catholic tradition.
There is yet another aspect of these texts, not treated above, which
relates to the Christians outside Alexandria. In 1912 Wallis Budge
published a volume containing Coptic versions of Deuteronomy,
Jonah, and Acts contained in a papyrus codex which he dated to no
later than the middle of the fourth century.[1] Budge argues that the
codex proves that Coptic versions of the Bible were being circulated
among Egyptian Christians at least as early as the beginning of the
century, and that the original translation cannot be later than the
third century.[2] He indicates a clear desire to assign the codex an
earlier date, but at the time there were no other texts from the same
period to which it could be compared.[3] H.I. Bell examined the papyri
forming the cover of the codex and dated them to as early as the late
third century,[4] confirming and enhancing Budge's estimate. Concerning the book of Acts, Budge notes that the scribe is the same as for
the previous books in the codex, and the Coptic is written in a "good
hand." Nevertheless,

> Mistakes in spelling both Greek and Coptic words are numerous, and
> there are many blunders in writing, which could only be made by a very
> careless copyist, or by one who was copying from an old and partly
> obliterated text. Omissions of words and whole lines are frequent, and
> only rarely are there signs that the copyist was conscious of the mistakes
> which he had made.[5]

One must conclude that the scribe was working from an older text in
this instance, for he is much more accurate in the previous two books
(Deuteronomy and Jonah).[6]

Since Budge's publication in 1912, other Coptic Biblical papyri
dating to the early fourth century have been found, and the editors of
the texts believe them to be copies of earlier texts rather than the first
translation from the Greek.[7] Two other texts are even more
significant than those mentioned above, and are important for a
number of reasons. The Chester Beatty Isaiah text (P. Beatty 7) has
been dated to the first half of the third century, and has marginal
glosses in Coptic which are not thought to be much later in date.[8] The

Coptic in the margins is of such early date that the five letters borrowed from demotic to supplement the Greek alphabet are not em-
ployed, making it perhaps the only Christian writing extant in Old
Coptic.[9] Although A. Atiya mistakenly refers to the Chester Beatty
collection of Paul's letters as written in Coptic,[10] the evidence of P.
Beatty 7 is quite convincing that at least part of the library was in the
possession of Coptic hands and, from the nature of the language, at
quite an early date. One might observe that the library also contained,
in addition to nine Old Testament books and fifteen New Testament
writings, the Book of Enoch, an Apocalyptic work rejected in the
Western Church.

The second of the very early texts comes from the verso (reverse
side) of a land register, which dates from the late second or early third
century, and contains a Greek-Coptic glossary to Hosea and Amos.[11]
Both texts indicate "the presence of Christians whose native tongue
was Coptic and who found Greek only imperfectly intelligible."[12]
Both texts also give convincing evidence that by the end of the second
century not only were there Christian proselytes in Upper Egypt but
Christianity was also making inroads into the native population.

Somewhat less convincing evidence to this author, but worth mentioning in the present context, is a tradition reported by Budge
concerning a monk named Frontonius, who is reported to have
collected seventy brethren together and to have led them into the
Nitrian Desert during the reign of Antoninus Pius (138–161). There
they lived simple lives of devotion, only cultivating sufficient ground
to meet their needs.[13] It seems quite unlikely that so large a group
could have made such an exodus into the desert to lead a Christian
monastic existence and yet be completely unknown or omitted in all
the literature dealing with the subject except this seventeenth century
reference.[14]

The evidence of the Biblical texts thus proves the existence of
Christianity in the second century throughout the length of the Nile
and also, to some extent, among the native population. Nevertheless,
there is no indication in those texts (beyond the inclusion of The Book
of Enoch and the other non-canonical writings mentioned earlier) of
the doctrines or organization in the non-Alexandrian congregations.
Clement remarks that Christianity had spread throughout the world,
to every nation, village, and town, converting entire households.[15]
Clement perhaps exaggerates the extent of the spread of Christianity,

but his words certainly must have applied to Egypt. Clement was also speaking of Christianity in a broader sense than that imposed on Alexandria during the episcopacy of a Demetrius or Dionysius, however, and it was shown in the last chapter that not even in Dionysius' time was all of Egypt securely controlled by the Alexandrian bishop. One might expect, therefore, that Christianity in Egypt outside of Alexandria would be comprised, in large measure, of that which would later be defined as heresies in doctrine and ritual practice.

If Epiphanius had access to accurate information, one may gain some insight into the doctrinal nature of some Christians in non-Alexandrian Egypt. According to that heresiologist, Basilides proselyted (evidently with success) in Egypt:

ἐν τῇ τῶν Αἰγυπτίων χώρᾳ στειλάμενος τὴν πορείαν, ἐκεῖσε τὰς διατριβὰς ἐποιεῖτο, εἶτα ἔρχεται εἰς τὰ μέρη τοῦ Προσωπίτου καὶ Ἀθριβίτου, οὐ μὴν ἀλλὰ καὶ περὶ τὸν Σαΐτην καὶ Ἀλεξάνδρειαν καὶ Ἀλεξανδρειοπολίτην χῶρον ἤτοι νομόν· νομὸν γὰρ οἱ Αἰγύπτιοί φασι τὴν ἑκάστης πόλεως περιοικίδα ἤτοι περίχωρον.[16]

He (Basilides) journeyed to Egypt and spent time there. He then went into the regions of Prosopitis and Athribis, and further to the neighborhoods of Sais and of Alexandria, and into the region or nome of Alexandria. For the Egyptians name the country or land around each city a nome.

The named cities and areas are all within the delta of the Nile, so one assumes that Basilides began in Upper Egypt and worked his way down the Nile, stopping along the way. There is absolutely no indication whether the missionary activity was the primary reason for the journey or was only subsidiary to some personal business. The Alexandrian bishops of the third century would not have recognized his efforts in either case, but he may have been more acceptable to a second century Alexandrian church not yet caught up in heresy-hunting.

Later in the same account, Epiphanius states that Valentinus was likely born in Pharbaithus, a nome capital city midway up the Pelusian branch of the Nile in the eastern part of the delta:

ἔφασαν γὰρ αὐτόν τινες γεγενῆσθαι Φαρβαιθίτην τῆς Αἰγύπτου παραλιώτην, ἐν Ἀλεξανδρείᾳ δὲ πεπαιδεῦσθαι τὴν τῶν Ἑλλήνων παιδείαν.[17]

Some say that he (Valentinus) was born in Pharbaithus, near the seacoast of Egypt, but was educated in Alexandria in the education of the Greeks.

The concluding statement of the famous Muratorian fragment (the earliest known list of New Testament writings, which dates from the second century) makes some connection between Valentinus and the city Arsinoë, perhaps suggesting an origin near the Fayyum, but the language is not clear on that point.[18] Epiphanius makes particular mention of the preaching of Valentinus, emphasizing his success by noting that Valentinians still could be found in his own time (the middle of the fourth century):

> ἐποιήσατο δὲ οὗτος τὸ κήρυγμα καὶ ἐν Αἰγύπτῳ ὅθεν δὴ καὶ ὡς λείψανα ἐχίδνης ὀστέων ἔτι ἐν Αἰγύπτῳ περιλείπεται τούτου ἡ σπορά ἔν τε τῷ Ἀθριβίτῃ καὶ Προσωπίτῃ καὶ Ἀρσινοΐτῃ καὶ Θηβαΐδῃ καὶ τοῖς κάτω μέρεσι τῆς παραλίας καὶ Ἀλεξανδρειοπολίτῃ.[19]

> *This one (Valentinus) preached in Egypt, for which reason even now, as the remains of the bones of a viper, the seed of this man yet survive in Egypt, in Athribis and Prosopitis and Arsinoë and Thebes and in the coastal areas and in Alexandria.*

From the last statement it is clear that much of Egypt for a long time continued to have a sizable portion of its Christian population following what later came to be defined as heretical doctrines and practices. Origen provides another example of one who, although excommunicated and exiled from Alexandria, continued to be very popular for years with a number of the monks throughout Egypt.[20] Although Origen's excommunication occurred ostensibly because of his irregular ordination, his doctrinal writings were condemned over a century later, and a persecution of Origenists in Egypt was instituted by Theophilus, bishop of Alexandria. Harnack suggested that the connection between Origen and the Coptic monks is best seen in Hieracas, an ascetic Copt of the late third and early fourth centuries.[21] In addition to teaching the doctrines of Origen to the monastic societies he founded, Hieracas promoted theological speculations concerning Melchizedek and the worship of the Holy Spirit (with whom he identified Melchizedek.)[22] By the time of Theophilus' persecution, Origenism would thus have flourished for up to a century in sympathetic monastic societies. It is a tribute to the tenacity of such Egyptian monks who, under the leadership of the Tall Brothers, resisted the anti-Origenist movement and persisted in the newly-defined heresy of Origenism, although the majority of the monks were anti-Origenist. This example illustrates how reluctant identifiable segments of the native Egyptian population were to change in their Christian beliefs. As the Alexandrian church became more aligned with Catholicism, much of the native population would appear to be increasingly heretical in religious matters.

One little-known aspect of the Nag Hammadi Library discovered in Upper Egypt in 1945 is the strong anti-heretical language found in some of the tractates. The object of these statements, however, is usually the Catholic Church, although there are some polemics aimed at other Christian groups. In particular, *The Second Treatise of the Great Seth* (VII,2) contains strong statements against Catholic Christians because they worship the dead or crucified Jesus without true knowledge, and they persecute the true Gnostics who know the Eternal Christ.

ЄΛΝЄΙ ЄΒΟΛ 2Μ ΠЄΝΗЄΙ · ЄΛΝЄΙ Є2ΡΛΪ ЄΠЄΪΚΟCΜΟC · ΛΥШ ΛΝШШΠЄ 2Μ
ΠΙΚΟCΜΟC 2Ν ΝΙCШΜΛ · ΛΥΜЄCΤШΝ ΛΥШ ΛΥΠШΤ ΝCШΝ · ΟΥ ΜΟΝΟΝ ΝΗ ЄΤЄ
ΝΛΤCΟΟΥΝ · ΛΛΛΛ ЄΒΟΛ 2ΙΤΝ ΝΗ ΟΝ ЄΤΜЄЄΥЄ ХЄ CЄΡЄΥΠΟΡΙ ΜΠΡΛΝ
ΜΠЄХC ЄΥШΟΥЄΙΤ 2Ν ΟΥΜΝΤΛΤCΟΟΥΝ ЄΝCЄCΟΟΥΝ ΜΜΟΟΥ ΛΝ ХЄ ΝΙΜ
ΝЄ .²³

After we came out of our house we came down to this world. And we came to be in the world in bodies, and they hated and persecuted us; not only those who were unknowing, but also those who think that they are prospering in the name of Christ, those who are vain in their ignorance, and they do not know who they are.

The false Christians who persecute these "true believers" are also depicted as being slaves to their own lustful appetites for worldly wealth and power:

ΟΥ ΓΛΡ ΜΠΟΥCΟΥШΝ ΤΓΝШCΙC ΝΤЄ ΤΜΝΤΝΟ6 · ХЄ ЄCШΟΟΠ ЄΒΟΛ ΜΠCΛ
ΝΤΠЄ ΜΝ ΟΥΠΗΓΗ ΝΤЄ ΤΜЄ · ΛΥШ ΟΥЄΒΟΛ 2Ν ΟΥΜΝΤ2Μ2ΛΛ ΛΝ ΤЄ ΜΝ
ΟΥΚШ2 · ΛΥШ ΟΥ2ΟΤЄ ΜΝ ΟΥШШΠЄ ΝΤЄ ΟΥ2ΥΛΗ ΝΚΟCΜΙΚΟΝ · ΠΗ ΓΛΡ ЄΤЄ
ΜΠШΟΥ ΛΝ ΠЄ ΜΝ ΠΗ ЄΤЄ ΠШΟΥ ΠЄ ЄΥΡХΡΛCΘΛΙ Ν 2ΗΤ9 ЄХΝ ΟΥ2ΡΤЄ ΜΝ
ΟΥΜΝΤΡΜ2Є · ΜΛΥΡЄΠΙΘΥΜΙ ХЄ ΟΥΝΤΛΥ ЄХΟΥCΙΛ · ΛΥШ ΟΥΝΟΜΟC ЄΒΟΛ
ΜΜΟΟΥ ЄХΝ ΝΗ ЄΤΟΥΝΛΟΥΟШΟΥ .²⁴

For they did not know the knowledge of the greatness, that it is from above and a spring of truth, and not out of slavery and envy, or fear and desire of worldly material. For that which does not belong to them, and that which does belong to them they use without fear and freely. They do not desire because they have authority and a law from themselves over whatever they will desire.

Similarly, the *Apocalypse of Peter* from the Nag Hammadi library contains polemic language directed against the Catholics, particularly those who claim Peter as their source of authority:

ⲀⲨⲰ ⲚⲀⲒ ⲈⲒ̈ⲬⲰ ⲘⲘⲞⲞⲨ ⲠⲈⲬⲈ ⲠⲤⲰⲦⲎⲢ ⲬⲈ ⲀⲈⲒⲬⲞⲞⲤ ⲚⲀⲔ ⲬⲈ ⲚⲀⲒ̈ ⲌⲈⲚ—
ⲂⲖ̄ⲖⲈⲈⲨⲈ ⲚⲈ ⲀⲨⲰ ⲌⲈⲚⲔⲞⲨⲢ ⲚⲈ · ⲤⲰⲦⲘ̄ ϬⲈ ⲦⲚⲞⲨ ⲈⲚⲎ ⲈⲦⲞⲨⲬⲰ ⲘⲘⲞⲞⲨ
ⲚⲀⲔ ⲌⲚ̄ ⲞⲚⲘⲨⲤⲦⲎⲢⲒⲞⲚ · ⲀⲨⲰ ⲀⲢⲈⲌ ⲈⲢⲞⲞⲨ Ⲙ̄ⲠⲢ̄ⲬⲞⲞⲨ ⲈⲚⲒϢⲎⲢⲈ Ⲛ̄ⲦⲈ ⲠⲒ—
ⲀⲒⲰⲚ · ⲈⲔⲈϢⲰⲠⲈ ⲄⲀⲢ Ⲛ̄ⲦⲞⲔ ⲈⲨⲬⲈ ⲞⲨⲀ ⲈⲢⲞⲔ Ⲛ̄ⲌⲢⲀⲒ̈ ⲌⲚ̄ ⲚⲈⲒ̈ⲀⲒⲰⲚ · ⲈⲨⲈ
ⲚⲀⲦⲤⲞⲞⲨⲚ ⲈⲢⲞⲔ · ⲈⲨⲦⲈⲞⲞⲨ ⲀⲈ ⲚⲀⲔ ⲌⲚ̄ ⲞⲨⲄⲚⲰⲤⲒⲤ · ⲞⲨⲚ̄ ⲞⲨⲘⲎⲎϢⲈ ⲄⲀⲢ
ⲚⲀⲬⲒ ⲈⲂⲞⲖ ⲌⲚ̄ ⲦⲀⲢⲬⲎ Ⲛ̄ⲦⲈ ⲠⲈⲚϢⲀⲬⲈ · ⲀⲨⲰ ⲤⲈⲚⲀⲔⲞⲦⲞⲨ ⲈⲢⲞⲞⲨ ⲞⲚ ⲌⲘ̄
ⲠⲞⲨⲰϢ Ⲛ̄ⲦⲈ ⲠⲒⲰⲦ Ⲛ̄ⲦⲈ ⲦⲞⲨⲠⲖⲀⲚⲎ ⲬⲈ ⲀⲨⲈⲒⲢⲈ Ⲙ̄ⲠⲈⲦⲈⲌⲚⲀϤ .[25]

And when I said these things, the Savior said: "I have told you that these are blind and deaf. Now hear the things which they are saying to you in a mystery, and guard them and do not tell them to the children of this age. For they will blaspheme you in these ages because they do not know you. But they will give honor to you in a knowledge, for a multitude will accept our doctrine in the beginning, and then they will turn from them again by the will of the father of their deception because they have done what was pleasing to him.

As was the situation elsewhere in early Christianity, the real threat to believers was considered to be from within the organization. Church members who had turned from the true faith and were in rebellion (the meaning of the Greek word *apostasia*) were a much greater threat to the Church than were external forces. The *Apocalypse of Peter* identifies the real apostates with those who have ecclesiastical authority:

ⲈⲨⲈϢⲰⲠⲈ ⲀⲈ Ⲛ̄ϬⲒ ⲌⲈⲚⲔⲞⲞⲨⲈ Ⲛ̄ⲦⲈ ⲚⲎ ⲈⲦⲤⲀⲂⲞⲖ Ⲛ̄ⲦⲈ ⲦⲈⲚⲎⲠⲈ · ⲈⲨⲦ ⲢⲀⲚ
ⲈⲢⲞⲞⲨ ⲬⲈ ⲈⲠⲒⲤⲔⲞⲠⲞⲤ · ⲈⲦⲒ ⲀⲈ ⲌⲈⲚⲀⲒⲀⲔⲰⲚ ⲌⲰⲤ ⲈⲀⲨⲬⲒ Ⲛ̄ⲚⲞⲨⲈⲬⲞⲨⲤⲒⲀ
ⲈⲂⲞⲖ ⲌⲒ̄ⲦⲘ̄ ⲠⲚⲞⲨⲦⲈ ⲈⲨⲢⲒⲔⲈ ⲘⲘⲞⲞⲨ ⲌⲀ ⲠⲒⲌⲀⲠ Ⲛ̄ⲦⲈ ⲚⲒϢⲞⲢⲠ̄ ⲘⲘⲀ Ⲛ̄ⲌⲘⲞⲞⲤ
ⲚⲎ ⲈⲦⲘ̄ⲘⲀⲨ ⲚⲈ ⲚⲒⲞⲞⲢ Ⲛ̄ⲀⲦⲘⲞⲞⲨ .[26]

And there will some of these outside of our number who will be called "bishop", and yet others "deacons", since they received their authorities from God. Yet they have bowed themselves under the judgment of the first thrones. These are waterless canals.

In a recent study on Gnostic polemics against the Christian Church, Klaus Koschorke presents arguments suggesting that the *Apocalypse of Peter* is directed against those who claim the Apostle Paul as their spiritual progenitor.[27] The main difficulty in proposing and maintaining such hypotheses arises from the fact that one cannot identify with certainty who wrote or translated the documents, or who accepted the writings as authoritative.

Birger Pearson has also found some evidence of anti-heretical feeling in both the *Melchizedek* tractate and the *Testimony of Truth* in Codex IX, some of which he believes to be directed against other Gnostic groups.[28] If these identifications are correct, the undifferentiated Christianity in Egypt during most of the first two centuries had, by the third century, become separated into competing sects, each claiming the others to be heretical.

The best available source for understanding the organization of Christian churches outside Alexandria in the third century is Dionysius, the bishop of Alexandria in the middle of the century. Dionysius was seen in an earlier context to be the first Alexandrian bishop to exhibit full harmony and fellowship with the other catholic bishops, but his letters and activities directed toward the rest of Egypt (that is, outside of Alexandria) provide insights into the nature of the Christian religion along the Nile and Alexandria's relationship to the rest of Egypt. In his defense against the charges of a certain Germanus, Dionysius answers criticisms that he had fled during the persecutions to avoid suffering.[29] This defense, which Lawlor and Oulton identify[30] with the letter written "to his fellow-presbyters and at the same time to others in different places,"[31] indicates widespread criticism of the bishop, and a need for him to give his fellow clergy a detailed accounting of his actions. On another occasion, after returning from exile in the Cephro Oasis following the persecution of Valerian, Dionysius was able to communicate with "the brethren" in Alexandria only by letter, since they were too torn by factions to gather in a meeting with the bishop:

... πάλιν δ' ἐνταῦθα στάσεως καὶ πολέμου συστάντος, ὡς οὐχ οἷόν τε ἦν αὐτῷ τοὺς κατὰ τὴν πόλιν ἅπαντας ἀδελφούς, εἰς ἑκάτερον τῆς στάσεως μέρος διῃρημένους, ἐπισκοπεῖν, αὖθις ἐν τῇ τοῦ πάσχα ἑορτῇ, ὥσπερ τις ὑπερόριος, ἐξ αὐτῆς τῆς Ἀλεξανδρείας διὰ γραμμάτων αὐτοῖς ὡμίλει.[32]

And when faction and war broke out there again, since it was not possible for him to watch over all the brethren in the city, inasmuch as they were divided into either one part or the other of the faction, he again at the festival of the Pascha (Easter), as if he were in a foreign country, communicated with them by letter from Alexandria itself.

The extent to which Dionysius felt as if he were a foreigner to those factious clergy in Alexandria must have been increased when he wrote to the churches elsewhere in Egypt. When he was exiled to Cephro in Libya, the bishop says:

... καὶ πολλὴ συνεπεδήμησεν ἡμῖν ἐκκλησία, τῶν μὲν ἀπὸ τῆς πόλεως ἀδελφῶν ἑπομένων, τῶν δὲ συνιόντων ἀπ' Αἰγύπτου.[33]

And a large church traveled with us, some of the brethren following us from the city, and others joining us from Egypt.

The significant distinction between "The brethren from the city" and "Those joining us from Egypt" is also implied elsewhere in Dionysius' writings.[34] Part of his difficulty in dealing with Christians who differed with him lay in the fact that some could remember the time before the "new order" was established. One such instance is clearly evident from a letter written to Xystus, bishop of Rome.[35] Dionysius relates how, as he was presiding at a communion service, one brother came to him who had been a member of the congregation since before the episcopacy of Heraclas. The man in question had recently attended a baptismal service for new converts, and when he heard the catechetical dialogue associated with the ritual, the member observed that it was quite different from his own. He had thus come to Dionysius to be baptized anew into the true faith. Dionysius, undoubtedly grateful for the show of unity, nevertheless confesses to Xystus that he did not dare ἐξ ὑπαρχῆς ἀνασκευάζειν,[36] (to build again from the beginning), although his predecessor, Heraclas, had instituted a rule which stated that any who had been baptized by heretics had to be rebaptized.[37] In this instance Dionysius was reluctant to make the rule retroactive beyond the time of Heraclas, and there may well have been a serious question whether the man had been baptized by heretics or simply under a less well-defined catechism. It is also possible that his reluctance to rebaptize heretics was a passive attempt to show conciliation and avoid increased animosity toward the divided Christians in the land over which he was attempting to preside.

Finally, as Eusebius explains the setting for Dionysius' work, On Promises, one can partly determine the organization of the churches in Egypt. A certain Nepos, identified as a bishop of those in Egypt, probably Arsinoë,[38] had taught a chiliastic interpretation of the Apocalypse which Dionysius journeyed to Arsinoë to refute. The seriousness of his task he emphasizes by saying that entire congregations had been split off from the truth by Nepos' doctrines. After arriving in Arsinoë,

συγκαλέσας τοὺς πρεσβυτέρους καὶ διδασκάλους τῶν ἐν ταῖς κώμαις ἀδελφῶν, παρόντων καὶ τῶν βουλομένων ἀδελφῶν, δημοσίᾳ τὴν ἐξέτασιν ποιήσασθαι τοῦ λόγου προετρεψάμην.[39]

After I convened the elders and teachers of the brethren in the villages, and as many of the brethren who wished were present, I urged them to hold a public examination of the doctrine.

One notes that Dionysius did not call a bishop, or local group of bishops, to this meeting, indicating that no bishop had been elected for Arsinoë to replace Nepos. If Nepos had been dead for some time, a new bishop should have been chosen, but perhaps due to the factions none could be elected. On the other hand, if bishops at this time were selected by the Alexandrian bishop and Dionysius were not in control of the churches in the area (as is obvious from the account), the purpose of his visit might have been to establish order so that a bishop might be appointed.[40] The rest of the language in the quoted passage is conciliatory, for "as many of the brethren who wished" were present, and Dionysius "urged them to hold a public examination of the doctrine." And, as he continues the account, he had to spend three full days arguing the issue with them, and even then many were not convinced at the conclusion of his visit.[41] Therefore, he left the conference able to admire them for "their firmness, love of truth, ability to follow an argument, and intelligence," but he was not able to capture the loyalty and obedience of more than a portion of the members. Even by the middle of the third century the bishop appears to be more successful in interfering in the affairs of other catholic churches elsewhere in the Mediterranean than in controlling the churches which, according to Canon VI of the later Nicene Council, were decreed to be part of his jurisdiction and domain.

Some slight evidence for identifying specific Christians in third century Egypt can be gleaned from the accounts of the persecutions and the materials related to them. The persecution of Severus in 202, which was aimed at limiting, rather than exterminating, Christianity, affected all of Egypt, according to Eusebius:

Ὡς δὲ καὶ Σευῆρος διωγμὸν κατὰ τῶν ἐκκλησιῶν ἐκίνει . . . μάλιστα δ' ἐπλήθυεν ἐπ' Ἀλεξανδρείας, τῶν ἀπ' Αἰγύπτου καὶ Θηβαΐδος ἁπάσης αὐτόθι ὥσπερ ἐπὶ μέγιστον ἀθλητῶν θεοῦ παραπεμπομένων στάδιον . . .[42]

And when Severus set in motion a persecution against the churches . . . and it was especially increased in Alexandria, where the champions of god were conducted from Egypt and the entire Thebaid, as if to a very great arena . . .

The historian is probably describing accurately the geographical diffusion of Christianity at the beginning of the third century, but he must certainly be exaggerating the numbers who were martyred when he says μυρίοι (*[they were] numberless*).[43] Origen made some qualified statements about the numbers of Christians in third century Egypt ("not so many at first, in comparison with the multitudes who subsequently became Christian" and yet, when all things are considered, καίτοι οὐ πάντη ἦσαν ὀλίγοι—*And indeed, they were not altogether few in number*)[44] and he also admitted that the Christian martyrs were not very numerous.[45]

The persecution of Decius in 250–251 was caused as the result of a summons made for all the people in the empire to participate in a sacrifice to the Roman gods.[46] An edict was published requiring certificates of sacrifice to be shown to a commission which was established for that purpose, and if the certificate, or *libellus*, were not exhibited by a given date an individual became liable to imprisonment, "where attempts were often made to break his resistance by torture."[47] The decree of Decius did not mention Christians specifically, and some scholars doubt that he really intended the extermination of that group. They suggest that he primarily was attempting to force a return to the old state religion in celebration of Rome's millenial anniversary—the persecution of the Christians was an unfortunate side-effect.[48] Eusebius states that Decius instigated the persecution of the churches because of his hatred toward Philip, the preceding emperor who had been quite tolerant toward the Christians.[49] Whatever the motivation, there is no question that this persecution constituted the greatest attack from external sources that Christianity had suffered.

There is no way to determine what percentage of the Christians in Egypt obtained *libelli* through sacrifice, how many may have obtained the certificates by bribes or intrigue, or how effective the method was for determining who had a *libellus*. Hardy argues that one cannot even be certain who of the population were required to have a *libellus*,[50] and thus any that are found have uncertain value for one trying to determine where Christians lived in Egypt. Baus stated that 43 *libelli* have been found in Egypt,[51] but an article by Knipfing lists only 41.[52] Of those found, the majority came from the Fayyum, but two came from the vicinity of the Oxyrhynchus. The fact that one was from a pagan priestess[53] makes it difficult to believe that only suspected Christians had to obtain *libelli*. There are some instances, furthermore, where entire families obtained a single *libellus*,[54] further suggesting that the decree applied to the general population rather than specifically to individual suspected Christians. The few number of *libelli* recovered, and the fact that they are associated with the adult population in general, preclude any determination being made from them concerning the strength of Christianity in any locality in Egypt.

There can be no question that the Decian persecution did have an effect on the Christian church, but more because of those who did sacrifice than of those who did not. Dionysius is clearly disturbed in his letter to Fabian at Antioch, claiming that the edict fulfilled the prophecy in Matthew 24:24 that even the elect would be deceived.[55] It would appear from his letter that many of the Alexandrian church lapsed in some way, either by sacrificing or fleeing to avoid imprisonment and punishment.[56] Even of those who went to prison, Dionysius said many capitulated under torture and sacrificed in accord with the decree. His own flight has been mentioned above, and the reproach which he hurls at those who are designated "cowards in everything, cowards both to die and to sacrifice" must have been similar to charges leveled against him, judging by his defense against Germanus to the presbyters in Alexandria. A.H.M. Jones suggests that most of the resentment against the lapsed or those who fled persecution likely came from the lower classes (meaning primarily the natives? On this point he is not clear.) who refused thereafter "to submit to clergy whose record they regarded as suspect."[57] Such statements, however attractive and supportive they are of the picture emerging from this study, are somewhat difficult to defend from the meager evidence available in the sources.

In a letter written to Fabian, bishop of Antioch, Dionysius recounts the narrative of the persecutions, in which he gives eighteen specific names of martyrs.[58] Of these, one is identified as Libyan[59] and four as Egyptians,[60] but beyond showing a mixture of races in the Alexandrian church one would wisely avoid using these figures in a statistical analysis of the ethnic makeup of church membership. Except for a name which gives a specific reference to one's racial origins, Bell correctly notes that even a study of names cannot yield certain results in determining someone's roots.[61] The evidence from the persecutions in the first half of the third century is tantalizing, but as yet cannot be pressed for much information concerning the organization which the persecution primarily affected.

One should also take into consideration what is known concerning the bishops attested outside Alexandria in the third century when assessing the strength of the Christian movement in the nomes. A tenth century patriarch of Alexandria, Eutychius, records information concerning the early episcopates not found anywhere else.[62] His Melkite (accepting the decision of Chalcedon in 451) bias was answered from the Monophysite position by Severus, son of El-Mukaffa and bishop at El-Ushmunain,[63] who gathered the records from the monasteries in order to compile his history.[64] Severus tells how he implored educated Christians to assist him in translating the Greek and Coptic records,[65] and one of the records was certainly that of Eusebius whom he quotes freely. As might be expected from these decidedly biased authors who oppose each other's position, the two accounts of these late historians differ in many respects, but nowhere more conspicuously than in the history of the bishops. Severus gives the Eusebian list of bishops, but has much more information than the Caesarean historian. In the account Severus gives to the end of the second century the miracle stories and fabulous tales should probably be considered to be much later inventions, for Eusebius would not have omitted entirely such a wealth of material had it been available to him. It is possible, however, that this material existed in sources older than the time of Eusebius and were simply unavailable to the non-Egyptian historian from Caesarea.

When Severus tells of the third patriarch of Alexandria, Avilius (Abilius in Euseb.), he mentions bishops in the land,[66] and the plurality of Egyptian bishops is repeated in the episcopates of Celadion and Julian.[67] There is an obvious defect in the account, though, for Severus mentions that Julian did not remain always in Alexandria, but went *secretly* (at the end of the second century, which is too early for the fear of persecutions) throughout the land and ordained priests. This strange account is inconsistent in its claim of secret ordinations, for Julian surely would not be going through Egypt ordaining priests without the knowledge of the local bishops—who are said to have gathered in a synod and appointed and consecrated Julian as bishop of Alexandria. It is possible that Julian was ordaining priests in a somewhat covert manner to upstage a developing and competing ecclesiastical tradition.

If Julian did ordain priests in Egypt, indirect support can be claimed for the accuracy of Eutychius' account, where he states that prior to Demetrius there were no other bishops in Egypt.[68] Eutychius is generally considered to be a blundering and incompetent historian,[69] but the inability of Severus to refute his statement that there were no bishops in Egypt outside Alexandria for the first two centuries C.E. (beyond stating that "the bishops" met together on three occasions) lends some credence to his statement that Demetrius first consecrated bishops in Egypt. Even as late as the middle of the third century, Dionysius could journey to Arsinoë where entire local churches had gone astray, but no living bishop is mentioned or associated with them.[70] Eutychius gives more detail, adding that Demetrius ordained three bishops,[71] and that his successor Heraclas ordained twenty.[72] The organizational development of the church implicit in Eusebius and Severus, but explicit in Eutychius, is the gradual imposition upon local Egyptian churches of the authoritative ecclesiastical structure of Alexandria through the increasingly frequent appointment of bishops by the bishop of Alexandria beginning in the episcopacy of Demetrius. Again one turns to Jerome's Epistle where he implies that there was a change in the manner of episcopal succession during the third century in Alexandria. He states that until the episcopates of Heraclas and Dionysius, the presbyters named as bishop one of their own number.[73] The change which occurred afterward was that bishops were consecrated by other bishops, thus limiting the power of the presbyters. Kemp notes that prior to the new method of selecting the Alexandrian bishop,

> The presbyters of Alexandria had exceptional powers not now possessed by presbyters . . . and at the outbreak of the Arian controversy we find presbyters in charge of churches and districts of the city with a position of independence which does not seem to be paralleled elsewhere in Christendom at that date.[74]

Local churches, then, appear to have depended more upon a leadership composed of deacons and presbyters before the entrance of the Western ecclesiastical system with its emphasis upon episcopal rule. This explanation would also account for the so-called "heretical" movements which continue to thrive for a long time in Egypt, being considered heretical as much for their recalcitrance in ecclesiastical affairs as for heterodoxy in doctrine.

Eusebius mentions but a few bishops in Egypt during Dionysius' episcopacy,[75] and that is in keeping with the small number suggested by Eutychius for the period just before Dionysius. Just as one could not push the evidence from the Decian persecution to say what it does not about the number of Christians in Egypt, so also one cannot use the relative silence of Eusebius to prove that there were few bishops in Egypt during the third century. The evidence tends to support that position, but the argument is still sustained in great measure by an argument from silence, not at all sufficient for arriving at certainty.

The picture of developing ecclesiastical Christianity in Egypt, which was illuminated rather well from the time of Demetrius to that of Dionysius due to a significantly greater number of sources, becomes much dimmer again until the Diocletianic persecutions in the early fourth century. This obscurity should not be understood as an indication that the organization declined in strength or vitality, for Alexander, bishop of Alexandria from 313 to 328, stated in an encyclical letter that nearly 100 bishops were gathered in a synod in c. 320 C.E., excluding some apostates who were once called bishops.[76] Athanasius, writing after the synods of Alexandria in 339 and of Sardica in c. 343, corroborates the earlier figure given by Alexander, for he says "There are in Egypt, Libya, and Pentapolis, nearly one hundred bishops."[77] The Egyptian ecclesiastical organization had grown, then, from a very few bishops in the first half of the third century to nearly 100 by the first quarter of the fourth, and had apparently remained somewhat stable over the next two decades to near the middle of the century. The organization of dioceses and ordination of bishops outside Alexandria took place, for the most part, during the period when information concerning them is almost totally absent. The lack of evidence makes moot the issue of whether the change from presbyter rule to episcopal rule occurred simply as a result of growth in numbers of Christians or as the outcome of the Alexandrian prelate trying to extend his hegemony over the Egyptian Christians by imposing an ecclesiastical structure of new offices and officers upon them.

Dionysius died before the Synod of Antioch in 268 was held, but he had previously sent a letter to the meeting of bishops expressing his views on the monarchianism of Paul of Samosata, the bishop of Antioch who was deposed by the Synod.[78] The Alexandrian prelate would have concurred both in the decision of the Synod and in the concept expressed by Eusebius, that Paul τῆς ὑπὸ τὸν οὐρανὸν καθολικῆς ἐκκλησίας ἀποκηρύττεται[79] (*was excommunicated from the Catholic Church under heaven*). Dionysius' successor, Maximus apparently did not attend the meeting of bishops (perhaps the invitation offered to Dionysius was not extended to him?),[80] for the synod sent a letter outlining the work and decision of the pastors in considerable detail both to him and to Dionysius, the bishop of Rome, who also did not attend the meeting (no Roman bishop attended eastern councils).[81] It would be instructive to know if *any* bishops from Egypt attended the Synod, and if not, why they were omitted from the greeting in the letter. The natural inference from Eusebius' narrative is that the bishops elsewhere assumed that addressing a missive to the

Alexandrian bishop was the same as addressing it to all within his spiritual domain.[82]

One note of interest comes from an otherwise sparse account of Maximus' reign as bishop. A certain Eusebius, a native of Alexandria, who had gone to Syria because of matters concerning Paul of Samosata, was chosen to succeed Socrates as the bishop of Laodicea.[83] He had been a deacon in Alexandria and had earned a good reputation for compassionate service rendered to Christian prisoners during the persecutions, even taking care of the burial tasks for the corpses of the martyrs.[84] Eusebius' successor at Laodicea, a certain Anatolius, also was an Alexandrian, well known for his achievements in Greek education and philosophy, so that he was selected to become the founder and head of an Aristotelian school at Alexandria.[85] Anatolius was so well-liked that the bishop who ordained him, Theotecnus of Caesarea, sought to have Anatolius succeed him in his own see. The Alexandrian was passing through Laodicea on his way to Caesarea (where he did preside for a short time with Theotecnus) soon after Eusebius died, however, and he was retained by "the brethren" to be the bishop there.[86] It had taken less than a century for Alexandria to import Ecclesiastical Christianity and nurture it to the point that Alexandrians were properly trained to be exported to other cities with long Christian traditions and be appointed bishops there. It was now also apparently all right for an Alexandrian to be ordained by a Palestinian bishop, especially since he was not returning to Egypt.

A less positive note for ecclesiastical Christianity is also sounded during this same period, for from Persia came the Christian heresy of Manichaios, or Mani as a short form.[87] Mani, born in 216 C.E. near Seleucia-Ctesiphon, the capital of the Persian Empire, was raised in a Babylonian Baptist community.[88] Remarkable spiritual manifestations beginning at age 12, including heavenly visits from his celestial alter-ego, led Mani, at age 24 in 240 C.E., to make his first public appearance as a preacher of a new gospel of hope and salvation.[89] The success of this religious leader, who called himself an Apostle of Jesus Christ,[90] was phenomenal even during his own lifetime. He suffered martyrdom in 276 under Bahram I of Persia, who had him put to death by being flayed alive.[91] Missionaries were sent both to the east and to the west, and Manichaeism became a major threat to Christianity in the Roman Empire during the fourth and fifth centuries.[92]

It is impossible to state precisely when Manichaeism first arrived in Egypt, but R. M. Grant argues that Manichaean missionaries were there before 262 C.E.[93] Before the end of the third century, Alexander of Lykopolis, a Platonist mistakenly thought by some to have been a bishop in that city,[94] was writing against the Manichees in Egypt.[95] Iranian sources state that Adda, one of Mani's intimate associates and disciples, eventually arrived at Alexandria during his missionary travels, but Alexander claims that his instructor in Manichaeism was a certain Pappos.[96] The two traditions may not be mutually exclusive, however, for Alexander does not (contrary to Lieu's statement on the matter) claim that Pappos was the first missionary to Egypt, and Alexander may have met Pappos in Lykopolis, rather than Alexandria.[97]

Yet another account of the arrival of Manichaeism to Egypt is suggested by Epiphanius, who links the trading of goods to the trading of ideas in the person of Scythianus.[98] Trading between India and Egypt, Scythianus called at the ports of Ailat, Castle-on-the-Beach, and Berenice on the Red Sea, and made his way to the Thebaid in the Nile Valley from Berenice. Epiphanius further names a city in the Thebaid, Hypseles, as the place where Scythianus found his wife, and Lieu makes a connection between the sub-Achmimic dialect of Coptic associated with the Hypseles region and some Manichaean codices written in the sub-Achmimic dialect and found in the Fayum in 1930.[99] The evidence probably cannot support such a story in all its details, or the geographical origin and limitation of Coptic dialects to Manuscripts found elsewhere. All accounts thus far presented, however, do support the image of a successful and widespread reception which Manichaeism enjoyed in Egypt.

The early arrival and rapid spread of Manichaeism in Egypt in the latter half of the third century is compatible with the portrayal of Egypt as a land where a strong and centralized ecclesiastical organization does not yet exist with power to resist this foreign heresy. Furthermore, Lieu makes a good case for the influence of Valentinian influences on the origins and doctrines of Manichaeism,[100] and the similarities of the two systems may account, in part at least, for the success Manichaean missionaries enjoyed along the Nile.

Significant manuscript discoveries of Manichaean writings in Egypt during the twentieth century attest that the so-called Christian heresy was well established in that country.

The discovery of Syriac fragments in Manichaean script at Oxyrhynchos shows that the earliest Manichaean communities were Syrian implantations, but names like Jmmoute, Pshai, and Apa Panai in the Coptic *Psalm-Book* attest to the Egyptian origin of some of the sect's earliest martyrs and followers in Egypt.[101]

In 1930 Carl Schmidt was shown a number of Coptic codices in Cairo which he identified as Manichaean, and the site of their discovery was traced to Medinet Medi in the Fayum.[102] Many of the sect's authoritative liturgical and homiletic writings are in this collection, and the fact that those writings were translated from Syriac originals (generally via Greek translations) shows they were intended for the native population, just as was the case with the Nag Hammadi writings being translated from Greek to Coptic.

The most sensational manuscript discovery of Manichaean writings during this century came to light with the decipherment of the Cologne Mani Codex in 1969 by A. Henrichs.[103] This miniature parchment codex, the smallest manuscript known from antiquity (measuring 3.5 by 4.5 centimeters, or 1.4 by 1.8 inches)[104] was written on vellum of very high quality, contains both corroborative and new material concerning the life and disciples of Mani, as well as synopses of five previously unknown Jewish Apocalypses and a brief synopsis of Pauline Apocalyptic references in the New Testament.[105] Although no certain provenance can be assigned to this remarkable find,

> Rumor has it that the remains of the codex were located several decades ago in Luxor, and it is a reasonable guess that they were found in the vicinity of ancient Lykopolis, a stronghold of Manichaeism in Upper Egypt.[106] In other words, next to nothing is known about the fate of the Mani Codex before it reached Cologne.[107]

The CMC has clarified the origin and nature of this offshoot of this sect, showing that it had a "predominantly Jewish-Christian, rather than Gnostic, basis."[108] Henrichs avers that the materials in the codex were likely collected soon after Mani's death from sources written during his lifetime.[109] Elsewhere he notes:

> The Coptic Manichaica . . . are separated from the lost Syriac originals by the interposition of Greek translations from the Syriac, equally lost, with the exception of the Cologne Codex, which is the first witness for the existence of this intermediate Greek stage of Manichaean literature in Egypt.[110]

Like many Christian groups scattered throughout Egypt, Manichaeism emphasized an on-going Apocalyptic tradition, gnosis required for salvation, and a broad-based literary tradition. The spiritual climate of Egypt, even Christian Egypt, in the third century was conducive to the spread of Manichaeism, and remnants of the movement lingered on for some centuries, as is indicated by these manuscripts discovered in recent years.

Not much is known concerning episcopal activity in Egypt during the reign of Maximus, and even less is known of Theonas, who succeeded him in 282. Eusebius records this segment of the Alexandrian succession in a style as stark and barren as that of the first bishops down to the time of Demetrius, and the only additional information available concerning Theonas is a letter written by the bishop to one Lucianus, the chief chamberlain, and one who enjoyed high favor with the emperor. There is even some question as to whether the author is Theonas, bishop of Alexandria, or another of the same name, perhaps the bishop of Cyzicus.[111] Beyond indicating that the bishop of Alexandria had contact and correspondence with people in high government circles, the letter does not give any information concerning the church in his episcopacy. Although nothing more is known about the ministry of Theonas, a note is added concerning the presbyter Achillas, who had become head of τῆς ἱερᾶς πίστεως τὸ διδασκαλεῖον[112] (*the school of the holy faith*). Theonas was succeeded in 300 by Peter, who led the Egyptian churches through the greater part of the Diocletianic persecutions.[113] He was unexpectedly beheaded in the renewed persecution of Maximin in 311,[114] and a number of other local bishops and presbyters also were beheaded at the time.[115]

Quite certainly the most significant aspect of Peter's episcopacy was the persecution begun by Diocletian, and this time there was no question concerning the motive: the edicts related to the persecution were directed against the Christian movement. His motives remain unknown (not from lack of speculation concerning them), and the outbreak of the persecution on 23 February 303 was as unexpected as it was harsh. When Eusebius turns his attention to Egypt to recount the persecution there, he separates the country into the Thebaid and Egypt,[116] and later into three parts, adding Alexandria to the other two.[117] The emphasis on the Thebaid in the martyrdom accounts is somewhat surprising, for Eusebius had devoted very little space to that area earlier in his narrative. The explanation, of course, is that Eusebius was an eyewitness of events in the Thebaid during a visit there in 311–312, but the detailed glimpse at Upper Egypt serves to show how limited were sources relating to Christian history outside of Alexandria.

For much of his material relating to Lower Egypt, Eusebius makes Phileas, the bishop of Thmuis in the delta and who was later beheaded, his example for what was happening in the entire region.[118] Little enough is known of Phileas, although the "Acts of the martyrdom of Phileas and Philoromus . . . are generally regarded as in the main authentic."[119] From the Acts, one learns that Phileas was wealthy,[120] and that at the time of his martyrdom his wife and children were pagans.[121] The latter fact suggests that he may have become a Christian later in life, an idea supported also by Jerome, who states that Phileas was born into nobility, held high political offices, and was trained in philosophy.[122] Two letters generally accepted as originating from Phileas have been preserved in fragmentary form, one to the people of Thmuis and recorded by Eusebius,[123] and the other a letter to Melitius, bishop of Lycopolis.[124] The second letter was written from prison, where Phileas and three other bishops joined in condemning Melitius for performing episcopal activities in their churches. In the first letter, Phileas gives an account of the persecution to the people of Thmuis, suggesting by its language that they had little knowledge of it there. One cannot fault Eusebius' zeal for his faith nor his good literary taste in avoiding a morbid avalanche of blood and gore in his narrative even if much more material were available to him, but the phrase, μυρίοι τε ἐπὶ τούτοις ἄλλοι διαφανεῖς[125] (*and countless other distinguished people in addition to these*), is difficult to defend in view of the limited number of examples he gives and also his apparent dependence upon one source for the bulk of his evidence. Eusebius' own eyewitness account of the martyrdoms in the Thebaid seems to be exaggerated, especially when he speaks of so many being decapitated that the axe was dulled and finally broken, and also that the executioners grew weary at the task and had to be replaced or rotated in turns.[126] Frend accepts the picture as accurate, however, stating that it is "confirmed from other sources,"[127] and then gives but one—Eusebius.[128]

The problem of those who sacrificed or fraudulently avoided prison and torture (by bribing officials, etc.), which Cyprian faced in the Decian persecution and to which Dionysius of Alexandria addressed himself in letters, erupted in great measure in the church of

Egypt during a lull in the Diocletianic persecution. A more detailed analysis of the Melitian schism will be given in the following chapter, but the significance of the dispute underlines the difficulty facing the bishop of Alexandria and the bishops elsewhere appointed by him, namely, that even having a well-organized episcopal system in Egypt by the end of the third century was no guarantee of ecclesiastical unity or control by the Alexandrian bishop. The Melitian problem began in c. 305, not over any doctrinal differences, but over the question how much to demand of the "lapsed" who desired to be readmitted to communion and fellowship in the church.[129] During the imprisonment of Phileas and the three other bishops mentioned above, Melitius, the bishop of Lycopolis, had profited at their expense by invading their churches and ordaining men loyal to him. Despite the bishops' letter of protest before their martyrdom, Melitius even went to Alexandria and strengthened his position at the expense of the imprisoned bishop of that city, Peter. As the persecution abated, Peter resumed control of his church, but the controversy over the treatment of the "lapsed" caused a lasting schism, with each side seeking power and authority in the churches.

Peter, the bishop in Alexandria, favored a more lenient disciplinary action, but Melitius represented a rigorous attitude. As Bell notes, "Neither party proposed to exclude the *lapsi* permanently from communion, neither thought of readmitting them unconditionally; it was merely a question of the interval to be allowed before readmission and the status to be accorded after it."[130] The dispute should not be thought of as simply one individual disagreeing with another, however, for Melitius was able to present a brief before the Council of Tyre in 335 in which he listed some 29 or 30 bishops from Egypt whom he could count among his supporters.[131] Melitian groups continued for at least three centuries,[132] and their influence extended beyond their own group as they later became associated with Arians. The point to be made here is that the ecclesiastical organization superimposed upon the already existing local and autonomous Christian congregations was unable to command their loyalty and devotion, especially when the structure was somewhat weakened by the Diocletianic persecution. A.H.M. Jones gives a good summary of the weakness of the system which the persecution brought to light:

> The only permanent damage done to the Church was the formation of two dissident sects, the Donatists in Africa and the Melitians in Egypt. In

these areas, where resistance had been strong, mainly amongst the lower classes, there was bitter feeling against those who had compromised or lapsed, and large numbers of rigorists refused to readmit them or to submit to clergy whose record they regarded as suspect.[133]

Dionysius' idealistic picture of the bishop of Alexandria being securely in command of the Christian churches of Egypt a half century earlier is seen to be exaggerated and overstated when one looks carefully at the evidence, and that portrayal is only superficially more realistic at the beginning of the fourth century, although the organization through the appointment and ordination of local bishops by the Alexandrian prelate by then had become widespread throughout Egypt.

The concluding portion of this chapter will treat the one major development of third century Egyptian Christianity which best illustrates the local nature of the religion in that country. Monasticism, an extreme form of asceticism adopted as a way of life for devotional reasons, is a gift of the Egyptian church to the Christian world, but the expression of that idea does little to account for its development in the third century or to explain why the Church would accept and embrace monasticism as part of its own program. Near the beginning of the third century Clement distinguished all the heresies against which he wrote according to their tendency toward asceticism or toward licentiousness.[134] He fought both tendencies, arguing in the case of the former that ascetics "proclaim the necessity of continence on the ground of opinions which are godless and arise from hatred of what God has created."[135] Again one notes, as was noted earlier, that the so-called heretics are designated by Clement primarily because of their non-ethical way of life (as determined by Clement), rather than by their doctrinal positions, some of which Clement accepts.[136] He thus is most concerned with the Carpocratians "as the outstanding examples of libertine gnosticism,"[137] but is somewhat sympathetic to the Valentinians (although there are significant differences between Clement and the Valentinians),[138] while the western heresiologists seem to reverse the order of importance between ethics and doctrines to emphasize the doctrinal heresies of the Valentinians.

Clement's successor, Origen, did not share his predecessor's distaste for ascetic ways, since according to Eusebius, he lived like a philosopher, working by day and studying the scriptures through the night. He disciplined his appetites, and slept on the floor for short periods of time rather than in a bed.[139] The picture thus depicted could well be applied to any monk of the fourth century or later, and the further details of his living in poverty, eating only what was necessary for life, and disdaining the material goods of the world would surely have been remembered in future centuries by the monks, many of whom were Origenists in the later controversies concerning him.[140] Origen's work *De Oratione* is entirely consistent with the picture of the man drawn by Eusebius, for often the works of Origen exhibit a conviction that the mortal body is negligible, especially for a spiritual man.[141] According to Eusebius' account, it was the asceticism of Origen which enhanced his popularity and was responsible for bringing people to be instructed by him.[142]

Another example of ascetic piety in the early third century is related by Eusebius, and although it comes from Palestine, its similarity to accounts from Egypt make it worth mentioning. Eusebius writes of Narcissus, bishop of Jerusalem around the beginning of the third century, and his piety and spiritual greatness are related in the account of his ascetic practices.[143] As in the case of the later famous Egyptian monks, miracle stories gravitated to the legend of Narcissus, and similar stories are common stock in the monastic world: the miracle of changing water to oil for lamps is reminiscent of Elijah and the miraculous providing of oil, and also of Jesus changing water to wine at a wedding feast in Cana; the divine vengeance against those who slander the reputation or work of the prophet-figure; the near-miraculous disappearance and reappearance of Narcissus, and the vision at night associated with his successor. All these accounts can be paralleled many times over from the *Apophthegmata Patrum* or any of the other surviving monastic accounts, as will be noted later in this work. In the case of Narcissus, just as with Origen, Eusebius declares that his retirement to a life of solitude and the philosophic life caused the brethren "to admire him to an even greater degree."[144]

The point to be emphasized from these two examples from the early third century is that the piety of these men is not linked to an office in the church, even in a bishop's history, but rather is tied to a way of life practised alongside (even outside) the ecclesiastical organization. There are non-Christian precedents in Egypt for the idea of withdrawal from the world to seek spiritual perfection, although no connection between the earlier ascetic movements and Christian monasticism can be ascertained.[145] While many Christians may have fled to the desert to avoid persecution in the third century, the primary motivation of the earliest monks, according to the accounts of their biographers, was to escape the corrupting influences of society and to lead "a life of perfection in greater security than is normally possible in the world."[146] Implicit in such a statement is the corollary that one could strive for sanctification in monasticism to a degree not normally possible in the church. This ideal of monasticism, that of achieving the highest degree of personal perfection possible in solitude, or at least through withdrawal from the world, can perhaps best be seen in Jerome's writings. Although ordained a presbyter in 379, Jerome did not consider his ecclesiastical office to be on the same level with the seemingly higher calling of being a monk:

> I, a poor wretch of a man, told Bishop Paulinus of blessed memory: "Did I ask to be ordained by you? If in bestowing the ranks of presbyter you do not strip us of the monastic state, you can bestow or withhold ordination as you think best. But if your intention on giving the name presbyter was to take from me that for which I forsook the world, I must still claim to be what I always was . . ."[147]

The monastic ideal, not to be confused with the sometimes less than ideal monastic practice, was to be free from the ecclesiastical establishment as well as from the world. "Until . . . the end of the fifth century the monk was generally regarded as a layman,"[148] having little concern for, if not opposition to, the clerical orders of the church or the pressures of a developing ecclesiastical organization.

The third century in Egypt has been shown as a time, especially from the episcopacy of Demetrius to that of Dionysius, when the Alexandrian bishop began to exert himself as the arbiter of Church doctrine (in defining orthodoxy and heresy), church education (in the gradual absorption of the catechetical school into the direct control of the bishop), and in Church authority (through the appointment of bishops for the congregations outside Alexandria). As the pressures of the new organization began to be felt throughout Egypt, Christians whose religious heritage had accustomed them to freedom and autonomy in their local congregations could be expected to follow a successful method for returning to more freedom. The most successful of those who achieved a piety in a setting not established or controlled by ecclesiastical offices would also become the most famous under the circumstances, and even if he were not the first in time, he would be the first in prominence.[149] Saint Anthony was not the first in time,[150] but he quickly became the exemplar for those who would withdraw from the church, society, and the world.[151]

"The most famous of the early monks was Anthony."[152] Anthony's fame, like that of Odysseus, was due to another telling of his exploits, and the "Homer" for Anthony was the great and controversial Athanasius. H. Queffélec emphasized the extent to which knowledge of Anthony is dependent upon Athanasius:

> Almost all the essential knowledge we have about Anthony is contained in the *Vita Antonii* of Saint Athanasius, who knew him and was very probably initiated by him into the ways of asceticism. But Athanasius cannot be said to have overloaded his biography with tangible details.[153]

Although the *Vita Antonii* was translated into Latin no later than 375 by Evagrius, bishop of Antioch, and subsequently played an important role in spreading the monastic ideal through the west,[154] considerable debate exists as to when and for whom Athanasius originally wrote the biography.[155] Analyzing the first and third person narrative passages in the biography, as well as a passage referring to the Roman Emperors in a tone described as "decidedly cool,"[156] Barnard concludes that Athanasius wrote the biography in 357 or 358 and, further, that it "was written for private circulation among the Egyptian monks."[157] B. R. Brennan responds to the position taken by Barnard, noting that in the preface to the *Vita*, Athanasius is writing to monks outside Egypt who are seeking to imitate the already famous Egyptian solitaries.[158] Concluding from the Preface that Athanasius was writing for a large audience, perhaps focusing on monks in the western provinces, Brennan also notes that the "decidedly cool" attitude of *VA* 81 is really a reserved opinion of the Emperor written by a hunted bishop who "does not have the degree of freedom to voice his real opinion of the Emperor, as he does in the secret *Historia Arianorum*."[159] The dating of the work is therefore uncertain, and the question of audience beyond the monastic world also has not been determined with certainty. Questions have also been raised in the past concerning the authenticity of Athanasius' account, but the work is generally accepted as accurate at present.[160] Even those who may not wish to accept the work at face value must concede that very few external checks exist with which to challenge Athanasius.

Anthony was a native Egyptian, was born in c. 251 in the village of Coma near the Thebaid,[161] and was reared amid considerable wealth by his Christian parents.[162] While still a young man, Anthony was orphaned, and soon afterward attended a service where he heard the passage from the Gospel, "If you wish to be perfect, go and sell what you own and give the proceeds to the poor, and you will have a treasure in heaven. Come follow me."[163] He accepted the command literally, sold his patrimony, and gave all to the poor, keeping only a portion to sustain his sister. He later even gave up the reserve for his sister and placed her in a convent, while he himself joined the ascetics in villages, first those nearby, and then those more distant. Athanasius reports that wherever Anthony went he garnered to himself the ascetic attributes of those whom he met, and in later practice excelled them all in his zealous application of those attributes. Providing a model for the hagiography of the monks who would follow Anthony's way of life, Athanasius recounts the spiritual struggles of the young man in vivid terms, having the devil first whisper to Anthony's soul, then come to him in dreams and during devotions, and then finally to confront him physically.[164] The enemy took many forms in order to tempt the monk, even—especially—that of a woman with her attendant sexual temptation.[165] Athanasius stresses the uniqueness of Anthony's subsequent departure to live in the desert:

τῇ δὲ ἑξῆς προελθὼν ἔτι μᾶλλον προθυμότερος ἦν εἰς τὴν θεοσέβειαν, καὶ γενόμενος πρὸς τὸν γέροντα τὸν παλαιὸν ἐκεῖνον, ἠξίου τὴν ἔρημον οἰκῆσαι σὺν αὐτῷ· τοῦ δὲ παραιτησαμένου διά τε τὴν ἡλικίαν, καὶ διὰ τὸ μηδέπω εἶναι τοιαύτην συνήθειαν, εὐθὺς αὐτὸς ὥρμησεν εἰς τὸ ὄρος.[166]

And on the next day as he went out he was even more zealous for the service of God, and after he met with the old man mentioned before, he asked him to live with him in the desert. But when the old man declined because of his age, and also because there was not as yet such a custom, Anthony himself immediately set out for the mountain.

Anthony occupied an abandoned fort at the mountain he found, which is called the 'Outer Mountain', and which is at Pispir, some 50 miles south of Memphis on the east bank of the Nile. Athanasius states that Anthony remained there for twenty years,[167] during which time many began to emulate his style of life as that of one "initiated into sacred mysteries and filled with the spirit of God." He rejected not only the attacks of the devil, but also the temptation to assume the leadership of a monastic organization. Desiring to be alone, Anthony journeyed to Upper Egypt, and there found another mountain, the 'Inner Mountain', to live out his days.[168]

This second mountain, identified with the modern Deir Anba Antonios near the Red Sea, became the unofficial headquarters for this new movement in Christianity, and both those who wished to ask the monk for advice and those who wished to follow his example journeyed there.[169] Anthony was accepted without question as the leader of the movement of individual and independent piety καὶ πάντων αὐτῶν ὡς πατὴρ καθηγεῖτο.[170] (and for all of them he led the way as a father). The Life of Anthony also contains a rather lengthy discourse by Anthony to the monks of Egypt, undoubtedly looked upon as the monastic equivalent of The Sermon on the Mount.[171] Anthony's visits to Alexandria appear to be infrequent, although he is reported to have gone during the persecution of Maximin to obtain martyrdom, only to be foiled because nobody would have anything to do with the holy and unkempt monk.[172]

Anthony is credited with the gifts and powers of exorcism, healing, prophecy, and virtually all the prophetic functions traditionally associated with the church, but he was not ordained to any clerical office. Duchesne remarked that he was unable to see any evidence that Anthony had received the Eucharist at any time during his twenty years of seclusion,[173] and Workman stated the same idea in rather stronger terms: "Anthony is not only a mere layman; he neither goes to church, nor receives the Sacrament for years, and yet continues in the closest intercession with God."[174] Even the bishops asked for his assistance in combatting the Arians, and he was given the epithet ὁ τοῦ θεοῦ ἄνθρωτος, ("The man of God"), a poignant substitute for any ecclesiastical title.[175] The reader cannot help sensing both admiration of bishop Athanasius and also his yearning for the same sanctity as that associated with the monk.

Anthony's death occurred in 356, and just before his death he asked that a sheepskin garment given to him by Athanasius be returned.[176] The individualism and independence from the world which epitomized his life were also thus in evidence at his death. Peter Brown notes in a recent work that the rapid growth of monasticism during the third and fourth centuries can be linked to tensions and crises in human relations, which cause men to seek autarchy through detachment from society.[177] Although his work emphasizes these tensions and crises as caused by acutely changing social conditions such as greatly increased taxation and the rejection by Christians of the social power wielded by pagans, Brown also notes that the monks sought "to be certain of oneself and one's fellows" by withdrawal from society, including "the increasingly unmanageable Christian communities of the third century."[178] Monasticism is thus viewed as "an institution . . . to search hearts," the achievement of which the bishops and other religious leaders of the third century had not attained.[179] Put another way, the appearance and growth of monasticism in third century Egypt is another expression of the perceived inadequacies of the ecclesiastical organization spreading from Alexandria into the rest of the country. It is not surprising, therefore, that the institution of monasticism caused some concern to Christian bishops of the time. It was both natural and necessary that the Church eventually would seek to recover and control this aspect of Egyptian Christianity, and the attempt was made, with varying degrees of success, during the century following Anthony's death.

The third century was one of conflict in Egyptian Christianity, for the growing ecclesiastical authority of the Alexandrian bishop met with various kinds of resistance in the long-established churches and local groups of Christians scattered throughout Egypt. The scene is now set to allow one to observe and appreciate the drama of schism and consolidation which was acted out in Egyptian Christianity down to the Council of Chalcedon in 451. The leading characters and the roles they played will be the focus of the following chapters.

ENDNOTES

[1] Wallis Budge, *Coptic Biblical Texts in the dialect of Upper Egypt* (London: Oxford Univ. Press, 1912. Reprinted in New York by AMS Press, 1977), p.v. The dating is based on the script in a greek hand which occurs at the end of Acts in the Codex. The first collection is identified as British Museum Codex Oriental No. 7594, and the second is British Museum Oriental No. 6803. The Codex was acquired in 1911, the manuscript in 1907. The exact site of discovery is unknown, although both are catalogued "from Upper Egypt." One should note that the Greek hand by which the codex was dated is at the end of the book and could have been added somewhat later, but it appears to be the colophon of the scribe of the codex.

[2] *Ibid.*

[3] *Ibid.*, p. xiii.

[4] *Ibid.*, p. xvi. The papyri and piece of vellum in the cover, used as cartonnage to stiffen the book, are all Greek and mostly contain accounts, although the vellum contained a text of Daniel and two of the papyri contain contracts. The inflated sums mentioned in the accounts may argue for a date no earlier than Diocletian, and none of the fragments contains dates or references to Christianity. A few unidentifiable scraps of Coptic papyri were also glued into the cover.

[5] *Ibid.*, p. xxxi.

[6] Budge observed that each of the three texts in the codex had separate pagination, although all were copied by the same scribe. This led him to the conclusion that the scribe copied them at different times, and further, that the collection was made for an individual rather than a church (pp. lxxxiiif.).

[7] Two examples are illustrative: Sir Herbert Thompson, *The Gospel of John According to the Earliest Coptic Manuscript* (London: The British School of Archaeology in Egypt, 1924), pp. xxiif. The dating was determined by F. C. Kenyon in comparison with Greek manuscripts. Rodolphe Kasser, *Papyrus Bodmer III, Evangile de Jean et Genèse I-IV, 2 en bohaïrique* (Louvain: CSCO, Scriptores Coptici, vols. 25–26, 1960). In vol. 25, p. v, Kasser gives the date in the fourth century, and in vol. 26, p. i, says that P. Bodmer III is "le seul document littéraire écrit en bohaïrique avant le IXe siecle."

[8] H. I. Bell, *Evidences*, op. cit., p. 203. Cp. Bell, *Recent Discoveries*, op. cit., p. 10.

[9] F. Ll. Griffith, "The Old Coptic Horoscope of the Stobart Collection," *ZÄS* 38 (1900), p. 71. "There is a very rare class of *pagan* texts in which the native Egyptian language is written out with full vocalization by the aid of Greek letters" (emphasis added). Speaking of Old Coptic texts, Griffith adds that "They give us vocalized Egyptian one or two centuries older than the earliest Christian Coptic MSS." (p. 72). P. Beatty 7 simply closes that gap, and allows one to argue that the Christians were likely responsible for the development from Old Coptic to the Upper and Lower Valley dialects.

[10] A. Atiya, *History of Eastern Christianity* (Notre Dame: Univ. of Notre Dame Press, 1968), p. 18. Atiya cites J. Finegan, *Light from the Ancient Past* (Princeton: Princeton Univ. Press, 1951), pp. 332ff., but must have misunderstood the place of discovery (Egypt) for the language (Egyptian). The Pauline corpus is written in Greek.

[11] Bell and Thompson, "A Greek-Coptic Glossary to Hosea and Amos," *JEA* 11 (1925), pp. 241–246. The authors argue for a date at the end of the second century or beginning of the third century, while Hunt pushed for the fourth century. The hand (Greek) fits the early third best, and should not be dated later than the first quarter of that century.

[12] Bell, *Early Christians*, op. cit., p. 203.

[13] Budge, *op. cit.*, p. lxxvi. Budge appears to accept the accuracy of this account from the *Acta Sanctorum*, April 14, since he remarks in conclusion: "For one systematically arranged 'flight from the world' such as this, there must have been hundreds carried out by individuals, or small groups of men, of which no record now exists."

[14] On the publication of the *Acta Sanctorum*, see Cross, *op. cit.*, p. 11. Budge uses the incident as a basis for arguing the necessity of translating the scriptures from Greek to Coptic in order to be used by such men who elected to forsake the world. The argument is fallacious for a number of reasons: 1) Coptic was not sufficiently attested as a language of translation for literature at that early date to support the translation argument; 2) those Christians who "withdrew from the world" are not known to have moved to the desert to practice their asceticism at this early date; 3) many of the later monks relied as much on memory as on books, considerably weakening the argument that translations were necessary for all such groups.

[15] Clement, *Stromateis* VI.18.

[16] Epiphanius, *Panarion* 24.1.

[17] *Ibid.*, 31.2.

[18] The text was published by F. W. Grosheide, *Some Early Lists of the Books of The New Testament, Textus Minores*, Vol. 1 (Leiden, 1948).

[19] Epiphanius, *Panarion* 31.7.

[20] Jerome, *Select Letters* (Cambridge: Harvard Univ. Press, 1963), p. 456, and n.1. The editor, F. A. Wright, comments on this passage from Ep. CXXVII.9: "Origen's works had always been much admired in his native country, Egypt, and many of the monks there were Origenists" (p. 498). Jerome himself had once been a defender of Origen, but was persuaded by a visit from Epiphanius to Jerusalem in 395 to change his opinion.

[21] Harnack, *Dogma*, *op. cit.*; III.98f.

[22] Epiphanius, *Adv. Haer.* 67.3, 55.5.

[23] *The Second Treatise of The Great Seth N.H.* VII.2.59:19–29.

[24] *Ibid.*, 60:36–61:14.

[25] *The Apocalypse of Peter*, N.H. VII.3.73:10–28.

[26] *Ibid.*, 79:21–31.

[27] Klaus Koschorke, *Die Polemik der Gnostiker gegen das kirchliche Christentum*. Leiden: E.J. Brill, *Nag Hammadi Studies*, Vol. XII, 1978, pp.39–42. Those who posit such divisions among disciples of Peter and Paul usually attempt to trace them back to I Cor. 1:11–13 and Galatians 2:11ff. That distinction cannot hold for the entire Nag Hammadi library, even if some try to apply it here, for some tractates quote from the Pauline Epistles in a favorable setting.

[28] Birger Pearson, "Anti-Heretical Warnings from Codex IX from Nag Hammadi," *Essays on The Nag Hammadi Texts* (Leiden: E.J. Brill. Nag Hammadi Studies, Vol. VI, 1975), pp. 145–154. The difficulty in much of this literature, as Pearson admits, is understanding who is meant by some of the cryptic terms and vague references.

[29] Eusebius, *Eccl. Hist.*, VI.40.

[30] Lawlor and Oulton, *op. cit.*, II,p. 250.

[31] Eusebius, *Hist. Eccl.*, VII.20.

[32] *Ibid.*, VII.21.1.

[33] *Ibid.*, VII.11.12.

[34] *Ibid.*, VII.21.2; 22.11; 24.

[35] *Ibid.*, VII.8.1–5.

[36] *Ibid.*, VII.9.4. Although the member believed that his baptism was performed by heretics because it had so little in common with the baptism performed under Dionysius' authority, Dionysius does not hint his agreement in the letter. The contrast with

Paul and the disciples of Apollos near Ephesus (Acts 19:1–6) is worth noting: Paul did not feel the need to concede simply because the disciples of Ephesus had been baptized once, and he rebaptized them after teaching them more correctly.

[37] *Ibid.*, VII.4.

[38] *Ibid.*, VII.24.1. The specific seat of Nepos' bishopric is not given in this text, but the doctrine which Dionysius is attacking was especially prevalent at Arsinoë, suggesting that Nepos had been bishop there. Furthermore, Dionysius implies that Nepos had not died recently ("gone to his rest"), for he speaks of many being cheered by the psalms of Nepos "even to this day." It would be natural for the man's influence to linger on more in the place where he presided than elsewhere.

[39] *Ibid.*, 24.6.

[40] Harnack, *Mission, op. cit.*, II, p. 164, gives support for this interpretation: "Alexandria at first and alone had a monarchical bishop, who very soon came to rank himself and to act as the counterpart of 'The chief priest of Alexandria and all Egypt.' This bishop then began to consecrate other bishops for the chief towns in the various nomes . . . According to one account (Eutychius, I.332), which is not to be despised, Demetrius only consecrated three such bishops at first, while Heraclas, his successor, created as many as twenty. During the third century, perhaps all the leading towns in the nomes came to have bishops of their own, under the autocratic supervision of the metropolitan. . . "

[41] Eusebius, *Hist. Eccl.*, VII.24.9. The sentence is incomplete: τῶν τε ἄλλων ἀδελφῶν οἳ μὲν ἔχαιρον . . ., but there is no expected οἳ δὲ . . .

[42] *Ibid.*, VI.1.1. It is in this context that Eusebius introduces Leonides. The father of Origen: ἐν οἷς καὶ Λεωνίδης, ὁ λεγόμενος Ὠριγένους πατήρ, making it appear that he was not a native of Alexandria.

[43] *Ibid.*, VI.2.3. Shifting the accent, μύριοι, would mean 10,000, but the problem of exaggeration would hardly be lessened, and the distinction between the two forms of the word was blurred and confused in later Greek.

[44] Origen, *Contra Celsum* III.10.

[45] *Ibid.*, III.8. E. Gibbon, in chp. 16 of *The Decline and Fall of The Roman Empire* (footnote 72) understands this sentence to say that "the number of martyrs was very inconsiderable." It depends on one's perspective whether "not many and easily counted" means "not many" or "hardly any." That Origen appears to mean "not many and easily counted" is suggested in his next phrase, that "God prohibited the entire nation from being exterminated." That is a strange sentiment if there were "hardly any" martyrs. In any case Eusebius exaggerated in his account.

[46] Karl Baus, *From The Apostolic Community to Constantine* (London: Burns & Oates, 1965), pp. 222f., states that the first arrests took place in December, 249. The beginning of the persecution is often taken as beginning with the execution of Fabian, bishop of Rome, in January, 250.

[47] *Ibid.*, p. 223.

[48] M. Cary and H. H. Scullard take the latter view in *A History of Rome*, 3rd ed. (New York: St. Martin's Press, 1975), p. 546: "In a wild attempt to crush the general insubordination and anarchy of his time and to create a greater unity within the Empire under its ruler. . ." Baus, more suspicious of Decius' motivation, sagely notes that even if the summons of sacrifice were only to invoke the blessings of the gods for the well-being of the Empire, "it was significant that, at the same time, exact supervision of the edict's implementation was ordered throughout the empire" (*op. cit.*, p. 223). The ascription of a motive with any degree of certainty, however, is impossible, and in this instance the effect is the same as if the destruction of the Christians were the motive.

[49] Eusebius, *Hist. Eccl.* VI.39.1.

[50] E. R. Hardy, *Christian Egypt: Church and People* (New York: Oxford Univ. Press, 1952), p. 24: "It is uncertain whether these *libelli* were demanded of the whole population, or at least of adult Roman citizens (which by now meant most of the free population), or only of those suspected of Christianity or some other neglect of their religo-civic duties."

[51] Baus, *op. cit.*, p. 223.

[52] R. Knipfing, "The Libelli of the Decian Persecution," *Harv. Theol. Rev.* 16 (1923), pp. 345–390. Bell, *Cults, op. cit.*, p. 85, does not know of any more by the 1950's and it is possible that Baus simply was mistaken, perhaps by adding the two from Oxyrhynchus to the total a second time.

[53] No. 3 in Knipfing, quoted in Bell, *Cults, op. cit.*, p. 85: "To the commissioners chosen to superintend the sacrifices, from Aurelia Ammonous daughter of Mystes, priestess of Petesuchus, the great, great, ever-living god, and the gods at Moeris, of the Moeris quarter. I have always throughout my life sacrificed to the gods, and now, in accordance with the order and your presence, I have sacrificed and poured a libation, and have tasted of the victims, and I request you to append your subscriptions." As Bell notes, it is impossible that an acting priestess could be suspected of being a Christian, and one must argue that libelli were required of the general population.

[54] E.g. no. 7 in Knipfing, cited in Bell, *Cults, op. cit.*, pp. 85–86. The best preserved example of a family libellus is published in H. MacLennan, *Oxyrhynchus* (Amsterdam; AM Hakkert, 1968), p. 31 (p. Oxy. XII.1464): "To the commissioners of sacrifices at Oxyrhynchus from Aurelius Gaion, son of Ammonius and Taeus. It has ever been my habit to make sacrifices and libations and pay reverence to the gods in accordance with the divine decree. And now I have in your presence sacrificed and made libations and tasted the offerings with Taos my wife, Ammonius and Ammonianus my sons, and Thecla my daughter, acting through me, and I request that you certify my statement. The first year of the emperor Caesar Gaius Messius Trajanus Decius Pius Felix Augustus, Epeiph 3. I, Aurelius Gaison, have presented this application. I, Aurelius Sarapion, also called Chaeremon, wrote on his behalf, as he is illiterate."

[55] Either Dionysius or Eusebius modified the text slightly, for Matthew uses the word πλανᾶσθαι and Eusebius had σκανδαλίσαι.

[56] Eusebius, *Eccl. Hist.* VI.41.10–13.

[57] A. H. M. Jones, *The Later Roman Empire* (Norman: Univ. of Oklahoma Press, 1964), Vol. 1., pp. 75–76. While his statement is made generally with regard to the Diocletianic persecution, he holds the same to be true for the earlier persecutions, and in this context says (p. 75) "As with the Decian and Valerianic persecution the general effect was to strengthen the Church." That may be so, but only at the expense of the bishop; who would have to recover his *potestas et auctoritas* and attempt to unite the "rigorists" and the "lapsed."

[58] Eusebius, *Hist. Eccl.* VI.41.3ff; 41.14–22. In one instance (41.18) he says καὶ σὺν αὐτοῖς γυναῖκες τέσσαρες, but then proceeds to name but three. One assumes that in his groupings, the fourth woman was a Greek, i.e. not identified as a Libyan or an Egyptian.

[59] Macar, in VI.41.17.

[60] Hero, Ater, and Isidore in VI.41.19, and Nemesion in 41.21.

[61] Bell, *Cults, op. cit.*, p. 61: "Thus, as time went on, a mixed culture became more and more characteristic of Egypt, and it is increasingly unsafe to rely on nomenclature as a guide to race, or to take the names of Greek gods, when they occur, as referring to Hellenic deities."

[62] Eutychius, *Annales, Patrol. Graecae* CXI.894–1156. See the preface to his work in Migne, *Patrol. Graecae* CXI, 889–894. The Patriarch's real name was Sa'id Ibn Batrik, and he wrote in Arabic for Christians speaking that language, as did Severus who answered him. A Latin translation is given in the *P.G.*

[63] Severus, *History of The Patriarchs of the Coptic Church of Alexandria*, *Patrol. Orientalis* I.101–214 and 381–518. The Arabic text was edited with an English translation by B. Evetts.

[64] *Ibid.*, p. 106.

[65] *Ibid.*, p. 115. One might naturally assume that two admittedly late accounts, especially written from positions developed through centuries of polemic tradition, should be discounted as giving dependable or authentic information about a period far removed in time and cultural environment. Nevertheless, one cannot entirely reject Severus' claim in the First Preface, that he collected histories from the monasteries, especially those of Macarius and Najya. He also speaks of collecting other scattered fragments from Christian sources. All such sources remain unknown in modern times, but the account of Severus must be considered as possibly reflecting ancient traditions, and also as giving some strength or limitation to the witness of non-Egyptian sources as Eusebius or Jerome. Telfer, *op. cit.*, pp. 6–7, gives a rather positive recommendation for Severus, as being more capable than Eutychius (cf. note 64 below). "As a historical writer, Severus had the better qualities. His documentation was the historical works to be found in the monastic libraries of Upper Egypt. Severus enlisted the aid of clerks learned in Greek and Coptic, who made translations for him to which he seems to have been faithful."

[66] *Ibid.*, p. 150.

[67] *Ibid.*, pp. 152–153.

[68] Eutychius, *Annales* 332: Et primus fuit hic patriarcha Alexandrinus qui episcopos fecit.

[69] E. W. Kemp, "Bishops and Presbyters at Alexandria," *JEH* 6(1955), p. 138. Cp. Telfer, *op. cit.*, p. 6. Despite his deficiencies as an historian, however, even Kemp asserts that Eutychius cannot be ignored: "We are bound, however, to take note of those points in which he appears to share a common tradition with Jerome and Severus, and we may now examine the precise nature of the evidence of these three writers." (Note: the Severus here mentioned was a Monophysite patriarch of Antioch from 512–518).

[70] Eusebius, *Hist. Eccl.* VII. 24.6: ὡς καὶ σχίσματα καὶ ἀποστασίας ὅλων ἐκκλησιῶν γεγονέναι·

[71] Eutychius, *Annales* 332: Ille autem factus patriarcha tres constituit episcopos.

[72] *Ibid.*, Mortuo Demetrio suffectus est Heraclas patriarcha Alexandrinus, qui episcopos constituit viginti.

[73] Jerome, *Epistle* CXLVI, *Ad Evangelum*: Nam et Alexandriae a Marco evangelista usque ad Heraclam et Dionysium episcopos, presbyteri semper unum ex se electum, in excelsiori gradu collocatum, episcopum nominabant.

[74] Kemp, *op. cit.*, p. 138. See also Harnack, *Mission, op. cit.*, II, p. 166–170, for the list of nomes or cities in which evidence is certain that Christians were present during the third century. On p. 170, Harnack speaks of organization in the local churches: ". . . each nome had at first only one bishop, while many large churches, in town and country alike, were governed by presbyters, and small villages had not even so much as a presbyter." Cf. Athanasius, *Apol. c. Arianos* 85, and Socrates, *Hist. Eccl.* I.27, for statements about Mareotis being within the jurisdiction of the Alexandrian bishop because they had never had a bishop. If they had a bishop the Christians would have been under the rule of Alexandria, even if just indirectly so. Even if churches were not actually controlled by Alexandria, that alone did not diminish Alexandria's claim of hegemony.

[75] Eusebius, *Hist. Eccl.* VI.42.3. Chaeremon, bp. of Nilopolis, near the Fayyum; VI.46.2. Colon, bp. of Hermopolis (probably parva, near Alexandria, although possibly magna, near Antinoë); VII.13. Pinnas and Demetrius, no place mentioned; VII.21.2 Hierax, "bp. of those in Egypt," with no city or nome mentioned; VII.22 Nepos, probably in Arsinoë (see VII.24.6); VIII.13.7. Phileas, bp. of Thmuis (cf.VIII.9.7), Hesychius, Pachymius, and Theodore, bps. of Churches, in Egypt; X.6.2. When Peter was beheaded, "many other bishops" suffered the same penalty.

[76] Socrates, *Hist. Eccl.* I.6. The effect of the letter was opposite to the hopes of Alexander, for it caused a greater division (over the Arian problem) than existed before.

[77] Athanasius, *Apologia Contra Arianos* 71. Cp. Intro.1. "First of all it was tried in my own country in an assembly of nearly 100 of its bishops . . ." A. Robertson, in a note on the second passage, said that there were about 90 bishops in Egypt, the Thebaid, and Libya (*NPNF*, Second Series, IV.100).

[78] Eusebius, *Hist. Eccl.* VII.27.2.

[79] *Ibid.*, VII.29.1.

[80] Lawlor and Oulton, *op. cit.*, II.p.257, state that Dionysius "died 26 December 268. Thus the letter must have been dispatched at the latest early in 269, before the report of his death reached Antioch." This would explain why the letter was addressed to these absentee members, although certainly other bishops were also missing from the Synod. Consequently, one may assume that the names of Dionysius of Rome and Maximus of Alexandria, perhaps by now seen to be two of the most important bishops in the church, would lend prestige and gravity to the council's decision, for it was sent ἐπὶ πάσας τὰς ἐπαρχίας.

[81] Eusebius, *Hist. Eccl.* VII.30.1.

[82] *Ibid.*, 30.2: The address of the letter may be understood to include bishops in Egypt, although the Eusebian preface suggests that "Maximus" was equivalent to saying Egypt.

[83] *Ibid.*, VII.32.5.

[84] *Ibid.*, VII.11.3, 24. The earlier reference states that Eusebius was a fellow-sufferer with Dionysius in the persecution of Valerian, and the latter tells of his service to the confessors in the Decian persecution.

[85] *Ibid.*, VII.32.6. Lawlor and Oulton comment on this passage (*op. cit.*, II, p. 262): "It is remarkable to find an Alexandrian Christian founding an Aristotelian School in his own city, the special home of Platonism—and that not long after the death of Dionysius and Origen. It is also remarkable that his fellow-citizens—most of whom, no doubt, were pagans—elected him principal of the school."

[86] *Ibid.*, VII.32.20–21.

[87] *Ibid.*, VII.31.

[88] A. Henrichs, "Mani and the Babylonian Baptists: A Historical Confrontation", *HSCP* 77 (1973), pp.44–45.

[89] *Ibid.*, p.32.

[90] A. Henrichs, "The Cologne Mani Codex Reconsidered", *HSCP* 83 (1979), p.349.

[91] Cross, *op. cit.*, p.864.

[92] Samuel N.C. Lieu, *Manichaeism in the Later Roman Empire and Medieval China, a Historical Survey*. Manchester: Manchester Univ. Press, 1985. One of the most famous of the Manichees during the earlier part of his life, Augustine, became one of their greatest foes after his conversion to Catholic Christianity (see pp.117–153). During his nine years as a Manichee, Augustine was in the company of groups of Manichees in Rome, and their presence is attested for centuries afterward in various parts of the empire.

[93] R.M. Grant, "Manichees and Christians in the Third and Early Fourth Centuries", *Ex Orbe Religionum, Studia Geo Widengren Oblata*. Leiden: E.J. Brill, 1972, Vol. 1, p.431.

[94] P.W. van der Horst and J. Mansfield, *An Alexandrian Platonist Against Dualism*. Leiden: E. J. Brill, 1974, p.3. Photius is the source for naming Alexander to the bishopric of Lykopolis (*Epist*. de Manich.), and van der Horst notes that on the strength of Photius alone, that view has been held well into the nineteenth century and accounts for Alexander's treatise against the Manichees being included in Migne's *Patrologia Graeca* and a translation in the *Ante-Nicene Fathers*, Vol. 6. The same author considers the arguments of A. Brinkmann, *Alexandri Lycopolitani contra Manichaei opiniones disputatio* (Leipzig, 1895, introduction), to be decisively against Alexander being a Christian, let alone a bishop.

[95] *Ibid.*, p. 4. For a translation of Alexander's work, see the *Ante-Nicene* Fathers, (Grand Rapids: Eerdmans, 1971 reprint), Vol. 6, pp.239–253.

[96] Lieu, *op. cit.*, p.74.

[97] Alexander, *contra Manich*. 2.

[98] Epiphanius, *Panarion* 66.8.1–12.

[99] Lieu, *op. cit.*, p.73.

[100] *Ibid.*, pp.50f.

[101] *Ibid.*, p.88. See also F.C. Burkitt, *The Religion of the Manichees*. Cambridge, Cambridge Univ. Press, 1925, pp.111–119. C.R.C. Allberry, *A Manichaean Psalm-Book*. Stuttgart: W. Kohlhammer, 1938, Vol. 1, part 2, Index C, p.44 (cited in Lieu, p.286, note 180).

[102] *Ibid.*, p.7. Most of the collection was divided between Chester Beatty and the Berlin Academy. Publication of these texts is as yet incomplete, but includes the following: H.J. Polotsky, ed. *Manichäische Homilien*. Stuttgart, 1934. C.R.C. Allberry, ed. *A Manichaean Psalm-Book* (Part II). Stuttgart, 1938. H.J. Polotsky and A. Böhlig, eds. *Kephalaia*, Vol. 1, Part 1. Stuttgart, 1940. A. Böhlig, ed. *Kephalaia*, Vol 1, Part 2. Stuttgart, 1966. See also Torgny Säve-Söderbergh, *Studies in the Coptic Manichaean Psalm-Book*. Uppsala: Almquist and Wiksells, 1949.

[103] A. Henrichs, "The CMC Reconsidered," *op. cit.*, esp. pp.342–351 for an account of the process of decipherment. For publication of the text, see A. Henrichs and L. Koenen, "Ein griechischer Mani-Codex" (P. Colon. inv. nr. 4780), *Zeitschrift für Papyrologie und Epigraphik* (ZPE) 5 1970), pp.97–214, and ZPE 19 (1975), pp.1–85.

[104] *Ibid.*, p.351.

[105] The Apocalypses of Adam, Seth, Enos, Shem, and Enoch are Jewish, with no uniquely gnostic characteristics. The longer texts, from which these synopses were made, are not from any other source, either singly or in a collection. A complete translation into English of the codex was made by Ron Cameron and Arthur Dewey and published by Scholars Press in 1979.

[106] See L. Koenen, "Zur Herkunft des Kölner Mani-Codex," *Zeitschrift für Papyrologie und Epigraphik* 11 (1973), pp.240–1.

[107] Henrichs, "the CMC Reconsidered," *op. cit.*, p.349.

[108] Henrichs, "Mani and the Babylonian Baptists," *op. cit.*, p.44.

[109] Henrichs, "The CMC Reconsidered," *op. cit.*, p.352.

[110] Henrichs, "Mani and the Babylonian Baptists," *op. cit.*, p.36.

[111] S. D. Salmond, "Theonas of Alexandria," *The Ante-Nicene Fathers*, Vol. VI (Grand Rapids: Eerdmans, 1971 reprint), p. 158.

[112] Eusebius, *Hist. Eccl*. VII.32.30. The very title given to the old catechetical school indicates its new direction and status with the bishop since the days of Origen.

[113] *Ibid.*, VII.32.31.

[114] *Ibid.*, IX.6.2.

[115] *Ibid.*, VIII.13.7. Of the four mentioned, only in the case of Phileas is the place (Thmuis) of his bishopric known. The other three are simply "bishops of the churches in Egypt." Three presbyters, Faustus, Dius, and Ammonius, are also named as Egyptian martyrs during the same persecution.

[116] *Ibid.*, VIII.6.10.

[117] *Ibid.*, VIII.13.7: τῶν δ' ἐπ' 'Αλεξανδρείας καθ' ὅλης τε Αἰγύπτου καὶ Θηβαῖδος ...

[118] *Ibid.*, VIII.9.7ff.

[119] Lawlor and Oulton, *op. cit.*, II, p. 276. W.H.C. Frend, *Martyrdom and Persecution in the Early Church* (New York: N.Y. Univ. Press, 1967), p. 519, speaks generally of this period in Egypt and of the Phileas account: "The dating, like most of the events in Egypt at this period, is uncertain."

[120] *Acta* 2, cited in Lawlor and Oulton, *op. cit.*, II, 276. The Acts of the Martyrs were translated and published by R.P.D. Thierry Ruinart, *Les véritables Actes des Martyrs*. Paris: A Besançon, 1818 (reprint). The Acts of Phileas and Philoromus are in Vol. 2, pp.200–206. A modern study of the Acts of Phileas, including editions of the Latin and Greek texts, esp. of P. Chester Beatty XV, was edited by Albert Pietersma, *The Acts of Phileas, Bishop of Thmuis*. Geneva, 1984. The P. Bodmer XX account of the martyrdom of Phileas has been dated to within 50 years of the date of the martyrdom (Pietersma, p.14).

[121] *Ibid.*, 1,2. This is only implied in the text of Pietersma *op. cit.*, plate 9, lines 15–23 (p.48).

[122] Jerome, *De vir. Illustr.* 78.

[123] Eusebius, *Hist. Eccl.*, VIII.10.

[124] *Patrol. Graec.* X. 1565–1568.

[125] Eusebius, *Hist. Eccl.* VIII.13.7.

[126] *Ibid.*, VIII.9.4.

[127] Frend, *op. cit.*, p. 388.

[128] *Ibid.*, p. 519, n.152: "In the *Mart. Pal.* ii.1, Eusebius refers to 'mere boys' being among the Egyptian prisoners whom he encountered in Palestine in 310." This quote does not exactly support the picture Eusebius draws of numberless executions in the Thebaid.

[129] Lebreton and Zeiller, *History of the Primitive Church* (New York: MacMillan, 1949), pp. 1047–1049. See also H. I. Bell, *Jews and Christians in Egypt* (London: Oxford Univ. Press, 1924), pp. 38–39.

[130] Bell, *op. cit.*, p. 39.

[131] Athanasius, *Apologia contra Arianos* 71.

[132] Bell, *Jews and Christians*, *op. cit.*, p. 42.

[133] Jones, *op. cit.*, I,p. 75.

[134] Clement, *Stromateis* III, 40.

[135] *Ibid.*

[136] Smith, *op. cit.*, p. 92, passim.

[137] *Ibid.*, p. 82.

[138] Chadwick, *op. cit.*, p. 31.

[139] Eusebius, *Hist. Eccl.* VI. 3.9–12.

[140] Sulpicius Severus, *Dialogues* I.6.

[141] Origen, *De Oratione* XVII; XIX.3; XXV; *De Princip.* I.8.1. One should note, however, that Origen believed in the resurrection of bodies, but glorified and infinitely better ones. See *De Princ.*) II.3.10; III.6.4, etc.

[142] Eusebius, *Hist. Eccl.* VI.3.13: ὥστε ἤδη καὶ τῶν ἀπίστων ἐθνῶν τῶν τε ἀπὸ παιδείας καὶ φιλοσοφίας οὐ τοὺς τυχόντας ὑπάγεσθαι τῇ δι' αὐτοῦ διδασκαλίᾳ. This all happened, the historian mentioned just earlier, because Origen was such a good example of the philosophical (ascetic) life.

[143] *Ibid.*, VI.9–11.

[144] *Ibid.*, VI.10.

[145] E. Hardy, *op. cit.*, pp. 35–36.

[146] Gross, *op. cit.*, p. 930.

[147] Jerome, *Contra Joan. Jerus.* 41 (trans. by W. H. Fremantle in *NPNF*, Second Series, Vol. 6, p.446). Cf. *Epistle* 58.5: "If you wish to take duty as a presbyter, and are attracted by the work or dignity which falls to the lot of a bishop, live in cities and walled towns . . . But if you desire to be indeed what you are in name—a monk, . . . what have you to do with cities which are the homes not of solitaries but of crowds? . . . because after the freedom of the lonely life (we) found confinement in a city as bad as imprisonment."

[148] Herbert B. Workman, *The Evolution of the Monastic Ideal* (Boston: Beacon Press, 1962. Reprint of 1913 edition), p. 13.

[149] Sozomen, *Hist. Eccl.* I.13. The historian admits that it really did not matter who was first, ὡς εἰς ἄκρον ἀκριβείας καὶ τελειότητος ἤθεσι, καὶ γυμνασίοις τοῖςπρέπουσιν ἐξήσκησε ταυτηνι τοῦ βίου τὴν διαγωγὴν Ἀντώνιος ὁ μέγας μοναχός. Yet Athanasius, *Vita Antonii* 3, says the desert was unknown to monks before Anthony, but that ascetics stayed close to their villages.

[150] Eusebius, *Hist. Eccl.* VI.42, states that during the Decian persecution many Christians wandered off into the deserts and mountains, not always escaping an awful death by their flight. Some could not survive the wilderness and others were taken captive by Saracens or other tribes. Cf. Sozomen, *Hist. Eccl.* I.12, who gives a rather more idyllic description of the pre-Anthonian monks.

[151] Sozomen, *Hist. Eccl.* I.13, states that Anthony's fame was so great that word of his piety reached Constantine, a plausible claim. It is less plausible that the Emperor wrote letters to the monk seeking his advice on various matters (*Vita Antonii* 81).

[152] Kenneth S. Latourette, *A History of Christianity* (New York: Harper and Row, 1953), p. 225.

[153] Henri Queffélec, *Saint Anthony of the Desert* (New York: E.P. Dutton & Co., 1954), p. 9.

[154] L. W. Barnard, "The Date of S. Athanasius' *Vita Antonii*," *Vigiliae Christianae* 27 (1974), p. 169.

[155] For a survey of the form and purpose of the work, see Hermann Dörries, "Die Vita Antonii als Geschichtsquelle," *Wort und Stunde* (Gesammelte, Studien zur Kirchenges-chichte des vierten Jahrhunderts). Göttingen: Vandenhoeck & Ruprecht, 1966, Erster Band, pp.145–224 (Originally published: Nachrichten der Akad. der Wissenschaften Göttingen, Philosoph.-hist. Kl., Abh. 14, 1949). A succinct bibliography is given on p.145 which lists works especially treating the literary analysis of the *Vita*. See also Martin Tetz, "Athanasius und die Vita Antonii," *Zeitschrift für die neutestamentliche Wissenschaft* 73 (1982), pp.1–30. For a recent translation of the text into English with annotations, see Robert T. Meyer, *St. Athanasius, the Life of Saint Antony* (Ancient Christian Writers, Vol. 10). New York: Newman Press, 1950. The Coptic (Sahidic) version of the Life of Anthony was edited by G. Garitte, *S. Antonii Vitae, Versio Sahidica* (Corpus Scriptorum Christianorum Orientalium, vols. 117–118). Paris-Louvain, 1949.

[156] *Ibid.*, pp. 170–172. The change of person in the narratives occurs in *VA* 82, and the passage referring to the emperors is *VA* 81.

[157] *Ibid.*, pp. 174–175.

[158] B. R. Brennan, "Dating Athanasius' *Vita Antonii*," *Vigiliae Christianae* 30 (1976), pp. 52–53.

[159] *Ibid.*, p. 54.

[160] Tetz, *op. cit.*, pp.1–2. See also G.J.M. Bartelink, "Die literarische Gattung der *Vita Antonii*, Struktur und Motive," *Vigiliae Christianae* 36 (1982), pp.38–62, for the historical and literary context of the *VA*.

[161] Sozomen, *Hist. Eccl.* I.13. Meyer (*op. cit.*, p.106, n.5) notes that "this may be a confusion arising from the fact that Athanasius repeatedly speaks of the home 'town' or 'village' (κώμη) of Antony.

[162] Athanasius, *Vita Antonii* 1.

[163] Matthew 19:21. This incident gives strong, but indirect evidence that the scriptures had been translated into Coptic by this time. Both sources for his life argue that Anthony knew no Greek (Athanasius, *VA* 1 and Sozomen, *HE* I.13), although one is then pressed to reconcile a later story of his coming to Alexandria to help Athanasius war against the Arians. Still, Anthony needed an interpreter, according to Ath. *VA* 44 when Greeks visited him, and Athanasius may have interpolated the eloquence of Anthony in the disputations with the Arians. If the story of his "call" has any truth to it, Budge's argument is worth consideration (*Coptic Biblical Texts*, *op. cit.*, p. lxxviii): "The reader in a village church in Upper Egypt towards the close of the third century is far more likely to have been a native of the district, who knew no Greek, or at least not enough to translate it at sight, than one who knew Greek well. Anthony himself was, according to St. Athanasius, an uneducated man, but this can only mean that he could not read or write Greek, for Athanasius himself tells us that Anthony wrote letters to Imperial Personages, though he could not write quickly. When certain men who knew no Egyptian came to consult him about the Christian religion, he was obliged to send for a skilled interpreter to translate his answers to their questions into Greek, but there is good reason for thinking that Anthony could read and write his native language."

[164] See Dörries, *op. cit.*, pp.171f. See also Meyer, *op. cit.*, pp.13f. and notes.

[165] Athanasius, *Vita Antonii* 5: καὶ ὁ διάβολος ὑπέμενεν ὁ ἄθλιος καὶ ὡς γυνὴ σχηματίζεσθαι νυκτὸς καὶ πάντα τρόπον μιμεῖσθαι, μόνον ἵνα τὸν Ἀντώνιον ἀπατήσῃ. On another occasion the devil appeared to Anthony as a "Black boy, taking a visible shape in accordance with the color of his mind" (*VA* 6).

[166] *Ibid.*, 11.

[167] *Ibid.*, 14.

[168] *Ibid.*, 49–50.

[169] *Ibid.*, 14, 16, 48, 49, etc.

[170] *Ibid.*, 15.

[171] *Ibid.*, 16–43.

[172] *Ibid.*, 46. Cf. 23, 30. While in Alexandria Anthony also exhorted condemned Christians on their way to martyrdom, just as Origen had earlier encouraged his father Leonides to have a good martyrdom. Cp. also Euseb., *Hist. Eccl.* 5.1.49, where Alexander exhorts Christians to remain true to their faith.

[173] L. Duchesne, *Early History of the Christian Church* (London, 1910–11), II.390.

[174] Workman, *op. cit.*, p. 14.

[175] Athanasius, *Vita Antonii* 69.

[176] *Ibid.*, 91.

[177] Peter Brown, *The Making of Late Antiquity* (Cambridge: Harvard Univ. Press, 1978), pp. 81–84.

[178] *Ibid.*, p. 95.

[179] *Ibid.*, p. 96.

CHAPTER V

THE FOURTH CENTURY: SCHISMS AND CONSOLIDATION

The Melitian schism, mentioned briefly in the last chapter within the context of the Alexandrian and non-Alexandrian episcopal relationships, was the first of the difficulties which threatened the fourth century ecclesiastical structure of Egypt. Conflicting accounts exist relating when and how the dispute arose but, unlike later controversies during the next century and a half, it was not based on a doctrinal disagreement. During the persecution of Diocletian both Peter, bishop of Alexandria, and Melitius, bishop of Lycopolis, were in prison at Alexandria, and the question concerning readmission of the *lapsi* arose between them. Peter favored a more lenient process for admitting those who had sacrificed to pagan gods, but Melitius held a more rigid position for harsher requirements. As noted in the preceding chapter, the question concerned the interval of time before readmission and the status afterward of those who returned, not whether to readmit them to communion or deny it from them permanently. As the argument in prison grew more heated, Peter reportedly drew a curtain across the middle of the cell so as to avoid looking at Melitius. According to the same account, moreover, most of the bishops and monks in the prison sided with Melitius rather than Peter.[1] Athanasius' assertion that Melitius was convicted by Peter of many crimes, especially of sacrificing to idols,[2] is inconsistent with the Melitian position in the dispute and should not be taken seriously, even though Athanasius was closer both in time and geography to the issue than was Epiphanius. Bias is not determined solely by proximity.

Of somewhat more importance in this study than the details of the dispute relating to the readmission of the *lapsi* are two letters edited and published by H. I. Bell.[3] They supply evidence concerning the dispute between these two bishops which casts the issue in a clearer light. Both are Latin translations of earlier Greek texts, one being a letter from four Egyptian bishops to Melitius, and the other a letter from Peter to the Alexandrian church. Both Peter and Melitius were freed soon after their disagreement began, but when the persecutions flared up anew, Melitius went into the dioceses of four imprisoned bishops and began to ordain others in their stead. The letter from the imprisoned bishops is a protest against his activity, but Melitius disregarded their objections. Soon afterward, in 306, Melitius traveled down the Nile from Lycopolis to Alexandria and, since Peter was in hiding because of the persecution, he began to excommunicate priests and lay members. Peter's letter to the church was an excommunication order against Melitius, and later "Melitius was arrested and banished, with several of his followers, to the mines of Palestine, where he remained till the edict of toleration promulgated by Galerius in 311."[4] Galerius died in the same year the edict was published, and his successor Maximin renewed the persecution of the Christians. Peter was beheaded during the early stages of the unexpected violence,[5] but the controversy did not end with his death. According to Epiphanius, the recently-freed Melitius went throughout the land and "established clerics, bishops, elders, and deacons, and built up churches of his own."[6] So that the Melitian groups would be distinguished from the Alexandrian church and its satellites, the former even assumed a new name:

> Ἐπέγραφον δὲ ἕκαστος ἐν τῇ ἰδίᾳ ἐκκλησίᾳ, οἱ μὲν ἀπὸ τοῦ Πέτρου διαδεξάμενοι ἔχοντες τὰς οὔσας ἀρχαίας ἐκκλησίας, ὅτι Ἐκκλησία καθολική, οἱ δὲ Μελητίου, Ἐκκλησία μαρτύρων.[7]
>
> *And they assumed names, each one in his own church: the successors of Peter, because they possessed the churches that were ancient, claimed the Catholic Church; and those of Melitius, the Church of the Martyrs.*

Neither group had fellowship with the other, but Bell states that "under the episcopate of Alexander relations between the two parties were apparently not entirely hostile."[8] The evidence he gives for that observation also comes from Epiphanius, who stated that it was Melitius himself who, while spending some time in Alexandria, took occasion to point out the heretical nature of Arius' teaching to Alexander.[9] Bell accepts this account, suggesting that the motive of Melitius was either to take vengeance on Arius for leaving Melitius and becoming reconciled to the Catholics, or to embarrass Alexander because of his association with Arius, assuming the bishop would not be anxious to lose Arius' loyalty. The last possibility would not have been realized, according to the continuation of Epiphanius' account, for the heresiologist states that Alexander soon afterward convoked a synod and deposed Arius for his heretical teaching, not a typical action for a bishop worried about losing a supporter.

The entire episode is difficult to evaluate, for the evidence concerning the early connection of Melitius and Arius is ambiguous, both in chronology and in the nature of the relationship.[10] The first association between Arius and Melitius is mentioned by Sozomen. According to this fifth century account, Arius was one

ὃς ἐξ ἀρχῆς σπουδαῖος εἶναι περὶ τὸ δόγμα δόξας, νεωτερίζοντι Μελιτίῳ συνέπραττε.[11]

who from the beginning was zealous in his opinions concerning doctrine, and he joined with Melitius who was trying to make revolutionary changes.

No specific changes are mentioned, but they may have included the ordinations Melitius performed in churches throughout Egypt, and they may also have included the rigorous penances which Melitius required of the *lapsi* upon their readmission to the church.[12] Sozomen is the only ancient source to link Arius and Melitius at this early period, but they clearly act in concert later on.

The early harmony between Melitius and Arius did not last, for Arius made peace with Peter and was ordained a deacon by the Alexandrian bishop.[13] In yet another shift in alliances that reminds one of the constantly changing political alignments in Greece during the age of Peisistratus and the Peisistratidae in Greek History,[14] Arius defended the Melitians when Peter excommunicated them. For his disloyalty to Peter, Arius and his followers were also cast out of the church.[15]

Following Peter's martyrdom, Sozomen states that Arius sought forgiveness from Achillas, Peter's successor, but Socrates (also writing in the early fifth century) notes that Melitius simply transferred his attacks to the new bishop of Alexandria.[16] During Achillas' short episcopacy (following Peter's martyrdom in November, 311 through much of 312) Arius was not only reinstated as a deacon, but was later ordained a presbyter.[17] Even if Melitius and Arius were united in the early part of Peter's episcopacy, they suffered a falling-out before Arius preached his 'heretical' understanding of the Godhead. Their quarrel did not last long, however, for Socrates states that Melitians again mingled with the Arians during Alexander's bishopric, even though they had earlier been separated from the Church.[18] No reason is given for the reconciliation, no exact date can be assigned to it, and some even doubt that it occurred, arguing that the Nicaean Council would have anathematized both if they were friendly with each other. Not enough is known to substantiate such reasoning, and one should not dismiss an ancient source simply on the basis of difficulty or disagreement.

Socrates' account states that it was during Achillas' episcopacy that Arius delivered his so-called heretical discourse on the nature of Christ, and that it was given in response to an earlier sermon by Achillas on the same subject.[19] Far from bringing forth a negative reaction from Achillas, however, Arius continued in favor with him, and also for a time with Alexander (bishop of Alexandria 312–328), Achillas' successor.[20] Both Epiphanius and Sozomen agree that Alexander took action against Arius only when forced to do so by the reports and criticisms of others, whether by Melitius[21] or "those who heard these doctrines being taught."[22] Sozomen adds that Alexander held Arius in high esteem for the latter's erudition and speaking ability.[23]

It is possible that Alexander's reluctance to prosecute Arius earlier was due to the similarity of their philosophical position, as both were basically Origenists,[24] while there is no indication that Melitius or his followers were sympathetic to Origenist thinking. Despite the great monastic following built up by Melitius, there is no evidence that they became identified or assimilated with the Origenist monks during the next century. It is worth noting, in passing, that in the next century the monastic movement was not united in its position regarding Origen, for there were Origenist monks as well as those opposed to Origen, especially notable during the episcopacy of Theophilus, and there were certain numbers of the non-Origenist monks who also continued in the Melitian schism.

This confused state of affairs between Melitians and Arians continued for a time, at least through the Council of Nicaea, for in that Synod of bishops the Arians were condemned, while the Melitians were admitted into fellowship with the Catholics.[25] Although accepted back into the church, Melitius really gained nothing beyond being distinguished formally from the Arians. He was sent to his own see as a bishop, but was stripped of the authority to act within his office. Furthermore, all who were ordained by him could only retain their office and authority if they submitted to a second ordination by the Catholic authorities.

It should be clear at this point that the *real* or *underlying* basis for the excommunication of Melitius by Peter had little, if anything, to do with the requirements stipulated for readmission of the *lapsi*, although that appears to have been the origin of their dispute. Neither is it to be connected with the Arian heresy, for the Melitians were not excommunicated by the Council of Nicaea, nor is there any hint in the sources of an early alignment with the Arian doctrine. Karl Baus perhaps pushed the use of penance by the Melitians as a propaganda issue beyond the evidence, but he correctly identified the basic issue:

> The question of penance was, however, not the starting-point of this division in the Egyptian church; it was provoked rather by Melitius, bishop of Lycopolis, in the Thebaid, who encroached upon the bishop of Alexandria's rights of consecration. Melitius, however, used the question of penance to win supporters in the struggle against the bishop of the Egyptian capital and to give the churches dependent on himself a distinctive and effective slogan. After a few years the question of penance ceased to be topical in the Melitian disorders and Melitius' supports soon joined the Arians and made common cause with them against Athanasius.[26]

Melitius' greatest sin was to challenge the authority of the Alexandrian bishop, and Theodoret states that Melitius was undermining the stability of the Church in Egypt by rebelling against the primacy of the Alexandrian bishop.[27] Although he was not considered sufficiently heretical that his followers had to be rebaptized if they wished to return to Catholicism (the method of reclaiming heretics according to the rule of Heraclas more than a half century earlier[28]), those ordained by him had to be ordained again so there would be no question about where they received authority or owed allegiance.

The question of ordination and consecration by the Alexandrian bishop brings into focus the primary significance of the Melitians for this work. Were the Melitians powerful and numerous enough to unite the Christians under their leadership, or were they simply an annoying diversion in the inevitable march toward domination by the Alexandrian patriarchs? Chadwick states that the Melitian schism, "though long-lived, never became large."[29] Accurate figures for the size of the sect are not available, but Chadwick's statement does not well accord with the Nicene attempt to reconcile the dissidents. They were sufficiently numerous to make reconciliation an important issue to the Nicene Council, and the possibility of adding their numbers to the Arians made accommodation easier than condemnation.[30] Frend perhaps goes too far in the opposite direction of ascribing popularity and influence to the Melitians, for he makes the Melitians the moving force to bring about Arius' condemnation at Nicaea, stating that they were powerful enough to threaten the bishop with heresy if he failed to act against Arius.[31] He does note, moreover, that the Melitians "had a good deal of popular Egyptian backing,"[32] and Lietzmann adds that the popularity of the sect was found mostly in the monasteries.[33] The movement did gain sufficient strength in Upper Egypt that "by *circa* 325 the Melitians had their bishops in every second or third city in Middle and Upper Egypt, compared with only one out of every six or seven cities in the Delta. There was an extensive network of Melitian monasteries."[34] The Melitian schism, therefore, is best seen as a nationalistic movement based in the Thebaid, carrying with it the possibility of turning the hegemony of the Egyptian Christian movement from Alexandria to the Thebaid.[35] That it did not do so, in spite of a long-standing and popular Egyptian opinion that Alexandria represented foreign domination, was due largely to the efforts of Athanasius.[36] The Alexandrian bishop's friendship with Anthony and Pachomius, the two leading monastic figures of Egypt, gave him a checkmate against the Melitian (and competing monastic) bid for power.

The Melitian schism did not end with the settlement of Nicaea, for, as Bell suggests, "very possibly neither Alexander nor Melitius was particularly anxious to carry out the Nicene decision," as it related to Melitius' loss of authority.[37] If there is any truth to Epiphanius' account that Melitius was the one who brought Arius' heretical teaching to the bishop's attention, Alexander may have been reluctant to implement such a harsh decision on his Thebaid counterpart. Melitius certainly would have no desire to accept the decision of the Council which effectively nullified his episcopal standing. Difficulties do exist, nevertheless, in the attempt to reconstruct the sequence of events following the Council of Nicaea.

Soon after Alexander returned to Alexandria from Nicaea, Melitius turned over to him a list of the bishops and churches as the council had decreed.[38] Not long afterward, however, Melitius ordained one of his associates, John, to be his successor, and John began ordaining bishops and priests in Egypt.[39] Although the followers of Athanasius attempted to destroy the Melitian hierarchy, both by civil complaints to the Emperor[40] and by fomenting riots and violence against their opponents,[41] there is evidence of Melitian bishops still active in Letopolis (near Memphis) and Alexandria as late as 334.[42]

Determining precisely whether Alexander or Athanasius was responsible for the immediate post-Nicene troubles in Egypt depends upon the date one accepts for Alexander's death. In his defense against the Arians, Athanasius makes the following statement concerning the death of his predecessor:

Οὔπω γὰρ πέντε μῆνες παρῆλθον, καὶ ὁ μὲν μακαρίτης Ἀλέξανδρος τετελεύτηκεν.[43]

For five months had not yet passed (sc. after the Council of Nicaea), and the blessed Alexander had died.

This statement, which implies that Alexander died some five months after the Nicene Council, does not agree with the Chronological preface to Athanasius' Festal Letters, which clearly states that Alexander died on 22 Pharmuthi (17 April), 328 C.E., and that Athanasius succeeded him on 14 Pauni (8 June) of the same year.[44] Epiphanius states that Alexander persecuted the Melitians after the death of Melitius,[45] which also must have occurred after Nicaea, for Melitius was required after the Council to give Alexander a list of bishops, presbyters, and deacons who were supporting him.[46] The later date for Alexander's death is preferable, although Epiphanius might have been confused as to the relative persecutions of the Melitians by Alexander and Athanasius, and the *Chronicum* for Athanasius' Festal Letters may be erroneous on the death of Alexander (which would admit the *Apol. contra Arianos* passage in its natural sense of the death coming right after Nicaea to be correct). A final decision on which chronology to choose is not presently possible.

Sozomen implies that the real rupture of relations between the Melitians and the Catholics occurred after Alexander's death, for he recounts a meeting following the prelate's death attended by 54 bishops of both factions from Thebes, and all over Egypt for the purpose of choosing his successor.[47] Apollinaris of Laodicaea is quoted by Sozomen as claiming that Athanasius was Alexander's choice for the bishopric, but the historian states that the bishops who gathered simply agreed by oath to choose the best man for the position. Seven of the bishops violated their oath and, according to yet another fifth century historian, Philostorgius, went to the church of Dionysius in Alexandria, locked the doors, and secretly ordained Athanasius the bishop of Alexandria.[48] Sozomen writes that such an irregular ordination caused many of the clergy and laity in Egypt to secede from communion with Athanasius. The new bishop responded to the calumnies of the Melitians and Arians both in his defence against the Arians[49] and in a letter to the Emperor Constantine, claiming in the latter that he had been elected unanimously to the bishopric and citing a decree passed in Alexandria as evidence of his veracity.[50] Whatever really happened in the meeting of the bishops is lost beyond recovery, but the meeting of Melitians and Catholics to choose Alexander's successor indicates that the recently-deceased bishop was not so divisive and antagonistic toward the Melitians as was Athanasius.

Because the Council of Nicaea did not solve the Egyptian ecclesiastical problems, Eusebius states that Constantine summoned the bishops (of Egypt alone?) to his presence a second time and tried to mediate their differences:

Ἀλλὰ γὰρ ἁπάντων εἰρηνευομένων μόνοις Αἰγυπτίοις ἄμικτος ἦν ἡ πρὸς ἀλλήλους φιλονεικία, ὡς καὶ αὖθις ἐνοχλεῖν βασιλέα, οὐ μὴν καὶ πρὸς ὀργὴν ἐγείρειν. Οἷα γοῦν πατέρας ἢ καὶ μᾶλλον προφήτας θεοῦ πάσῃ περιέπων τιμῇ καὶ δεύτερον ἐκάλει καὶ πάλιν ἐμεσίτευε τοῖς αὐτοῖς ἀνεξικάκως, καὶ δώροις ἐτίμα πάλιν, ἐδήλου τε τὴν δίαιταν δι᾽ ἐπιστολῆς. καὶ τὰ τῆς συνόδου δόγματα κυρῶν ἐπεσφραγίζετο, παρεκάλει τε συμφωνίας ἔχεσθαι, μηδὲ διασπᾶν καὶ κατατέμνειν τὴν ἐκκλησίαν, τῆς δὲ τοῦ θεοῦ κρίσεως ἐν νῷ τὴν μνήμην λαμβάνειν. καὶ ταῦτα δὲ βασιλεὺς δι᾽ οἰκείας ἐπέστελλε γραφῆς.[51]

For although all others were living peaceably, only among the Egyptians the contention toward one another was savage, so that the emperor was annoyed, though he was not angry. Constantine, treating them with every honor just like fathers, or even more like prophets of God, summoned them a second time and again patiently acted as mediator between them. He even honored them again with gifts and disclosed the result of his arbitration by letter. He confirmed and ratified the decrees of the council, and he appealed to them to strive for harmony and not to tear down or cut in pieces the church, but rather to hold in mind the memory of the judgment of God. And these matters the emperor sent by personal letter.

Bell believes that a second meeting of the council was called to settle the Melitian controversy, although it is at least equally possible that the major issue continued to focus on the excommunicated Arians.[52] Of greater difficulty is the fact that a second meeting of the Council (either of the Nicene participants or of the Egyptian delegation) is not mentioned by most commentators, and its existence is suggested only by the passage quoted above.

Even if the Melitians were somewhat mollified by the decision of the Nicene Council, and if the further statement of Epiphanius concerning persecution of the Melitians is erroneous, there is no question that open antagonism existed between the Melitians and Athanasius, whose election to the bishopric they claimed to be entirely irregular and invalid.[53] A Melitian embassy was sent to Nicomedia to complain to the emperor and to ask "that they be permitted to hold meetings without violent disruption.[54] After being unable to get an audience with Constantine except through Eusebius, the bishop of Nicomedia, Epiphanius states that they were brought into an alliance with Arius through the machinations of that same bishop.[55] Put another way, it appears that the price of Eusebius' cooperation with the Melitians in obtaining an audience with the emperor was to join with the Arians. It has been seen earlier that the Arians and the Melitians had little in common from a doctrinal perspective, but they were joined together in a common cause *against* Athanasius. Sozomen is explicitly in accord with this analysis of the strange alliance:

> ὡς εἶδον τὸ πλῆθος ἑπόμενον τοῖς ἱερεῦσι τῆς καθόλου ᾽Εκκλησίας, εἰς φθόνον κατέστησαν. καὶ πρὸς ἀλλήλους ἐσπείσαντο, καὶ κοινὴν τὴν ἔχθραν ἀνεδέξαντο πρὸς τὸν κλῆρον ᾽Αλεξανδρείας.[56]

> *When they saw the great number of people following the priests of the Catholic Church, they became jealous and made peace with each other, and they undertook a common hatred toward the clergy of Alexandria.*

No matter what differences the parties brought with them to their alliance, Sozomen further states that in the process of time their differences became less apparent and that, for the most part, Melitians in Egypt even came to be called Arians.[57] The uneven nature of the relationship, indicated by the fact that the Arian appellation was dominant for both groups and not the other way around, supports Bell's statement, that "during the later stages of the Arian controversy the Melitians played a quite secondary part."[58] Bell further asserts that a number of the Melitians absolved their differences with the Catholics and were later counted among the partisans of Athanasius.[59]

The sect was not entirely wiped out by absorption into Arianism or reinstatement into Catholicism, however, for groups of Melitian Monks are still known to Theodoret in the fifth century, who speaks of them in terms of heretical doctrines picked up from Samaritans and Jews.[60] The association with Egyptian monks further emphasizes the local, or Egyptian, nature of the Melitian problem, since from its inception it was a revolt against the Alexandrian prelate. The fight against Alexandria even drove the Melitians into a strange alliance with the Arians against the Catholics and, finally, the Melitian schism became almost entirely an Egyptian monastic movement which had no connection with the ecclesiastical organization of Christian Egypt.

Of particular importance in understanding Melitian monasticism during the time of Athanasius are the papyri containing the correspondence of a certain Apa Paieous and acquired by the British Museum in 1922 and 1923.[61] In P.1920, Apa Paieous is addressed by Hatres (author of the letter) as "Confessor," which indicates that he suffered in the Diocletianic persecution,[62] and the context of the collection indicates that he is in charge of a sizable Melitian Monastic community,[63] perhaps in the decade from 330–340.[64] P.1920 mentions in the greeting that the community of monks is at Hathor,[65] and in P.1913, Hathor is said to be "situated in the eastern desert of the Upper Cynopolite nome."[66] P.1917 also implies that related monastic communities were located at Memphis and in the Thebaid.[67] The Egyptian nature of the sect is seen in the Egyptian names in the letters, the Coptic note at the end of one text,[68] and the fact that three of the letters are written in Coptic.[69] Although the Greek in the correspondence "is mostly of a vulgar kind,"[70] the bilingual abilities of the monks cannot be overlooked. W.E. Crum went so far as to suggest a connection between this collection of the papyri and the Coptic texts of the Rylands papyri, but Bell argues that the similarity of one or two names is insufficient to support Crum's hypothesis.[71]

P.1913 and P.1914 deal specifically with the Melitian struggles against Athanasius during the time of the Synod of Caesarea in 334 and the Synod of Tyre in 335. Athanasius had been charged with violence against the Melitians,[72] and Sozomen claims to have found specific evidences of the charges in the record of the Synod of Tyre.[73] In the case of the council at Caesarea, Sozomen states that Athanasius refused to attend because he felt that Eusebius of Caesarea, Eusebius of Nicomedia, and their associates would be united against him.[74] The council was called because of charges made against Athanasius, and some of them (for example, the case of Arsenius and the concocted murder charge concerning this man who in fact was not dead[75]) were admittedly ridiculous. Other charges had sufficient evidence or testimony associated with them to warrant calling together the councils of Caesarea and Tyre. Athanasius, of course, argued that the charges were all manufactured against him unjustly, but it is at least possible that he did not attend the council to avoid having to answer to real crimes, as at least one modern commentator believes.[76] It is worth noting in this regard that Athanasius nowhere makes any mention of the council of Caesarea. The two British Museum papyri not only shed light on the dating and circumstances surrounding the synods, but they make possible for the first time a glimpse at the issue from the Melitian point of view.

P.1913 is internally dated to a date corresponding to 19 March, 334.[77] Aurelius Pageus, the author, is a priest in Hipponon of the Heracleopolite nome, and he has received letters from the emperor Constantine:

κελευόντων τινὰς τῆς Αἰγύπτου ἐπισκόπους τε καὶ πρεσβυτέρους καὶ ἑτέρους πολλοὺς καὶ ἐμὲ σὺν αὐτοῖς . . . ἀπαντῆσαι εἰς Καισάριαν τῆς Παλαιστίνης Συρίας πρὸς διάκρισιν περὶ καθαρισμοῦ τοῦ ἁγίου Χρηστιανικοῦ . . .[78]

(letters from the Emperor Constantine) ordering certain persons from Egypt, both Bishops and priests and many others and myself among them . . . to proceed to Caesarea in Palestinian Syria to come to a decision concerning the purgation of the holy Christian body . . .

The council appears to be made up of Egyptian bishops, at least according to this letter, and indeed Athanasius may have had more to fear in the charges against him from his "local" area than from the bishops from other cities. Furthermore, the purpose of the council was to render a decision concerning the purification of the Egyptian church, and Athanasius was the focal point of the purifying effort. Contrary to Athanasius, who clearly wished to avoid going to such a meeting, this small-town priest admits that he is anxious to go and do his duty for the benefit of the church.[79] The purpose of the document is to acknowledge to the presiding monks at the monastery at Hathor that a temporary deputy has been selected to serve in Pageus' absence.[80] The part of this contract which is significant for understanding the organization of Egyptian Christian congregations has to do with the manner of choosing officers. Pageus called the group together, but they "unanimously, voluntarily and spontaneously" selected his brother to stand in his stead, and the *decision* was being sent to the officials at Hathor. This method of choosing local officers, just as was the case in Alexandria much earlier and throughout the congregations in Egypt which can be observed down to the imposition of Catholic ecclesiasticism, depends on local initiative and individual congregations making decisions. No indication exists in this contract to indicate a conspiracy on the part of the Melitian monks to overthrow Athanasius, but Pageus' remarks are placed clearly in the context of one who is willing to do his duty for "the purification of the church," whatever that might require.

P. 1914 is best introduced by giving Bell's own summary of its importance in understanding the Melitian schism:

This letter is historically the most important of the whole archive and indeed may well claim to rank among the primary authorities for the ecclesiastical history of Egypt in the fourth century. The writer, Callistus, was doubtless a Melitian monk or cleric, and he gives a circumstantial account of the sufferings of his fellow Melitians at the hands of Athanasius' adherents and of Athanasius himself.[81]

The date of the letter is not so easily determined as in the case of P.1913, but Bell brings enough circumstantial evidence to bear on the internal clues to yield a probable date before the beginning of Athanasius' exile in March, 339 or 340, and even as early as 335, just before the Council of Tyre.[82] Because the letter is private and because the writer suggests that his story can be verified by others known to the recipient, the events mentioned in the text are less liable to distortion for propaganda purposes than the public letters of a metropolitan bishop.

A Melitian bishop of Letopolis in the Thebaid, Isaac, went to Alexandria and planned to have dinner with a bishop there.[83] Word of the dinner got to followers of Athanasius, who came with some drunken soldiers to break up the meeting and "rough up" the Melitians. When the bishops could not be found (for they quickly had been hidden in the camp storeroom by some soldiers partisan to the Melitian cause), the soldiers of Athanasius went out from the camps, found some other Melitians, and beat them up.[84] The soldiers then went to the hotel or monastery (μονή) where the Melitian brethren were staying, and there seized other men and imprisoned them for the night simply because they had received Melitians as guests.[85] In the midst of all this, Callistus states that Athanasius was very despondent because of the reports he had received concerning his intrigues abroad.[86] According to the letter, the bishop of Alexandria had been planning a trip away from Egypt, and even had his baggage on board a ship, but changed his mind and took it off again.[87] The text states that Athanasius probably suffered frustration at having his friends Archelaus and Macarius imprisoned in Antioch, and as a result he was venting his frustration by taking violent measures against the Melitians,[88] even to the extent of kicking seven Melitian bishops out of the country.[89] Perhaps Athanasius felt justified in taking the action mentioned in this letter, but the denial of the charges of violence and persecution of the Melitians which appears in his own writings and in the church histories cannot stand as accurate history.[90]

The case for Melitian monasticism in later times is strengthened considerably by papyri discovered in recent years. In the Pierpont Morgan Library, New York, is a manuscript containing a Panegyric on Apollo, an otherwise unknown monk of the sixth century who was expelled from the Monastery of Pbow (modern Faw Qibli, not far from Nag Hammadi) for his Monophysite beliefs.[91] The monk journeyed northward and founded a new monastery, the Monastery of Isaac, in an unknown location, but conjectured to be near Heracleopolis Magna.[92] The new monastery was not founded without a struggle:

ΝΑΪ ΔΕ ΕϥΜΕΕΥΕ ΕΡΟΟΥ Ν̄ϬΙ ΠΧΑΧΕ ΕϥϹΟΠϹ ΝΕΤΕΝϢϢΝΕ ΕΤΡΕΥΡΠΟΛΥ-
ΜΟϹ ΜΝ ΠΕΙΡϢΜΕ ΕΤΟΥΑΑΒ... ΕΙϢΑΧΕ ΕΝΕΜΕΛΕϮΑΝΟϹ ΝΑΙ ΕΤΧΡΗΜΑΤΙΖΕ
2Μ ΠΕΙΤΟΟΥ ΜΠΕΥΟΕΙϢ ΕΤΜΑΑΥ.[93]

And when the enemy thought about these things, he urged his followers to wage war against this holy man ... I am referring to the Melitians who were present in this mountain at that time, impeding by every means the settling of this saint.

The text does not give any details about the number or organization of the Melitians, but one might suspect that a monk who had been expelled from one monastery might not be too anxious to settle near a very large monastic community of his enemies.

Another reference to Melitians in the late sixth and early seventh centuries comes from the Arabic text of the *History of the Patriarchs of the Coptic Church of Alexandria*. This work cannot be dated before the tenth century, although it is clearly drawn from early sources. The author of the life of Damian (Patriarch from 569–605) within the history states that Damian had lived in one of four monasteries in the Wadi Habib during his youth. The author adds that "there were among them Melitians, I mean the followers of Meletius, who used to receive the Chalice many times in the night, before they came to the church."[94] When Damian became the patriarch, he wrote to the monasteries and commanded that the Melitians should be expelled. What happened is not at all clear, but the text states that "after a short time, a voice came from heaven upon that desert, saying: 'Flee! Flee!' And when the inhabitants of the four monasteries had left them, they were laid waste. When news of this reached the Patriarch Damian, he was exceedingly sad."[95] It would appear that the Melitians were not easily or successfully dislodged, and that the attempt resulted in a total dissolution of the monastic communities.

The material presented here on the Melitians may at first appear to be treated disproportionately to the importance of that movement when compared to the major theological controversies of the third and fourth centuries, but a closer examination reveals the Melitians to be one of the major groups of the local Egyptian Christianity which fought for its existence against an expanding Catholicism. The bishops of Alexandria did not begin ordaining bishops outside Alexandria until Demetrius, according to Eutychius,[96] and only a century later they had attempted to usurp the right of controlling bishops and their ordinations throughout Egypt.

The Melitian problem (at least from the Catholic point of view) began with Melitius going into the dioceses of other bishops to ordain or excommunicate, but he was unable to win this war for power by himself. Arius was one supporter of Melitius early on, but for reasons not fully understood he vacillated in his loyalty between Melitius and the Alexandrian bishop, finally being reconciled to the latter until after the Nicene Council. Although separated from Arius and his movement until as late as the Council of Nicaea, Melitius was committed by Eusebius of Nicomedia to join forces with the Arians some few years later in a common cause against Athanasius and Catholicism.[97] Some Melitians were lost by attrition over the years to Arianism and Catholicism, but many enclaves of the sect accepted a uniquely Egyptian format of Christianity capable of maintaining a separate existence from the Catholic Church, namely monasticism, and continued on as Melitian groups for some centuries. The papyri found earlier in the century which relate to the Melitians give concrete evidence that the Melitians were primarily an Egyptian sect with followers scattered through all the length of Egypt, and yet a congregational autonomy reminiscent of early Egyptian Christianity continues to be evident in the movement.

Other than the "rigorism" of Melitius with respect to readmitting *lapsi* into communion and fellowship in the church, the sect does not appear to have strong doctrinal definition, as is evidenced by the fact that some were absorbed into Arianism and others into Catholicism. Even the bond established with the Arians by much of the movement after the Council of Nicaea was political at first, rather than doctrinal. This is to be expected, considering the rather undefined orthodoxy of early Egyptian Christianity. Doctrinal definition came with the imposition of a centralized ecclesiastical authority. One sees in the Melitian movement, therefore, one of the best available examples of a local Egyptian sect resisting the encroachment of an outside religious power.

It is within this context that the Sixth Canon of the Nicene Council can be properly evaluated. This canon, which was prompted by the determination to avoid a repetition of the Melitian problem, is translated as follows:

> Let the ancient customs in Egypt, Libya and Pentapolis prevail, that the Bishop of Alexandria have jurisdiction in all these, since the like is customary for the Bishop of Rome also. Likewise in Antioch and the other provinces, let the Churches retain their privileges. And this is to be universally understood, that if any one be made bishop without the consent of the Metropolitan, the great Synod has declared that such a man ought not to be a bishop. If, however, two or three bishops shall from natural love of contradiction, oppose the common suffrage of the rest, it being reasonable and in accordance with the ecclesiastical law, then let the choice of the majority prevail.[98]

In a commentary cited by Percival, W. A. Hannon declared that the purpose of a canon was not to introduce new powers, but rather "to confirm and establish ancient customs already existing."[99] Kidd surprisingly takes the same position, stating that "The bishop of Alexandria, by ancient custom, ruled over a district . . . including five 'provinces,' . . . The bishop of Alexandria was sole metropolitan in Egypt; and, as such, consecrated each and all of the hundred bishops there."[100] As has been shown in numerous examples above, the declaration of the canon that this ecclesiastical order in Egypt accords with "ancient custom" was no more than wishful thinking on the part of the Catholic bishops following Demetrius. The Alexandrian bishop had not been able to establish such effective power or authority over Christian Egypt as claimed in this canon even by the time of the Council of Nicaea. Nearly a half century after Nicaea, in 369, Athanasius implies the inability of Alexandria to control the Egyptian churches, for he wrote to the Catholic bishop of Carthage "stressing that one object of the Council of Nicaea had been to prevent local synods being summoned to solve problems regarding the Faith. Nicaea was the sole point of reference."[101]

The novelty of Canon VI is not overlooked by Telfer, however, who in an insightful argument claims that the canon was "adequate solace" for the method of ordaining bishops required in Canon IV.[102] Canon IV reads as follows:

It is by all means proper that a bishop should be appointed by all the bishops in the province; but should this be difficult, either on account of urgent necessity or because of distance, three at least should meet together, and the consent of the absent bishops also being given and communicated in writing, then the ordination should take place. But in every province the ratification of what is done should be left to the Metropolitan.

The method of selecting bishops down to the time of Alexander included selection by presbyters rather than by bishops, and Telfer states "that Alexander was the last Alexandrine pope to take office without the imposition of living episcopal hands, and that a new order came in with Athanasius."[103] The reference to "living episcopal hands" in Telfer's article relates to a description of episcopal ordination found in Liberatus, a Carthaginian deacon, who wrote a *Breviarum* in the sixth century. Liberatus described the ritual of episcopal succession, during which the body of the deceased bishop was present. The newly consecrated bishop therefore received his authority through the imposition upon his own head of the right hand of the deceased bishop.[104] Whether the authority was transmitted through a council of presbyters or by the literal transfer of the bishop's power from the deceased bishop to his successor, it is obvious that the new order of ordination in Egypt by living bishops, under the aegis of the Alexandrian Metropolitan Bishop, would be difficult to accept. The "solace" offered by Canon VI, that the Alexandrian prelates had exercised such authority over the entire province by ancient custom would be scant indeed for churches accustomed to local autonomy in the selection of their leaders.

Epiphanius had also noted a difference in the method of choosing bishops in Egypt from the procedure followed elsewhere. He states that in Alexandria it had been the custom to choose a bishop *without delay* to avoid dissension and party strife in a campaign of various nominees.[105] In the pre-Nicene era, the lack of delay in Egypt may simply indicate local activity without having to wait for Metropolitan approval and a convocation of bishops to perform the ordination. By placing the authority for episcopal succession in Egypt in the hands of the Alexandrian bishop, Canons IV and VI of Nicaea would effectively replace the tradition of immediate selection and ordination in local churches, and in theory should have removed the possibility of local competition for the office. Because of the continued presence of schismatic groups (such as the Melitians and Arians and others later), the theory of peaceful episcopal succession was not fully realized in succeeding centuries. To be sure, Athanasius did not achieve during his episcopacy the complete hegemony of the Alexandrian bishop described in the Nicene Canons.

While the Melitian issue was extremely important in the history of early Egyptian Christianity, it is not generally so well known or understood by students of Christian history because it was essentially a local problem. The confrontation between Arius and the Alexandrian bishops had considerably greater impact on the history of Christianity in general than did the Melitian schism, for the battles over Arianism were fought not only in Alexandria but in other major eastern cities of the Roman Empire as well. Both movements were influential in Egyptian ecclesiastical politics, but Arianism exhibited a theological dimension which was never a significant aspect of Melitianism.

Some of the major historical sources do not give a unified picture of Arius, since they represent a strong interest in either a favorable or a negative point of view, or are far removed in time from the events themselves, or both.

Eusebius of Caesarea is contemporary with many events relating to the Arian controversy, but his relationship to the issues is complex. The legacy of Origen was widespread in the eastern provinces of the Empire, and both Alexander, bishop of Alexandria, and Eusebius of Caesarea are heirs of that legacy, even if at somewhat opposite ends of the theological spectrum in Origenistic thought. Alexander was quite conservative in his attacks against Arius while reproducing such elements of Origen's teaching as the eternal generation of the Son from the Father and the Word or Son as an individual being, distinguishable from the Father.[106] Eusebius, on the other hand, "reflects Origen in his most subordinationist mood," and, even before Arius came into prominence, accepted "the unique, transcendent Father, the indivisible Monad Who is 'above and beyond reality' . . . and who is alone self-existent and without beginning."[107] The Father, according to Eusebius, "is prior to and pre-exists the Son,"[108] thus refusing to admit that the Son is co-eternal with the Father. As will be seen below, the position of Eusebius (and that of many Eastern bishops) is very much like that of Arius, and one might therefore expect to find the real source of Arius' difficulties elsewhere than in the popular idea that he was a theological innovator or heretic (at least if he is compared to the dominant theology of the East). Despite his sympathy with the theology of Arius, Eusebius pursued an ambivalent course in the proceedings of Nicaea and afterward. He accepted the Creed of the Council, yet wrote a letter to his flock at Caesarea in which he explains with some embarrassment over why he acted in such unexpected fashion.[109] His admiration for the Emperor and perhaps concern for his own position after being censured some months earlier at the Council of Antioch (December, 324) may have made the Caesarean bishop cautious in defending beliefs which he expounds in his other writings.[110] Greenslade suggests a connection between Eusebius' Origenistic theology and his defense of the Emperor:

> There are no reserves in the stilted encomium with which Eusebius closes his history (10.9.6–9) . . . no prophetic fear of imperial control of the Church. His heart is full of gratitude to God and Constantine . . . He is ready with a theory, indeed a theology, of the Christian Emperor . . . As Christ, the Word of God, the Logos, is the archetypal image of the Father, so on earth Constantine is the image of the Logos.[111]

Barnes' work on Constantine and Eusebius illustrates the apparent paradox when in one place he says "Constantine ridicules Arius' theology at length,"[112] and elsewhere, that Eusebius "(took) up his pen in the Arian cause."[113] The solution to the problem is to be seen in yet another observation: "Eusebius presents the reign of Constantine as the culmination of human history."[114] Even if Constantine held theological views different from those of Eusebius, political reality helped the Church historian to harmonize his Arian tendencies with an unabashed esteem for the Emperor. This brief picture of Eusebius illustrates the difficulties one faces in assessing the Arian controversy, even with sources which should be sympathetic. "Ecclesiastical politics after Nicaea are party politics."[115]

Much information concerning Arianism is also contained in the fifth-century historians, Sozomen, Socrates and Theodoret, but their distance in time from the events is accompanied by partiality to a considerable degree.[116] Socrates admits his (or anybody's) difficulty in dealing with the Arian controversy and the Nicene Council when he noted that the debates resembled a contest in the dark, where neither side understood clearly the issues, and thus did not really know whether he was attacking friend or enemy.[117] Theodoret is a fifth-century bishop of Cyrrhus in Syria, who wrote a continuation of Eusebius' history, and notwithstanding his orthodox bias against Arianism, his work is worth noting because of a number of primary sources quoted within it.[118] The work of yet another fifth-century historian,

Philostorgius, survives only in fragments, but it is one of the few works representing history from the Arian point of view.[119] As biased and unreliable as are many anti-Arian sources, Philostorgius is nevertheless valuable for sources he includes and information regarding Arians not recorded elsewhere.

Epiphanius is closer in time to the beginnings of the Arian problem, and this fourth-century bishop of Salamis is not only known for intolerance of any suspected heresy, but his work against heresies is uncritically receptive to any material which supports his position.[120] Epiphanius was also anti-Origenist in his theology and some believe that his influence contributed to the growth of anti-Origenism beginning in the late fourth century and continuing through the fifth.[121] The heresiologist blamed Origen for the rise of Arianism and spent much of his life opposing Origenists, even leading to the conversion of Jerome, formerly an ardent supporter of Origen, to his position. Jerome's writings also thus contain material relating to Arianism, as do the extant writings of most of the Fathers in these critical centuries. Credibility is, of course, a vexing problem among authors of both sides whose partisan feelings result in distortion, exaggeration, fabrication, and mendacity. Athanasius has been shown above to be unreliable in the affairs of the Melitians, and his credibility certainly must not be considered greater in the matter of his greatest personal opponent. Despite the difficulties presented by the available sources concerning the Arian controversy, general agreement exists relative to the life of Arius, and the basic charges can be outlined, especially as they affected Egyptian Christianity.[122]

Arius (c.255-c.336) was apparently a Libyan by birth,[123] and later a student of Lucian of Antioch.[124] He was subsequently appointed to be a presbyter at Baucalis in Alexandria during the episcopacy of Peter,[125] and Sozomen alone suggests that he had an early connection with the Melitians.[126] This connection is not clearly understood, as pointed out above in the Melitian context, but Peter's ordination of Arius to the deaconate is probably accurate. The real difficulty arose during the ministry of Alexander,[127] when he began to teach concerning the Son of God:

καὶ εἶναί ποτε ὅτε οὐκ ἦν.[128]

And there was a time when He was not.

Because of the similarities of Arius' teaching with the subordinationism of Origen, who was popular throughout the churches of Egypt and the East, it should not be surprising that Socrates could write of the rapid diffusion of Arianism that "the evil which began in the Church at Alexandria ran throughout all Egypt, Libya, and the upper Thebes; and at length diffused itself over the rest of the provinces and cities."[129] The chronology of the beginning of the Arian 'heresy' and the question of whether at first personalities or doctrinal issues played the major part are disputed,[130] but in c. 321 Alexander called a synod of bishops to Alexandria to consider the teachings of Arius, and the result was excommunication for Arius and his followers.[131] After his excommunication, Arius went to other major cities in the East, looking for support in his cause,[132] and the ensuing disorders were of such magnitude that the emperor Constantine intervened and sent his Christian advisor, Hosius, bishop of Cordova, to Alexandria to mediate the difficulty.[133] Hosius was also to look into the Melitian problem and the Pashcal question which was raging at the time.[134] Neither the visit of the emperor's confidant nor a synod in Alexandria in 324 was able to solve the problems at hand, so the emperor called an ecumenical council to meet in Nicaea in Bithynia in 325. The council convened in the summer of 325, coinciding with the *Vicennalia* of Constantine, and there were approximately 220 bishops present (probably more correct than the traditional 318).[135] The council was essentially Eastern in its geographical makeup, but it was an especially significant episode in church history, both for its size and for the geographical range of its members. Only four or five bishops represented the Latin Church, in addition to the Emperor's confidant, Hosius of Cordova, and two presbyters sent by Pope Sylvester of Rome.[136] The majority of the council members were thus generally sympathetic to Origenistic theology, but diversity still existed within that broad category of thought. For example, the Alexandrians and their supporters generally accepted a position often described as "Word-flesh" Christology, meaning that Christ's being was defined as a human body animated by the Word, but not having a human soul.[137] Unity or clarity on this position is not entirely possible, leaving room for differences of opinion. While Athanasius taught that the Word was fully divine and was not changed when inhabiting the human body,[138] Arius stated that the Word was a creature of God, susceptible of change, although superior to all other creatures.[139] Some of the Nicene supporters, while allies of Athanasius and opposed to Arius, were anti-Origen, notably the Antiochenes, who, for the most part, believed in a "Word-man" Christology, meaning that the Word inhabited a complete human, that is, one composed of both body and a human soul.[140] Despite these differences (and others, such as the influence of Platonic and Aristotelian thought on various positions), the preponderance of Origenistic influence in the council caused one modern commentator to state that, "the victory of Nicaea was rather a surprise than a solid conquest."[141] An uneasy truce prevailed in Egypt after the Council, with both Alexander and Melitius parrying for position, and the Arians needed time to regroup after such a resounding defeat in the Council.

One should observe at this point that the theological aspect of the Arian controversy is only an Egyptian problem because it occurred in Alexandria. Both Alexander and Arius were Origenists, as was much of the Eastern Christian world, Antioch being a notable exception. Thus Origenists elsewhere in the East could have disputed one with another over how to interpret the theology of the great Alexandrian scholar, and in fact many did. The dispute in Alexandria was primarily political at first, and became doctrinally significant only afterward. Frend notes that the real problem facing the drafting committee of the council of Nicaea was how to state a position which excluded Arius' ideas.[142] Chadwick is implicitly in agreement, for he states the resulting creed was sufficiently ambiguous "that the crucial terms of the creed were not understood in a precisely identical sense by all the signatories."[143] It is noteworthy that in the ensuing debates and councils concerning the Arian heresy the Egyptian churches outside Alexandria are not known for being divided and fighting over the doctrinal issues. Of course, sources are scarce for what was happening in most of the churches, and there may have been more struggles over doctrine than is presently known.

Alexander's successor, Athanasius, was autocratic in his rule as the bishop of Alexandria from 328 to 373, but he was exiled on a number of occasions, which is indicative of the difficulties he faced in attempting to establish Catholic unity throughout his diocese. There is no question that Athanasius was supported by a large group of devoted followers in Alexandria, and Barnes states that the bishops whom he controlled constituted a majority in Egypt.[144] His influence outside Egypt was significant, although the support of bishops elsewhere for Melitius and Arius (whether politically or doctrinally motivated) effectively weakened the dominant role Alexandria had played in eastern ecclesiastical circles for nearly two centuries. One can surmise that if Athanasius had been more like his predecessor, that is to say, more conciliatory and less ruthless and violent toward any who disagreed with him, he might have avoided being exiled so many times, and the widening theological gulf of the fourth century might not have occurred. The latter point is especially suggested by the difficulty which the bishops of the Church faced in trying to define the terms of the argument so as not to alienate colleagues inadvertently and also by attempts to settle the dispute by the use of new words or phrases in efforts to compromise or meet on common ground. Such a surmise only reinforces the impression of an implacable leader, one "who seemed to revel in controversy,"[145] yet one whose episcopacy was pivotal in the course of Egyptian Christian history.

Athanasius had been well trained for the position to which he was elected. He probably acquired his 'liberal education' in the Alexandrian school[146] and he later became the deacon and secretary to Bishop Alexander.[147] Although reputed for his wealth,[148] Athanasius was nevertheless ascetic in nature.[149] As noted just above, Athanasius was incapable of adapting to the less dogmatic and structured groups of Christians which still existed in Egypt. It is likely that only his own ascetic tendencies permitted him to enjoy a friendship and association with Anthony and Pachomius, the leading representatives of the Egyptian monastic movement. This alliance with the leading monks ensured the allegiance of much of the Egyptian Christian movement to Athanasius, however, even if most Egyptian Christians did not accept or understand the theology of the bishop. The natives were fiercely loyal to their own leaders, and the benefits to Athanasius because of his association with Anthony and Pachomius are illustrated by the fact that when exiled in 356, the bishop was protected and defended by the monks as he moved from monastery to monastery.[150] His difficulties with other people or groups, especially the Arians, kept him from having a peaceful reign, but his own intractability, combined with a streak of violence directed at least toward the Melitians, was as responsible as their heretical beliefs and activities. One should note, however, that Athanasius did not continue to confront the same people or issues throughout his nearly half-century long episcopacy. Death claimed some of his enemies, others were exiled, and even the issue of Arianism appeared to decrease in Egypt, if not elsewhere, for a time during the last decade of Athanasius' life. C. Kannengiesser perhaps has gone beyond the evidence when he attempts to solve the problem of when Athanasius wrote his anti-Arian tractates,[151] but he is probably correct to ask:

> Why do we no longer find the *Thalia* quoted in the dogmatical writings of Athanasius after his Alexandrian synod of 362?...the "Arian" crisis no longer affects the local church of Alexandria after the departure of Aetius and the exile of Eunomius, nor does it mobilize any more its elderly bishop. The Cappadocians, especially Basil of Caesarea, are the new anti-Arian fighters.[152]

The sources available for an analysis of Athanasius' patriarchate as it relates to Egyptian Christianity vary considerably in their value to the modern historian. Athanasius himself is a valuable source, despite the limitations and criticisms noted previously, especially in a number of polemical tracts written on religious controversies during the last decade of Constantine's reign.[153] In addition to his numerous apologetic works, Athanasius had a voluminous correspondence of which only a portion remains. The most significant of these for the historian are the Festal letters, written each year to announce the beginning of Lent and establish the correct date for Easter. Athanasius wrote such letters, even when he was in exile, and many are preserved in Syriac or Coptic, with a few Greek fragments.[154] In the later part of his rule, Athanasius also wrote letters in the name of the Alexandrian synod,[155] suggesting that he was then more secure in his own archdiocese. This suggestion is perhaps tempered by two letters written to the monks ca. 358–360, in which Athanasius says he is compelled to write, "because there are certain persons who hold with Arius and are going throughout the monasteries with no other object save that under color of visiting you and returning from us they may deceive the simple."[156] The threat from Arians infiltrating the monasteries must not have been too great, however, since the letters were written during the third exile of Athanasius, and he was protected during that exile in the monasteries by the very monks to whom he wrote his epistle. Athanasius' *Life of Anthony* is important, not only for the information which it gives concerning the early monastic movement in Egypt, but also for the insights gained about the author. It becomes obvious to the reader that Athanasius wrote both to glorify the saintly Anthony whose ascetic life he admired, and to cement his alliance with the monks of Egypt by his portrayal of Anthony's respect and friendship for the bishop. Frend states that the move by Athanasius to secure the allegiance of the monks to himself "was a stroke of genius, as far-reaching in its effects as his championship of Nicaea."[157]

Other major historical sources for this period include Rufinus, who translated Eusebius into Latin near the close of the fourth century, and added a fragmentary account of uneven value down to 395.[158] The evaluation of the fifth-century writers Sozomen, Socrates, Philostorgius, and Theodoret made above with regard to Arianism continues to be valid in the case of Athanasius, but one should further note that Athanasius is a prime source for these authors.[159] Significant documents, such as "imperial letters on religious questions, letters of bishops and canons of councils," are found scattered through various writers and collections of a later period.[160] In summary, available sources are not lacking for the fourth century Egyptian Church, but they tend to be quite biased in their viewpoint and often give incomplete reports or contradictory information on such matters as the chronology and activities of leading personalities.

The first years of Athanasius' episcopacy seem relatively calm, and his Festal Letter for 329 is concerned entirely with the feast, fasting, and the salvation of the Christian through the Word of God.[161] In the autumn of that year, Athanasius apparently made a journey throughout Egypt "to strengthen the churches of God," or perhaps to strengthen their allegiance to him.[162] The Festal Letter for 330 makes reference to heretics,[163] but it is not until the third year that Athanasius says it is "the time of tribulation, which the heretics excite against us."[164] This year, 331, might possibly be the year when the Melitians and the Arians joined forces, and also possibly the year when Arius was recalled to Alexandria with the permission of the Emperor.[165] Athanasius did not receive him, but tried to have him thrown out of the city. Arius wrote to the emperor, who in turn wrote to Athanasius and ordered him to receive Arius back into the church.[166] Athanasius refused, and again Constantine wrote, this time a sharply worded rebuke:

Ἔχων τοίνυν τῆς ἐμῆς βουλήσεως τὸ γνώρισμα, ἅπασι τοῖς βουλομένοις εἰς τὴν Ἐκκλησίαν εἰσελθεῖν ἀκώλυτον παράσχου τὴν εἴσοδον.[167]

Therefore, because you have knowledge of my desire, allow all who wish to enter into the Church unhindered entry.

Athanasius refused again, although the reason may be different from the one suggested by Thomson, who argues that the basis for refusal was the archbishop's greater knowledge "of the dogmatic issues at stake."[168] The real reason may well have been Athanasius' desire to keep Arius away from Egypt, especially since the Arian cause had been strengthened by the Melitians, who had joined them primarily to fight Athanasius. Athanasius' problems with the Arians were not lessened by his refusal to readmit Arius, however, for he found himself out of favor with the emperor, and this led to his exile in 336.

The Council of Tyre was held in 335, and it was called by Constantine who was on his way to Jerusalem to dedicate the Church of the Resurrection as part of his *tricennalia* festivities.[169] The Eusebian (of Nicomedia) party had been stirring up feelings against the Egyptian Metropolitan Bishop, and Constantine was acceding increasingly to their demands for a trial of Athanasius. The council was packed with opponents of the Alexandrian bishop, and the 48 bishops who accompanied Athanasius were not even admitted as members of the Council.[170] Given the charges against him and the biased court hearing his case, one cannot fault Athanasius for attending "with reluctance, nominally as a participating bishop, substantially as a defendant."[171]

The Emperor's primary concern was the unity of the Church, and he told the disputants to settle their differences, reminding them that they could not serve God while harboring animosity.[172] The council was anything but peaceful, however, according to Epiphanius[173] and Rufinus.[174] Charges and accusations were hurled back and forth, and finally a commission was appointed to go to Mareotis and ascertain what had really happened.[175] Athanasius was against this action, since the commission consisted of six Arians, and soon afterward he departed for Constantinople to complain to the Emperor.[176] In his absence the Council deposed Athanasius,[177] while the bishop's success with the emperor is suggested by Constantine's call for a review to be held in Constantinople in 336.[178] The council met in the capital, but Athanasius was responsible for his own defeat because of his violent activities in Egypt,[179] coupled with a charge against him that he had threatened to interfere with grain shipments from Alexandria to Constantinople unless Constantine gave a favorable decision.[180] It is impossible to tell whether the emperor was convinced of Athanasius' guilt on the charges raised against him, or whether he simply saw the bishop as an intransigent obstacle standing in the way of peace, but the result was Athanasius' exile to Trier in Gaul.[181]

Athanasius was not replaced by the emperor during his exile, unlike other bishops suffering the same fate,[182] and that indicates that his position was sufficiently secure to discourage the emperor causing a rebellion by choosing another archbishop. Athanasius remained in contact with his supporters in Alexandria through letters, and the Arians were not able to destroy the popular base of his power in his absence. Even the Melitian leader, John Arkaph, was banished during this period,[183] further keeping effective opposition to Athanasius in check. The opposition did continue with vigor, however, as can be observed in the events related to the archbishop's return to Alexandria.

Upon Constantine's death in 337, Constantine II (the eldest of the three sons of Constantine, ruler of the Western part of the Empire after his father's death, and an adherent of Nicaea) wrote to Alexandria and informed the church that he intended to send Athanasius back to that city.[184] Athanasius had two interviews with Constantius (the second of the sons, ruler of the East, and an Origenist in his theological leanings), in whose part of the empire Alexandria was situated,[185] and with peace established between them the bishop entered his diocese after an absence of nearly two years. The peace did not extend from the bishop to his enemies the Arians, however, and new recriminations arose from both sides, the truth of which is impossible to establish. The one charge raised during this time which Athanasius could not overcome was that he had been deposed by a council and not restored by one.[186] Arian sympathizers attempted to install bishops in the supposedly vacated see. Athanasius traveled to Rome to state his case there,[187] and he remained in virtual exile in Rome for three years. Earlier, when the circumstances were reversed and Athanasius was in Alexandria keeping the opposition in exile, the hope certainly was to enhance his own position at the expense of those who were out of the country. The Arians must have harbored the same hopes, and the absences of Athanasius from Alexandria, including this three year visit to Rome, show how incapable they were of bringing the balance of power into their favor, even with a sympathetic Emperor over that part of the Empire. Athanasius' friendship and alliance with the Egyptian monks gave considerable strength to his cause, and Athanasius demonstrated his awareness of their importance to him by taking two monks with him to Rome, a certain Ammonius and one whose name was Isidore.[188] The effect of this flight to Rome,[189] according to Jerome, was to establish the monastic movement in the west.[190]

Councils were held during this period, including those of Rome in 340, Antioch in 341, and Sardica in 342 or 343.[191] It should not be surprising that the Council in Rome (where Constantine II, who favored Nicaea, ruled) found Athanasius innocent of all charges made against him in the Council of Tyre, and further accepted him as the authorized bishop of Alexandria. Julius, the Roman Pope, further exerted himself on behalf of Athanasius in a most amazing way, sending a letter to Eastern bishops which denounces actions taken against Athanasius by a Council of bishops, and also continues at length defending his friend and other anti-Arians who had fled to Rome during the period of Arian ascendancy in the East.[192] By this time, the eastern bishops had nominated Gregory, a Cappadocian, to become the bishop of Alexandria in Athanasius' absence. The intruding bishop was established through military intervention with the aid of the prefect of Egypt, who just happened also to be a Cappadocian.[193]

Perhaps most amazing in this letter is the claim of Roman primacy in affairs concerning the Egyptian church.

> Διὰ τί δὲ περὶ τῆς Ἀλεξανδρέων Ἐκκλησίας μάλιστα οὐκ ἐγράφετο ἡμῖν; Ἢ ἀγνοεῖτε ὅτι τοῦτο ἔθος ἦν, πρότερον γράφεσθαι ἡμῖν, καὶ οὕτως ἔνθεν ὁρίζεσθαι τὰ δίκαια; . . . ἃ γὰρ παρειλήφαμεν παρὰ τοῦ μακαρίου Πέτρου τοῦ ἀποστόλου ταῦτα καὶ ὑμῖν δηλῶ.[194]

> *And why especially concerning the Church of the Alexandrians was nothing written to us? Or are you unaware that this was the custom, to write first to us, and then for a just decision to be determined from this place? . . . For what we have received from the blessed Apostle Peter, this I also signify to you.*

Frend notes that "No trace of the custom claimed by Julius has been preserved in the previous history of the Church."[195] It has neverthe-less been shown earlier in this study that as early as Valentinus and later Demetrius, there were attempts to impose ecclesiastical author-ity from Alexandria to Rome or from Rome to Alexandria. Perhaps the Roman Pope is tracing the asserted custom back to the end of the second century when Demetrius became the bishop of Alexandria and attempted to establish Catholic Christianity in Egypt.

The letter of Julius did not go unchallenged. In 341, nearly 100 eastern bishops met at Antioch and formulated a new creed of faith (omitting *homoousios*, but in other respects being similar to the Nicene Creed), and declared that it was unheard of for eastern bishops to be judged by western bishops.[196] The Council also confirmed the deci-sions of the Council of Tyre and added some canons concerning disciplinary matters.[197]

Constans, ruler of the entire West, or nearly two-thirds of the Roman Empire after Constantine II's defeat and death in 340, was a supporter of Athanasius, and called the Council of Sardica in 342 or 343 with the hope that the archbishop would be found innocent of all charges and returned to his see. Constantius favored the Arians, however, and also sided against Athanasius were the Origenist bishops in attendance at the Council.[198] The result was a deadlock, and the eastern bishops withdrew to the East and excommunicated Athanasius, Julius of Rome, and all who supported Athanasius' return to communion.[199] The Western bishops in turn excommunicated Gregory, the Anatolian chosen by the Arians to replace Athanasius in 339, and the split continued until Gregory's death in June, 345.[200]

Athanasius had been staying at Aquileia[201] and while there had a number of interviews with Constans,[202] who finally persuaded his brother with threats of war to permit Athanasius to return to Alexandria.[203] The exile finally returned to Alexandria in 346 to a triumphant welcome, and was able to remain there for the next ten years, often called the Golden Decade of Athanasius. Athanasius was not free from attack by the Arians and the Arian Emperor during this period, but he continued to enjoy the support of many of the Egyptian monks and, when pressed, he went to the desert and stayed with them.[204] The preoccupation of Constantius with the Persian wars and the threat of Constans to attack if Athanasius were disturbed were sufficient causes to allow Athanasius to strengthen his hold on the church during this period. An early commentator noted that, "Strong as was the position of Athanasius in Egypt upon his return from exile, his hold *upon the country* grew with each year of the decade"[205] (emphasis added). His position was somewhat precarious, nevertheless, since Constantius still favored the Arians. When Constans died in 350, Constantius defeated Magnentius of Gaul in the civil war which followed, and emerged as sole ruler in the Empire. The emperor himself did not officially remove Athanasius from Alexandria, but local troops led by Syrianus and accompanied by the Egyptian Prefect, Maximus, invaded the church of Theonas on 8 February, 356, hoping to capture the bishop.[206] Supporters removed him first, however, and he made his escape to the desert monasteries, where he was in hiding during the next six years. The military then attempted, within the year, to place George of Cappadocia as another intrusion bishop on the bishop's throne.[207] This radical Arian[208] was the major reason for the Arians not being able to increase in influence at the expense of the Athanasian party. Not only a profiteering pork contractor for the army, George was also an oppressive administrator in Egypt, and he aroused such resistance to his policies that he had to leave Alexandria within a year out of fear for his life.[209] Even Ammianus Marcellinus refers to George as a rather obnoxious person without a noble character.[210] George returned to Alexandria when Julian was proclaimed Augustus by Constantius, but when news of the latter's death reached Alexandria a mob murdered the Arian bishop.[211] Athanasius was unable to make a lasting return to Alexandria until after Julian's death in 363, suggesting the turbulent state of affairs in Egyptian Christianity during this time.

It is appropriate at this point to consider the nature of the Athanasian-Arian struggle for superiority to the middle of the fourth century. Frances Young characterizes the legend of Athanasius in the following terms: "...a steadfast saint and theologian who almost single-handed (sic) defended the Nicene formula through the reigns of Arian emperors, and finally engineered a reconciliation among anti-Arian parties in the East."[212] The legend implies that Arius was the theological innovator, when just the opposite was more likely the case. Young presents two major facts to show that "It is not impossible that he was simply a die-hard conservative who was not afraid to challenge what he considered the innovations of his bishop, and who attracted a following merely on the grounds that he voiced what so many others felt about dangerous theological developments."[213] These facts are:

> (i) His position could be presented as thoroughly scriptural—at Nicaea his opponents were forced to adopt the non-scriptural, philosophical term *homoousios* (of the same substance) in order to exclude his views. He proved during his career that he had no difficulty in accepting creeds couched in traditional scriptural language.
> (ii) The argument with Arius revolved around certain key texts of scripture, and often his opponents had to produce very forced exegesis to counter his position.[214]

Despite the legend of Athanasius as the great defender of the Nicene Creed, there is no mention of Nicaea or *homoousios* in his early works, *Contra Gentes* and *De Incarnatione*, even though he was writing against Eusebius' *Theophania*.[215] The speeches against the Arians contain *homoousius* only once in the opening of the work, and the word never appears again.[216] As Thompson notes, "less precise terms were acceptable, and in later life he was willing to admit different interpretations of the important word *hypostasis*."[217] Many of the technical terms adopted in the Nicene Creed were at first disliked by many of the allies of Athanasius from Antioch and the West who signed the Creed, as well as by Arius and Eustathius. It is probable that precise articulation of the different positions taken at Nicaea (as can be seen in the numerous creeds drawn up during succeeding decades) was possible only after considerable time for reflection and correspondence, but the differences may also have become magnified in time as each side continued to react against the other. The real theological differences in the positions taken by Athanasius and his Arian opposition may have been less than is often assumed. It is true that Athanasius became more specific in defining the Nicene position as quite different from the Arian one, but the early decades of the controversy resemble a battle for power between two competing camps rather than a theological war. The seesaw nature of the dispute did not cease with the death of the principals, for Peter, named a successor to Athanasius just before the latter's death in May, 373,[218] was forced by the Arian candidate for succession, Lucius, to take refuge with Damasus of Rome until the death of Valens in 378.

A most important aspect of Athanasius' rule has to do with his close ties to monasticism, the most visible component of Egyptian Christianity. As the dominance of the ecclesiastical and doctrinally dogmatic church increased over the local churches of Egypt, a less structured movement such as monasticism would naturally tend to become separated from the ruling institution. That it did not do so completely during this critical period, according to Frend, is a tribute to the efforts of Athanasius and Cyril, who "needed all their prestige and then skill to win the acceptance of these (theological assumptions based on the Nicene Creed which could be at variance with the literal doctrines of the Bible) by the monks."[219] The importance to the Alexandrian bishop of acquiring and keeping the allegiance of the monks in the matters of the church and its orthodoxy is obvious. One notes, for example, how Athanasius took the monks into his confidence and wrote in three major works his reasons for refusing fellowship and communion with the Melitians and the Arians.[220] He also wrote a letter to a Nitrian monk, Amun, in 354, in which he formally attempts to reconcile the monk to the idea that God approves of marriage and procreation in the church, even if monastic celibacy is of a higher spiritual order before the Lord:

Δύο γὰρ οὐσῶν ὁδῶν ἐν τῷ βίῳ περὶ τούτων, μιᾶς μὲν μετριωτέρας καὶ βιωτικῆς, τοῦ γάμου λέγω· τῆς δὲ ἑτέρας ἀγγελικῆς καὶ ἀνυπερβλήτου, τῆς παρθενίας.[221]

for of the two ways which exist in life concerning these things, one is more moderate and popular—I am speaking of marriage; but the other is angelic and unsurpassed, that is virginity.

Athanasius continues, saying that those in the church who choose marriage, or the way of the world, will not be condemned, even though they will not receive such great gifts as those who are monastic and celibate.[222]

In 354 or 355, Athanasius wrote to a certain monk, Dracontius, asking him not to refuse ordination to the episcopacy of Hermopolis Parva, to which he had just been elected and appointed. Although Dracontius ultimately accepted the position, the letter is remarkable for showing the anti-clerical tendencies of his fellow monks. Athanasius asks, "For if all were of the same mind as your present advisers, how would you have become a Christian, since there would be no bishops?"[223] And again, "Perhaps there are some who are advising you to hide because you have sworn an oath not to accept the office if you are elected."[224] Was the oath typical of some monastic communities, perhaps to prevent the intrusion of ecclesiastical authority into monasticism, or was this unique to Dracontius, as he was pressured by associates to promise a refusal to leave his order for a church office? Although others may have preceded Dracontius in making a change in vocation, it was not that common, for Athanasius has to remind him that he was "not the only one who has been elected from among monks."[225] The reasons which Dracontius apparently put forth, or at least the ones which Athanasius refutes, are that he found the organizing of the churches distasteful and that he did not think the ministry of his episcopate to have a heavenly reward.[226] The archbishop's passionate discourse infers that others feel the same way, and he acknowledges the difficulty which monasticism presents to the church:

Ἐὰν δὲ καὶ οἱ μεθ᾽ ἡμᾶς ἀναλάβωσι τὸν τοιοῦτον νοῦν, πῶς ἂν συστῆναι δυνήσωνται αἱ Ἐκκλησίαι;[227]

And if they who come after us take up such a state of mind, how would the Churches be able to come together?

As will be seen below, the Alexandrian patriarchs on occasion even sought out reluctant monks to ordain them deacons or presbyters, thereby ensuring a bond between Catholicism and monasticism, and minimizing the tendency of the latter to become a non-ecclesiastical and independent Egyptian Christian institution.[228] In the examples given above and elsewhere, Athanasius was successful in his unifying efforts, so that he "called back into the service of the church the monastic movement which had begun by taking some of the most earnest believers away from the common life."[229]

Athanasius was the leading representative of Catholicism in Egypt for nearly half a century before his death, and in that long tenure he was thus able to consolidate his ecclesiastical authority primarily in two ways. He was more tenacious than his opponents[230] and outlived them as well. He also was able to bring monasticism within the grasp of the church, thus minimizing the autonomous existence of Christian groups that were the hallmark of early Christianity in Egypt. The 39th Festal Letter (for 367) is usually studied for the list of canonical books which it contains, but the first part of the letter shows that Athanasius is still struggling to impose a stringent doctrinal position upon Egyptian Christians who were reluctant to follow along:

> They have fabricated books which they call books of tables, in which they show stars, to which they give the names of saints . . .[231]
> I fear lest, as Paul wrote to the Corinthians, some few of the simple should be beguiled from their simplicity and purity, and by the subtlety of certain men, and should henceforth read other books—those called apocryphal—led astray by the similarity of their names with the true books . . .[232]

Despite Athanasius' efforts, the development of monasticism in the fourth century persisted in being relatively independent of the control of ecclesiastical leaders. Alexandrian bishops during that century and the following one continued to have difficulty assuring the allegiance of the movement as a whole. That was true at least until it was united by such leaders as Pachomius, Schenoute, and their successors.

The sources available today which permit a glimpse into fourth century Egyptian monasticism have a complex textual history and are uneven in historical value. The *Life of Anthony* by Athanasius mentioned previously was certainly a model which stimulated the later hagiographers to immortalize monastic leaders with biographies. Pachomius, the acknowledged founder of coenobitic, or communal, monasticism,[233] was so honored shortly after his death. His disciples, with the approbation of Pachomius' spiritual successor, Theodore, composed accounts of his life, although it is disputed whether they were first written in Coptic or Greek.[234] These works quickly became popular and were subsequently transmitted in Sahidic, Bohairic, Greek, Latin, Syriac, Ethiopic, and Arabic.[235] The Rule of monastic life which began with Pachomius and later became the basis for monastic regulations throughout the East and West, was also copied, translated, and distributed in numerous languages, as were letters and other writings attributed to the great monk.[236] Writings of his successors also became popular, particularly those of Theodore and Horsiesios.[237]

At the end of the fourth century or the beginning of the fifth, a history of the monks in Egypt was also compiled by a group of seven pilgrims who journeyed to Egypt from a monastery on the Mount of Olives in order to visit the great monastic communities along the Nile. Authorship of this work is attributed to Rufinus, the leader of the Palestinian monastery, although that author's Latin translation from a Greek original does not actually make him the original author.[238] Another source from nearly the same time, the *Lausiac History* written by Palladius of Galatia (c.363–431) who traveled to Egypt in 388 to gain a firsthand knowledge of monasticism, is problematic in both its textual tradition and in historical credibility.[239] Like other works just mentioned, the *Lausiac History* was so popular that it was translated from Greek into Latin, Coptic, Syriac, Armenian, Ethiopic, Arabic, and Old Sogdian, and distributed widely throughout the Occident and the Orient.[240] Generally discredited in the nineteenth century,[241] the work has regained considerable respect in the twentieth as the best historical source relating to Egyptian Monasticism:

> So it seems most likely that Palladius was a contemporary observer of much that he describes, and that his work must be regarded as a most important source for the study of the early monastic movements, its ideals and its mentality.[242]

Jerome, best known for being a translator of the Bible, also traveled to Egypt early in his life and later wrote "three biographic 'novelettes', (in which) he outlines the monastic ideal in typically Eastern colors and motives such as were exemplified in the famous *Life of Anthony*."[243] His works contain material relating to his own monastic experiences in Egypt and Syria, but do not otherwise contain historical information concerning specific Egyptian monks, except in his Preface to the Rule of Pachomius.[244]

Finally, of the major sources relating to fourth century monasticism, there are also the non-literary collections of sayings of the desert fathers, or the *Apophthegmata Patrum*. These anonymous writings contain spiritual aphorisms and anecdotes of the miracles and virtues of both famous and unknown monks.[245] No better source exists for giving the flavor and spirit of Egyptian monasticism.

The popularity of the monastic movement is thus well attested, although Rufinus must be exaggerating when he claims that by the late fourth century "the multitude of monks in the deserts equals the population of the cities."[246] Palladius also appears to many to be exaggerating when he states that there were in excess of 5000 monks at Nitria and that Pachomius ruled over 3000 in his monasteries.[247] These numbers, moreover, are associated with the Antonian or Pachomian monks, who, primarily because of Athanasius, were strongly or even violently Catholic. The Melitian monks likely would not be included in these records, nor would any others considered schismatic by later authors having Catholic sympathies. Any pretense of accuracy in defining the size of the monastic movement must therefore be considered impossible at present, even though Lietzmann is safe in saying that by the end of the fourth century," there were places in south Egypt in which monasteries dominated the life of the towns."[248]

Anthony was not the first to adopt the eremitic life, although specific monks who preceded him, such as Paul of Thebes,[249] are not easily identified. Athanasius' *Vita Antonii* speaks of the monk's fame reaching all the monks in Egypt, and that many came to emulate his ascetic deeds and way of life.[250] A later contemporary of Anthony, and the spiritual leader of a colony of monks in the desert of Scetis (west of the Delta), Macarius (c.300–390) the Great attracted many to the desert life.[251] Writings of uncertain authorship have been attributed to Macarius, including "sayings, letters, prayers, homilies, and treatises."[252] Another Macarius, designated "the Alexandrian," lived in the famous colony of Kellia[253] from c.335 to c.394, except perhaps some time spent in the Nitrian desert. He was a priest, one of the few monks known to hold clerical office in the eremitic monasticism.[254]

Evagrius of Pontus was a disciple of the two Macarii,[255] living in Nitria and later in Kellia. He was well-known for his writing skills,[256] and perhaps because of that, bishop Theophilus of Alexandria wished to ordain him a bishop. Evagrius had earlier been ordained a deacon in Constantinople, but after embarking on his monastic way of life refused to accept any further ecclesiastical appointment.[257] Others of the eremitic tradition could be mentioned, but these are sufficient to suggest the popularity of this expression of Christianity which was outside the control of ecclesiastical authorities.

To call eremitic monasticism the Antonian system or order is to go beyond the evidence, for the emphasis was on the individuality rather than organization. Palladius describes the monastic existence among the Nitrian monks as follows: "There live excellent men who are adorned with divers kinds of ascetic virtues, and every monk leadeth the ascetic life as he wishes and as he is able, either by himself or in a community."[258] Athanasius emphasized Anthony's obedience to all clerical orders,[259] but the theology of a monk was primarily one "in which Christ serves only as an example and the Bible only as a textbook, and in which church and sacrament were regarded merely as subsidiary aids."[260] Frend notes that there were twenty years of Anthony's career when he could not have partaken of a Eucharist administered by a priest,[261] and Palladius clearly indicates that service in the church was secondary to the sanctity of the solitary life:

τὴν δὲ ἐκκλησίαν σαββάτῳ καταλαμβάνουσι μόνῳ καὶ κυριακῇ. ὀκτὼ δὲ ἀφηγούμενοι πρεσβύτεροι ταύτης τῆς ἐκκλησίας εἰσίν, ἐν ᾗ μέχρις οὗ ζῇ ὁ πρῶτος πρεσβύτερος ἄλλος οὐδεὶς προσφέρει, οὐχ ὁμιλεῖ, οὐ δικάζει, ἀλλ' ἡσύχως αὐτῷ προσκαθέζονται μόνον.[262]

They (the monks) arrive at the church only on the Sabbath and on the Lord's Day. There are eight elders who are leaders of this church, and as long as the first elder is living, no one else either ministers in the church or speaks or sits in judgment, but they only sit at his feet in tranquillity.

Within this "loosely knit community" the monks lived in cells, coming together only for common worship, occasionally to meet and study scriptures, or periodically to visit one another concerning health and personal welfare.[263] There was an order of authority, but the early development of monasticism emphasized the Bible as being a sufficient guide to redemption and sanctity,[264] apart from the Church. It is noteworthy, however, that a popular tradition of monks receiving visions and visitations from heavenly messengers is found throughout monastic literature.[265] In addition to the revelations (continuing in varying degrees an Apocalyptic tradition long since considered past history in Catholicism), the constant warring with the devil and the extreme denial of the flesh are two more examples of the characteristic qualities of their religious sanctity which, for the monks, replaced the more worldly honor and glory associated with episcopacies and other clerical offices. Frend notes this basic difference between the Egyptian ascetic's theological outlook and the Logos-theology of Alexandria, stating that the reconciliation of "the Spirit-inspired hopes of the converted Copt" with "the predominant Logos-theology of the Greek Christian intellectual in Alexandria" was an immense problem.[266] The basically unstructured nature of early monasticism, coupled with a continuing Apocalyptic tradition, well illustrates the following assessment of Egyptian Christianity at the beginning of the fourth century:

> All this shows us that Egyptian Christianity in the second and third centuries was very open and was characterized by a pluriformity of currents within the one Church.[267]

The ability of Athanasius to accomplish such a reconciliation of the seemingly opposite currents mentioned by Frend is one of the major factors leading to the consolidation of the Egyptian Christian churches and movements under the authority of the Alexandrian archbishop.

The other person whose influence on monasticism was eventually to make that institution more serviceable and accessible to the church was himself a monk, St. Pachomius. Pachomius was born of pagan parents in the Thebaid, perhaps in Diospolis Parva of the nome of Esneh.[268] When Pachomius' parents went to the river to sacrifice on one occasion, the divine creatures in the water fled at the sight of the youth with his parents. Because of this miraculous rejection by the Gods of Egypt, Pachomius was protected from paganism so that he might be better prepared to receive Christianity.[269] An Egyptian conscript in the Roman army during Maximinus' campaign against Licinius,[270] Pachomius was incarcerated with his fellow conscripts for a time in a village in the Thebaid, where he was the recipient of Christian charity.[271] Following Licinius' defeat of Maximinus in 313, the draftees were set free from prison and discharged from the army. After his discharge, Pachomius went to the village of Chenoboskion, was baptized, and then entered into the ascetic life as an Antonian Anchorite under his teacher Palamon.[272] A few years afterward, Pachomius received a vision in which he was commanded to go upstream to Tabennesi and there build a monastery.[273] Although none of the monks in the rapidly-growing monastery had any priesthood, a priest from one of the nearby churches was called in on occasion to administer the Eucharist.[274] The Bohairic *Life* states that Pachomius "did not want any clerics in his monasteries, for fear of jealousy and vainglory."[275] The possibility of tying the monastery of Pachomius formally to the ecclesiastical organization was not over-looked by Serapion, bishop of Tentyra, or by Athanasius. When the latter journeyed to the Thebaid, Serapion requested that Pachomius be ordained a priest over the monks, but Pachomius was forewarned of the request and went into hiding to avoid the ordination.[276]

Pachomius' biographer portrays him as a paragon of orthodoxy, but the visions of the monk and his general attitude toward the clergy temper the picture to some extent. The Apocalypticism of Pachomius is well illustrated by the account of his receiving the monastic rule.[277] The angel who gave the rule appeared to the monk sitting in his cell, and the rule itself was written upon a heavenly tablet. Both the angelic appearance and the heavenly record are well-known themes in Apoc-alyptic literature.[278] Pachomius' discourse on temple imagery and symbolism, briefly reported by a monk in Theodore's presence,[279] is similar to temple images and symbols found in Gnostic tractates, such as the *Apocryphon of John*,[280] the *Apocalypse of Peter*,[281] the *Gospel of Philip*,[282] and elsewhere. The tension which monastic Apocalypticism placed between the monks and the church is underscored by Frend: "it (monasticism) was to some extent associated at this time with apocalyptic, and . . . the spiritual claims of the prophet and martyr clashed with those of the bishop and clergy."[283]

The theology of monasticism is not easily reconstructed, and what may be considered orthodox for some would be heretical for others. For example, many monks read and accepted Origen's writings,[284] while others considered his works impious. Although Pachomius did not read Greek and was therefore unable to read Origen's works in their original language, he learned enough from some sources to gain a hatred for the theologian, and is said to have destroyed one of Origen's books when he learned what it was.[285] His position becomes even more significant in view of his friendship with Athanasius, who was an Origenist in much of his theology,[286] even if there are depar-tures in thought from the earlier theologian.[287] Athanasius was able to befriend and hold in balance men of opposite theological persua-sions, for he did not hesitate to place the ascetic teacher, Didymus the Blind, at the head of the Catechetical school in Alexandria,[288] and Didymus was an avowed Origenist. Again one perceives the diplomacy of the great bishop who was able to bring many disparate elements of Egyptian Christianity under one general head, the archbishop of Alexandria. Frend concludes that the strength of the position enjoyed by the patriarchs of Alexandria from Athanasius to Dioscoros was derived in great measure from the alliance between the patriarchate of Alexandria and the monks.[289]

Beyond the typical miracles of healing, speaking in tongues, exorcism, and related prophetic powers ascribed to many monks, Pachomius is most famous for establishing the monastic rule by which the monasteries were governed. The rule stipulates vigorous labor for the able-bodied, a limit of three brothers to a cell, common meals, a regimen for sleeping and studying, and grades for distinguishing the advancement of the monks. Atiya speaks of the Rule as prescribing every detail of a monk's life by day and night,[290] and he is following a position taken also by others who emphasize the strictness of the Rule.[291] Not all agree that the Rule was so strictly observed, for Palladius states that meals were served at irregular times to accommodate monks with delicate health, and Jerome speaks of the voluntary abstinence from the common meals.[292] The Rule even stated in such instances, "Allow them either to eat or to fast."[293] John Cassian stressed the strictness of the Rule,[294] but that may be due to his attempt to establish monasteries in Gaul and also his having to give special attention to the need for discipline and renunciation of worldly goods and values. Even Walters admits that the Rule is tolerant and flexible in some areas, allowing for more or less asceticism, depending on the individual monks.[295]

The strictness of observance of the Pachomian rule is secondary to the significance which the rule had for Egyptian Christianity. Monasticism was transformed from a movement which relied on individual observance of the Biblical faith and living as an anchorite, to a formidable organization with a monastic hierarchy and a tightly governed community of monks.[296] The influence of the rule is reflected in the spectacular growth of monasteries during the fourth century, both in Egypt and elsewhere in the Christian world. Frend conjectures that in the fourth century there were nearly 490 monasteries in Upper Egypt alone.[297] Monasteries were also established for women, with Pachomius' sister appointed to be their leader at first, although a monk was assigned to look after their welfare and visit them and teach them.[298]

Notwithstanding the popularity of the Pachomian monasteries and the Rule which organized the communities and established order in monastic life, the continuation of the system after its founder's death was far from assured.[299] On one occasion when Pachomius was very sick, the monks approached Theodore and asked him to become archimandrite if Pachomius died. Theodore agreed, but the leader recovered and punished the perceived ambition of Theodore by stripping him of power within the monasteries.[300] Whether this episode insinuates an incipient problem of jealousy and ambition concerning leadership or describes a unique situation cannot be determined. Theodore had earlier been given significant leadership responsibilities over monasteries,[301] but as Pachomius lay on his deathbed in May, 346, he selected another monk, Petronius, to succeed him, even though he was also ill.[302]

Petronius survived only two months as archimandrite,[303] and he was succeeded by Horsiesios.[304] One cannot learn from the *Life of Pachomius* when Horsiesios became acquainted with the monastic leader, but Bacht cites evidence in a papyrus codex published by W. Crum which suggests that Horsiesios became a monk in 320.[305] Horsiesios ruled over the monasteries for approximately four years, but a growing revolt of monks who would not accept his leadership led to his resignation in c.350.[306] The Greek account of the revolt states that a major cause of disaffection was the desire of some monks to enjoy a less strict application of the Pachomian Rule (especially with regard to its austere lifestyle). At any rate, Theodore, who had been passed over by Pachomius and Petronius in the selection of a new archimandrite, replaced Horsiesios in that position.[307] Few writings remain which can be attributed to Horsiesios, and they consist of additions to the Rule, letters, a Testament (The *Book of Horsiesios*), and some fragments.[308]

Theodore was able to restore peace and order in the monasteries, and he ruled over them for about 18 years, dying in April, 368.[309] During his tenure, Theodore was visited by Athanasius, apparently often enough that when the archbishop was a fugitive in 360, the Arian search party thought they might find him hiding out with the monks of Tabennesis.[310] Another such flight took place in 363, during the reign of Julian,[311] and the description in the *Life* of the bishop's visit to the monasteries shows deference given by the monks to Athanasius, but not subservience.[312] The bishop even seemed somewhat surprised at the warmth of the reception he received:

καὶ βλέπων τὴν διάθεσιν τῶν ἀδελφῶν γνησίαν σφόδρα εἰς αὐτόν, ἐχάρη δοξάζων τὸν κύριον.[313]

And when he saw the disposition of the brethren to be exceedingly sincere toward him, he rejoiced and gave glory to the Lord.

Athanasius also sent a letter to Horsiesios after Theodore's death, eulogizing the latter and encouraging the former.[314] The tone of the letter is of one Christian brother to another, rather than of a superior to his subordinates, further indicating that the consolidation of the monasteries under the control of the bishop was not complete by the death of Athanasius. One could also wish to know more of the second and successful succession to leadership by Horsiesios after the death of Theodore. Had he mellowed since the rebellion that caused his earlier resignation, or was the method of succession so widely accepted by Theodore's death that competing claimants had no forum? The evidence is not sufficiently clear to help answer such questions.

The continuation of the Pachomian monastic communities was now ensured, and another facet of the earlier unstructured Christian faith in Egypt was organized and became more susceptible to the growing influence of the Alexandrian patriarch. Pachomius' death preceded that of his ecclesiastical counterpart by nearly 30 years, but both great leaders were responsible for the consolidation of monastic and ecclesiastical authority, respectively. Considerable evidence of schismatic movements in both areas can be noticed, but the essential task of providing the organizational framework for a national Egyptian Church was nearly complete.

The emphasis must now shift somewhat toward doctrinal definition and unity. With the organizational structure for an Egyptian Christian Church fairly well established, it was necessary to deal with the diversity of beliefs which could be found throughout Egypt and all of Eastern Christianity. "What constituted 'orthodox Christianity'? This was the question that dominated East Roman politics and theology in the first half of the fifth century and beyond."[315] A major move toward doctrinal limitation and unification was taken by Athanasius, as will be seen in the next chapter. All that remained was for strong and autocratic personalities to arise in both the monastic and ecclesiastical realms of Christianity, and the early undifferentiated Christian religion of Egypt would face a certain demise. The two leaders did arise, in the person of Cyril for the church and of Shenoute for the monks. The final act leading to the establishment of a national church was about to take place.

ENDNOTES

1 Epiphanius, *Panarion* 2.68.3. The account is written nearly a century after the alleged experience in prison, but Epiphanius claims to have been briefed by Egyptian bishops who had been exiled to Palestine by the Emperor Valens. The account is third-hand, then, and its trustworthiness in details is clearly suspect.

2 Athanasius, *Apologia contra Arianos* 59. Socrates, *Hist. Eccl.* I.6, gives the same general charges as Athanasius, who was likely the source for Socrates. The bias of Socrates in this matter is clearly seen by the style with which he "defends" Melitius: Ἀπολογίαν τε οὐδὲ μίαν εὔλογον ἔχων τοῦ κεχωρίσθαι τῆς ἐκκλησίας, ἠδικῆσθαι μὲν ἔλεγεν ἑαυτὸν ἁπλῶς. Ἐκακηγόρει δὲ καὶ ἐλοιδόρει τὸν Πέτρον. Ἀλλὰ Πέτρος μὲν ἐν τῷ διωγμῷ μαρτυρήσας, ἐτελεύτησεν. That seems to be the proof: Peter died as a martyr, so he must have been right.

3 Bell, *Jews and Christians*, *op. cit.*, p. 38f., citing editions of the texts by Maffei and later M.J. Routh (*Reliquiae Sacrae*, ed. altera, iv. 91–4).

4 *Ibid.*, p. 39.

5 Eusebius, *Hist. Eccl.* VII.32.31; IX.6.2.

6 Epiphanius., *Panarion* 2.68.3: καθίστα κληρικοὺς, ἐπισκόπους τε καὶ πρεσβυτέρους, καὶ διακόνους, καὶ ᾠκοδόμει ἐκκλησίας ἰδίας· Baus, *op. cit.*, p.345, states that the real division between Peter and Melitius, was *not* the issue of the *lapsi*, but was caused by Melitius, "who encroached upon the bishop of Alexandria's rights of consecration." This will not be the only occasion when there is a distinction between apparent and real causes.

7 *Ibid.*

8 Bell, *Jews and Christians*, *op. cit.*, p. 39.

9 Epiphanius, *Panarion* 2.68.4. See also 2.69.3f.

10 Athanasius, *Apol. contra Arianos* 59, was inimical to both groups (Arians and Melitians) and would be expected to mention any earlier collusion or agreement between them if such existed. He instead states in this passage that it was while the Melitian schism was raging that the Arian heresy arose. Socrates' account of the rise of the Arian heresy also lacks any reference to Melitius, but states (I.5) that the heresy began simply because of a talk given on the Godhead in response to an earlier talk on the same subject by Achillas.

11 Sozomen, *Hist. Eccl.* I.15.

12 Epistle of Peter of Alexandria to the Church, in M. J. Routh, ed., *Reliquiae Sacrae*. Oxford: Oxford Press, 1815, iii, p.84, ll.306–311.

13 Sozomen, *Hist. Eccl.* I.15.

14 This period of Greek history has much in common with the subject presently being considered. Both are attested by numerous but conflicting sources, and both are often misunderstood in modern reconstructions. For Peisistratus and his sons, see Herodotus I.59–64; V.55–65, 94–95; Thucydides I.20.2 and VI.54–59; Aristotle, *Ath. Polit.* 13–19. For a modern discussion of the issues, see R. Sealey, *A History of the Greek City States, 700–338 B.C.* Berkeley: Univ. of Calif. Press, 1976, pp.123–160. Nothing less than control of the government of Athens was at stake in the age of Peisistratus, and competing factions would change sides both to enhance their own fortunes and to diminish those of others, seemingly quite apart from purely ideological considerations. Similarly, one sees in the Arian controversy of the fourth century many shifting alliances and maneuverings for political advantage which do not reflect ideological consistency.

15 Sozomen, *Hist. Eccl.* I.15.

[16] Socrates, *Hist. Eccl*. I.6.

[17] Sozomen, *Hist. Eccl*. I.15.

[18] Socrates, *Hist. Eccl*. I.6.

[19] Socrates, *Hist. Eccl*. I.5.

[20] Sozomen, *Hist. Eccl*. I.15.

[21] Epiphanius, *Panarion* 2.68.4. The role of Melitius is not clear. T. Barnes, *Constantine and Eusebius* (Cambridge: Harvard Univ. Press, 1981), p.204, suggests a doubting attitude: "Several clerics (among whom, it was later alleged, Melitius took a leading role) objected to Arius' teaching and complained to the bishop." The words "later alleged" leave the reader to choose whatever he wishes in the matter.

[22] Sozomen, *Hist. Eccl*. I.15.

[23] *Ibid*.

[24] Kelly, *op, cit*., pp. 224-230.

[25] Socrates, *Hist. Eccl*. I.9; Sozomen I.24; Athanasius, *Apol. contra Arianos* 59.

[26] Baus, *op. cit*., p. 345.

[27] Theodoret, *Hist. Eccles*., I.8.

[28] Eusebius, *Hist. Eccl*. VII.7.4.

[29] Chadwick, *op. cit*., p. 124.

[30] Athanasius, *Apol. contra Arianos* 59, refuses to discuss the reasons for accepting them back, as if he were not certain they were valid.

[31] W.H.C. Frend, *The Early Church* (Philadelphia: J.B. Lippincott, 1966), p. 136.

[32] *Ibid*.

[33] H. Lietzmann, *A History of the Early Church* (London: Butterworth Press, 1951, p. 152.

[34] Frend, *Martyrdom*, *op. cit*., p. 397. Cp. Hardy, *op. cit*., pp. 52–53, and Bell, *Jews and Christians*, pp. 38ff.

[35] W.H.C. Frend, *The rise of the Monophysite Movement* (Cambridge: Cambridge U. Press, 1972), pp. 81f.

[36] *Ibid*., p. 82.

[37] Bell, *Jews and Christians*, *op. cit*., p. 40.

[38] Sozomen, *Hist. Eccl*. II.21.

[39] *Ibid*., II.22.

[40] *Ibid*.

[41] Charges abound against Athanasius in the historical sources of the period. While many were fabrications, enough are believed true that Barner can say: "In Alexandria itself, he maintained the popular support which he enjoyed from the outset and buttressed his position by organizing an ecclesiastical mafia. In later years, if he so desired, he could instigate a riot or prevent the orderly administration of the city. Athanasius possessed a power independent of the emperor which he built up and perpetuated by violence. That was both the strength and the weakness of his position. Like a modern gangster, he evoked widespread mistrust, proclaimed total innocence— and usually succeeded in evading conviction on specific charges" (*Constantine and Eusebius, op. cit*., p.230).

[42] *P. Lond. 1914*, ll.6ff. (Bell, *Jews and Christians, op. cit*., pp.58ff.).

[43] Athanasius, *Apol. contra Arianos* 59.

[44] *Epistolae Festales Domini Sancti Athanasii cum Chronico Praerio* (*Patr. Gr*. 26.1351): "capto initio anno XLIV arae Diocletiani, quo anno Paschatis festum erat die XVI Pharmuthi . . . Cum enim vita excessisset praecessor eius Alexander die XXII Pharmuthi, successit ei (Athanasius) post Pascha, die XIV Pauni . . ." For a chart converting Egyptian calendar dates to Julian calendar dates, see Finegan, *Handbook of Biblical Chronology* (Princeton: Princeton Univ. Press, 1964), p. 29.

⁴⁵ Epiphanius, *Panarion* 2.68: Ἀλέξανδρος ὁ ἐν Ἀλεξανδρείᾳ μετὰ τὴν τελευτὴν Μελητίου τοῦ προειρημένου ὁμολογητοῦ, ζῆλον ἀνειληφὼς κατὰ τοῦ σχίσματος τῆς Ἐκκλησίας, πάντη τοὺς ἰδίᾳ συνάγοντας, ὑπὸ δὲ Μελητίου καταλειφθέντας, ἐδόκει ταράσσειν τε καὶ σνέχειν, βιάζεσθαί τε, ὅπως μὴ ἀφηνιάσωσι τῆς μιᾶς Ἐκκλησίας.

⁴⁶ Athanasius, *Apol. contra Arianos* 71–72.

⁴⁷ Sozomen, *Hist. Eccl.* II.17.

⁴⁸ Philostorgius, *Hist. Eccl.*, II.11.

⁴⁹ Athanasius, *Apol. contra Arianos* 6. Athanasius also quotes the story of the secret ordination being circulated by his Arian detractors, showing that Philostorgius did have and use some sources well from the period.

⁵⁰ Philostorgius, *Hist. Eccl.* II.11.

⁵¹ Eusebius, *Vita Constant.* III 23.

⁵² Bell, *Jews and Christians*, *op. cit.*, p. 40. Sozomen, *Hist. Eccl.* II.21, states that after the Council of Nicaea, Melitius appointed one John as his successor, contrary to the decree of the synod. This could have been the cause of the second council, as could have been Sozomen's further observation that both joined in harassing the churches under Catholic rule.

⁵³ *Ibid.*, p. 41. Frend, *Early Church*, *op. cit.*, p. 159, states that the Melitians also "were irked, as they seem to have been led to believe that they would share in the election of Alexander's successor."

⁵⁴ Barnes, *op. cit.*, p.231

⁵⁵ Epiphanius, *Panarion*. 2.68: ὁ δὲ, μετὰ τὸ ὑποσχέσθαι αὐτοὺς ἀνοίσειν τῷ βασιλεῖ, καὶ ποιῆσαι αὐτοῖς τὸ πρᾶγμα τῆς δεήσεως, αἰτεῖται παρ' αὐτῶν τὸ αἴτημα τοῦτο, ὅπως δέξωνται Ἄρειον μετ' αὐτῶν εἰς κοινωνίαν... οἱ δὲ ὑπισχνοῦνται αὐτόν.

⁵⁶ Sozomen, *Hist. Eccl.* II.21.

⁵⁷ *Ibid.*: ὡς προϊόντος τοῦ χρόνου, Μελιτιανοὺς ἐν Αἰγύπτῳ παρὰ τῶν πολλῶν ὀνομάζεσθαι τοὺς τὰ Ἀρείου φρονοῦντας.

⁵⁸ Bell, *Jews and Christians*, *op. cit.*, p. 41.

⁵⁹ *Ibid.*, citing Gwatkin, *Studies of Arianism* (Cambridge: Cambridge Univ. Press, 1900), p. 71.

⁶⁰ Theodoret, *Hist. Eccl.* I.8.14: οὔτε τοῖς ὑγιαίνουσι πειθόμενα δόγμασι καὶ κατὰ τὴν πολιτείαν κενοῖς τισὶν ἐπιτηδεύμασι κεχρημένα, τῇ Σαμαρειτῶν καὶ Ἰουδαίων φρενοβλαβείᾳ συμβαίνοντα. Socrates, *Hist. Eccl.* I.9, also knows of Melitians who are alive in his day: ἄχρι νῦν κεχωρίσθαι τῆς ἐκκλησίας τοὺς ἐν Αἰγύπτῳ Μελιτιανούς.

⁶¹ These papyri constitute the major sources for Bell's chapter on the Melitian schism in his *Jews and Christians*, *op. cit.* While he correctly identifies the Melitian problem as non-doctrinal at first, Bell nowhere makes the connection between Melitius and the local Christian movements as distinct from Alexandrian, or Catholic, Christianity. The closest he comes to such an identification is when he notes the link between Melitians and Arians after 328, and then he says the connection is simply due to a common hatred for Athanasius.

⁶² P. 1920, verso: ⲁⲡ' ⲡⲁⲓ̈ⲏⲩ ⲍⲟⲙⲟⲗⲟⲅ'(ornament) ⲡⲁⲣⲁ' ⲁ[ⲧⲣⲏⲧⲟⲥ]

⁶³ In P. 1920, Hatre sends greetings to the brethren with Paieous, and the monastic industries of shoe-making and cloak-making are mentioned in the text. P. 1921 contains a number of greetings to some monks and also makes reference to the sending of provisions from the monastery to unknown recipients.

⁶⁴ Bell, *Jews and Christians*, *op. cit.*, p.43.

⁶⁵ P. 1920, ll. 1–2.: . . . ⲉⲓⲱⲧ ⲡⲁⲉⲓⲏⲩ ⲛ̅ⲡ2ⲁⲧ2ⲱⲣ

⁶⁶ P. 1913, l.3.

⁶⁷ P. 1917, l.9: "When we were in the island of Memphis with the Holy brethren . . ." Ll. 17–18: ἔγραψα . . . εἰς τὰ ἄνω μαίρη πρὸς Μικαλώνην . . . Bell (p.44) is surely right to

understand "the upper regions" as the Thebaid, or perhaps the region near Pboou where a monk was expelled a century later and moved to found a monastery near a Melitian stronghold. See below, note 91.

[68] P. 1915, verso near bottom of page.

[69] P. 1920, P. 1921, and P. 1922.

[70] Bell, *Jews and Christians*, *op. cit.*, p. 44.

[71] *Ibid.*, p. 45. Paphnutius is common to both, but the more rare name of Paieous is not found in the Rylands letters.

[72] Sozomen, *Hist. Eccl.* II.22.

[73] *Ibid.*, II.25.

[74] *Ibid.* Theodoret, *Hist. Eccl.* I.26, also makes reference to the synod of Caesarea: πείθουσι δὴ οὖν τὸν βασιλέα σύνοδον ἐν Καισαρείᾳ τῆς Παλαιστίνης ἀθροῖσαι, ἔνθα δὴ πλείους ἦσαν οἱ δυσμενεῖς, κἀκεῖσε κριθῆναι κελεῦσαι τὸν Ἀθανάσιον. Cf. also the *Index to the Festal Letters of Athanasius*, *Patrol. Graecae XXVI*. 1352–3: quo tempore vocatus fuit Caesarem Palaestinae ad synodum, ubi eius inimici fraudulentas machinas struebant . . ."

[75] Sozomen, *Hist. Eccl.* II. 23. The Melitians hid Arsenius and then claimed that Athanasius had killed him. Although the populace readily received and believed the rumor and passed it along to the emperor, Athanasius was able to track down the non-corpse and destroy the charge. The strangest part of this story is that the same charge over the same person was later raised again by the Arians and the Melitians (Sozomen, *H.E.* II.25).

[76] Frend, *Early church*, *op. cit.*, p. 160: "there was substance in all these charges, and together they add up to a picture of tyranny and lack of charity."

[77] Bell, *Jews and Christians*, *op. cit.*, p. 48. The incipit of the letter contains the date: Ὑπατίας Φλαυίου Ὀπτάτου πατρικίου καὶ Ἀνικίου Παυλίνου τῶν λαμπροτάτων Φαμενὼθ κγ.

[78] P. 1913, ll.4–7, Bell's translation.

[79] *Ibid.*, ll.7–8.

[80] *Ibid.*, ll.9–13.

[81] Bell, *Jews and Christians*, *op. cit.*, p. 53.

[82] *Ibid.*, p. 54, 56. The dating depends on the proposed journey of Athanasius to answer the summons of the emperor, and also knowing the frame of mind of Athanasius at any given time, since he is described as "despondent" in the letter. Although tenuous, Bell's dates have not been revised by subsequent commentators.

[83] P. 1914, ll.7–8.

[84] *Ibid.*, ll.8–15.

[85] *Ibid.*, ll.15–21. The threatening attitude is seen in the statement, κατὰ ποίαν ἐτίαν τοὺς μοναχοὺς τῶν Μελιτιανῶν ἤασας ἐν τῇ μονῇ; Heraiscus, the bishop with whom Isaac was having dinner, is called πάπα in 1.25. but because he is unknown in other sources, one cannot tell whether he was really a bishop or a priest. The term can be used for the latter office, as is seen from P.Lond. ii, 417,3. That Heraiscus was a bishop is inferred from 11.42ff., where Callistus states that Athanasius locked up a bishop from Lower Egypt.

[86] *Ibid.*, ll.29ff.

[87] *Ibid.*, ll.39ff.

[88] *Ibid.*, ll.32–38,41ff.

[89] *Ibid.*, ll.47–48.

[90] Athanasius, *Apol. contra Arianos* 60–85. Athanasius spends so much time defending himself against the obviously sham charges relating to the incident of the broken chalice and the murder of Arsenius which never took place, and so little on the other

charges of violence and persecution mentioned in Sozomen, *Hist. Eccl.* I.26; II.6, elsewhere, that one cannot help seeing his defense to be a smokescreen hiding real crimes.

⁹¹ K.H. Kuhn, ed. *A Panegyric on Apollo: Corpus Scriptorum Christianorum Orientalium*, vol. 394. Louvain, 1978, pp.xiiif.

⁹² *Ibid.*, section 10 of the text, and p.xiv for the conjecture of the site's proximity to Heracleopolis Magna.

⁹³ *Ibid.*, section 11. The translation given here is that of Kuhn, editor of the text.

⁹⁴ B. Evetts, transl. and ed. *History of the Patriarchs of the Coptic Church of Alexandria (II)*. *Patrologia Orientalis* I, p.473.

⁹⁵ *Ibid.*, pp.473–4.

⁹⁶ Eutychius, *Annales* 332.

⁹⁷ Athanasius, *Apol. contra Arianos* 59: Εὐσέβιος τοίνυν, τοῦτο μαθὼν καὶ προϊστάμενος τῆς ᾽Αρειανῆς αἱρέσεως, πέμπει καὶ ὠνεῖται τοὺς Μελιτιανοὺς ἐπὶ πολλοῖς ἐπαγγελίαις· καὶ γίνεται μὲν αὐτῶν κρύφα φίλος, συντάττεται δὲ αὐτοῖς εἰς ὃν ἐβούλετο καιρόν.

⁹⁸ Translation by Henry R. Percival in *The Seven Ecumenical Councils*, NPNF 14 (Grand Rapids: Eerdmans Pub. Co., 1971, reprint), p. 15.

⁹⁹ *Ibid.*

¹⁰⁰ B. J. Kidd, *A History of the Church to A.D. 461* (Oxford: Clarendon Press, 1922), Vol. II, p. 46.

¹⁰¹ Frend, *The Monophysite Movement*, *op. cit.*, p. 20, n. 3. Cf. Athanasius, *Ep. ad Afros* 2 (*Patrol. Graec.* 26.1032).

¹⁰² Canon IV (trans. by Percival in *NPNF* 14, p. 11).

¹⁰³ Telfer, "Episcopal Succession in Egypt," *Journ. of Eccles. Hist.* 3 (1952), p.11.

¹⁰⁴ Liberatus, *Breviarium*, *Patrol. Lat.* 68:1036: Consuetudo quidem est Alexandriae illum qui defuncto succedit excubias super defuncti corpus agere, manumque dextram eius capiti suo imponere, et sepulto manibus suis, accipere collo suo beati Marci pallium, et tunc legitime sedere.

¹⁰⁵ Epiphanius, *Panarion* 69.11.

¹⁰⁶ JND Kelly, *Early Christian Doctrines*, *op. cit.*, pp.224-225.

¹⁰⁷ *Ibid.*, p.225.

¹⁰⁸ *Ibid.*, p.226, quoting Eusebius, *Demonst. Evang.* 5.1.20.

¹⁰⁹ The letter is quoted in Socrates, *Hist. Eccl.* 1.8.

¹¹⁰ Frend, *Monophysite Movement*, *op. cit.*, p.110.

¹¹¹ S.L. Greenslade, *Church and State from Constantine to Theodosius*. Wesport: Greenwood Press, 1981 (Reprint of 1954 ed.), p.10.

¹¹² Barnes, *op. cit.*, p.233.

¹¹³ *Ibid.*, p.264.

¹¹⁴ *Ibid.*, p.249.

¹¹⁵ *Ibid.*, p.225.

¹¹⁶ Frend, *Early Church*, *op. cit.*, p. 152.

¹¹⁷ Socrates, *Hist. Eccl.* I.23.

¹¹⁸ Cross, *op. cit.*, p. 464.

¹¹⁹ Philostorgius, *Hist. Eccl.*, ed. by F. Winkelmann. Berlin, Akademie Verlag (*GCS*), 1981.

¹²⁰ Frank Williams, ed. and transl. *The Panarion of Epiphanius of Salamis, Book I*. (Nag Hammadi Studies 35). Leiden: E.J. Brill, 1987. For an overview of Epiphanius' life, see intro., pp.xi-xvi.

¹²¹ *Ibid.*, p.xiv.

¹²² For treatments of the theological issues relating to Arianism, see J.N.D. Kelly, *Early Christian Doctrines*, *op. cit.*; H.M. Gwatkin, *Studies of Arianism*. Cambridge:

Deighton Bell and Co., 1900; Gwatkin, *The Arian Controversy*. London: Longman's, Green and Co., 1891. Gwatkin is not disinterested in his works, for he says of them: "On one side their doctrine was a mass of presumptuous theorizing, supported by alternate scraps of obsolete traditionalism and uncritical text-mongering, on the other it was a lifeless system of unspiritual pride and hard unlovingness. And therefore Arianism perished," (*Studies*, p.274).

A recent attempt to reclaim Arius from such a typical denunciation was made by Robert C. Gregg and Dennis E. Groh, *Early Arianism: A View of Salvation* (Philadelphia: Fortress Press, 1981). These authors claim that early Arianism was primarily a soteriological movement rather than an attempt to redefine the Godhead. In such a major issue as Arianism, it is not possible to consider the immense amount of scholarship which has been devoted to it.

[123] Epiphanius, *Panarion*, 2.69; Socrates, *Hist. Eccl.*, I.5.

[124] Theodoret, *Hist. Eccl.*, I.4; Epiphanius, *Panarion* II.69.6.

[125] Epiphanius, *Panarion*, 2.69; Sozomen, *Hist. Eccl.* I.15.

[126] Sozomen, *Hist. Eccl.* I.15.

[127] *Ibid*. Cp. Socrates, *Hist. Eccl.*, I.5. Sozomen states that in the meantime Arius had been excommunicated by Peter, readmitted and ordained to the presbyterate by Achillas, and was held in high repute by Alexander because of his considerable abilities in philosophy.

[128] *Ibid*.

[129] Socrates, *Hist. Eccl.* I.6.

[130] W. Telfer, "When did the Arian Controversy begin," *JThS*. 47 (1946), pp. 129–142, says that the Arian controversy began in 323, while Norman Baynes, "Sozomen Ecclesiastica Historia, I.15," *JThs*. 49 (1948), pp. 165–168, generally opts for the earlier date of 318, agreeing with Opitz and others. The question of basic influences on early Arianism is a common problem, with commentators (e.g. Pollard, Kidd, Green, and Bardy) divided over Paul of Samosata and Origen as the greatest sources of influence. Theodoret, *Hist. Eccl.* I.1., states that the envy Arius had for Alexander was the primary force behind the difficulty, and that Arius went from house to house to gain supporters for his cause. See Kidd, *op. cit.*, Vol.II, p. 50: "But the struggle, as at first renewed, centered upon persons . . ."

[131] Socrates, *Hist. Eccl.*, I.6; Cp. Sozomen, *Hist. Eccl.* I.16: Ἐπεὶ δὲ καὶ ἐν Αἰγύπτῳ συνόδων περὶ τούτου πολλῶν γενομένων . . .

[132] Sozomen, *Hist. Eccl.* I.15; Theodoret, *Hist. Eccl.* I.4–5.

[133] Socrates, *Hist. Eccl.* I.7; Sozomen, *Hist. Eccl.* I.16. In both sources it is quite clear that Constantine's primary concern is for peace and unity, rather than for either side of the doctrinal dispute. While his emphasis on peace has led many to conclude that Constantine did not understand the subtleties of the theological issues under consideration, Barnes (*Constantine and Eusebius*, p.213) takes a different view: "Constantine has sometimes been accused of failing to appreciate what was at stake in the controversy, or of an inability to detect manifest heresy. The charge is unjust and anachronistic."

[134] *Ibid*., I.8.

[135] E. Honigmann, "The Original Lists of the Members of the Council of Nicaea, the Robber-Synod and the Council of Chalcedon," *Byzantion* 16 (1942), pp. 20–80. The traditional number of 318 bishops comes from Athanasius, *Ep. ad Afros* 2, and is perhaps based on the number of servants which Abraham had (Genesis 14:14).

[136] Chadwick, *op. cit.*, p. 130.

[137] Kelly, *op. cit.*, p. 281. J. G. Davies, *The Early Christian Church* (New York: Holt, Rinehart, and Winston, 1965), pp. 194f., notes that Athanasius never categorically denied the existence of a human soul in Christ, as did Apollinaris.

[138] *Ibid.*, pp. 284f.

[139] *Ibid.*, p. 282.

[140] *Ibid.*, p. 281.

[141] Gwatkin, *op. cit.*, p. 54.

[142] Frend, *Early Church*, *op. cit.*, p. 153.

[143] Chadwick, *Early Church*, *op. cit.*, p. 130.

[144] T. Barnes, *op. cit.*, p.230.

[145] Frend, *The Rise of Christianity*, *op. cit.*, p.524.

[146] Gregory Nazianzen, *In Laudem Athanasii*, Orat. 21.6.

[147] Sozomen, *Hist. Eccl.* II.17.

[148] Athanasius, *Apol. contra Arianos* 9.

[149] *Ibid.*, 6.

[150] Frend, *The Monophysite Movement*, *op. cit.*, p. 82.

[151] Charles Kannengiesser, *Athanase d'Alexandrie*, *Évêque et Écrivain*. Paris: Beauchesne Éditeur, 1983. In this work on Athanasius' *Discourses Against the Arians*, Kannengiesser believes he can demonstrate that Athanasius wrote only *Contra Arianos* 1–2, and not 3. He bases his conclusions on a structural and stylistic analysis of the work, including the overall theme of the theology of the Son. On the basis of his analysis, Kannengiesser also believes he can date the writing, and also the development of the Arian heresy in Egypt.

[152] Charles Kannengiesser, *Holy Scripture and Hellenistic Hermeneutics in Alexandrian Christology: The Arian Crisis*. Berkeley: The Center for Hermeneutical Studies, Colloquy 41, 1981, p.14 n.55.

[153] Jones, *op. cit.*, I, p. 77.

[154] Quasten, *op. cit.*, III, pp.52–53.

[155] *Ibid.*, pp. 55f.

[156] Athanasius, *Ep. ad Monachos* II, translation by Robertson.

[157] Frend, *The Monophysite Movement*, *op. cit.*, p. 82.

[158] Jones, *loc. cit.*

[159] N. H. Baynes, "Athanasiana," *JEA* 11 (1925), pp. 64–65.

[160] Jones, *loc. cit.*

[161] Athanasius, *Ep. Festalis*, I (*Patrol. Graecae* XXVI, 1360ff.)

[162] R. W. Thomson, *Athanasius*, *Contra Gentes and De Incarnatione* (Oxford: Clarendon Press, 1971), p. xiii. Cp. Amélineau, *Histoire de St. Pakhôme* etc. (Paris: Musée Guimet, Annales 17, 1889), pp. 39f. A. Athanassakis, ed. *The Life of Pachomius* (Missoula: Scholars Press, 1975), 30.

[163] Athanasius, *Ep. Festalis* II.6. The heretics mentioned in this letter are described as those who make use of the scriptures, but not in the traditional (i.e. Catholic) understanding. No specific examples are cited of those who "observe the traditions of men" rather than those of the bishop.

[164] *Ibid.*, III.5.

[165] Thomson, *op. cit.*, p. xiii. Arius had signed a declaration of faith which did not contain the term *homoousios*. Socrates, *Hist. Eccl.* I.23, 25–27. Socrates portrays Eusebius as the moving force behind the recall, and he relates how Arius and Euzoius went to Constantinople, presented an acceptable creed before the emperor, and received permission to return to Alexandria.

[166] Socrates, *Hist. Eccl.* I.27.

[167] Athanasius, *Apol. contra Arianos* 59.

[168] Thomson, *op. cit.*, p. xiv.

[169] Eusebius, *Vita Constantinii* IV.40.

[170] Frend, *Rise of Christianity, op. cit.*, pp.526–527; Greenslade, *op. cit.*, p.19; for ancient accounts of the Council of Tyre, see Socrates, *Hist. Eccl.* I.29–32; Sozomen, *Hist. Eccl.* II.25; Theodoret, *Hist. Eccl.* I.26–28; Athanasius, *Apol. Contra Arianos* 26–27,31,71–90. The Athanasian passage (71–90) contains documents gathered by the bishop which are meant to support his defense.

[171] Greenslade, *op. cit.*, p.19.

[172] *Ibid.*, IV.41.

[173] Epiphanius, *Panarion* 68, says that Potammon, an Egyptian Bishop, attacked the president of the Council. Sozomen, *Hist. Eccl.* II.25, also describes the Council as being "filled with tumult and confusion" during the later sessions. Athanasius himself may have been the source for later descriptions of the atmosphere of the Council. See *Apol. contra Arianos* 86, where the bishop had obviously told Constantine how riotous the meetings were.

[174] Rufinus, *Hist. Eccl.* I.17.

[175] Socrates, *Hist. Eccl.* I.31.

[176] *Ibid.*, I.32.

[177] *Ibid.*, Sozomen, *Hist. Eccl.* II.25.

[178] Athanasius, *Apol. contra Arianos* 86.

[179] Chadwick, *op. cit.*, p. 135.

[180] Thomson, *loc. cit.*

[181] Athanasius, *Apol. contra Arianos* 87–88.

[182] Thomson, *loc. cit.*

[183] *Ibid.*

[184] Athanasius, *Apol. contra Arianos* 87.

[185] Athanasius, *Apol. ad Const.* 5.

[186] Athanasius, *Apol. contra Arianos* 7–8.

[187] Athanasius, *Apol. ad Const.* 4.

[188] Socrates, *Hist. Eccl.* IV.23. Kidd, *op. cit.*, II.74, mistakenly identifies this Ammonius with one of the later Tall Brothers of the same name, and the Isidore is otherwise unknown. Jerome, *Ep.* 127.5, implies that others associated with monasticism may have accompanied Athanasius, inasmuch as the bishop's associates are there said to have taught in Rome the virtues and life of Anthony the monk.

[189] Frend, *Early Church, op. cit.*, 162. Cp. J. Stevenson, *Creeds, Councils, and Controversies* (London: SPCK Press, 1966), p. 185, quoting Jerome, *Ep.* 127.

[190] Jerome, *Ep.* 127.5.

[191] Frend, *Early Church, op. cit.*, p. 163, chooses the earlier date, and Thomson, *op. cit.*, p.xv, selects the more traditional later date. The significance, obviously, is the issue at stake, and not the six months difference in chronology. See Athanasius, *Apol. contra Arianos* 20, 45–46. The arguments were based primarily on the evidence from the earlier Council of Tyre.

[192] Athanasius, *Apol. contra Arianos* 20–35. An account of the Council at Rome and the letter of Julius are included in this material. The letter is simply one piece of a continuing (and acrimonious) correspondence between Julius and his eastern counterparts.

[193] *Ibid.*, 29–30. See also Frend, *The Rise of Christianity, op. cit.*, pp.528–529.

[194] *Ibid.*, 35.

[195] Frend, *The Rise of Christianity, op. cit.*, p.529.

[196] *Ibid.*, p.530. Frend includes in a note part of a quote from Hilary of Poitiers, *Fragmenta historica* 4.1.12: "Novam legem introducere putaverunt, ut Orientales episcopi ab Occidentalibus iudicarentur." For the Creed of the Council, see Athanasius, *De Synodis* 22ff; Socrates, *Hist. Eccl.*, 2.10.4–8; and a translation in J. Stevenson, ed. *Creeds, Councils, and Controversies*. London: SPCK Press, 1966, pp.11–15.

[197] *Ibid*.

[198] *Ibid*.

[199] Thomson, *loc. cit*.

[200] *Ibid*.

[201] Athanasius, *Apol. contra Arianos* 51.

[202] Athanasius, *Apol. ad Const*. 3.

[203] Socrates, *Hist. Eccl*. II.22.

[204] Thomson, *op. cit*., p.xvi.

[205] Robertson, *op. cit*., p.xlviii.

[206] Athanasius, *Apol. ad Constant*. 24–26; *Apol. de Fuga* 24–25.

[207] Lietzmann, *op. cit*., III, p.217.

[208] Chadwick, *Early Church*, *op. cit*., p. 141.

[209] Thomson, *loc. cit*. Frend, *Rise of Christianity*, *op. cit*., p.595, describes George in an understated way: ". . . a man of humble background and tactless manner . . . an Origenist cleric whose richly endowed library contained both Christian works and Neo-Platonist commentaries on Plato and Aristotle."

[210] Ammianus Marcellinus 22.11.4.

[211] Thomson, *loc. cit*.

[212] Frances M. Young, *From Nicaea to Chalcedon, A Guide to the Literature and its Background*. Philadelphia: Fortress Press, 1983, p.65.

[213] *Ibid*., p.64.

[214] *Ibid*., p.62.

[215] Lietzmann, *op. cit*., III, p.222. Some have argued that these works were written before the outbreak of Arianism, but Young (*op. cit*., pp.68–69) gives telling reasons why they must have been written during the bishop's exile to Trier (335–337).

[216] *Ibid*.

[217] Thomson, *op. cit*., p.xx.

[218] Socrates, *Hist. Eccl*. IV.20; Theodoret, *Hist. Eccl*. IV.17.

[219] Frend, *The Monophysite Movement*, *op. cit*., pp. 138–139.

[220] *Ibid*., p.139.

[221] Athanasius, *Ep. ad Amun*, *Patr. Graec*. 26.1173.

[222] *Ibid*.

[223] Athanasius, *Ad Dracontium*, *Patr. Graec*. 25.528.

[224] *Ibid*.

[225] *Ibid*., 25.532.

[226] *Ibid*., 25.525.

[227] *Ibid*., 25.528.

[228] Frend, *Martyrdom*, *op. cit*., p. 348, writes of the monastic movement as "not anti-hierarchical, however; it was non-hierarchical involving complete rejection of the world and its institutions, including Christian institutions."

[229] Hardy, *op. cit*., pp. 75–76.

[230] Tenacity is not an untainted virtue in this instance, for F. Young (*op. cit*., pp.67–68) cites a study of Leroux ("Athanase et la seconde phase de la crise arienne, 345–373," *Politique et Theologie*, pp.145–156) in which the conclusion is reached that "Athanasius is out of touch: he went on fighting the old battle against Arius when everyone else was struggling with the much subtler issues raised by Aetius and Eunomius; he had no idea of the real situation in Antioch, Basil only appealed to him because he had influence in the West, and the *Tomus ad Antiochenos* was addressed only to the quarrelsome ultra-Nicenes. Thus, in Egypt alone did Athanasius have the ascendancy attributed to him, and even here he had had to defend himself; his apologetic works were a means of justifying his dubious career to his own flock and

were not widely disseminated elsewhere. Ecclesiastical politics in the East mostly passed him by." The judgment is probably too harsh, but it does temper the equally exaggerated adulation Athanasius often received in orthodox circles. The picture painted by Young (cited earlier re. Arius and here citing Leroux) is of a die-hard biblical conservative (Arius) struggling against a doctrinaire, ignorant, and ambitious bishop. The fire generated by two such embers would emit more heat than light.

[231] Athanasius, *Ep. Festalis* 39.1 (transl. by Newman in *NPNF* 4, *op. cit.*, p. 551). This portion of the letter is also found in the Bohairic Life of St. Theodore (Amelineau, *op. cit.*, p. 239), indicating the likelihood that many of the monks still had a much broader literary tradition than did the ecclesiastical church. This letter would have been sent to curtail that tradition, according to this view.

[232] *Ibid.*, 39.2. the reference to those who are simple and pure would appear to refer to monks, although that may be disputed. In any case, books such as those recently discovered in the Nag Hammadi Library would easily fit the category of the apocryphal books with "the similarity of their names with the true books." The *Apocalypse of Peter*, *Acts of Peter and the Twelve Apostles*, and the *Gospel of Thomas* are examples of such writings.

[233] See Jerome, *Preface to the Rule of Pachomius*.

[234] Armand Veilleux, *Pachomian Koinonia I: The Life of Saint Pachomius and His Disciples*. Kalamazoo: Cistercian Publications, 1980, pp.2–3.

[235] *Ibid.*, pp.1–18. See Heinrich Bacht, *Das Vermächtnis des Ursprungs II: Pachomius—Der Mann und sein Werk*. Würzburg: Echter Verlag, 1983, pp.10–11, 42–47. For editions and translations of these works, see Veilleux, pp.478ff., and Bacht, pp.297f. The Greek version of the life was edited by Apostolos Athanassakis, *The Life of Pachomius*. Missoula: Scholars Press, 1975.

[236] A. Veilleux, *Pachomian Koinonia II: Pachomian Chronicles and Rules*. Kalamazoo: Cistercian Publications, 1981, and *III: Instructions, Letters, and Other Writings of Saint Pachomius and His Disciples*, 1982. See also Johannes Quasten, *Patrology III*. Utrecht: Spectrum, 1960, pp.155ff; esp. 156: "This first rule had an extraordinary influence on all subsequent monastic legislation."

[237] *Ibid.*, III, pp.91–224, and Bacht, *Das Vermächtnis des Ursprungs I: Studien zum frühen Mönchtum*. Würzburg: Echter Verlag, 1972 (1984).

[238] F. Young, *op. cit.*, pp.38–39. See also A. Festugière, ed., *Historia Monachorum in Egypto*. *Subsidia Hagiographica* 34. Brussels, 1961.

[239] Palladius was bishop of Helenopolis (in Bithynia) after a life with the monks of Egypt, and he dedicated his history of the monks to Lausus, chamberlain in the court of Theodosius II. For a general introduction to the work, accompanied by an edition of the Greek text, see Dom Cuthbert Butler, *The Lausiac History of Palladius*, I and II (*Texts and Studies* 6). Cambridge: Cambridge University Press, 1898 and 1904. Volume 1 contains a lengthy discussion of opinions held by various authors concerning the recensions and versions of the text, including arguments about which is the original. Historical criticism is also attempted, being in large measure a rebuttal to Weingarten's negative evaluation. Volume 2 contains a Greek text, still considered the best, with notes. Butler showed that this work was joined with the *Historia Monachorum in Egypto* sometime soon after 400.

[240] Young, *op. cit.*, p.39.

[241] *Ibid.*, p.40.

[242] *Ibid.*, p.41.

[243] Johannes Quasten, *Patrology IV*. Westminster, Maryland: Christian Classics, 1986, p.237.

[244] A Veilleux, *Pachomian Koinonia II, op. cit.*, pp.141f.

[245] A translation from the Latin was made by Helen Waddell, *The Desert Fathers*. Ann Arbor: Univ. of Michigan Press, 1957. E.A.W. Budge translated from the Syriac, *The Book of Paradise II*. London: W. Drugulin, printer, 1907.

[246] Rufinus, *Hist. Monachorum* 5.

[247] Palladius, *Hist. Lausiaca* 7,32. Others generally considered guilty of exaggeration include Jerome, who states that there were 50,000 monks (Pref. to *Reg. Pachom.*) and in the *Vitae Patrum* (P.L. 73, p.433), a statement is made that the monastery of Macarius contained 15,000 monks.

[248] Lietzmann, *op. cit.*, IV, p. 148.

[249] The sole source for his life is Jerome's *Vita Pauli*, where he is said to have originated in the Thebaid. The story continues that he fled to the desert in the Decian persecutions and lived the life of a hermit for some 100 years. Much of this account is questionable, though there is little reason to doubt the reality of his life.

[250] Budge, trans. of the Syriac text in *The Book of Paradise of Palladius*. London: W. Drugulin printer, 1904, Vol. 1, p.26. The Greek text is not so specific in 14 about all who came to Anthony being monks, but the inference is the same, and is supported by 16 and 54.

[251] Rufinus, *Hist. Monach.* 28; Palladius, *Hist. Lausiaca* 17; *Apophthegmata Patrum*, passim.

[252] Johannes Quasten, *Patrology III*, *op. cit.*, pp.162ff.

[253] C.C. Walters, *Monastic Archaeology in Egypt*. Warminster: Aris and Phillips, 1974, pp.7–12, passim. For the excavation report and illustrations, see F. Daumas et A. Guillaumont et al., *Kellia I, Kom 219*. Cairo: l'Institut Francais d'Archéologie orientale du Caire. Vol. 28, 1969.

[254] Palladius, *Hist. Lausiaca* 18.

[255] Socrates, *Hist. Eccl.* 4.23.

[256] Palladius, *Hist. Lausiaca* 38.

[257] Socrates, *Hist. Eccl.* 4.23.

[258] Palladius, *Hist. Lausiaca* 7.

[259] Athanasius, *Vita Antonii* 67. Each order is mentioned in this passage, including the deacon to whom Anthony showed deference in prayer and teaching.

[260] Lietzmann, *op. cit.*, IV, p. 138.

[261] Frend, *Martyrdom*, *op. cit.*, p. 348. See Athanasius *Vita Antonii* 1 and 16.

[262] Palladius, *Hist. Lausiaca* 7. Typical of the disdain for holding office in the church is the story of Ammonius in Nitria, who even mutilated himself to avoid being made bishop, and yet he still was nearly forced into the office (*Ibid.*, 11).

[263] Jones, *op. cit.*, II, p. 929. Cp. Palladius, *Hist. Lausiaca* 13, passim.

[264] Frend, *Martyrdom*, *op. cit.*, p. 348.

[265] See esp. M. Chaine, *Le Manuscrit de la Version Copte en Dialecte Sahidique des 'Apophthegmata Patrum'* (Cairo: L'Institut Francais d'Archéologie Orientale, 1960) passim.

[266] Frend, *Martyrdom*, *op. cit.*, pp. 348–349.

[267] Quispel, "Origen," *op. cit.*, p. 33.

[268] E. Amelineau, *Vie de Pakhôme* (Paris: Annales du Musée Guimet, 1889), Vol. 17, p.2: ⲚⲈ ⲞⲨⲞⲚ ⲞⲨⲀⲒ ⲆⲈ ⲬⲈ ⲠⲀϢⲰⲘ ϨⲈⲚⲦϨⲞⲨ ⲤⲚⲎ ⲚⲈ ⲌⲀⲚϨⲈⲖⲖⲎⲚⲞⲤ ⲆⲈ ⲚⲈ ⲚⲈϤⲒⲞⲦ The Greek version, transl. by A. Athanassakis, *Life of Pachomius* (Missoula: Scholars Press, 1975), p. 4, reads: καὶ αὐτὸς ἑλλήνων γονέων ὑπάρχων ἐν θηβαΐδι.

[269] *Bohairic Life* 4. The Greek version (hereafter *Vita Prima*) 3.

[270] The *Bohairic Life* 7 states that Pachomius was drafted by order of Constantine for a war against the Persians, but chronology and context require the correction offered by Veilleux, *op. cit.*, I, p.267, note 1.

[271] *Ibid.*, 7. *Vita Prima* 4–5.

[272] *Ibid.*, 10. *Vita Prima* 5–6. The Bohairic text states that it was three years after his baptism that Pachomius found Palamon, but the Greek text gives no length of time.

[273] *Ibid.*, 17. *Vita Prima* 12. The Coptic version states that Pachomius had been with Palamon for seven years, and the founding of the monastery at Tabennesi (Phboou) is thus dated to c.323, or perhaps a little earlier. If one accepts the priority of the Greek text, however, (as some do) the dates in the Coptic version are highly suspect.

[274] *Ibid.*, 25. *Vita Prima* 27.

[275] *Ibid.*, Veilleux translation.

[276] *Ibid.*, 28. *Vita Prima* 30.

[277] Palladius, *Hist. Lausiaca*, *The Monks of Tabenna*, 33.

[278] On angels, e.g. Daniel 8:16; 9:21–22; Rev. 1, *passim* (the bulk of the revelation was given to John by an angelus interpres); Shepherd of Hermes, *passim*; I Enoch 93. The heavenly record or tablet is also common: Rev. 5; I Enoch 82.1; 93.2; 103.2; 106; 19; Test. Levi 5.4; etc.

[279] *Bohairic Life of Pachom.*, 29.

[280] *The Apocryphon of John*, C.G. II *1*, 1, 29, 30ff.

[281] *The Apocalypse of Peter*, C.G. VII, *3*, 70, 72.

[282] *The Gospel of Philip*, C.G. II, *3*, 69, 84f.

[283] Frend, *Early Church*, *op. cit.*, p. 201.

[284] Palladius, *Lausiac History*, 11.

[285] Vita Prima 31.

[286] Quasten, *op. cit.*, III, p. 66, speaks of Athanasius as "a true disciple of Origen." Bigg, *op. cit.*, p. 322, observes that Athanasius gave high approval to Origen's doctrine of the Trinity, although a shift had clearly taken place, for (p. 240) "the church of Origen is no more the church of the Athanasian Creed than the Parliament of Charles I is the Parliament of Queen Victoria."

[287] Lietzmann, *op. cit.*, III, p. 248, distinguishes Athanasius from Origen: "His way of thought was not that of Origen's school as was the case with those who opposed him wholly or in part."

[288] Rufinus, *Hist. Eccl.* 2.7.

[289] Frend, *Early Church*, *op. cit.*, p. 205.

[290] Atiya, *op. cit.*, p. 63.

[291] C. C. Walters, *op. cit.*, p. 8: "In his system the needs of the individual were subjugated to the requirements of the community, and the life of each monk was governed by a precise set of rules and code of discipline."

[292] C. Butler, *op. cit.*, I. p. 236.

[293] *Ibid.*

[294] John Cassian, *Institutes*. IV.1ff.

[295] Walters, *op. cit.*, p. 205.

[296] Lietzmann, *op. cit.*, p. 142. "It was with the matter of having 'rules' that Pachomius introduced a new feature and one that was to prove of unbounded significance for future ages."

[297] Frend, *Early Church*, *op. cit.*, p. 205.

[298] *Bohairic Life of Pachom.*, 27. *Vita Prima* 32.

[299] *Ibid.*, 66. Pachomius experienced a vision in which the crisis of continuation of the monasteries after his death was vividly portrayed. He was obviously concerned for the future of his organization.

[300] *Ibid.*, 94. *Vita Prima* 106–107.

[301] *Ibid.*, 70, 78. *Vita Prima* 78.

[302] *Ibid.*, 121. *Vita Prima* 114, 117. The date of Pachomius' death is disputed, with

Amelineau choosing 348, Kruger and others opting for 345, and Achelis believing 340 to be correct. One of the later dates (traditional 346) seems more likely correct to this author, since it would allow for the development of the coenobitic system and also for the sequence of events following the visit of Athanasius in 329. The exact date, however, is of little consequence for this study.

[303] *Ibid.*, 123, 130. *Vita Prima* 117. The Greek source differs by two days from the death date given in the Bohairic Life, but that cannot be considered a significant textual or historical problem.

[304] *Ibid.*, 131–132. *Vita Prima* 117–118. For a survey of the life and work of Horsiesios, see Bacht, *Das Vermächtnis des Ursprungs, op. cit.*, I, pp.9–28.

[305] Bacht, *op. cit.*, I, pp.14–15. See W. E. Crum, *Der Papyruscodex saec. VI-VII der Phillippsbibliothek in Cheltenham.* Strassburg, 1915. The papyrus tells of a meeting between Horsiesios and Theophilus, bishop of Alexandria (385–412), in 386, during which Horsiesios said he had been a monk for 66 years. It is strange that Quasten knows the Crum publication (*op. cit.*, III, p.102), yet still gives the death date of Horsiesios as c.380 (III,p.159).

[306] *Bohairic Life of Pachomius* 139. *Vita Prima* 127–129.

[307] *Ibid*.

[308] These are published and translated (German) in Bacht, *op. cit.* I. See also the translation (English) in Veilleux, *op. cit*. III.

[309] *Bohairic Life of Pachomius* 206. *Vita Prima* 148.

[310] *Ibid.*, 185. *Vita Prima* 137–138.

[311] Veilleux, *op. cit.*, I, p.293, ref. 201.

[312] *Bohairic Life of Pachomius* 201. *Vita Prima* 143–144.

[313] *Vita Prima* 144.

[314] *Bohairic Life of Pachomius* 210. *Vita Prima* 150.

[315] Frend, *Rise of Christianity, op. cit.*, p. 745.

CHAPTER VI

AUTOCRACY IN CHRISTIAN EGYPT AND THE SEPARATION

FROM CATHOLICISM

Athanasius and Pachomius were responsible for much consolidation within the ecclesiastical organization and monasticism, respectively, but one should not understand this to mean that absolute unity was established, or that the acknowledged friendship between the bishop and the monks signified that complete harmony existed between them, or even that one was entirely subservient to the other. A number of monks, including Pachomius, sought to avoid ordination to clerical offices, and this is true of monks outside of Egypt as well. While the ostensible reason was to avoid the assumption of earthly honors and glory, the practical benefit (and perhaps the real motivation to avoid ordination) in Egypt was clearly a measure of continued independence from the ecclesiastical organization increasing in dominance along the length of the Nile. The goal of unifying all segments of Christianity into an orthodox structure under the Alexandrian patriarch, as envisioned by Athanasius in his Festal Letters, was still not entirely achieved nearly a century later at the time of the Council of Chalcedon. Nevertheless, the emergence of powerful figures in Alexandria and within the system of monasteries was sufficient to provide a strong and powerful organization which separated from the Catholic Church at that time and became a national Egyptian Christian movement.

Although Athanasius was quite successful in his attempt to bring Egyptian Christianity under the leadership of the Alexandrian patriarch, due in great measure both to his lengthy episcopacy and his proven ability to harness disparate elements of the burgeoning monasticism, a brief survey of the problems faced by fourth and fifth century Alexandrian bishops will illustrate the tenacity of diverse Christian sects along the Nile. The Arians were often the most visible of these sects, but it has been noted before that Melitians continued to exist for a few centuries, and discoveries during the last century of great numbers of manuscripts representing so-called Gnostic groups and Manichaeans also give evidence of substantial numbers who persisted in non-Catholic Christianity. Recently-found evidence confirming the presence of these groups logically infers the possible presence of other yet unidentified non-Catholic groups in Egypt during and following the episcopacy of Athanasius.

Although Athanasius made considerable progress toward the goal of unifying various segments of Christianity under the authority of the Alexandrian bishop, his successes were uneven for most of the years of his rule. A survey of the extant Festal letters (written to establish the date of the Easter celebration each year) reveals a bishop who is beleaguered by heretics and schismatics.[1] The specific identity of the heretical groups is not given until in later epistles,[2] and only general denunciations of particular doctrines are given. Athanasius did not produce theological works using the word *homoousios* or otherwise clarifying his theological position until a generation after Nicaea. Whether his avoidance of the term *homoousios* was due to tact toward other Christians (both avowed enemies and uncommitted groups) or because he had not yet come to a strong position still cannot be determined.[3] What can be determined, however, is that the prelate had all he could handle during the first decades of his episcopacy just to hold on to his office, let alone develop and delineate a sophisticated theology. From his appointment in 328 to the end of his fifth and final exile in 366, Athanasius had spent approximately one half of his time in some type of exile, either among the monks of Egypt or outside of the country altogether. His greatest concern during this troublesome period was to strengthen his hold over the Christians in Egypt, and only then would he be free to attempt an imposition of doctrinal limitations to any significant degree.

Perhaps one of the greatest indications of his success in efforts at unification was Athanasius' ability to integrate the natives with the foreign ruling population. The examples of Anthony and other monks have already been given, and Frend explains that "this was a rare, if not a unique, partnership in the ancient world between the civilization of the conquerors, the Alexandrians, and a subject people."[4] The same author notes that by mid-fourth century, this integration resulted in Coptic becoming a language for composing as well as translating texts.[5] Appreciation for the Alexandrian's accomplishment is increased by repeating that the monks of the fourth century often resisted the overtures of the ecclesiastical foreigners, preferring to strive for individual sanctity within the cells of the monasteries rather than accept ordination and office. As late as Chalcedon, Frend can speak of "particularist tendencies among the native Christians of Egypt," although loyalty to specific patriarchs and the empire was great.[6] The strength of monasticism was growing, and Athanasius, who was struggling for power and unity against a formidable Arian movement, was undoubtedly very interested in keeping as many of the monks as possible sympathetic to himself and opposed to Arianism. Arians also made an appeal, primarily in the person of Eusebius of Nicomedia, to the Melitian monks to join them, but the monks' tenacity to the Melitian cause is demonstrated by their continued presence in the fifth century.[7] The Alexandrian archbishop could ill afford a large scale alienation of the desert and monastery dwellers, even if he could not convince them to accept fully the responsibilities of the Church ministry or control the orthodoxy of their doctrines. It is in connection with the last subject that Coptic Gnostic documents of the fourth century and later should be considered.

When Athanasius returned to Alexandria in 366 at the end of his fifth exile, he was sufficiently secure from his enemies that he was able to spend his last years in office. His own sense of security is best seen in the Festal Letter he wrote for 367 (Festal Letter Number 39, though many early ones are either missing or were not written. The letters are numbered according to the years of his bishopric). In this letter Athanasius becomes the arbiter of doctrinal limitation and orthodoxy on a grand scale, a move that he most likely could not have made with success during the early decades of his episcopacy.

The 39th Festal Letter of Athanasius contains the list of books deemed canonical by the bishop, but the list is preceded by a warning to the local Egyptian Christians to avoid apocryphal works which were apparently popular among them. Specific names of such books are not given, but Athanasius notes that some were "led astray by the similarity of their names with the true books."[8] The contents of the apocryphal books are likewise not given specifically, but are said to be a mixture of scripture and speculative thought.[9] Those who read the apocryphal books are not named, but monks are implied:

> καὶ φοβοῦμαι μήπως ὡς ἔγραψε Κορινθίοις Παῦλος, ὀλίγοι τῶν ἀκεραίων ἀπὸ τῆς ἁπλότητος καὶ τῆς ἁγνότητος πλανηθῶσιν ἀπὸ τῆς πανουργίας τῶν ἀνθρώπων καὶ λοιπὸν ἐντυγχάνειν ἑτέροις ἄρξωνται τοῖς λεγομένοις ἀποκρύφοις ἀπατώμενοι τῇ ὁμωνυμίᾳ τῶν ἀληθινῶν βιβλίων· παρακαλῶ ἀνέχεσθαι εἰ περὶ ὧν ἐπίστασθε περὶ τούτων κἀγὼ μνημονεύων γράφω διά τε τὴν ἀνάγκην καὶ τὸ χρήσιμον τῆς ἐκκλησίας.

And I am afraid lest, as Paul wrote to the Corinthians, a few of the uncontaminated ones should be led astray from their simplicity and their purity by the knavery of men, and thereafter begin to read other books, those called apocryphal, being deceived by their use of the same names as the true books. I appeal to you to be patient if, concerning matters with which you are acquainted, I also write and bring to mind these things for the sake of the need and advantage of the Church.[10]

Following this warning and appeal, Athanasius gives what is now the earliest extant list of the canonical New Testament writings (following a similar listing of the Old Testament books). In his reference to apocryphal books, two major items stand out: (1) there is an abundance of writings still circulating in Egypt which, in name and apparent similarity of form to the canonized works, claim to be of equal authority and antiquity with the accepted writings. (2) the so-called apocryphal works contain doctrines or rituals which Athanasius recognizes will be appealing to many Christians, potentially providing as great a threat to his control over Egyptian Christianity as did his competitors.[11] Part of the appeal of such writings is contained in the term *apocrypha*. The word means *hidden* or *concealed* (and does not imply doubt as to accuracy or authenticity), and continues a tradition of the secrets or mysteries of Christianity known only to initiated faithful members. This tradition of apocryphal teachings can be seen in the New Testament and has been shown to occur in Egyptian Christianity from its origins down to the time of Athanasius.[12] The bishop is not attacking a new heresy or movement in the letter. He is attempting to eradicate an aspect of the faith as old as the fist appearance of Christianity in Egypt.

In addition to his references to the readers of the apocryphal works as the simple and pure, as well as to those who are aware of "the need and advantage of the Church," one notes that generally the language of the letter is not harsh, but rather explanatory and entreating in tone. Athanasius had spent his third exile from 356–362 with the monks, and he suffered two further exiles after that, from 362–363 and from 365–366. Only during the last seven years of his life could Athanasius enjoy the freedom to bring the monastic movement into greater doctrinal unity with the Church, and the Festal Letter for 367 may mark the beginning of an attempt to bring those who had sympathized with him in the Arian controversy also into doctrinal harmony on other issues.

Although the 39*th* Festal Letter of Athanasius was intended to define the limits of the canon, conformity to the bishop's prescription did not occur immediately, even in Alexandria. Bart Ehrman has made a recent study of the extant writings of Didymus the Blind (c.313–398), the blind monk appointed by Athanasius to be the director of the Catechetical School, to see which works the erudite teacher accepted as scripture.[13] Limiting the evidence to positive assertions that a book is scriptural (therefore leaving open the possibility that other works may have been equally authoritative for Didymus), Ehrman concludes that Didymus not only recognized virtually all of the Athanasian list of 27 books as scriptural, but also accepted explicitly such writings as *The Shepherd of Hermas*, *Barnabas*, *The Didache*, and *I Clement* in his canon of scripture.[14] Ehrman thus concludes

> ...the idea of a fixed canon in Alexandria during Athanasius' lifetime to be a fantasy. One of the leading Alexandrian scholars of Athanasius' day—the very man he appointed as head of the famed catechetical school—believed that the NT canon extended beyond the bounds advocated by the bishop.[15]

It is relevant to note that two significant codices of the Bible produced in Alexandria during or after the time of Athanasius, namely Sinaiticus and Alexandrinus, include not only the canonical New Testament writings, but Sinaiticus adds Barnabas and Hermas and Alexandrinus 1 and 2 Clement, all works accepted by Didymus.[16] This example, conservatively presented by Ehrman, shows that the fluidity of the canon, and, by extension, the diversity of doctrine, was not ended with the publication of Athanasius' letter.

Evidence that this Epistle was directed toward the monks is found in the *Life of Theodore*, Theodore being the spiritual successor to Pachomius as leader of the coenobitic monasteries. In that work, Athanasius' letter is quoted in a context which indicates it is being sent to the monasteries:

ЄϤϪⲰ ⲘⲘⲞⲤ ⲘⲠⲀⲒⲢⲎϯ ϪЄ ⲀⲨЄⲢⲠⲖⲀⲤⲤЄⲒⲚ ⲚⲰⲞⲨ ⲚⲚⲎ ЄⲦⲞⲨⲘⲞⲨϯ ЄⲢⲰⲞⲨ ϪЄ ⲚⲒϪⲰⲘ ⲚⲀⲠⲞⲢⲄⲀⲘⲘⲞⲚ ЄⲨⲞⲨⲞⲚⲌ ЄⲢⲰⲞⲨ ⲚⲌⲀⲚ ⲤⲎⲞⲨ ЄⲨϯ ⲘⲪⲢⲀⲚ ⲚⲚⲎ ЄⲐⲞⲨⲀⲂ ЄⲢⲰⲞⲨ ЄⲂⲞⲖ ⲄⲀⲢ ϪЄⲚ ⲪⲀⲒ ⲀⲖⲎⲐⲰⲤ ⲀⲨⲰⲞⲨϤⲞⲨ ⲘⲘⲒⲚ ⲘⲘⲰⲞⲨ ϪЄⲚ ⲰⲰⲰ ⲃ̄ ⲚϪЄ ⲚⲎ ЄⲦⲀⲨЄⲢⲦⲞⲖⲘⲀⲚ ЄⲤϪⲀⲒ ⲚⲚⲀⲒϪⲰⲘ ⲘⲠⲀⲒⲢⲎϯ ЄⲐⲂЄ ϪЄ ⲚⲎ ЄⲦϪⲎⲔ ЄⲂⲞⲖ ϪЄⲚ ⲞⲨЄⲘⲒ ⲘⲘЄⲐⲚⲞⲨϪ ⲞⲨⲞⲌ ЄⲦⲀϤⲰⲞⲨϤ ⲚⲒⲀⲦЄⲘⲒ ⲄⲀⲢ ⲞⲨⲞⲌ ⲚⲀⲦⲔⲀⲔⲒⲀ ⲚⲦЄ ⲠⲒⲖⲀⲞⲤ ⲀⲨⲤⲞⲢⲘⲞⲨ ϪЄⲚ ⲦⲞⲨⲠⲖⲀⲚⲎ ЄⲦⲌⲰⲞⲨ ЄⲂⲞⲖⲌⲀ ⲠⲒⲚⲀⲌϯ ЄⲦⲤⲞⲨⲦⲰⲚ ⲞⲨⲞⲌ ЄⲦⲦⲀϪⲢⲎⲞⲨⲦ ϪЄⲚ ⲘЄⲐⲘⲎⲒ ⲚⲒⲂЄⲚ ⲞⲨⲞⲌ ЄϤⲤⲞⲨ—ⲦⲰⲚ ⲘⲠЄⲘⲐⲞ Ⲙ̄Ⲫϯ.[17]

He (Athanasius) wrote in this (letter) that they have made books they name the Books of Charts which show some stars (var., the text says seasons) to which they give the names of the Saints. And in this they truly have brought upon themselves a double reproach: first, because they have undertaken to write those books in this way

> *because they have become perfect in a false and despised knowledge; second, as for those who are ignorant and without malice among the people, they (the apostates) have misled them by reason of their deception, taking them away from the correct faith which is strengthened in every truth and which is correct in the presence of God.*

The disciple writing the life follows this quotation with a long exhortation to the monks that they avoid reading the heretical, godless, and impious works to which Athanasius alludes, but read only the orthodox (i.e. approved by the bishop) writings which are able to lead men to salvation.[18] Theodore even had Athanasius' letter translated into Coptic and had it displayed in the monastery to serve as a rule for the monks. It seems that such a move would have been quite unnecessary had the monks been reading only the so-called canonical or approved works and not also non-canonical writings. The march toward doctrinal orthodoxy was in progress, but what were the books to which Athanasius and the Pachomian monks made reference? Threats against those who followed heretical teachings and orders to burn books[19] account for the nearly complete loss of such works over the centuries, but some works and collections of non-canonical writings were either discarded or buried in the Egyptian desert. Especially within the past century, an unexpected multitude of new finds of Christian apocryphal manuscripts in Egypt allows, or rather demands, a new assessment of the works implied by Athanasius' letter. While most of the discoveries cannot be linked to the monastic movement directly, the spectacular Coptic Gnostic library from Upper Egypt, known today as the Nag Hammadi Library, is thought by some to have been connected with monasticism. According to a story published in a number of sources,[20] some peasants were digging in December, 1945, on the talus of the Jabal al-Tarif near Nag Hammadi for nitrates to use for fertilizer on their crops. They were digging near a fallen boulder (which is well up the talus, high above the level of the valley floor and certainly higher than where such digging usually takes place) and found a jar with a lid sealed upon it. Muhammed Ali, one of the two discoverers smashed the jar with his mattock (but had the presence of mind to save the lid, so the story goes), was frightened by some gold-like particles which flew into the sky, and found a collection of old books which he took home. Muhammed's mother is supposed to have burned a volume in her oven because she thought them "worthless, or perhaps even a source of bad luck."[21] Despite the fantastic nature of his discovery, the discoverer could not be enticed to return to the site of the discovery until 1975. Even then he had to be disguised, escorted by a government official, and given a financial gift, all because of his involvement in a blood feud with the neighboring village which dated to May, 1945. A number of discovery sites were pointed out to an excavation team in 1975, of which the author was a member, but that season, as well as the two succeeding ones, yielded no supporting evidence for any of the sites or the story in general. It must therefore be admitted that the precise site of discovery has not been determined, although some evidence from within the covers of the volumes has led some to identify the library with one of the nearby Pachomian monasteries.

John Barns, whose death in 1974 prevented his completing a thorough study of the cartonnage in the covers of the codices, published a preliminary study concerning these papyri, and concluded that the books were made in a Pachomian monastery, probably Pboou or Chenoboskion.[22] While Barns claimed to see the word μονή (*monastery*) in the fragments,[23] Eric Turner appended a note to his article stating that careful examination of the fragments failed to yield the term, and that had Barns lived, "he would have incorporated a modification in his paper."[24] Turner does not reject Barns' identification of the local origin of the codices at or near Chenoboskion, however, for part of the name of that village is mentioned on a fragment.[25]

Since the preliminary work of Barns and Turner appeared in 1975, a complete study of the papyri in the cartonnage of the covers for the codices has appeared.[26] After a careful examination of the 153 Greek fragments and the 19 Coptic fragments found in 8 of the 13 codex covers of the library, Shelton and Browne make a number of observations concerning the monastic connection with the codices, especially that:

> . . . the theory that the codices themselves once belonged to the library of a Pachomian monastery requires new consideration. This question was answered in the positive by Barns in his *Preliminary Report*, but it will be seen below that evidence for monasticism in general in these papers is less frequent than was supposed in that work, and there are no texts in which a specifically Pachomian background comes plainly to the fore.[27]

Cartonnage cannot be a decisive element in determining ownership, for the materials can be gathered from sources unrelated to the owners or readers of books. The probability of monastic fabrication of the codex covers nevertheless might be greater if there were numerous pieces of papyri which have clear ties to the monks, either through the names or the contents of the texts. As seen in the quotation given above, Shelton argues that the lack of such associations decreases considerably the possibility of monastic ownership of the codices. The cartonnage of codices I, IV, V, and VI contains only secular material, including tax-related documents dealing with wine, wheat, barley, oil, etc.[28]

The cartonnage from Codex VII does contain religious writings as well as business documents, including fragments of Genesis and perhaps of a homily, and some private letters (some by Christians).[29] Among the last group "there are only two letters which beyond all reasonable doubt came from or into the hands of monks . . ."[30] In one, a woman wrote to two monks, asking them to find some chaff for her donkeys and to tell her how much it costs per wagonload. Such correspondence between a woman and monks in a Pachomian monastery is not possible, according to Shelton, and he notes that "the point of Pachomian coenobitic life was to avoid just such secular concerns".[31] The other letter includes a request to transport wheat to a monk's dwelling for storage. The letter closes with a greeting to the recipient and the brothers with him from the author and those with him,[32] suggesting at least two groups of monks and perhaps monasteries as well.

There are also two letters from the same codex cover written from presbyters to another presbyter, and other letters with the same name in them (Sansnos), but no proof that it is the same person.[33] There is also a Coptic letter which is from one Papnoute (Papnoutius) to a certain Pahome (Pachomius).[34] The address on the verso has been tentatively restored, "deliver it (the letter) to my prophet and father Pahome, from Papnoute,"[35] but Shelton (Browne?) is somewhat skeptical of the restoration of the mutilated text.[36] If the restoration is correct, it is possible that the monastic leader Pachomius could be the addressee, and Papnoutius might be the overseer of the monasteries. The *if*, *possible*, and *might* of the previous sentence show how tenuous such identifications are.

The remaining codices with cartonnage, VIII, IX, and XI, do not contain materials relevant to the monastic ownership question, except that a fragment of a letter from Codex XI is written by a resident of Chenoboskia, a village in the neighborhood of a famous Pachomian monastery. Shelton thus concludes his introductory essay concerning the cartonnage:

> On the basis of place names mentioned in the cartonnage it may be concluded that at least Codices I, V, VII, and XI were bound using material from the general neighborhood of the place where the codices were found. A terminus a quo for Codex VII can safely be set: it was bound on or after October of A.D. 348 (Deed of Surety, #65). There are no certain traces of classical Pachomian monasticism in the cartonnage.[37]

The evidence which some had earlier sought and thought to have found among the papyri of the cartonnage to demonstrate a Pachomian tie to the Nag Hammadi library proved to be illusory. The codices do come from the general area in which the most famous monastery existed, and they were bound about the middle of the fourth century, but the Nile valley is not so wide that any Christian document found along its length can be identified with a nearby monastery or church. Neither can it be ruled out that the monks of one of the monasteries could have obtained discaraed papyri from the neighboring village with which to stiffen book covers for a collection of sacred writings. To complicate the matter further, even if one argues that the codices are to be associated with a Pachomian monastery, it is not necessary to conclude that the monks to whom they belonged were of that order. Shelton notes "that Pachomius himself made provision for the reception of visiting monks who did not follow his order".[38] Mention was made in the previous chapter of Melitian monks, and others may well have lived in the area. There is no question that some Christian body held the writings of the library in high esteem,[39] and if the Athanasian letter which Theodore placed in the monastery also indicates a connection between the monks and this library or one like it, the earlier observation in this study concerning the broad literary base and undefined doctrinal orthodoxy of local Egyptian Christianity is greatly strengthened.

The writings of the codices have also led some to see a connection with monasticism, but again the evidence is inconclusive. In a paper delivered at the International Conference on Gnosticism at Yale University in 1978, Douglas Parrott suggested that the appeal of the Nag Hammadi library to Pachomian monks came from the emphasis on asceticism found in a number of the tractates.[40] He noted that The Acts of Peter and the Twelve Apostles (VI,1), Thomas the Contender (II,7), The Exegesis on the Soul (II,6), and the Authoritative Teaching (VI,3), all contain exhortations relating to "fasting, celibacy, and other sorts of mortifications of the flesh."[41] Parrott also identifies the struggle against the demonic forces, which is a common theme in the Nag Hammadi library, with the encounters which monks had with demonic forces.[42]

Despite Parrott's observations, difficulties arise in considering the association of the contents of this so-called Gnostic library with a monastery system allied, even if loosely, with the Catholic bishop of Alexandria. The charges of Catholic heterodoxy found in the library and discussed in chapter four of this work would be surprising, although the early history of monasticism showed that movement occasionally to be an escape from the Church, and that theme may not have been eradicated from otherwise popular writings. The docetic account of the crucifixion of Jesus in the *Apocalypse of Peter*,[43] as well as ascribing the creation of the world to an evil god in many of the tractates,[44] would also be unexpected in Christian circles sympathetic to Athanasius. One must remember, however, that Athanasius spent most of his energy fighting against the Arians, and *that* issue was the primary test of orthodoxy during most of his episcopacy. Before the exhortations contained in the Festal Letter for 367 were given, he was likely satisfied to have the sympathy of the monks without insisting on strict conformity to all the doctrinal limitations by then associated with the Catholic Church.

While the focus of Athanasius' attention during his episcopacy was directed primarily toward the Arian faction, the fortunes of the Arians were greatly influenced in the Eastern half of the Empire by the theological pressures exerted in the dioceses by the Emperors. From 364 to 378 the Emperor Valens ruled the Eastern half of the Empire, while his brother Valentinian I ruled the West. Valens was influenced by his wife to favor Eudoxius, the Arian bishop of Constantinople until 370, and then his slightly less Arian successor, Bishop Demophilus.[45] Athanasius and the Egyptian church do not appear to have suffered directly from any of the sporadic persecutions unleashed against the anti-Arians by the emperor, but one cannot say whether this was due to the preoccupation of Valens with repeated Gothic invasions of the East and similar problems, or simply because Athanasius' stronghold on the church was felt to be too great to attack it until after his death.[46] There had been an attempt by the Arians to place another intrusion bishop, Lucius, in the see of Alexandria in 367. He was ordained by the Arian faction at Antioch, but within 48 hours of his arrival in the city, a pro-Athanasian mob had gathered and escorted him out of Egypt.[47] Just before he died, Athanasius moved to ensure an orthodox succession by naming a companion of many years, Peter, as the next bishop.[48] No sooner had Athanasius died, however, than the Arians attempted again to place Lucius on the episcopal throne, as described by Socrates:

Εὐθὺς οὖν ἀνεθάρρουν οἱ Ἀρειανίζοντες τῇ τοῦ βασιλέως αὐχοῦντες θρησκείᾳ, καὶ μηδὲν μελλήσαντες γνωρίζουσι βασιλεῖ κατὰ τὴν Ἀντιόχειαν τότε διάγοντι, τότε δὴ καὶ Εὐζώιος, ὁ ἐν Ἀντιοχείᾳ τῆς Ἀρειανῆς προεστὼς θρησκείας, ἁρπάζει τὸ εὐεπιχείρητον τοῦ καιροῦ· κατασκευάζει τε αὐτὸς κατελθεῖν εἰς τὴν Ἀλεξάνδρειαν, ἐπὶ τῷ παραδοῦναι Λουκίῳ τῷ Ἀρειανῷ τὰς ἐκεῖ ἐκκλησίας. ταῦτ' ἐδόκει καὶ βασιλεῖ.[49]

Immediately afterward, the Arians began to take courage, having confidence in the religious preference of the emperor, and without delay they made known the circumstances (at Alexandria) to him as he was spending time at Antioch. And Euzoius in particularly, who was in charge of the Arian church in Antioch seized the favorable opportunity of that moment, and he himself prepared to go to Alexandria for the purpose of handing over the churches there to Lucius the Arian. The emperor also agreed to this action.

The irregularity of Lucius' selection is emphasized in a letter of Peter preserved in Theodoret, in which he states that Lucius had not been selected by a synod of bishops, sustained by a vote of the clergy, or acclaimed by the populace, all three of which the laws of the church enjoin for a proper succession to take place.[50] The tacit argument in the letter is that Peter had received all three affirmations of his consecration.

The Arians went to the pagan Prefect, Palladius, and after obtaining military assistance from him began to lay siege to the churches under Peter's authority.[51] Theodoret's account, taken primarily from the letter of Peter mentioned above, states that the mob accompanying Lucius was made up of Greeks and Jews and further, that the Arian used idolators as his attendants. The letter of Peter grudgingly admits that Lucius entered the city with a great parade of followers, but Peter is quick to argue that the Arian was not accompanied by any of the priesthood, monks, or the laity, implying that the group must have been primarily non-Christian. Euzoius, a former deacon in Alexandria who had been later excommunicated for Arianism, escorted Lucius into the city, however, and despite Peter's polemic innuendoes, it is most unlikely that a large body of pagans would have formed the core of Lucius' support. The Arians were probably more

numerous than Peter was willing to admit, and that would also help
explain the rather weak reaction of the supposedly overwhelming
majority of Nicene supporters. Exaggeration of the severity of events
by the authors with strong partisan interests cannot be ruled out,
further complicating the matter. Rufinus was in Alexandria at the
time, and even he claims to have been a victim of the Arian persecution,[52] but Jerome denounced and dismissed his claim as a shameless
lie.[53] Peter escaped the rioting, assaults, and general tumult which
accompanied Lucius' entry into Alexandria, but was later appre-
hended and thrown into prison.[54] He somehow escaped soon afterward and made good his escape to Rome, where he remained from
373–378 with Damasus, bishop of Rome, until the rule of Lucius
came to an end with the death of Valens during a battle against the
Goths near Adrianople.[55]

The significance of the monastic movement to both of the major
factions in this Arian takeover is obvious from the sources, for in
addition to the persecution in the churches which led to the exile of
some 19 presbyters and deacons to Heliopolis, a city notorious for
pagan practices and licentiousness,[56] all the sources note that the
monasteries and even the hermits suffered, resulting in 23 monks
being sent to the mines, and 11 bishops from Egypt who had ascetic
tendencies being exiled to Dio-Caesarea in Galilee.[57] Two monastic
leaders, both named Macarius, were exiled to a non-Christian island,[58] where they reportedly converted all the inhabitants. Didymus
the Blind, appointed by Athanasius to be the leader of the Catechetical school, also confronted the Arians at this time in Alexandria, but
there is no indication that he was beaten or otherwise persecuted for
his activities.[59] Socrates argues that although the Arians were able to
perpetrate such acts, they were nevertheless few in numbers,[60] and
the obvious implication is that such an uprising could not have taken
place without the backing of the Emperor and the Prefect. The
Emperor's Arian sympathies must have found considerable support
in Egypt, however, and the previously mentioned letters from
Athanasius to monks just a few years earlier state that Arianism was
still a problem in the monasteries.[61] The Arian takeover after Athanasius' death signifies that the success of his consolidation efforts was
due more to the strength of his position and personality than to his
achieving doctrinal or ecclesiastical unity among the Christians.

When Peter returned to Alexandria after the death of the Emperor Valens in 378, he enjoyed good relations with orthodox bishops elsewhere. In 379, however, he nominated an Egyptian, Maximus, to replace Gregory of Nazianzus as bishop of Constantinople.[62] Gregory himself had been recently invited by a Nicene faction to leave his bishopric in Sasima (Frend describes the place as "a wretched one-horse town near the Armenian frontier.") and assume the leading role in the capital city.[63] Peter's own ambition and desire to exert influence and control in the capital through his own candidate for the bishopric there demonstrate the continuing intensity of ecclesiastical politics and episcopal competition at the close of the fourth century. His ploy almost succeeded. By ingratiating himself with many in the church, and even gaining the confidence of Gregory,[64] Maximus was able to convince some of Gregory's clergy to join with Peter's envoys and consecrate him bishop. The meeting was supposedly secured from interruptions by some sailors from the Egyptian grain ships, and was in process in the church of the Anastasia (Church of the Resurrection), when Gregory, in bed because of illness, was informed of the proceedings.[65] Gregory's supporters showed up at the church before the consecration was completed, and the usurpers went to the house of a flute-player and completed their meeting there.[66]

Consecration alone did not secure the episcopacy, so Maximus began traveling to other cities in 380 to seek support and recognition. The emperor would not receive him,[67] and Damasus of Rome joined in denouncing his claim.[68] Even his attempted return to Alexandria to obtain support from Peter was thwarted, for the Prefect caught him first and exiled him.[69]

Peter's motives for backing Maximus at the outset of this bizarre chain of events can only be conjectured, although Constantinople had been in the control of Arians for forty years, and with Gratian's accession in 378 and his edict of toleration in 379 (which made possible a revival of Catholicism in the eastern capital),[70] the religious fortune of the city was a tempting prize for competing parties.[71] It is possible that Peter's opposition to Gregory was based on Canon 15 of the Nicene Creed which forbade the translations of bishops to new dioceses (Gregory had been consecrated bishop over Sasima before he was summoned to Constantinople),[72] or perhaps his opposition was based on a difference of opinion with the Cappadocians (notably Basil and the two Gregorys) concerning Trinitarian terminology, for they taught that the godhead was comprised of three *hypostases* in one *ousia*, or essence.[73] As will be observed below, this position essentially discarded the Word-flesh Christology generally associated with Alexandrian theologians in favor of the Word-man Christology of the Antiochenes.

The best possibility for explaining the disagreement would be to note the beginnings of envy at the increasing importance of Constantinople as a Christian center, obviously at the expense of Alexandria. The dual capitals were Rome and Constantinople, and while Rome and Alexandria enjoyed the leadership among dioceses from as early as Dionysius, who even counseled the Novatianists to become reconciled to the Roman bishop, there can be no question that the bishop whose see was at the emperor's court would have increasingly greater prestige in the East. The increased importance of Constantinople at the expense of Alexandria by 380 should not be exaggerated, however, for an edict of the Emperor Theodosius dated 27 February of that year indicates the continuing leadership exerted by Rome and Alexandria at that time:

> It is our pleasure that all the nations which are governed by our clemency and moderation should steadfastly adhere to the Religion which was taught by St. Peter to the Romans, which faithful tradition has continued, and is now professed by pope Damasus and by Peter, bishop of Alexandria . . .[74]

The date of Peter's death is not specified in the histories but by the time the second general Council was called together in Constantinople in the spring-summer of 381, Peter's brother, Timothy, had succeeded him as bishop of Alexandria.[75] The purpose of the Council was twofold: to confirm the decisions of the Council of Nicaea and to appoint a bishop for Constantinople.[76] The first purpose was realized, although the Cappadocian influence in the reaffirmed creed was felt, for the consubstantiality of the Spirit was accepted, as well as the expression, 'one *ousia* in three *hypostases*'.[77] The position of Apollinaris (a friend of Athanasius and bishop of Laodicea from 361), that the Word replaced the mind as the animating force of Christ, was also rejected at the Council.[78] Davies observed that this settlement had the effect of discarding the Word-flesh Christology in favor of a Word-man Christology,[79] demonstrating the lessening influence of Alexandrian theology in the Council. The settlement of Constantinople must be viewed as a partial compromise, however, for Chadwick notes that even though Apollinarianism was condemned, no clauses were written into the creed which Apollinarians could not accept.[80]

The nearly 150 bishops who assembled at Constantinople were all from the Eastern part of the Empire and, although the Egyptian contingent arrived late, the histories of Socrates and Sozomen state that Timothy was a leader of the Nicene bishops of the Council.[81] If Peter had fears two years earlier that Constantinople was gaining in prestige at the expense of Alexandria, the results of the Council show that they were not entirely groundless. The third Canon of the Council specified that henceforth Constantinople was to enjoy the right of primacy after Rome:

ὥστε τὸν Κωνσταντίνου πόλεως ἐπίσκοπον τὰ πρεσβεῖα ἔχειν τῆς τιμῆς μετὰ τὸν Ῥώμης ἐπίσκοπον, διὰ τὸ εἶναι αὐτὴν νέαν Ῥώμην.[82]

(The canon states) that the bishop of the city of Constantinople is to have the prerogatives of honor after the bishop of Rome, because that city is the new Rome.

Such a change in the order of precedence could not be taken lightly by the Egyptian church, even though the Sixth Canon of Nicaea was reaffirmed, giving control of all the Egyptian churches to Timothy of Alexandria.[83] Even this renewal was included in a Canon which was intended as a rebuff to the Alexandrian bishop, for the Second Canon commands that, "The bishops are not to go beyond their dioceses to churches lying outside their bounds, nor bring confusion on the Churches; but let the Bishop of Alexandria, according to the canons, alone administer the affairs of Egypt . . ."[84] It has been assumed that the manner in which Peter of Alexandria had supported the consecration of Maximus as bishop of Constantinople was the immediate cause of this canon.[85] These two canons clearly provide the stimulus which would eventually lead to the separation of Christianity in Egypt from the Catholic Church. Rome, not represented at the Council, also expressed resentment at the canons, especially the third, for "although it conceded that Rome was the first see of Christendom, it implied that Roman primacy depended on the city's secular standing."[86]

The desire of the Alexandrian bishop to regain his status as the ranking prelate behind the bishop of Rome can be clearly observed in the case of Timothy's successor, Theophilus (bishop from 385 to 412). The bishops of Alexandria desired to have weak bishops at Constantinople and, after the death in 397 of the neophyte bishop of Constantinople, Nectarius, it was only with reluctance that Theophilus traveled to consecrate his successor, John Chrysostom.[87] Not only did he oppose John's ordination by trying to "detract from his reputation," but he also attempted to accomplish what Peter had tried in 379, namely to install Isidore, one of his own presbyters, as bishop of the Eastern Capital. Little is known of Isidore, and even Sozomen doubts the authenticity of the story he relates concerning that Egyptian on a mission of intrigue to the emperor.[88] Theophilus' motives in opposing John appear to be obvious, especially from the account given in Socrates,[89] since the gifted and popular orator would further decrease the prestige of the Alexandrian bishop. John was from Antioch, and coming from that city which had experienced some ecclesiastical battles with Alexandria[90] would have perhaps made him especially unpopular with Theophilus. Chadwick notes that Theophilus attempted to cooperate with John at first, "e.g. in settling the long-standing schism at Antioch that had divided the Church there since the fall of Eustace soon after the council of Nicaea,"[91] but the early appearance of harmony was not to last, and other problems arose which led to John's downfall. Unfortunately for Chrysostom, his grandiloquent speaking talent was not matched by a similar ostentation in the display of wealth and an easy-going attitude which were the marks of his predecessor, and he was unpopular with many in Constantinople.[92] In addition to making numerous enemies, John also made some grand errors which played into the hands of Theophilus who wished to overthrow him. The confrontation between Theophilus and John resulted directly from the Alexandrian bishop's difficulties with some monks concerning the theology of Origen.

The Origenist Controversy, which had been fanned into flame in Palestine near the end of the fourth century by the invectives of Epiphanius, broke out in 400–401 in Egypt between Theophilus and the Origenist monks of Nitria. The leading monks on the Origenist side in the controversy were the Tall Brothers, Ammonius, Eusebius, Euthymius, and Dioscorus, the bishop of Hermopolis Minor from 399-c.403.[93] On an earlier occasion relations between Theophilus and these monks were very good, and Theophilus had even consecrated Dioscorus to his bishopric in Hermopolis.[94] In his Festal Letter of 399, however, Theophilus denounced the idea that God has human form and thus offended many anti-Origenist monks who thought of God as anthropomorphic.[95] The field was now prepared for a major confrontation over the theological dispute.

Some of the Origenist monks living under the leadership of the Tall Brothers in the Nitrian desert on the southwest edge of the Nile delta were joined by one Evagrius, formerly an archdeacon at Constantinople, who published much of the group's theology in his writings. "Despite obscurities they were clear in teaching that in prayer the imagination must not admit any pictures of God as having human form or any kind of spatial localization 'up there'."[96] Reacting against these 'Origenists' were simple believers, for whom God could be imagined as a Being with human form living in the sky.[97] The 'anthropomorphites' rushed to Alexandria and made threats against the bishop, and in fear Theophilus did an about-face, formally denouncing Origen's books and doctrines. Kelly states simply that Theophilus' motive for his sudden change was to placate the desert monks, the great majority of whom were anti-Origenist in theology.[98] In pointed language, Kelly argues:

> More interested in power politics than in dogmatic truth, he at once sensed the importance of having the formidable army of monks as his devoted storm-troopers, and hastened to assure them that he too pictured God as bodily and rejected Origen's intellectualism.[99]

Theophilus' dispute with the Origenist monks was exacerbated by his problems with Isidore, the unsuccessful candidate earlier put forward by the Alexandrian prelate for the bishopric of Constantinople, since Isidore also was an Origenist.[100] Isidore had been appointed to represent the Alexandrian patriarch as a mediator between bishop John of Jerusalem and Jerome in 396,[101] but the attempt had ended in failure, due in part to Isidore's partisanship as an arbitrator. At that time, Theophilus was also sympathetic to Origenistic theology, but soon after his "change of heart" he became inimical toward his former confidant and candidate, alleging that Isidore had admitted a Manichaean woman to communion, and also that he was unwilling to give money from his poor-box to the bishop for the building of churches.[102]

Isidore was excommunicated by the patriarch, and he fled to his Origenist friends, the Tall Brothers, who in turn petitioned Theophilus to receive Isidore back into communion. For his reply, Theophilus jailed one of the monks,[103] and in the summer of 399 he issued letters expelling the Origenist monks from Nitria.[104] The success of the expulsion order has been questioned,[105] but it is clear from the ancient sources that at least some of the monks left Egypt and later made their way to Constantinople in order to complain at the Imperial Court and before the bishop, John Chrysostom.[106] Theophilus wrote a synod letter in 400 attacking the monks of Nitria and Scetis and condemning the errors of Origen,[107] and he also drove Dioscorus from his bishopric at Hermopolis. The Egyptian version of the Origenist controversy to this point was political in nature, as Theophilus had been willing to take that position which would ensure for him the greatest amount of support from the monastic movement. The appeal of some of the Origenist monks before the Imperial Court and the bishop of Constantinople, John Chrysostom from Antioch, brought more forces into play, and the focus of the storm shifted from Egypt to the capital.

One cannot help feeling sympathy for the Alexandrian patriarch at this strange turn of events. The obvious discomfiture of Theophilus is explained by his having to go to the "New Rome" to defend his actions toward insubordinate monks who were once good friends, and present his defense in the diocese of the bishop whose ordination he had earlier opposed. Without question, the dominating influence enjoyed by the Alexandrian metropolitan in the East, was being replaced by that of the ascendant Constantinople. Theophilus was not one who would accept a position of lesser influence than his predecessors had enjoyed, however, and his actions demonstrate his desire to maintain the Alexandrian patriarchate as the leading see in the East.

Frend states that the Imperial court had agreed that the accusations against the monks would be heard by the Praetorian Prefects, and that Theophilus would be called to defend his actions before John.[108] He doesn't cite a source, but Palladius, the historian of Egyptian monasticism, states that such a decision was granted to the monks by Eudoxia, the emperor's wife.[109] Palladius was both a close friend of John and a hated critic of Theophilus, so his information is at least suspect on this matter, and perhaps should be discounted completely. Theophilus journeyed to the Bosporus in 403, ostensibly for the purpose of defending his treatment of the expelled monks, but it is generally agreed that his real intention was to put John on trial.[110] With a group of Egyptian bishops and a few local malcontents, Theophilus held a council on the Asiatic shore opposite Constantinople, in the Palace of the Oak, once the villa of a prefect. John refused to leave Constantinople and his own diocese to attend such a partisan council, for obvious reasons, and his deposition was a foregone conclusion.

Chrysostom's own speaking abilities abetted the Alexandrian and his colleagues at the Synod in their attempt to depose him, for he had earlier eloquently offended the empress Eudoxia in a sermon on feminine frailty, and the emperor accordingly stood by his wife, upheld the partisan decision of the Synod to depose John, and decreed an exile for the bishop.[111] Although the first exile was of brief duration, John later again insulted the emperor's wife after the inauguration of a silver statue of Eudoxia near the Church of St. Sophia,[112] and his enemies were able to obtain his banishment, which this time lasted from 404 to his death in 407.[113] Theophilus did not attend the second trial of John, but sent others to represent his interest and to keep pressing John's adversaries into action.

Theophilus' action against the Origenist monks in Egypt was tacitly upheld, and the incident provided an opportunity to interfere in the affairs of the diocese at Constantinople, which at the time was the major obstacle in the way of enhancing the declining prestige of the Alexandrian diocese. It was a further blow to the Alexandrian patriarchs to have an Antiochene on the episcopal throne at Constantinople, since Alexandria and Antioch were long-standing rivals in the East. Repeated failure to establish Alexandrians in the see of Constantinople did not lessen the desire of the Alexandrian prelates to interfere there, as seen in the case of Chrysostom's deposition.

Moreover, the schism in Egypt which led to the episode gives a further lesson relating to the power of the Alexandrian bishop. The consolidation of the episcopal power was not entirely secure as long as monks could appeal to the Imperial Court and See in the hope of curtailing the bishop's control over Egypt.[114] Furthermore, the strength of the monastic movement was too great for a bishop to ignore, and the monks' friendship and allegiance were courted by Theophilus and his successors.[115] One cannot state with certainty how many monks there were in Egypt by the end of the fourth century, but

> Rufinus's estimate of ten thousand monks in the monasteries and twenty thousand virgins in and around Oxyrhynchus c.390, and Jerome's claim that "nearly fifty thousand monks" took part in the annual convention of Pachomian monasteries, indicate that they were very numerous.[116]

The social, political, and religious impact of such great numbers of monks and nuns can hardly be overstated. The importance of the Athanasian attempt to bring them into doctrinal harmony with the Alexandrian Church through a list of approved books is also illustrated in the rebellion of the Egyptian Origenist monks and their subsequent appeal to the bishop of the rival see at Constantinople.

Theophilus died on 15 October 412, and three days after his death his nephew Cyril was made bishop, after winning a minor skirmish with a faction trying to place Timothy the archdeacon on the episcopal throne.[117] Cyril is characterized by Frend as "utterly unscrupulous, overbearing, turbulent and greedy for power, ready to use the mob and the monks to do his bidding against his opponents such as the Alexandrian Jews and the pagans."[118] In many ways the tactics of Athanasius were renewed during his episcopacy. It is not only in doctrinal matters that one can say with Frend, "Cyril was a dedicated follower of Athanasius".[119] The failures of Theophilus to have his way in selecting a bishop at Constantinople or in maintaining strict control over all facets of Christianity in Egypt were compensated by the strong measures taken against heretics and pagans successfully by Cyril:

καὶ γὰρ ἐξ ἐκείνου, ἡ ἐπισκοπὴ Ἀλεξανδρείας παρὰ τῆς ἱερατικῆς τάξεως καταδυναστεύειν τῶν πραγμάτων ἔλαβε τὴν ἀρχήν. Εὐθέως οὖν Κύριλλος τὰς ἐν Ἀλεξανδρείᾳ Ναυατιανῶν ἐκκλησίας ἀποκλείσας, πάντα μὲν αὐτῶν τὰ ἱερὰ κειμήλια ἔλαβεν· τὸν δὲ ἐπίσκοπον αὐτῶν θεόπεμπτον, πάντων ὧν εἶχεν ἀφείλετο.[120]

For from that time, the bishopric of Alexandria, beyond sacerdotal order, seized the administrative authority to rule in secular matters. Immediately thereafter, Cyril closed the churches of the Novatians in Alexandria, and carried off all their sacred treasures. And as for their bishop, Theopemptos, Cyril took from him all that he had.

Cyril's attempts to usurp civil authority naturally caused animosity between himself and the Prefect, Orestes, and the attack on the Novatians, in which the Novatianist bishop was deprived of his property, was the first incident which filled the Prefect with indignation. Not content with attacking schismatic Christians in the city, Cyril turned his wrath against the Jews. The Jews had comprised a substantial portion of the Alexandrian population for centuries, and had represented both wealth and authority in that city.[121] Christian antipathy toward Judaism had grown in time, and Socrates states that disturbances between the two groups were constantly occurring.[122] The pretext for the Jewish expulsion in 415 arose because of some Jews going to the theater to watch dance performances on the sabbath. Because the shows were disorderly, the Prefect was present on one particular occasion to publish regulatory edicts for the shows.

Some of Cyril's supporters were also present, and one of them, Hierax, was boisterous in his applauding the Prefect's edicts, where-upon the Jews proclaimed that Hierax and others were spies and riot-mongers. Orestes, portrayed as growing more jealous of the bishop's powers anyway, used the tumult as an excuse to seize and torture Hierax in the theater. Cyril reacted by threatening the Jews, and, when they banded together for small group attacks at night against the Christians, he expelled them from the city.[123] Both Orestes and Cyril then sent accounts of the action to the emperor Theodosius II (408–450), and some people convinced Cyril to try to pacify the Prefect, but the attempt failed because of yet another incident.

Many monks in Nitria were filled with an ardent zeal to fight for Cyril, and hundreds came to Alexandria and confronted the Prefect as he was driving around in his chariot. Verbal abuses were followed by a stone-throwing incident on the part of one of the monks named Ammonius. Orestes was hit on the head and was soon "covered with the blood which flowed from the wound." His guards reportedly fled to escape injury, but a gathering crowd soon put the monks to flight. Ammonius was tortured to death, and Cyril nearly had his name enrolled among the martyrs before more cautious and sober opinions prevailed.[124] This event might also have faded into forgetfulness and the Jewish problem perhaps diminished in importance, were it not for still another episode which followed.

An Alexandrian philosopher, Theon, had a daughter named Hypatia who was widely known for her "attainments in literature and science, as to far surpass all the philosophers of her own time."[125] Students came from many regions of the Empire to hear her lectures, and she also enjoyed a close association with Orestes, having frequent interviews with him. Some Christians thought she kept Orestes from being reconciled to Cyril, and a mob of zealous fanatics led by a reader named Peter waylaid her on the way home, took her to the church of Caesareum, stripped her, killed her with roof-tiles, and dismembered the corpse.[126] While no direct blame can be placed on Cyril for the crime, Socrates notes, "This affair brought not the least opprobrium, not only upon Cyril, but also upon the whole Alexandrian church."[127] The violence which Cyril had unleashed first against the Jews was getting out of control, and in 416 Theodosius II published an edict forbidding the clergy to take part in public affairs, and otherwise limited the powers of the archbishop.[128] The despotic powers now held and exercised within the Alexandrian church, however, were still greater than at any time in the past.

The next severe test for the prestige and authority of Cyril had to do with the episcopate of the Eastern Capital. The death of Sisinnius, bishop of Constantinople, in December 427, caused such intense rivalries for the throne that Theodosius II appointed Nestorius of Antioch to fill the vacancy and end the quarrels.[129] The rivalry between Antioch and Alexandria, and also more recently between Constantinople and Alexandria, was a major factor in Theophilus' earlier attack on John Chrysostom, and Theophilus' nephew Cyril, now likewise must have felt Nestorius' appointment a blow to the prestige and influence of the Alexandrian bishop. A suitable note of caution concerning motives must be added here. Evidence available for this study has shown repeatedly how ecclesiastical leaders have acted in ways which suggest that they were motivated by lust for power to secure political advantage. Personal ambition may thus explain much of the competitive animosity and contention between rival sees, but Baus reminds readers that another factor cannot be excluded:

> Cyril sought to put across his ideas with adept and often highly questional (sic) diplomacy, in which a certain antagonism of Alexandria with regard to the see of Constantinople may have played a role. However, it will not do to see in these traits, especially on Cyril's part, the real motivating forces for the theological discussion and to undervalue it as mere logomachy. Despite all the at times depressing human foibles which can be established in the course of the conflict, it dealt with questions of high theological and religious relevance.[130]

Not even for one so unscrupulous and violent at times as was Cyril can religious belief and faith be ruled out as the driving force in his life.

Consecrated in April 428, Nestorius immediately established himself as a zealot with his famous speech concerning heretics:

> Δός μοι, φησὶν, ὦ βασιλεῦ, καθαρὰν τὴν γῆν τῶν αἱρετικῶν, κἀγώ σοι τὸν οὐρανὸν ἀντιδώσω. Συγκάθελέ μοι τοὺς αἱρετικούς, κἀγὼ συγκαθελῶ σοι τοὺς Πέρσας.[131]

> *"Give to me," he said, "O king, the earth cleansed of heretics, and I in turn will give you heaven. Join me in putting down the heretics, and I will join you in conquering the Persians."*

Nestorius thus shared the violent opinions of Cyril concerning pagans and heretics, and some indications exist that the two were friendly toward each other in the early period of Nestorius' rule. Nestorius established a yearly festival at Constantinople in honor of

John Chrysostom, and he was able to gain Cyril's consent to place John's name in the Alexandrian diptychs,[132] even if the latter was reluctant to do so.[133] As late as 429, when Cyril was trying to provoke Nestorius over his refusal to use the word *theotokos* (Mother of God), Nestorius responded, saying, "There is a good deal, as I must confess, in your letter which ill befits brotherly charity; but I prefer, if possible, to persist in our old friendly relations."[134]

The major issue usually raised in Cyril's dispute with Nestorius is the latter's Christology. Socrates states that a presbyter named Anastasius accompanied Nestorius from Antioch to Constantinople, and he preached in church one day that nobody should call Mary *theotokos* (Mother of God), "for Mary was only a woman, and it is impossible for God to be born of a woman."[135] Many in the church were offended, but Nestorius did not wish his friend and associate deemed guilty of error, and he subsequently delivered a number of discourses on the subject and rejected the term *theotokos*.[136] It is generally admitted that Cyril was a far more astute theologian than was Nestorius, and it is also generally conceded that Nestorius was not a "Nestorian" in the classic sense of the term, i.e. he did not teach the doctrine of two Sons or of Adoptionism.[137] He nevertheless did insist, in the tradition of Antiochene Christology, that the two natures of the incarnate Christ (Godhead and manhood)[138] "remained unaltered and distinct in the union."[139] The Alexandrian school recognized the distinction of divinity and humanity in Christ, and Cyril admitted that the *two natures* brought together in the union are different and are not destroyed in the resulting union that became the *one* Christ.[140] For Nestorius, the " 'natural' or 'hypostatic' union envisaged by Cyril" appeared to destroy the separateness of the natures,[141] while Cyril perceived Nestorius' doctrine as teaching that two persons were artificially linked together.[142] Indicative of the differences found among modern commentators on the issue, Kelly emphasizes the differences of the two positions, noting that Cyril "found a compromise with moderate Antiochenism possible,"[143] while Sellers states,

> that so far as fundamentals are concerned, there is no difference between the Christological teaching of the Antiochenes, and that of the Alexandrians, though, when set beside that raised by the latter, the Antiochene doctrinal structure must appear crude and unfinished.[144]

The discovery early in this century of the *Book of Heraclides*, an apology written by Nestorius some twenty years after he was deposed, caused Loofs to speculate that if Nestorius had flourished at the Council of Chalcedon, he would have been a pillar of orthodoxy.[145] The intransigent character of both Nestorius and Cyril made compromise on the doctrinal issue unlikely, however, even if the differences were minimal.

Beyond the question of the differences in Christology and not withstanding Baus' warning not to ignore theological issues, ecclesiastical politics and episcopal rivalry still appear as primary motives leading to confrontation in the actions of the bishops.[146] Around the end of 428, some Alexandrians in Constantinople were induced by Nestorius to complain to the emperor that Cyril had treated them harshly and unfairly,[147] suggesting that Nestorius was trying to undermine Cyril's power and authority. Cyril retaliated against the possible influence of Nestorius in his diocese, for in his Festal Letter for 429, *Ad Monachos Aegypti*, Cyril berates some of the monks for even questioning the use of the term *theotokos*, "for it really amounts to asking, Is her Son God, or is He not?"[148] From that time the battle became more vigorous and vicious, and in 430 Cyril wrote a series of treatises to Theodosius II and the Imperial Women in the court to swing them from their support of Nestorius.[149] These works were not successful in turning the Imperial household, for Theodosius' life was dominated alternately by his sister and his wife. Nestorius was popular with the Emperor's wife, Eudokia, but Theodosius' sister, Pulcheria was opposed to the bishop, and Cyril's treatises had the effect of dividing the household and "making his (Theodosius') own life a misery."[150]

Cyril had not succeeded in swaying Imperial opinion away from Nestorius, but he did succeed in winning the Roman bishop as an ally. Celestine was already disturbed that Nestorius had received in Constantinople some of the Pelagian heretics who had been condemned at Rome,[151] and after calling in John Cassian to clarify the Nestorian doctrine,[152] he then sided with Cyril against Nestorius. Cyril was not equally successful in trying to line up Eastern bishops for his cause, for Acacius, bishop of Beroea (in Syria), wrote to Cyril and said, "A phrase ought not to set us by the ears,"[153] and added that the feeling in the East was that Cyril should not be hasty in his actions.

Matters moved rather quickly, though, and in the summer of 430 Celestine called a Council in Rome, after which he wrote letters to a number of Eastern bishops, condemning Nestorius' heresy. Cyril called together a Council in Alexandria for late 430, consisting primarily of Egyptian bishops.[154] He also sent a strongly worded letter to Nestorius soon afterward, including the threat of excommunication if he did not comply with the stringent demands of the letter.[155] As if to preclude the possibility of compliance, twelve anathemas were also attached to the letter which, as Kelly observes, were "deliberately provocative" and "most ill-judged."[156]

The anathemas, or statements to which Nestorius was to subscribe or be anathematized, were not only meant to provoke the bishop of Constantinople (if indeed that was the purpose), but they also spelled out in detail the Christology of Cyril. Increasingly stringent in defining doctrines concerning Christ from earlier Alexandrian theologians, the anathemas also alienated other once-friendly bishops, including John of Antioch, Andrew of Samosata, and Theodoret of Cyprus.[157] The moderate Antiochenes perceived Cyril's theology to be distinctly Apollinarian, and the result of this skirmish was to take Alexandria yet another step in the direction toward a formal separation. The anathemas therefore "served but to defeat the project they were intended to promote".[158]

The first anathema requires the term *theotokos* to be used for Mary, who "in the flesh bore the Word of God made flesh".[159] The second and third define the Word as being united hypostatically to flesh and denies that there can be any division of the hypostases (the Word and flesh) after their union.[160] The fourth repudiates any attempt to apply scriptural or theological statements to Christ as if referring either to the man separate from the Word or to the Word alone apart from the man.[161] The fifth denies that Christ is Theophoros (God-bearing or God-inspired), stating rather that the Word is God who was made flesh (as distinguished from prophets or others who were men in whom God dwelt).[162] The sixth denies that the Word is the Lord or God of Christ, since the Word became flesh, and the Word is thus at the same time both God and man.[163] Likewise, the seventh denies that Jesus is a man energized by the Word, as if to separate the glory of the Word from the man.[164] The eighth rejects worship of the "assumed man" together with the Word, as if they are different or one with the other.[165] The ninth denies that Jesus was empowered by the Holy Ghost to work miracles as through a spirit apart not His own. Put another way, it was Jesus' own power and Spirit through which He performed divine works, and not an external source of power which he received.[166]

The tenth, eleventh, and twelfth emphasize the divinization of the flesh of the Word, with the tenth denying that the great High Priest and Apostle was a man separate from the Word, since the Word became flesh.[167] The eleventh avers that it is the flesh of the Word which gives life, because the flesh is of the Word and not simply a dwelling-place for divinity.[168] The twelfth affirms that the Word suffered, died, and came forth from death in the flesh, emphasizing the unity of the flesh with the Word.[169] Such strenuous defining of the Word-flesh Christology by Cyril could lead only to a hardening of positions, although the Alexandrian bishop did move toward a some-what more moderate position in the years immediately following the Council of Ephesus.[170]

The extremely strained situation in 430, however, caused by Cyril's aggressiveness and Celestine's unwise decision to have Cyril carry out the excommunication of Nestorius if the latter did not renounce his teachings, brought a strong letter of rebuke from Theodosius II to Cyril in November of the year.[171] The emperor also called a general council to be held in Ephesus at Pentecost, 431,[172] and Nestorius, with the backing of the court, might reasonably have expected to be the victor in the Council,[173] especially since Cyril's acceptance of the emperor's summons superseded his claim "to be the Pope's executor against Nestorius."[174] Such was not the case, however, for Cyril turned the decision to his favor through a large retinue of sailors, bishops, and monks, including the archimandrite Shenoute from the White Monastery.[175] The Ephesian church, under the leadership of the bishop Memmon, was also solidly sympathetic to Cyril, being jealously independent of Constantinople and also more harmonious in theology with Cyril than with Nestorius.[176]

Celestine, according to Roman custom, did not attend the Council, but sent legates to represent him. Cyril was accompanied by a contingent of bishops and arrived in early June.[177] A delayed arrival by John of Antioch caused postponement of the Council's beginning until 10 July, but the two factions met ahead of time. Baus observes that "It does not help Cyril's reputation that he awaited the arrival neither of the papal delegation nor of the Antiochene bishops," but began the council on his own authority.[178] Cyril's partisans first met on 22 June and deposed Nestorius, and then Nestorius, upon John's arrival, met on 26 June with his supporters and deposed Cyril and Memmon, bishop of Ephesus.[179] When the Papal legates arrived on 10 July,

Cyril's meeting was the one recognized by them as being official, and it is also the one which historically is called the Third General Council.[180]

Following the fiasco of Ephesus, some attempts were made during the next two years to unify the Church, and Celestine's death in 432 opened the way for his successor, Xystus III, to seek reconciliation of the parties. Now that Nestorius was deposed, exiled (first to Antioch and later to the Great Oasis in Egypt), and no longer a threat or a thorn to Cyril, the Alexandrian was conciliatory, and in April 433 he wrote John of Antioch a letter stating how useless dissension was, and concludes with the *Formulary of Reunion* which earlier had been sent to him.[181]

The evidence thus considered shows that Cyril was tyrannical and forceful, both at home and in the Imperial Court. He was not scrupulous in his means to achieve goals, and he wielded more power in his see than any of his predecessors. It is likely that the differences in theology with Nestorius derived from his envy of the bishop of Constantinople, for he jealously guarded the autonomy of his own diocese, as well as trying to interfere in the operations of bishops elsewhere.[182] His death of 9 June 444 ended a sixty year dynasty for Theophilus and his nephew. The development of absolute power in the episcopate, combined with growing jealousy toward other bishops, especially at Constantinople, made a break with Catholicism a real possibility, and it was not long in coming. Such a break depended upon unified support from the monastic movement, however, and while Pachomius had been responsible for much consolidation through the establishment of monastic communities, it has been noted that by the time Athanasius had published his Festal Letter of 367, the monks still exhibited considerable independence in matters of doctrine and submission to ecclesiastical authority.

Three years after the publication of Athanasius' 39th Festal Letter, an event took place in the monastic world that eventually would lead to the orthodoxy in doctrine and the consolidation in organization toward which Athanasius was striving. A young boy, Shenoute, entered the White Monastery south of Achmim (it was in the Pachomian system of monasteries) to be taught by his uncle Pjol, who was over the monastery at the time.[183] Shenoute became the head of the monastery in 388,[184] and soon produced rules for the monks to follow which were much more strict than those of Pachomius.[185] In addition to sending a murderer to be executed who had come to confess an old crime and seek spiritual solace,[186] Shenoute wrote a letter to a convent of nuns in which he stipulates the exact number of blows of a rod to be given the sisters for various infractions of the convent rules.[187] One monk who was beaten by Shenoute for breaking a regulation is said to have died,[188] and another entered a self-imposed exile away from the monastery for breaking one rule.[189]

The harshness of the archimandrite was not limited to his own monasteries, for Besa, his biographer and disciple who wrote in the second half of the fifth century, records a number of violent attacks made on "pagan" places of worship of the Greeks. Although one cannot be certain of their identity, it is entirely possible that those designated "Greeks" were really unorthodox Christians, as Shenoute would define that phrase. One such Hellene was attacked because he did not treat the poor with respect,[190] and the biographer states that it was the hand of God that smote the Greek. Shenoute grabbed another by the hair of his head, struck him a blow in the face, and dragged the unfortunate victim to the Nile and baptized him two times. The bystanders were amazed and said:

ΘΑΙ ΟΥΕΧΟΥϹΙΑ ΝΤΕΦΤΤΕ ΕΤΑϤΟΥΟΡПϹ ΕϬΙ ΜПϢΙϢ ΜПΙΑϹΕΒΗϹ Ν2ΕΛΗΝΟϹ ΕΤΕΜΜΑΥ.[191]

This is the authority of God, which He has sent to take vengeance upon that impious Greek.

On another occasion Shenoute attacked some idolatrous Greeks who had buried their books which contained magic spells and consequently hoped to avoid the monk's destructive wrath. Shenoute found the books, went into the church of the Greeks and expelled the perpetrators of evil, afterward destroying the heretical church and its furnishings.[192] This group which Shenoute attacked worshipped the demiurge, called itself kingless, and refused to accept Cyril the archbishop as their illuminator or teacher.[193] The inference Robinson draws from the text is that those whom Shenoute attacked were heterodox Christians who professed no allegiance to the Alexandrian church, although Shenoute calls them pagan heretics. After he seized their magical books (one should note that within the Nag Hammadi library and other so-called gnostic writings such as *First Jeu* and *Second Jeu* are strings of unintelligible vowels and words similar to those found in magical incantations) he also threatened them: "I shall make you acknowledge . . . the Archbishop Cyril, or else the sword will wipe out most of you, and moreover those of you who are spared will go into exile."[194]

Shenoute was also anti-Nestorian, and Cyril asked him to accompany the bishop's entourage to the Council of Ephesus in 431. Although the monks who accompanied Cyril effectively represented the Alexandrian cause which saw Nestorius deposed, a curious tale is given by Besa concerning the return journey. He relates that Cyril's servants would not allow the monk to go aboard the ship to go home, and the abbot had to depend on a miraculous means of getting to Egypt, which God fortunately provided.[195] This suggestion that some difficulty existed between Shenoute and the bishop is especially strange, since most evidence indicates strong support of one for the other. It almost appears from this account (possibly not correct in details) that Cyril's association with Shenoute is based primarily upon the usefulness of the monastic power in the bishop's programs. Besa also reports that at the Synod called to repudiate Nestorianism Shenoute attacked Nestorius, who in turn rebuked the monk:

ΟΥΠЄ ΠЄΚ2ѠΒ ΝΘΟΚ Ῑ2ЄΝΘΜΗϯ ΝΤΔΙϹΥΝΟΔΟϹ; 2ΟΛѠϹ ΡѠ ΝΘΟΚ ΟΥЄΠΙϹ—
ΚΟΠΟϹ ΔΝ ΟΥΔЄ ΝΘΟΚ ΟΥΔΡΧΗΜΔΝΔΡΙΤΗϹ ΔΝ ΟΥΔЄ ΟΥΠΡΟЄϹΤѠϹ ΔΛΛΔ
ΝΘΟΚ ΟΥΜΟΝΔΧΟϹ.[196]

What is your business in the presence of this synod? For to be sure you are neither a bishop nor an archimandrite nor even an administrator, but you are a monk.

Shenoute responded that he was sent by God, implying that such authority superseded any ecclesiastical or administrative authority which men could obtain or confer.

It was after Shenoute's response to Nestorius, as the text continues, that Cyril laid hands on Shenoute's head, kissed him, gave him the tokens of authority, and made him archimandrite on the spot. Although the action may have been performed as an immediate response to the monk's attack on Nestorius, there can be no doubt that it had the further effect of bringing the powerful monk and the monasteries which responded to his charisma and leadership into a closer relationship to the ecclesiastical organization and its equally powerful leader.

Further evidence that each leader was quite autonomous in his own realm is contained in the account of Cyril inviting Shenoute to attend a service in Alexandria. The abbot at first refused to go, and finally was persuaded only by the threat of damnation and excommunication extended by the bishop. He then made a perfunctory visit north and quickly returned to his monasteries.[197] The monasteries were beginning to resemble the Church in organization and doctrinal definition, but the reticence for the monastic communities to embrace the Church fully is still evident in the fifth century.

Shenoute still exhibits some of the trappings of the earlier Apocalyptic and less doctrinally defined Christianity in Egypt, if his biographer is not simply adding hagiographic legends to the archimandrite's vita. The visionary experiences of the monk are numerous, and the heavenly messengers are from both the Old Testament and the New Testament tradition. David the King makes more than one appearance, once to preach to the monks,[198] and another time to sing psalms with a choir of angels.[199] Jeremiah[200] and Ezekiel[201] both appear in vision to read and explain Old Testament passages, and unidentified angels appear, seal a covenant with a handclasp of right hands, and wear special garments, both common to Apocalyptic literature.[202] Three of the most notable figures within the monastic tradition also are said to have appeared to Shenoute, namely Elijah, Elisha, and John the Baptist.[203]

New Testament figures who reportedly appeared to Shenoute in vision include the Twelve Apostles[204] and Paul.[205] In confrontations between cosmic good and cosmic evil which are common to monastic writings, Shenoute also faces demons who try to destroy him[206] and Christ who instructs and rescues him.[207] It is not uncommon for the biographer to state that Shenoute spoke with Jesus face to face for extended periods of time. In the death scene of his *Life*, Shenoute is visited by a host of heavenly personages, including prophets, apostles, archbishops and especially the monks Pjol, Anthony, and Pachomius.[208]

Miracles are attributed to Shenoute, and they often resemble the miracles of Jesus in the New Testament. He multiplied loaves,[209] miraculously escaped a mob trying to kill him,[210] and he demonstrated a powerful influence over the flooding of the Nile.[211] The monk also enjoyed the spirit of prophecy,[212] was transported in vision to Constantinople and back,[213] and became famous by virtue of the many miracles he performed.[214]

Shenoute's influence in the monastic movement is best illustrated by the power and prestige he enjoyed in the world about him. Monks and laity came to him, rather than to the bishop, to receive counsel and blessings.[215] Besa also recounts a visit to the monastery by a

senator.[216] An account with miraculous elements is given, stating that
Shenoute received a letter from the Emperor Theodosius inviting
him to travel to Constantinople.[217] Shenoute did not wish to go, but
was transported to the capital in vision and visited with the emperor
before being returned to Egypt. Generals on their way to war stopped
at the monastery for the archimandrite's blessing, according to
Besa,[218] and when captives were in the area near the monasteries
Shenoute tells how much food and assistance was given to them.[219]
Allowing for exaggeration in amounts of food dispensed and
inflation in the economy, the point is made that the monasteries were
seen as a major part of Egyptian society by the fifth century, so that
groups as well as individuals could turn to them for assistance.[220] One
can understand easily why Cyril, who was autocratic and overbearing
in the Church, needed to cultivate a good relationship with his equally
autocratic and violent counterpart in the burgeoning monastic system. If Shenoute had been as gentle as Pachomius, the Church may
have completely absorbed the monasteries in the time of Cyril, but a
close association was all that could be achieved by the time of Chalcedon.

Dioscorus, the archdeacon to the Alexandrian patriarch, succeeded Cyril in 444 as Patriarch of Alexandria. Frend describes him
as an enigma,[221] and Baus states that he was "one of the most questionable figures of the century in the eastern episcopate."[222] One who
would later oppose Dioscorus, Theodoret, Bishop of Cyrrhus, wrote
to Alexandria to congratulate the new bishop, making mention of his
widespread reputation for modesty.[223] On the other hand, he is
described as one who extorted large sums of money from the relatives
of his predecessor in order to make no-interest loans to bakers and
vintners so they in turn might supply bread and wine to the populace
of Alexandria at low cost.[224] Although Dioscorus has been labeled as
one of the villains of ecclesiastical history, he does not appear so to
some of his contemporaries at the time of his consecration.[225] The
historian Theodoret congratulated him and praised his modesty and
reason,[226] and Domnus of Antioch "believed that at last Alexandria
had elected a bishop with whom he could work."[227] His enemies later
saw him as one who "had filled the whole world with storm and
tempest,"[228] or one who tried to force "devilish blasphemies on his
brethren."[229] In temperament and method of operation Dioscorus
was similar to his predecessor, if not his equal.[230] Both are further

characterized as bishops who "strove to make themselves the masters of Egypt and the leaders of the Church of the East . . . inasmuch as they aimed at making Egypt a sort of independent ecclesiastical state."[231]

Perhaps the comparison to his predecessor offers a clue to understanding how a bishop viewed with optimism at his consecration could become so despicable in such a short time. Frend cites a letter from a presbyter named Alypius to Cyril some years earlier, in which Athanasius was praised because he "had exalted the holy see of St. Mark the Evangelist to the highest degree, and Cyril was following in his footsteps."[232] Frend continues:

> This was Dioscorus' ambition. None would rival the see of Alexandria... 'He turned the see of St. Mark upside down,' it was said (Theodoret, Letter 86). To further his ambitions he gave full rein to his latent aggression in frenzied efforts to stamp out the embers of Nestorianism wherever they might be found.[233]

Whether or not Dioscorus acted under a conscious motivation to emulate and match the accomplishments of Athanasius and Cyril, historians have judged him by that standard and found him wanting.

Dioscorus needed help to keep the growing power of Constantinople at bay, and he sent Poseidonius as a legate to Leo of Rome to announce his consecration and further cement ties between those two Christian centers.[234] Leo also was interested in holding in check the power of the "New Rome" and responded favorably to Dioscorus' prestige. The real strength of his position depended upon his control within his own see. He was "well aware that to no small extent success depended on his having the support of the monastic world,"[235] and he continued the effort begun by Athanasius to secure the loyalty of the monks to the Alexandrian episcopate. Dioscorus' overbearing personality and unscrupulous methods nevertheless caused him to make mistakes and enemies in his own diocese. His brutal mistreatment of Cyril's nephew, the presbyter Athanasius, stirred up a strong reaction against him, and part of the church in Egypt allowed their indignation at the bishop to outweigh their theological loyalty to him.[236] One of Cyril's financial officers, Nestorius, even accused Dioscorus of using some 1400 lbs. of gold from Cyril's legacy for his own purposes.[237]

Despite such difficulties within his own see, Dioscorus remained sufficiently powerful to mount an aggressive attack against his opposition elsewhere in the East. Sellers states that, "unlike Cyril, he directed his attack, not against the see of Constantinople, but against that of Antioch."[238] Yet though Cyril was attacking the growing power of Constantinople at the expense of Alexandria, he was also assailing the Antiochene Nestorius (as his uncle earlier had done in the case of John Chrysostom), so the difference in opponents for Cyril and Dioscorus is not really so great as Sellers suggests. Within the ecclesiastical territory of Antioch, some who had supported Cyril at the Council of Ephesus had been deposed, such as Athanasius of Perrha,[239] or not appointed after an earlier nomination, as Alexander in Antaradus of Phoenicia.[240] Other 'Nestorianizers' were appointed in the see of Antioch,[241] and in view of such actions, the adherents of the Alexandrian position began to react.

Since 441, the most influential man in the Emperor's court had been the Grand Chamberlain, Chrysaphius.[242] Being essentially monastic in temperament, he and the other eunuchs of the court also tended to favor the Alexandrian point of view, perhaps due to the influence of Chrysaphius' godfather, the archimandrite Eutyches, who was especially sympathetic to Dioscorus' position.[243] Eutyches ruled over and was venerated by a large monastery of 300 monks and, coupled with the association he enjoyed with Chrysaphius, was an important figure in helping formulate Imperial Court policy on religious matters.[244] His influence was enhanced by the banishment of the Empress Eudoxia in 444 because of suspected infidelity to her husband,[245] and Chrysaphius became the real power behind the throne until Theodosius' death.[246]

As for Flavian, the bishop of Constantinople, Chrysaphius disliked him because the bishop had refused to send him an *eulogion* of gold at his consecration.[247] Flavian was nevertheless able to amass sufficient support to hold a 'Home Synod' in November, 448, in which Eutyches' refusal to accept the Antiochene two-nature formula of Christology caused his deposition and loss of priestly status.[248] Soon afterward, in a letter from Flavian to Leo, Eutyches' teaching was characterized as being that of an Appollinarian and also that of a Valentinian Gnostic.[249] The last-mentioned epithet is especially interesting, implying that perhaps Valentinian Gnosticism was still an issue in some areas of Christianity at this late date. It is tantalizing to observe that it is here associated with one of the most venerated monks of the time, even though certainly not as an indictment against monasticism. Furthermore, Eutyches did condemn Mani, Valentinus, and others in his defense at the Council of Ephesus in 449.[250]

Eutyches' fall from power and influence appeared to be a setback for the cause of Dioscorus, but Frend states that "as at Ephesus the anti-Alexandrian bishops had failed to read the tide of public opinion."[251] The Alexandrian patriarch was able to marshall great support from Egyptian and Syrian monks who venerated the fallen archimandrite, as well as to obtain the backing of Theodosius for Eutyches. Leo at first had also supported Eutyches, but, upon review of the materials sent by Flavian, was induced to change his mind and support the decision of the Home Synod,[252] although he regarded Eutyches more of a fool than a heretic.[253] The Roman prelate also tried to dissuade Theodosius from calling a Council, but Eutyches enjoyed the sympathy of the Court through his godson, Chrysaphius, and a Council was called for 1 August 449 at Ephesus.[254] Eutyches not only convinced Chrysaphius to persuade the emperor to call the Council, but was also able to have Dioscorus appointed president of the meeting.[255] Through this imperial intercessor, the Alexandrian episcopate was reasserting a leading role in the Church, but this apparent glory was fleeting, and the Alexandrian bishops would not exert such influence again within the Catholic Church.

"The decisions of the council were a foregone conclusion."[256] Some 135 bishops were in attendance, most of them solid supporters of Eutyches and Dioscorus. By the Council's end, Flavian and Eusebius of Dorylaeum were among those deposed, and Eutyches was declared orthodox.[257] The Roman legates could understand the proceedings in Greek only imperfectly and, combined with the tactics of Dioscorus in running the Council, they were ineffective in lodging any protests or exerting influence in the proceedings. Dioscorus had taken precautions of his own to ensure a favorable outcome in the Council. In addition to a strong imperial police force, the monastic followers of Eutyches, and a large group of Syrian monks, the Alexandrian "brought with him a detachment of Alexandrian *parabolani*—members of a guild of nurses of the sick, who could be used for other purposes also."[258] When he called for a vote of the bishops, and as some were hesitating, Dioscorus had the church doors opened and "soldiers, noisy monks, and a shouting mob streamed in."[259]

The *Latrocinium*, or Robber Council of Ephesus as it was called by Leo, concluded by deposing Theodoret of Cyrrhus, Domnus of Antioch, Ibas of Edessa, and others sympathetic to them. Dioscorus' success appeared complete, and he was able to have his own deacon and representative in the capital,[260] Anatolius, appointed bishop of Constantinople in the place of the deposed Flavian.[261] Another of the significant results of the Council of 449, according to Sellers, was that the Antiochene school never recovered from the severe blow.[262] One could almost refer to the Alexandrian successes as Pyrrhic victories, since the cost paid in hardened positions and questionable tactics used in winning a battle must be counted against immensely greater losses at Chalcedon in 451.

The triumph was short-lived. Leo had been alienated from Alexandria, perhaps in part by the letter of Eutyches to the Roman bishop in 448, in which the monk referred to Cyril as "the leader and chief of the holy synod of Ephesus," words certainly not in harmony with the views of Rome.[263] It could not have helped matters that Leo's *Tome*, written to influence the deliberations of the Council, had not been read.[264] The letter, written to Flavius, denounced Eutyches and the Alexandrian Christology of the day.[265] Dioscorus did not technically refuse to allow the letter to be read, but he made certain "that it was propelled down the agenda until lost sight of in the crowded moments that ensued."[266] The one-sided and volatile nature of the Council were so obvious that Frend suggests that "It was good that Leo's *Tome* was not read, for in that atmosphere its author and his representative's would have been excommunicated then and there."[267] In fact, when Flavius and Eusebius were deposed by the heavy-handed procedures of Dioscorus, the Roman deacon called out *contradicitur* into the church,[268] and it was unquestionably fortunate for him that not many present knew Latin very well.[269]

Leo may have held the opinion that Eutyches was unskilled and rash in his theology,[270] but the extreme 'One-Nature' Christology and the brutal tactics of the so-called Robber Council in 449 greatly increased Roman disaffection toward Alexandria.[271] The alienated bishop of Rome now led the opposition, and he sent seven letters protesting the proceedings of the Council to Pulcheria, Anastasius of Thessalonica, the monks at Constantinople, Flavian, Julian of Cos, Theodosius, and the clergy of Constantinople.[272] Leo apparently had not understood the gravity of the controversy for any length of time before the Council, for he wrote Flavian just before the first session urging that Eutyches be treated mildly if he repented of his error.[273] And within the Imperial Court after the Council, a reaction was setting in, for Pulcheria in early 450 indicated her disapproval of the Council's errors,[274] and even Anatolius, the new patriarch of Constantinople, "began to assert his independence from Dioscorus."[275] The real change in the state of affairs occurred on 28 July 450, when the Emperor Theodosius II fell from his horse and died.[276] The political situation was immediately reversed, as Chrysaphius was put to death by Marcian, who succeeded Theodosius on the throne.[277] The relationship between the patriarch of Constantinople and the new Emperor Marcian may have accounted for the former's cooler relationship with Dioscorus, for Anatolius was at least present at the coronation, and may have been the one who actually crowned Marcian.[278]

Marcian was determined to overthrow the old regime,[279] and Dioscorus obviously perceived his intent, for at Chalcedon he attempted to prevent the proclamation of Marcian's accession.[280] The bishops who had been banished by Dioscorus were recalled[281] and, at the suggestion of Anatolius, on 23 May 451, the Emperor called for a general council to be held in Nicaea that September.[282] Leo of Rome was reluctant to see a Council called in the East, where the bishop of Constantinople might acquire too much power, but since he knew the Emperor would not hold the Council in the West, he had to content himself with an appeal for postponement.[283] His request was refused, and the bishops began to arrive in Nicaea for the opening of the Council on 1 September.[284] For some reason Marcian and his consort Pulcheria were slow in making their arrival and the bishops complained at the delay. The result was an order for the bishops to journey to Chalcedon, so that the nearness of the meeting to the capital would allow Marcian to attend to matters of state as well as participate in the Council.[285]

Almost as a signal that the Council was not going to be peaceful, Dioscorus, with the 17 bishops from Egypt accompanying him, arrived early at Chalcedon and excommunicated Leo of Rome, being convinced that Leo's famous *Tome* was contaminated with Nestorianism.[286] A breakdown of the unity at the Ephesian Council of 449 began to appear, for Anatolius of Constantinople and Juvenal of Jerusalem refused to support Dioscorus in his action.[287] The Alexandrian bishop surely had a clear idea from that point what lay ahead of him, but he was undaunted in his determination to see the matter to the end.[288]

The first session of the Council was on 8 October. Leo's papal delegate, Bishop Paschasinus, spoke at the beginning of the session, moving that both a seat and a vote be denied Dioscorus in the proceedings.[289] Marcian may have moved to estrange Dioscorus' backers even more from the Alexandrian by establishing Jerusalem as a Patriarchate.[290] Juvenal and his associates were certainly not going to jeopardize such a move by standing beside Dioscorus against the Emperor. The first session was not all anti-Dioscorus, however. The uproar caused by the attempt to restore Theodoret to his see and admit him to the Council as an accuser of the Alexandrian bishop was stilled only through imperial pressure and intimidation.[291] Most of the bishops opposed Theodoret and repudiated his "Nestorian" theology. Still, the new emperor and his court had to be accommodated, and Theodoret was seated in the Council. After the reading of Flavian's doctrinal statement which had been given at the Home Synod in 448, further defections from the Alexandrian patriarch occurred, including Anatolius, Maximus of Antioch, the Palestinian bishops with Juvenal, the bishops of Illyricum, and even 4 of the 17 Egyptian bishops.[292] Dioscorus still refused to yield, although he was at that point nearly alone.[293] The split opinion evidenced within the Egyptian delegation, and which continued for many centuries between the competing factions of the pro-Chalcedonian "Melchites" and the Coptic Monophysites, shows that by the middle of the fifth century the bishop of Alexandria was still unable to claim complete ecclesiastical control in Egypt, even among the few bishops who accompanied him to this critical Council. His real source of power, as noticed earlier, lay with the monastic movement.

Contrary to the expectations of many present, the second session of the Council proceeded to deal with the formulation of right belief concerning the nature of Christ.[294] The Creeds of the earlier Councils of Nicaea and Constantinople were read, and two of Cyril's letters were also read to the assembled bishops. All these were accepted by acclamation, as was Leo's *Tome*.[295] The emperor still persisted in calling for a new creed, apparently believing that there was no alternative to achieving unity and a peaceful settlement.[296] The bishop resisted, arguing that the faith was adequately defined in the documents mentioned above. Finally, however, the emperor prevailed, and a committee of 23 bishops was appointed to draw up a creed, which they did in three days.[297] The crucial session of the Council concerning the statement of faith was the fifth.[298] The proposed creed had the phrase ἐκ δύο φύσεων *of* two natures, rather than ἐν δύο φύσεσιν *in* two natures, when discussing Christ. The Romans threatened to leave if it were changed. Because Dioscorus could accept *of* rather than *in*, the council nevertheless had to reword the Creed to try to satisfy the Romans, satisfy the East, and exclude Dioscorus.[299] The resulting creed included *in two natures*, but also qualified the phrase in such a way "as to exclude any hint of a strongly Antiochene (or 'Nestorian') interpretation."[300] The relevant portion of the creed thus reads: ". . . in two natures, without confusion, without change, without division, without separation . . ."[301]

During the Third session, all those who had presided at the Ephesian Council of 449, and who had been deposed in the first session at Chalcedon, were separated from Dioscorus, and he was charged with contumacious conduct because he had excommunicated Leo.[302] His deposition and exile were upheld by Marcian and Pulcheria, while in the fourth session the remaining bishops who had been deposed for their role at Ephesus now accepted Leo's *Tome* and were reinstated.[303] Dioscorus had thus been effectively separated from his erstwhile supporters, and in his exile was sent first to Cyzicus, then to Heraclea, and finally to Gangra, where he died 4 September, 454.[304]

The effect of the Council of Chalcedon was to unify most of Christianity, but the intransigent monophysites were severed from the church. Most important for this study is the observation that Alexandria's position as the favored Catholic see of the East had been effectively and officially replaced by Constantinople. In Seller's words, ". . . Theophilus, Cyril, and Dioscorus had governed Eastern Christendom like 'second pharaohs' but at Chalcedon the pretensions of the Alexandrian see came to an end."[305] Canon 28 of the Council ratified the Council of Constantinople Canon 3, establishing Constantinople as an equal in all ways to Rome, being second only in ecclesiastical matters. J. B. Bury sees the Council's action as the culmination of a process begun much earlier:

> Politically, the Council was a decisive triumph for Constantinople and a final blow to the pretensions of the see of Alexandria. Marcian completed what Theodosius the Great had begun. Three successive Patriarchs, Theophilus, Cyril, and Dioscorus, had aimed at attaining the supreme position in Eastern Christendom and at ruling Egypt like kings. Alexandria could never again claim to lead the Church in theology. But the defeat of Alexandria was accompanied by an exaltation of Byzantium which was far from acceptable to Rome.[306]

One should emphasize the political rather than the theological impli-
cations of the Council's action toward Dioscorus, for he was *not* condemned as a heretic, but was deposed for contumacy in excommuni-
cating Leo.[307] Far from losing his monastic support in Egypt, the
exiled bishop, "the 'valiant Dioscorus'. . . became the type of the em-
battled ascetic leader proof against the intellectual pitfalls laid by his
adversaries."[308]

It is obvious, at least in retrospect, that the Council of Chalcedon
was the decisive event which led to the establishment of the national
Coptic Egyptian Church. One must remember, however, that
Dioscorus and his immediate successors did not perceive themselves
as founders of the new church, and further attempts at unifying the
pro-Chalcedonians and the anti-Chalcedonians would take place over
the next century. Although the conclusion of the war was not in doubt
after Chalcedon, some skirmishes and battles yet remained to be
fought.

In the later sessions of Chalcedon, the bishops voted agreement to
canons which would subordinate the monastic movement even more
to the rule of the bishops. No monasteries could be built without
consent from the diocesan bishop, monks were to be subject to their
bishops, and they were not to enlist fugitive slaves as monks.[309] The
purpose of these enactments, states Frend, was to strengthen the
authority of the episcopal government against the growing power of
the monks.[310] When one remembers the role of the monks in assisting
the Alexandrian bishop achieve his conciliar aims, especially
Shenoute in the Council of Ephesus in 431 and the Syrian monks in
the so-called Latrocinium of 449, an additional dimension is added to
the canons of Chalcedon. Monasticism was clearly a formidable
power which must be tethered by the very ecclesiastical authority it
might otherwise overcome.

The difficulty of enforcing this legislated episcopal authority in
Egypt, however, is evident from the breakdown of group interests.
The great majority of Egyptian Christians were anti-Chalcedonian,
including a small number who were monastic enthusiasts of Eutyches
(as distinguished from Cyrillians, etc.). There was another small, but
powerful group which favored the Chalcedon decisions.[311] The anti-
Chalcedonian movement became visible when the four returning
pro-Chalcedonian bishops consecrated Proterius as bishop in place of
the deposed Dioscorus. The selection of Proterius appears to have

been an attempt to diminish the public reaction against the deposition and exile of Dioscorus, for it was to this arch-priest that Dioscorus had given control of the Church while the bishop attended the Council of Chalcedon.[312] The attempt was unsuccessful, however, and the public uproar so great that order was restored only with the assistance of military force,[313] and Proterius' position remained tenuous in the uneasy peace which followed. The popularity of Dioscorus among the monks might be given as a reason for Proterius' impotence in office,[314] but even after the former's death in 454, Proterius was unable to advance the Chalcedonian cause.[315] The patriarch's following was made up primarily from officials and foreigners[316] and isolated groups of Pachomian monks, for the "majority of the Egyptian Church and people had separated themselves from him in disgust."[317]

As soon as the death of Marcian became known in Egypt in early 457, a monophysite bishop named Timothy, nicknamed the Cat, was consecrated.[318] Timothy was a monk who had served as presbyter with Cyril, and was regarded as continuing in the succession of Cyril and Dioscorus.[319] A group of monks and clerics smuggled him into Alexandria for the consecration by Peter of Iberia, a Palestinian bishop in exile at the time.[320] The splitting of the Alexandrian bishopric is said by one commentator to have accelerated the progress of emerging Egyptian nationalism which would result in a national church.[321] Frend alludes to some slight evidence which suggests that the new emperor Leo I was favorably disposed toward Timothy at first,[322] but local military leaders acted in haste before rapprochement was established.[323] The *comes Aegypti* arrested Timothy, and a large mob responded to his arrest by lynching Proterius, and then dragging his body through the streets, and burning it in the Hippodrome.[324]

The episcopacy of Proterius was established and maintained only through imperial force, and the authority did not extend outside Alexandria to any great degree. Hardy states that only ten or twelve bishops outside the provincial capital and one Pachomian monastery in the delta supported him.[325] The distinction between the "foreign Church" in Alexandria and the local Egyptian Christians observed in earlier centuries was still evident after Chalcedon, but with a major difference: the important and powerful means of control in the provinces, namely an imported imperial civil service, was severely weakened in Egypt.[326] Local leaders exercised considerable autonomy and freedom in most aspects of their responsibility, and a corresponding sense of independence from imperial control is clearly evident in the Egyptian Church.[327] The fate of Proterius mirrors the fate of effective outside influence or control of Christianity along the Nile.

Timothy attempted to have the new Emperor, Leo, call a new general council in 457, but frantic maneuvering by Pope Leo and others prevented the proposed Council from taking place.[328] The western bishops, under Leo's theological guidance, were able to bring sufficient pressure against Timothy so that in 459 he was arrested and exiled to Gangra on the Black Sea.[329] Timothy's absence from Egypt gave his opposition a chance to exercise control over the Church for a time. Among those who had supported Proterius and Chalcedon were some "Pachomian monks at Canopus where memories of Dioscorus' tyranny died hard."[330] One of the monks, Timothy nicknamed Wobble-cap was consecrated bishop of Alexandria,[331] but despite his attempts to accommodate various factions of Christians, the greater part of the Church did not accept him in the place of Timothy the Cat.[332]

The emperor Leo died in 474, and a palace revolution occurred during the next year which caused his successor Zeno, an Isaurian who had risen rapidly in Leo's court and who had even married the emperor's daughter, to flee temporarily. The usurper Basiliscus was thus left on the throne, and he published an *Encyclion* which condemned Chalcedon and effectively gave control to the monophysites in Egypt.[333] After a seventeen-year exile Timothy the Cat was recalled, and was immediately received in triumph at Alexandria.[334] Although his return was pleasing to the majority of Egyptian Christians, Timothy was disappointing to some of the monks who favored the Eutychian position which stated that the divine nature of Christ had wholly absorbed the human nature, making the result an entirely heavenly Christ.[335] Timothy stated his own view that "the humanity of Christ was in all ways similar to our own,"[336] causing a continued split even among the anti-Chalcedonian monks. At Timothy's arrival in Egypt, Timothy Wobble-cap returned to his monastery with a small pension,[337] and 'the Cat' seemed securely in control of the Alexandrian see. Zeno was returned to power in the summer of 476, however, and only Timothy's death in the next summer prevented his being exiled again.[338]

The short reign of Basiliscus showed both to Zeno and to Acacius of Constantinople the strength of the monophysite movement in

Egypt,[339] and a further attempt to establish unity between Egypt and those accepting Chalcedon was made by Zeno. On Acacius' advice, Zeno drafted the famous *Henotikon* on 28 July, 482, and it "was addressed to the bishops, monks, and laymen of Alexandria, Egypt, and Cyrenaica."[340] Despite Frend's giving credit to Acacius for advising the emperor to produce the *Henotikon*, Gray writes that the real impetus "appears to have been a request made by the monks of Alexandria that Zeno give imperial approval to Peter Mongus' status as patriarch of Alexandria."[341] The decisions of the first three ecumenical councils were recognized, Nestorius and Eutyches were anathematized, the twelve anathemas of Cyril were accepted, and Mary was repeatedly designated *Theotokos*. The document is clearly an attempt at conciliation by returning to a pre-Chalcedonian theology, without explicit repudiation of that Council. The *Henotikon* was published by the authority of the Emperor without a council of bishops, was signed by the monophysite patriarchs in Alexandria and Antioch, and appeared to have brought the churches of the East back into harmony with each other.[342] The Roman see obviously did not approve of the *Henotikon*, and in 484 the Pope excommunicated both Acacius and the Emperor, and while Chadwick notes the regret felt at Constantinople over the Papal act, he further states that, "it was more important for the emperor to retain the loyalty of Egypt and Syria than to keep in step with Rome and the now disintegrating barbarian West."[343]

The primary weakness of the *Henotikon* lay with its origin, for it came from the emperor and not from the bishops whose action at Chalcedon had caused the break. Because of this, any attempt at reconciliation which did not include a denunciation of Chalcedon had no real chance of success in Egypt.[344] Peter Mongus, the successor to Timothy the Cat, was in the uncomfortable position of trying to placate extreme anti-Chalcedonian monks by denouncing Chalcedon and at the same time accepting the *Henotikon*.[345] Most people in Alexandria appeared to be satisfied with the *Henotikon*, and they formed the nucleus for a continued pro-Chalcedonian community in Alexandria, known as the Melchite (Imperial) Church of Egypt.[346] The dissident monks, to whom anything less than a formal condemnation of Chalcedon was unacceptable, became known among themselves as the *Akephaloi* (headless ones), indicating they were without a leader.[347] For them the *Henotikon* was not sufficient. Some 30,000 of these monks, led by bishop Theodore of Antinoë who had laid hands on Peter's head, are said to have confronted Peter Mongus concerning his theology, and while he was judged orthodox, they nevertheless rejected him because he remained in communion with "Chalcedonians."[348] Finally, however, Peter denounced both Chalcedon and Leo's *Tome* in order to achieve unity in Christian Egypt,[349] as did his successor, Athanasius II.[350] Despite this denunciation, communion was not broken with Constantinople, and no successors in the Proterian tradition were chosen.[351] Continued association with the imperial capital by the Alexandrian episcopate provided sufficient grounds for disaffection from the bishop by the *Akephaloi*, and thus the *Henotikon* had the dubious distinction of further alienating many whom it was meant to reconcile. Similar attempts with equally unsuccessful results occurred over the next century, but both the pro- and anti-Chalcedonian factions became more polarized and intransigent in their positions. Both sides could be found in Egypt, but the establishment of a dominant and separate monophysite movement had been realized.

Although the anti-Chalcedonian forces in other Eastern Patriarchates, as in Egypt, led ultimately to the formation of separate churches, no move to establish a separate hierarchy emerged for sixty years after Chalcedon except along the Nile.[352] As noted earlier, even in Egypt, where both pro- and anti-Chalcedonian bishops were competing for control on occasion,[353] "there was no thought of setting up a separate Egyptian Church" immediately after Chalcedon,[354] for then it was "a schism of minds and hearts but not of organizations."[355] Furthermore, the pro-Chalcedonian minority in Egypt cannot be identified strictly as the "foreign element" or the "city element." Some Pachomian monks were pro-Chalcedonian, although most monks in Egypt, including much of the cenobitic movement, repudiated the Council.[356] On the other hand, many people in Alexandria supported the anti-Chalcedonians,[357] and not all the officials and wealthy people who supported Chalcedon were foreigners.[358] Patterns explaining the division are difficult to establish, and Frend observes that the differences "ran through families and friends rather than along hard and fast community boundaries."[359]

The individual most responsible for establishing an ecclesiastical hierarchy to rival the Chalcedonians in the East was Severus of Antioch. Our knowledge of his life comes primarily from the two literary *lives* of Severus, one by Zacharias Scholasticus and the other by John of Beith-Aphthonia in Syria, which are preserved only in Syriac translations from the Greek originals.[360] Both are contemporary records, valuable for the information they give concerning their subject and also concerning pagan-Christian relations during the period. Born in c.465 into a wealthy landowning family whose members had wielded considerable power in their local communities for generations (his grandfather had been a bishop in Pisidia at the time of the Council of Ephesus in 431),[361] Severus traveled to Alexandria as a young man to study Greek and Latin grammar preparatory for studying law. He moved to Berytus in c.486 to begin legal training, but was drawn away from his studies to accept baptism and the monastic life through the influence of Peter of Iberia, who visited Berytus in 488.[362] While Severus himself did not leave a great treatise containing his theological reasoning in summary form, his voluminous correspondence covering some 30 years shows how he formulated and refined the monophysite distinctions from the pro-Chalcedonian position.[363] Severus was consecrated Patriarch of Antioch in November 512, but growing opposition to his rule in Syria and elsewhere in the eastern provinces made his position increasingly precarious. The death of Emperor Anastasius in July 518, and the accession of the pro-Chalcedonian Justin soon afterward, strengthened the position of the patriarch's opposition, and Severus was deposed by a synod held in Constantinople.[364] To avoid arrest, Severus fled to Egypt, arriving in Alexandria on 29 September 518, where, he stated, the Egyptians were preparing for active opposition to the new emperor's policies.[365] The deposed patriarch attempted to rule his diocese while in exile, and Frend believes that Severus then first began thinking of establishing a rival hierarchy to combat the Chalcedonians in Syria.[366] In a letter to one of his supporters, bishop Sergius of Cyrrhus, he stated that the archimandrites must accept the responsibility for appointment to ecclesiastical offices,[367] for much of the strength of his movement lay in the monastic movement. It is difficult to determine how much Severus was influenced by the anti-Chalcedonian organization beginning to be established in Egypt, or how much that organization was directly affected by the exiled patriarch in Alexandria. Clearly, however, the rise of a monophysite hierarchy outside Egypt strengthened the monophysite organization in that country.[368]

Just as Severus was beginning to establish a monophysite clerical system, a change in the government helped turn the fortunes of the hitherto persecuted movement. The Emperor Justin's successor, Justinian (527–565), did not deviate from supporting Chalcedon, but his own inclinations toward the monophysite theology caused him to cease persecuting the anti-Chalcedonians.[369] From that time, the monophysite hierarchy was permanently established and grew to become the national religion in the Churches of Egypt, Armenia, Nubia, Ethiopia, and much of Syria with the Arab tribes.[370]

In summary of the history of Christian Egypt in the late-Roman early-Byzantine period, one can see how the Council of Chalcedon and its aftermath saw the separation of Egyptian Christianity from Catholic Christianity. This separation was the natural result of an alienation stemming in large part from the founding and development of Constantinople as the Eastern Capital of the Roman Empire. Alexandria, which had played the leading role in ecclesiastical and theological affairs for the eastern portion of the Empire (at least that, and often more) for approximately three centuries, was relegated to an unaccustomed subservient status. The new and dominant role of the eastern imperial capital as stated in the Canons of both the Councils of Constantinople in 381 and Chalcedon in 451 struck unacceptable blows to the prestige of the Alexandrian Patriarchs. It is ironic that the Alexandrian bishops' international influence should decline just at the time their control over discrete elements of Christianity was finally becoming a reality.

In addition to a nationalistic response to the unacceptable demotion from first city in the East, Baus notes that a subsequent de-Hellenization of the ecclesiastical system accompanied the establishment of the Monophysite theology.[371] The ecclesiastical organization and doctrinal definition of Catholicism was by then firmly established in Egypt, however, and the earlier local Egyptian Christians had been transformed from a loosely organized and broad-based religion into a movement similar to and sympathetic with Egyptian Catholicism. In the centuries following Chalcedon they became even more united, driven together by external forces as well as internal similarities, and the resulting unity became the national Egyptian Christian Coptic Church.

ENDNOTES

[1] The first few letters, written between 330 and 335 contain general indictments against divisive forces among the Christians, meaning those who will not submit to the patriarch in Alexandria (or wherever he happened to be). ". . . and with him (the devil) are all inventors of unlawful heresies, who indeed refer to the scriptures, but do not hold such opinions as the saints have handed down . . ." (2.6 in A.D. 330); ". . . but especially now, when the time is one of tribulation, which the heretics excite against us . . ." (3.5 in 331); ". . . the schismatics keep it (the feast) in separate places, and with vain imaginations." (5.4 in 333); ". . . to the schismatics, in not rending the coat of Christ, but in one house, even in the Catholic Church, let us eat the Passover of the Lord . . ." (*ibid.*); ". . . at this same time the altogether wicked heretics and ignorant schismatics are in the same case; the one in that they deny the Word, the other that they rend the coat . . ." (6.6 in 334, all translations by Robertson).

[2] The Arians, for example, are mentioned in 11.13 of A.D. 339, the Melitians in 12.1, perhaps of the next year (the dating of 12 isn't entirely certain), etc.

[3] Young, *op. cit.*, p.79. "Athanasius' avoidance of the word *homoousios* is easily exaggerated, and certainly need not reflect 'tact' towards other parties: he himself may have only gradually recognized its usefulness."

[4] Frend, *Rise of Christianity*, *op. cit.*, p.577.

[5] *Ibid.*

[6] Frend, *Monophysite*, *op. cit.*, pp. 74, 82.

[7] Theodoret, *Hist. Eccl.* I.9.14.

[8] Athanasius, *Epist.* 39.2.

[9] *Ibid.*, 3.

[10] *Ibid.*, 2.

[11] For similar observations on the significance of Athanasius' 39*th* Letter, see Hennecke-Schneemelcher, *op. cit.*, I, pp.60–61.

[12] C. Wilfred Griggs, "The Origin and Formation of the Corpus of Apocryphal Literature," *Apocryphal Writings and the Latter-day Saints*. Provo: Brigham Young University Religious Studies Center, 1986, pp.35–52. *The Secret Gospel of Mark*, Clement, Origen, and the Nag Hammadi Library are major examples of authors and literature typifying this tradition in Egyptian Christianity.

[13] Bart Ehrman, "The New Testament Canon of Didymus the Blind," *Vigiliae Christianae* 37 (1983), pp.1–21. For a detailed study of the text of the Gospels used by Didymus, see Ehrman's *Didymus the Blind and the Text of the Gospels*. Atlanta: Scholar's Press, 1986. The work is a publication of his dissertation, submitted at Princeton in 1985.

[14] *Ibid.*, pp.11–18.

[15] *Ibid.*, p.18.

[16] *Ibid.*, p.19.

[17] Amelineau, *Vie de Theodore, Annales*, *op. cit.*, p. 239.

[18] *Ibid.*, pp. 240–241.

[19] Frend, *Monophysite*, *op. cit.*, p. 154, for the instance in 455 when Marcian promulgated such threats and orders. Cf. R. H. Charles, *op. cit.*, II, p. 163, for a similar observation in the case of I Enoch.

[20] James M. Robinson, ed., *The Nag Hammadi Library in English* (New York: Harper and Row, 1977), pp. 21ff. The same author published a pamphlet, *The Nag Hammadi Codices* (Claremont: The Ink Spot), with the story of the discovery on pp. 2ff. See also *The Facsimile Edition of the Nag Hammadi Codices* (Leiden: E. J. Brill, 1976), pref. vii. For

an earlier account of the discovery, see JeanDoresse, *The Secret Books of the Egyptian Gnostics* (New York: Viking Press, 1960), pp. 116ff. esp. from p. 128. The orthodox version has generally replaced the camel drivers story or the tea-makers story of the discovery, for witnesses of those two accounts have not been found in recent years. Furthermore, as noted later in the text, no archaeological evidence has been found supportive of any of the stories associated with the discovery. A ceramic dish was once displayed with a Nag Hammadi exhibit and was claimed to be the lid of the jar in which the library was found, but the lid was given to Robinson by a peasant and was not recovered through archaeological excavation at the site. The official report of the excavation is found in *The Facsimile Edition of the Nag Hammadi Codices, Introduction*, ed. James M. Robinson. Leiden: E. J. Brill, 1984. The doubts and concerns expressed by this author are similar to those held by Rodolphe Kasser and Martin Krause as expressed in a two-page long footnote on pp.3–4 of the volume: "Rodolphe Kasser and Martin Krause wish to make it known here that they have serious reasons to put in doubt the objective value of a number of important points of the Introduction that follows. They contest especially the detailed history of the discovery of the Coptic Gnostic manuscripts of Nag Hammadi resulting from the investigation of James M. Robinson." The note continues, stating that only the core of the story (general location and time of discovery) can be accepted as more than fable and gossip.

[21] Robinson, *N. H. in English*, *op. cit.*, p. 23. Cp. Robinson, *Facsimile Edition Intro.*, p.5.

[22] John W. B. Barns, "Greek and Coptic Papyri from the Covers of the Nag Hammadi Codices," *Essays on the Nag Hammadi Texts*, NHS VI (Leiden: E. J. Brill, 1975), pp. 9–17.

[23] *Ibid.*, p. 12.

[24] E. G. Turner, Comment of Barns' article, *op. cit.*, p. 18.

[25] *Ibid.*, pp. 17–18.

[26] J. W. B. Barns† , G.M. Browne, and J.C. Shelton, eds., *Nag Hammadi Codices: Greek and Coptic Papyri from the Cartonnage of the Covers*, NHS 16. Leiden: E.J. Brill, 1981. Barns was listed as a contributing author because his papers on the cartonnage were given to Browne and Shelton by his widow (see foreword, p.ix).

[27] *Ibid.*, p.2. John Shelton, editor of the Greek papyri in the collection, wrote the introductory essay which gives the overview and summary of the cartonnage.

[28] *Ibid.*, pp.2–4.

[29] *Ibid.*, pp.4–7.

[30] *Ibid.*, p.7.

[31] *Ibid.*

[32] *Ibid.*, p.61.

[33] *Ibid.*, pp.61–76.

[34] *Ibid.*, pp.139–142.

[35] *Ibid.*, p.141.

[36] *Ibid.*, pp.10–11.

[37] *Ibid.*, p.11.

[38] *Ibid.*, p.6, citing *Patrol. Lat.* 23.73 and *Patrol. Gr.* 40.949, and F. Halkin, ed., *Sancti Pachomii Vitae Graecae*. Brussels, 1932, pp.24–25.

[39] Robinson, *Nag Hammadi Library*, *op. cit.*, p.17. Robinson gives persuasive arguments to show that the writings were considered sacred.

[40] Douglas Parrott, "The Nag Hammadi Library and the Pachomian Monasteries," an unpublished paper read at the International Conference on Gnosticism held at Yale University on 28–31 March 1978, pp. 7ff. A copy of the paper was kindly furnished the author of this study at his request.

[41] *Ibid.*, p. 8.

[42] *Ibid.*, p. 7–8.

[43] *Apocalypse of Peter* VII, *3* 81, 3ff.

[44] *Apocalypse of Adam* V, 5, 65–66; *Hypostasis of the Archons* II, 4, 87, 10ff.; *The Origin of the World* II, 5; etc.

[45] Theodoret, *Hist. Eccl.* IV.11.

[46] Robertson, *op. cit.*, p. lxii, implies the latter reason by his statement that, "Little occurred to disturb his (Athanasius') peace at home, and if the confusion and distress of the Eastern Church under Valens could not but cause him anxiety, in Egypt at any rate, so long as he lived the Catholic Faith was secure from molestation." Cf. Socrates, *Hist. Eccl.* IV.20, where the historian states that Valens was restrained by God from troubling the Egyptian church so long as Athanasius was alive, especially because the bishop commanded a great following in the Church: πυνθανόμενος πλεῖστον εἶναι κατ᾿ αὐτὴν τὸ πλῆθος τῶν προσκειμένων ᾿Αθανασίῳ.

[47] *Ibid.*

[48] Socrates, *Hist. Eccl.* IV.20; Theodoret, *Hist. Eccl.* IV.27: "He had shared the heavy labors of Athanasius; at home and abroad he had always been at his side, and had undergone many perils with him."

[49] *Ibid.*, 21; Cf. Theodoret, *Hist. Eccl.* IV. 18.

[50] Theodoret, *Hist. Eccl.* IV.19. These items are also mentioned in Cyprian, *Epist.* 55.8: de clericorum testimonio, de plebis . . . suffragio, et de sacerdotum collegio."

[51] Socrates, *Hist. Eccl.* IV.21–22; Theodoret, *Hist. Eccl.* IV.18–19.

[52] Rufinus, *Hist. Eccl.* II.2–4; *Apol. ad Anast.* 2.

[53] Jerome, *Apology* 2,3.

[54] Socrates, *Hist. Eccl.* IV 21.

[55] Ammianus Marcellinus 31.13.18f.

[56] Theodoret, *Hist. Eccl.* IV.19. Even a deacon serving as a courier from Damasus in Rome was beaten and deported to work in copper mines. The evil reputation of Heliopolis is not widely attested, and a stock charge of paganism and loose living is not easily defended without specific details.

[57] *Ibid.*

[58] Socrates *Hist. Eccl.* IV.24; Sozomen, *Hist. Eccl.* VI.20.

[59] *Ibid.*, IV.25: Sozomen, *Hist. Eccl.* VI.20; Theodoret, *Hist. Eccl.* IV.26.

[60] *Ibid.* IV.22. Sozomen, *Hist. Eccl.* VI.20, agrees with Socrates but is clearly using the elder historian as his source.

[61] Athanasius, *Ad Monach.* 1 and 2.

[62] Gregory of Nazianzus, *Carmen* XI.844–847. For the religious ferment in Constantinople and the effect it had on the public, (see Gregory of Nyssa's famous portrayal of the interest shown in doctrinal issues at a popular level *On the Deity of the Son and the Holy Spirit*, P.G. 46.557).

[63] Frend, *Rise of Christianity, op. cit.*, p.636.

[64] *Ibid.*, 814; *Orat.* XXV. The latter was given in praise of Maximus by Gregory, illustrating the degree to which the Egyptian candidate had become attached to the bishop.

[65] *Ibid.*, 887.

[66] *Ibid.*, 909.

[67] *Ibid.*, 1001–1009.

[68] Damasus, *Epist.* 5.

[69] Gregory of Nazianzus, *Carmen* XI.1023.

[70] C. J. Hefele (transl. by H. Oxenham), *History of the Councils of the Church* (Edinburgh: T&T Clark, 1896), pp.340f.

[71] Frend, *Early Church, op. cit.*, p.221. See also, *Rise of Christianity, op. cit.*, p.636.

[72] *Ibid.*, p. 186.

[73] Chadwick, *op. cit.*, p.149.

[74] *Codex Theod*. XVI.1.2. This edict *(Cunctos populos)* not only recognizes the primacy of Rome and Alexandria but more importantly, makes Catholicism the official religion of the state. As Coleman-Norton suggests (*The Roman State and the Christian Church*. London: S.P.C.K. Press, 1966, I,pp.355f.), the earlier edict of Milan recognized Christianity as a legitimate religion, but this edict spells out what kind of Christianity is acceptable. Henceforth, all schismatics are considered not only a menace to Catholicism but also rebels against the state. The consolidation efforts of Athanasius and other Catholic bishops would be helped immeasurably by the backing of the state in this way. The force of this edict was strengthened by the *Nullus Haereticis* of 10 January 381, in which Theodosius ordered that no place be given for the heretics to hold meetings or exhibit their foolish errors (*Codex Theod*. XVI.5.6).

[75] Socrates, *Hist. Eccl*. V.3; Sozomen, *Hist. Eccl*. VII.7, specifies that Timothy was Peter's brother; Theodoret, *Hist. Eccl*. V.8, must be confused in his chronology, for he states that Timothy was the engineer of the Maximus fiasco in Constantinople. The error is obvious when one remembers that the illegal consecration took place in 379, but the edict of Theodosius in early 380 specifies that Peter is still the bishop of Alexandria.

[76] *Ibid.*, V.8; Sozomen, *Hist. Eccl*. VII.7; Theodoret, *Hist. Eccl*. V.6.

[77] Kelly, *op. cit*., pp.263f.

[78] Gregory Naz., *Dem Evang*. V.1.20. See Kelly, *op. cit*., pp.297f., and Chadwick, *op. cit*., pp.150f.

[79] J. G. Davies, *op. cit*., p.196. Cp. Kelly, *op. cit*., pp.295ff. "The chief objections advanced against Apollinarianism may be shortly summarized. One of the most damaging and lasting, based on the divinization of Christ's flesh which Apollinarius taught, was that it was virtually docetic, implying that the Saviour was not a real man but only 'appeared as a man' . . . Secondly, the underlying assumptions of the whole theory were queried. Was it necessarily the case, it was asked, that the two complete entities, divinity and humanity, could not coalesce so as to form a real unity? . . . Thirdly, if it is assumed that Christ lacked the most characteristic element in man's make-up, a rational mind and will, His alleged manhood was not in the strict sense human, but must have been something monstrous . . . Fourthly, the rejection of a normal human psychology clashes with the Gospel picture of a Saviour who developed, exhibited signs of ignorance, suffered and underwent all sorts of human experiences. Lastly, . . . for all its concern for soteriology, the Apollinarian Christology . . . failed to meet the essential conditions of redemption." (Kelly, p.296). Opposition to Apollinarianism concentrated on the Savior having two natures, God and man, which, though united, were identifiably distinct (Gregory of Nazianzus goes farther than some, by stating that the two are joined in substance to each other, *Epist*. 101.5).

Word-flesh Christology thus assumes that the only part of man in the Savior is the flesh, while Word-man Christology argues that the mind and will of the Savior were also part of His humanity, with which the divinity of Christ was joined. For a brief but useful survey of this technical matter, see also Karl Baus *et. al.*, *The Imperial Church from Constantine to the Early Middle Ages*. *History of the Church*, Vol. II (Eng. transl. by A. Biggs). New York: Seabury Press, 1980, pp.96–100.

[80] Chadwick, *op. cit*., p.151.

[81] *Ibid.*, V.8; Sozomen, *Hist. Eccl*. VII.7; Cf. Gregory of Nazianzus, *Carmen* XI.1802.

[82] Quoted in Socrates, *Hist. Eccl*. V.8.

[83] Socrates, *Hist. Eccl*. V.8.

[84] Percival, *op. cit*., (*NPNF*, Series 2, Vol.14), p.176.

[85] Hefele, *op. cit*., p.355.

[86] Henry Chadwick, *The Early Church* (Baltimore: Penguin Books, 1973), p.151.

[87] Socrates, *Hist. Eccl*. VI.2; Sozomen, *Hist. Eccl*. VIII.2; Theodoret, *Hist. Eccl*. V.27.

[88] Sozomen, *Hist. Eccl*. VIII.2.

[89] Socrates, *Hist. Eccl*. VI.2.

[90] See above, p. 171. Frend, *Early Church*, *op. cit*., pp.125–126, pp. 224ff. The same difficulty would arise later with Nestorius of Antioch being selected as Patriarch of Constantinople. For the importance of Antioch among the Eastern sees at this time, see Chadwick, *Early Church*, *op. cit*. p.165, Kelly, *op. cit*., pp.301ff., Frend, *Rise of Christianity*, *op. cit*., pp.641f.

[91] Chadwick, *Early Church*, *op. cit*., p.187.

[92] Socrates, *Hist. Eccl*. VI.4; Sozomen, *Hist. Eccl*. VIII.9; Palladius, *Vita* 19. John was a reformer, and although one can justify his reforms as necessary and for the well-being of the church, his actions caused many to dislike his "fault-finding" and his inhospitable nature.

[93] *Ibid*., VI.7; Sozomen, *Hist. Eccl*. VIII.12.

[94] Sozomen, *Hist. Eccl*. VIII.12.

[95] The letter is lost, but the details of its contents and their effect on the monks are found in Sozomen, *Hist. Eccl*. VIII.11. Reference is also made to the letter in Cassian, *Collatio* X.2.

[96] Chadwick, *Early Church*, *op. cit*., p.185.

[97] *Ibid*.

[98] J.N.D. Kelly, *Jerome, His Life, Writings and Controversies* (London: G. Duckworth & Co., Ltd., 1975), p. 243.

[99] *Ibid*.

[100] Socrates, *Hist. Eccl*. VI.9; Sozomen, *Hist. Eccl*. VIII.12.

[101] Kelly, *Jerome*, *op. cit*., pp.204f.

[102] Socrates, *Hist. Eccl*. VI.9; Sozomen, *Hist. Eccl*. VIII.12.

[103] Sozomen, *Hist. Eccl*., VIII.12.

[104] *Ibid*., VIII.13. See Kelly, *Jerome*, *op. cit*., p.244.

[105] Kelly, *Jerome*, *op. cit*., p.244.

[106] Socrates, *Hist. Eccl*. VI.9; Sozomen, *Hist. Eccl*. VIII.13; Jerome, *Epist*. XC. Some disagreement exists in the sources relating to just which monks came to Constantinople, although Sozomen states that besides the Tall Brothers, nearly eighty other monks went first to Jerusalem and then to Constantinople.

[107] In addition to addressing the bishops of Egypt, Theophilus sent the letter to bishops of Palestine and Cyprus. The copy available today is Jerome's translation (*Epist*. 92), and was written subsequent to a synod called by Theophilus in 400 to combat Origenism in his diocese. The specific teachings of Origen which are attacked include a definite Subordination doctrine of the Son, non-perfect resurrection bodies, a qualified acceptance of magic and astrology, etc. The tone is so polemic that the substance of the charges is highly suspect.

[108] Frend, *Early Church*, *op. cit*., p.222.

[109] Palladius, *Vita* 8.

[110] Socrates, *Hist. Eccl*. VI.15, states that an order from the emperor was given to Theophilus to convoke a synod against John, but this is certainly not true. The emperor would not have called the Alexandrian bishop to settle an issue in Constantinople, the capital. Chadwick, *Early Church*, *op. cit*., p.189, Cross, *op. cit*., p.987, and Frend, *Early Church*, *op. cit*., pp.222f., agree that the real purpose of Theophilus' journey was to embarrass his enemy from Antioch.

[111] *Ibid*., Sozomen, *Hist. Eccl*. VII.16–17.

[112] Chadwick, *Early Church*, *op. cit*., p.190. Frend, *Rise of Christianity*, *op. cit*., p.752.

[113] Socrates, *Hist. Eccl*. VI.18–21.

[114] The political, rather than religious, basis of the feud between Theophilus and Chrysostom is suggested in a letter from Synesius to Theophilus in c. 409. Synesius had been appointed bishop of Ptolemais and Metropolitan of the Pentapolis by Theophilus, and in a letter (LXVI), he tells the patriarch how he had entertained a bishop who had been consecrated by "John Chrysostom of happy memory: permit me to speak in this way, since he is dead, and all disputes ought to end with this life." No offense was taken by Theophilus, and he continues to support Synesius in regulating the affairs of the church. Synesius writes that he is "bound to carry out, as a sacred law, whatever the throne of the Evangelist should command" (Letter LXVII), showing the nearly monarchical power the bishop of Alexandria enjoyed within the Ecclesiastical organization.

[115] Frend, *Monophysite*, *op. cit*., p.82.

[116] Frend, *Rise of Christianity*, *op. cit*., pp.746–747. His sources include Rufinus, *Historia Monachorum* V, *Patrol. Lat*. 21.408–9; Jerome, *Regulae S. Pachomii translatio Latina*, Praefatio 7, *Patrol. Lat*. 23.68. He further notes that "Shenoute's White Monastery had a population of twenty-two hundred monks with eighteen hundred nuns in a dependent convent (J. Leipoldt, "Schenute von Atripe," *TU* [1904]:93)," p.777.

[117] Socrates, *Hist. Eccl*. VII.7.

[118] Frend, *Monophysite*, *op. cit*., p.16.

[119] Frend, *Rise of Christianity*, *op. cit*., p.753.

[120] Socrates, *Hist. Eccl*. VII.7. Socrates states that for the same reason, i.e. the Novatian problem, the Roman bishop also usurped secular authority as well as ecclesiastical power at the same time as Cyril acted in Alexandria.

[121] Origen, *Epist. ad Africanum* 14, where Origen states that the ethnarch had great authority. See Jones, *Later Roman Empire*, *op. cit*., pp.944–950 for a survey of Jews and Judaism in the Empire; particularly of privileges and offices in provincial urban centers. The fifth century saw a decrease in Jewish rights and privileges in the East. Still, Theodosius gave instructions in the East that Jews were to be protected in their religious activities (Jones, pp.166–167). See also p.473.

[122] Socrates, *Hist. Eccl*. VII.13.

[123] *Ibid*.

[124] *Ibid*., VII.14.

[125] *Ibid*., VII.15, Zenos' translation.

[126] *Ibid*.

[127] *Ibid*., Zenos' translation.

[128] *Codex Theod*. XVI.2.42.

[129] Socrates, *Hist. Eccl*. VII.29.

[130] Baus *et al*., *Hist of the Church*, Vol. II, *op. cit*., p.101.

[131] *Ibid*.

[132] Diptychs were lists of Christians, both living and deceased, for whom special prayer is made in the Eucharistic ritual of the Church (see Cross, *op. cit*., p.408). Special prayer rolls for the sick and spiritually needy are still similarly found in many Christian groups.

[133] Chadwick, *op. cit*., pp.191,195.

[134] Cyril, *Epist*. III.

[135] Socrates, *Hist. Eccl*. VII.32. Baus *et. al*., *Hist*. II, *op. cit*., p. 100, notes that in the dispute in Constantinople over whether to call Mary Theotokos (Mother of God) or Anthrōpotokos (Mother of The Man), Nestorius tried to bring unity to the opposing groups by calling her The Mother of Christ (see Nest. *Ep. ad Joann. Antioch*.). Nevertheless, because Theotokos was an accepted term in theology and liturgy since before Nicaea, the bishop's attempted compromise simply resulted in his being branded as one who deviated from custom and the accepted faith.

[136] *Ibid*.

[137] J.N.D. Kelly, *Early Christian Doctrines* (London: Adam and Charles Black, 1968, pp.311–317; Chadwick, *op. cit*., p.195; Kidd, *op. cit*., III, pp.207–208, is most reluctant to make such an admission, saying that despite Nestorius' emphasis on the singleness of the two distinct substances combined in one, he still should have been condemned as a heretic. Cross, *op. cit*., p. 962, suggests that he is probably more guilty of "unguarded language" than of real heresy, and even Socrates, *Hist. Eccl*. VII.32, states that after reading the writings of Nestorius he was convinced that he was not really a heretic. "But he seemed scared at the term *theotokos*, as though it were some terrible phantom." Socrates inveighs against Nestorius for his ignorance (and that of a man usually acclaimed for good education and ability!), and further adds that his greatest sin was vanity.

[138] R.V. Sellers, *The Council of Chalcedon* (London: SPCK Press, 1953), pp.158–181. See Kelly, *Doctrines*, *op. cit*., pp.310ff., where he explains how Nestorius fits into Antiochene theology.

[139] Kelly, *Doctrines*, *op. cit*., p. 312.

[140] Cyril, *Epist*. 4.

[141] Kelly, *Doctrines*, *op. cit*., p.314.

[142] *Ibid*., p.313.

[143] *Ibid*., pp.322–323.

[144] Sellers, *op. cit*., p.181.

[145] F. Loofs, *Nestorius and His Place in the History of Christian Doctrine* (Cambridge: Cambridge U. Press, 1914), Lecture 1.

[146] Kelly, *Doctrines*, *op. cit*., p.318, disagrees, saying, "While jealousy of the upstart see of Constantinople caused him (i.e. Cyril) to dip his pen in gall, he was also inspired by motives of a purely theological character."

[147] Cyril, *Apol. ad Theod. Imp*., *Epistles* IV,X.

[148] Cyril, *Epist*. I.

[149] Cyril, *De Recta Fide ad Theod. Imp*. All three bear the same name, the first being addressed to the emperor, and the latter two to the emperor's younger sisters.

[150] Chadwick, *op. cit*., p.196.

[151] *Ibid*.

[152] John Cassian, *De Incarnatione Domini contra Nestorianos*. This response to Celestine's request for information is seven books long, and was not completed until 431, just prior to the Council of Ephesus.

[153] Acacius, *Epist*. XV.

[154] Kelly, *Doctrines*, *op. cit*., pp.324.

[155] Cyril, *Epist*. XVIII.

[156] Kelly, *Doctrines*, *op. cit*., p.324–5.

[157] *Ibid*., p.325.

[158] Kidd, *op. cit*., III. p.228.

[159] Cyril's Third Letter, Henry R. Percival, ed. *The Seven Ecumenical Councils of the Undivided Church*. Grand Rapids: Eerdmans, 1971 (Reprint), p.206.

[160] *Ibid*., pp.210–211.

[161] *Ibid*., p.211.

[162] *Ibid*., p.212.

[163] *Ibid*., p.213.

[164] *Ibid*.

[165] *Ibid*., p.214.

[166] *Ibid*., pp.214–215.

[167] *Ibid*., p.216.

[168] *Ibid.*, p.217.

[169] *Ibid.*

[170] Kelly, *Doctrines, op. cit.*, pp.328–330.

[171] Frend, *Monophysite, op. cit.*, p.18.

[172] Eduard Schwartz, ed., *Acta Conciliorum Oecumenicorum.* Berlin: Walter de Gruyter & Co., 1922–1929. Tome 1, vols. 1–5. For the emperor's calling of the Council, see I, 32. Schwartz has collected and edited the sources relating to the Council of Ephesus, with subsequent volumes containing the sources for later Councils.

[173] Loofs, *op. cit.*, Lecture 2.

[174] Frend, *Early Church, op. cit.*, p.228.

[175] *Ibid.*

[176] *Ibid.*

[177] Socrates, *Hist. Eccl.* VII.34.

[178] Baus *et. al., Hist. II, op. cit.*, p. 104.

[179] *Ibid.*

[180] Kelly, *op. cit.*, p.237.

[181] Cyril, *Epist.* XXXIX. By enclosing the Formulary in the letter, Cyril signified his agreement with it. The original of the Formulary had been made by Theodoret, bishop of Cyprus, in 431, and was an Antiochene document in its theology, Cf. Harnack, *History of Dogma* (New York: Dover, 1961), Vol. IV, p.189.

[182] Socrates, *Hist. Eccl.* VII.34, emphasizes the political basis of the dispute in his account of the council at Ephesus. Nestorius, when he saw the contention was leading toward disunity cried out, "Let Mary be called *theotokos*, if you will, and let all disputing cease." Socrates claims that nobody paid any attention to this belated attempt toward reconciliation. While the details of the account may be fictitious, the nature of the disagreement is supported by Friedrick Loofs, *op. cit.* When Nestorius wrote to Celestine, he said that *theotokos* was tolerable, but not preferred. (Lecture II). Because an ecumenical Council was not held at Ephesus in 431, (only the partisans met), Nestorius would have been judged better as to his orthodoxy by Chalcedon in 451.

[183] J. Leipoldt, ed., *Sinuthii Archimandritae Vita A Besa Discipulo eius, CSCO, Scriptores Coptici* II.2 (Paris: C. Poussielque, 1906), 7 (hereafter cited Besa, *Shenoute*):

ЄΠΙΤΗ ΓΑΡ ΘΜΑΥ ΝΑΠΑ ϢΕΝΟΥϯ ΤϹϢΝΙ ΝΑΠΑ ΠΧϢΑΤΕ ΝϢΕΝΙϢΤ ϨΙΜΑΥ ΟΥΟϨ ΑϤΧΑϤ ϨΑΤΟΤϤ.

For the date, see Cross, *op. cit.*, p. 1269.

[184] Cross, *op. cit.*, p.1269.

[185] Besa, *Shenoute* 11.

[186] *Ibid.*, 15–16.

[187] Leipoldt, *Schenute von Atripe, TU* XXI (1903), pp.141–143.

[188] *Ibid.*

[189] Besa, *Shenoute*, 98.

[190] *Ibid.*, 81.

[191] *Ibid.*, 82.

[192] *Ibid.*, 83–84.

[193] Robinson, *Nag Hammadi in English, op. cit.*, p.19.

[194] *Ibid.*, p.20.

[195] Besa, *Shenoute* 17–21.

[196] *Ibid.*, 129.

[197] *Ibid.*, 70–72.

[198] *Ibid.*, 92.

[199] *Ibid.*, 93.

[200] *Ibid.*, 94.

[201] *Ibid.*, 95–97.

[202] *Ibid.*, 99–101.

[203] *Ibid.*, 117ff.

[204] *Ibid.*, 121.

[205] *Ibid.*, 138–144.

[206] *Ibid.*, 24,73, passim.

[207] *Ibid.*, 22,23,25,26 (voice only, with no personage), 30,32,70,115, 121,154–160. In many of these visions Shenoute is portrayed as being a casual companion of Jesus, rather than Jesus appearing as an *angelus interpres*. The overwhelming nature of the heavenly vision is not prominent in these accounts as it is in Jewish and Christian Apocalyptic literature.

[208] *Ibid.*, 184–185.

[209] *Ibid.*, 27f., 140–144 and Matt. 14:15ff, with parallels; Cf. Matt. 15:32ff and Mark 8:1ff.

[210] *Ibid.*, 89 and John 7:30, 44, etc.

[211] Ibid., 86, 102–105 and Matt. 8:23ff. with parallels; John 6:18–21, etc.

[212] *Ibid.*, 42.

[213] *Ibid.*, 58–69.

[214] *Ibid.*, 53. Prophecy, visionary travel, and miracles are common to Jesus and His disciples also. See Matt. 24–25 and parallels, Acts 8:28ff., and Mark 1:39ff. for examples.

[215] *Ibid.*, 68–69.

[216] *Ibid.*, 80.

[217] *Ibid.*, 54–59.

[218] *Ibid.*, 98, 102–108, 135, etc.

[219] W. C. Till, "Schenutes Werke," texts given in *Koptische Grammatik* (Leipzig: VEB VERLAG, 1966), pp.296ff.

[220] Besa, *Shenoute* 87. Wine and grain are given to groups and entire villages, according to this passage.

[221] Frend, *The Rise of Christianity, op. cit.*, pp.763f.

[222] Baus, *Hist.* II, *op. cit.*, p.111.

[223] Theodoret, *Ep.* LX, *Dioscoro Episcopo Alexandriae, Patrol. Gr.* 83.1232. Even allowing for exaggeration, the letter gives evidence for Dioscorus having a good reputation throughout the East.

[224] Kidd, *Hist.* III, *op. cit.*, p.284, citing Liberatus (Carthage), *Breviarium causae Nestorianae et Eutychianae* X (*Patrol. Lat.* 68.992).

[225] Frend, *Monophysite, op. cit.*, p.26.

[226] Theodoret, *Epist.*60.

[227] Frend, *Monophysite, op. cit.*, pp.26–27.

[228] Leo, *Epist.* 101.2, a letter of Anatolius to Leo.

[229] Leo, *Epist.* 109,123.

[230] Frend, *Early Church, op. cit.*, p.238, speaks of Dioscorus as "Altogether a man of lesser calibre," A. Harnack, *Hist., op. cit.*, IV, p.190, says that while Dioscorus was "not indeed the equal of his predecessor, he was not unlike him."

[231] A. Harnack, *Hist., op. cit.*, IV, pp.190–191.

[232] Frend, *Rise of Christianity, op. cit.*, p.764, citing Cyril, *Epistle* 29, *Patrol. Gr.* 77.148b.

[233] *Ibid.*

[234] Leo, *Epist.* IX (*Patrol. Lat.* 54.624ff.). This work of Leo's is well-known by the title *Quantum Dilectioni Tuae*, and specifically mentions the desirability of having good relations between the sees of St. Mark and St. Peter.

[235] Sellers, *op. cit.*, p.33.

[236] Frend, *Monophysite, op. cit.*, p.28, citing Mansi, *Collectio*, VI, col. 1021.

237 *Ibid*., citing Mansi, *Collectio* VI, col. 1044.

238 Sellers, *op. cit*., p.33.

239 J.D. Mansi, ed. *Sacrorum Conciliorum nova et amplissima Collectio* (Paris, 1901–1927), VII, 325–241. Hereafter *Collectio*.

240 Sellers, *op. cit*., p.33.

241 Count Irenaeus was made bishop of Tyre in 446. Aquilinus was appointed to Byblus, and Paul 'The Nestorian' to Antaradus in Phoenicia.

242 Frend, *Monophysite*, *op. cit*., p.29.

243 Sellers, *op. cit*., p.57.

244 Frend, *Monophysite*, *loc. cit*.

245 Chadwick, *Early Church*, *op. cit*., p. 196 n.2. Jones, *op. cit*., p.180, infers that the eunuch Chrysaphius was responsible for alienating the emperor from his wife.

246 Jones *op. cit*., p.180. "Chrysaphius exercised the supreme power for the rest of Theodosius' reign, apparently in conjunction with Nomus, who was master of the offices during the same period." Chadwick stated that Theodosius preferred to be dominated by the eunuch rather than by his sister, Pulcheria, after his wife's banishment.

247 Evagrius, *Hist. Eccl*. II.2.

248 Frend, *Monophysite*, *op. cit*., pp.31–33.

249 Flavin to Leo, in *Acta Conciliorum Oecumenicorum*. 2.11.1.

250 Frend, *Monophysite*, *op. cit*., p.41.

251 *Ibid*., p.34.

252 Leo, *Epist*. 36.

253 Frend, *Monophysite, op. cit*., p.32. See Leo, *Epist*. 29, ". . . imperite atque imprudenter errare detectus sit . . ."

254 Jones, *op. cit*., I, p.215. Frend, *Monophysite*, *op. cit*., p.36.

255 Frend, *Monophysite*, *op. cit*., pp.36,39.

256 Jones, *op. cit*., I. p.215.

257 Frend, *Monophysite*, *op. cit*., pp.41–43.

258 Baus, *Hist., op. cit*., II, p.113.

259 *Ibid*., p.214. J.B. Bury, *History of the Later Roman Empire*. New York: Dover, 1958 (Reprint), p.356, says of the Council: "The voting of many of the 115 bishops who signed the Acts was not free; they were overawed by the Imperial authorities and by the violence of a noisy crowd of monks from Syria. Yet it has been said, perhaps with truth, that this Council more than any other expressed the general religious feelings of the time, and would have permanently settled the controversy in the East if extraneous interests had not been involved."

260 Liberatus, *Brev*. 13.76.

261 There is some argument about the date, but November, 449, is most probably correct. See Frend, *Monophysite*, *op. cit*., p.43. Cf. Chadwick, *Early Church*, *op. cit*., p.202.

262 R.V. Sellers, *Two Ancient Christologies*. London: SPCK Press, 1954, p.241.

263 Leo, *Epist*. 21.

264 J. Stevenson, ed. *Creeds, Councils, and Controversies*. London: SPCK Press, 1966, pp.315–324. See also Schwartz, *ACO, op. cit*., II.2, pp.24–33.

265 Kidd, *Hist., op. cit*., III, pp.303–304.

266 Frend, *Monophysite*, *op. cit*., p.40.

267 Frend, *Rise of Christianity*, *op. cit*., p.768.

268 Baus, *Hist., op. cit*., II, p.114.

269 See Frend, *Monophysite*, *op. cit*., pp.41–42.

270 Leo, *Epist*. 28:1.

271 Frend, *Monophysite*, *op. cit*., pp.43ff. Kelly, *op. cit*., pp.333f.

[272] Leo, *Epist*. 44, 45, 47–51. See Schwartz, *ACO*, II.4, pp.19–27. Little resulted from these letters, but the sweeping changes in attitude of Rome toward Alexandria is significant, and essentially isolated the Egyptian church from a major source of power and support.

[273] Leo, *Epist*. 38.

[274] *Ibid*., *Epist*. 60.

[275] Frend, *Monophysite*, *op. cit*., p.45.

[276] Sellers, *Chalcedon*, *op. cit*., p.96.

[277] Jones, *op. cit*., I, p.218. Pulcheria married Marcian, bestowing upon him the prestige of the Theodosian dynasty, and the new emperor reversed the policies of Chyrsaphius in foreign, domestic and ecclesiastical affairs. Jones suggests that the ecclesiastical policy of Marcian was inspired by Pulcheria, although the influence of Leo was not inconsiderable.

[278] Frend, *Monophysite*, *op. cit*., p.46. See also J. B. Bury, *History of the Later Roman Empire*. New York: Dover, 1958 (Reprint), I, p.236.

[279] Sellers, *Chalcedon*, *op. cit*., p.97.

[280] Mansi, *Collectio* VI.1032.

[281] Leo, *Epist*. 77.

[282] Sellers, *Chalcedon*, *op. cit*., p.98.

[283] Leo, *Epist*. 83.2 Cf. *Epist*. 89.

[284] Mansi, *Collectio* VI.556.

[285] *Ibid*., VI.557. Forty years later, Pope Gelasius (*Gesta de nomine Acacii*) affirmed that the Council was held at Chalcedon just because it was close to the capital: "propter palatii vicinitatem."

[286] *Ibid*., VI.1009. Cf. Sellers, *Chalcedon*, *op. cit*., pp.102f., and Frend, *Monophysite*, *op. cit*., p.47

[287] Frend, *Monophysite*, *op. cit*., p.47.

[288] Sellers, *Chalcedon*, *op. cit*., p.103.

[289] Baus, *Hist*. II, *op. cit*., p.117.

[290] Zacharias Rhetor, *Hist. Eccl*. III.3, states that the decision making Jerusalem a patriarchate came in the first session.

[291] Schwartz, *ACO*, II. 1,1, pp.55–196.

[292] Mansi, *Collectio* VI.1032.

[293] Sellers, *Chalcedon*, *op. cit*., p.107.

[294] Mansi, *Collectio*, VI.953. Cp. Frend, *Monophysite*, *op. cit*., p.49. The protest came especially from the Roman delegation, who argued that it was improper to add to that which was taught by the fathers.

[295] Sellers, *Chalcedon*, *op. cit*., p.110.

[296] Baus, *Hist*. II, *op. cit*., p.118.

[297] *Ibid*., See Schwartz, *ACO* II. 2,2, pp.94–109.

[298] Mansi, *Collectio*, *op. cit*., VII. 97–118.

[299] For a discussion of this critical problem, see Patrick Gray, *The Defense of Chalcedon in the East*. Leiden: E.J. Brill, 1979, pp.10–16.

[300] *Ibid*., p.16. Cp. Kidd, *Hist., op. cit*., III, pp.324–326.

[301] Frend, *Rise of Christianity*, *op. cit*., p.771. Frend gives a translation of the complete Definition of Chalcedon. J. B. Bury, *op. cit*., p.357 describes the Creed thusly: ". . . the Council decreed that the true doctrine was contained in certain writings of Cyril as well as in Leo's epistle; and described Jesus Christ as complete in his humanity as well as in his divinity; one and the same Christ in two natures, without confusion or change, division or separation; each nature concurring into one person and one hypostasis."

[302] Sellers, *Chalcedon*, *op. cit*., p.112.

[303] *Ibid.*, p.113.

[304] Timothy Aelurus, *Patrol. Orient*. 13.2. p.210.

[305] Sellers, *Chalcedon*, *op. cit.*, p.125.

[306] J.B. Bury, *op. cit.*, p.357.

[307] Frend, *Monophysite*, *op. cit.*, p.47.

[308] *Ibid.*, p.141.

[309] *Ibid.*, p.143. See Schwartz, *ACO*, II, 1,2, p.157.

[310] *Ibid.*, p.144.

[311] *Ibid.*, pp.144f.

[312] Duchesne, *op. cit.*, III.329.

[313] Frend, *Monophysite*, *op. cit.*, p.149. Bury, *op. cit.*, p.358.

[314] *Chron. ad ann*. 856: "Postquam eiectus est Dioscorus in exilium, multi tamen clam eum proclamabant in monasteriis."

[315] The strength of anti-Chalcedonian opinion in Egypt is suggested by the statements of the Egyptian bishops at the Council that to sign Leo's *Tome* or repudiate the position of Dioscorus would mean certain death for them if they went back to Egypt (see Kidd, *Hist*. III, p.322).

[316] Liberatus, *Brev*. 14.98, and Michael, *Chron*. 8.12. Cf. Zacharias Rhetor, *Hist. Eccl*. III.2.

[317] Frend, *Monophysite*, *op. cit.*, p.155. On the other hand, Frend notes (p.163) that some Pachomian monks at Canopus favored Proterius because they remembered the tyranny of Dioscorus.

[318] Jones, *op. cit.*, p.221.

[319] Frend, *Monophysite*, *op. cit.*, p.155.

[320] Duchesne, *op. cit.*, III.332.

[321] Atiya, *op. cit.*, pp.70–71.

[322] Frend, *Monophysite*, *loc. cit.*, quoting *Vita Petri Iberi*, p.68.

[323] Duchesne, *op. cit.*, III.332.

[324] Frend, *Monophysite*, *op. cit.*, p.155.

[325] Hardy, *op. cit.*, p.115.

[326] Gray, *op. cit.*, p.19.

[327] *Ibid*.

[328] *Ibid.*, p.160.

[329] *Ibid.*, p.163.

[330] *Ibid*.

[331] Leo, *Epistles* 171–173.

[332] Frend, *Monophysite*, *op. cit.*, pp.163f.

[333] Jones, *op. cit.*, pp.224f. Cp. Baus, *Hist*. II, pp.424–425. The Encyclion defined the faith in terms of Nicaea, Constantinople, and Ephesus, and anathematized Leo's *Tome* and the *Horos* of Chalcedon. See also Gray, *op. cit.*, pp.25–26.

[334] Frend, *Monophysite*, *op. cit.*, p.173.

[335] *Ibid.*, p.171.

[336] Zacharias Rhetor, *Hist. Eccl*. V.4.

[337] *Ibid*.

[338] Baus, *Hist*. II, p.425. Frend, *Monophysite*, *op. cit.*, p.174.

[339] Atiya, *op. cit.*, p.72.

[340] Frend, *Monophysite*, *op. cit.*, p.177. Evagrius, *Hist. Eccl*. 3.14. For an English translation of the Henotikon, see Coleman-Norton, *Roman State and Christian Church*. London: SPCK, 1966, III, pp.924–933.

[341] Gray, *op. cit.*, p.28.

[342] Chadwick, *Early Church*, *op. cit.*, pp.205f.

[343] *Ibid*., p.206.

[344] Frend, *Monophysite*, *op. cit*., p.180.

[345] *Ibid*.

[346] *Ibid*.

[347] Zacharias Rhetor, *Hist. Eccl*. VI.2. Frend, *Monophysite*, *op. cit*., p. 180. Gray, *op. cit*., p.32.

[348] Duchesne, *op. cit*., III,350f. Cp. Frend, *Monophysite*, *op. cit*., p.187, who notes that the continuance of communion between Alexandria and the capital through the reigns of Zeno and Anastasius illustrates the lack of separatist intention in Egypt.

[349] Zacharias Rhetor, *Hist Eccl*. VII.1.

[350] *Ibid*.

[351] Frend, *Monophysite*, *op. cit*., p.193.

[352] W.H.C. Frend, "Severus of Antioch and the Origins of the Monophysite Hierarchy," *Orientalia Christiana Analecta* 195 (Rome: Pont. Inst. Stud. Orient., 1973), p.262. On p. 274, Frend lists the areas where national churches were established by the end of the sixth century: Armenia, Syria, Egypt, Nubia and Ethiopia.

[353] Atiya, *op. cit*., p.71. Atiya gives a brief list of the competitors from both factions, noting the confusion which existed in the half century following Chalcedon.

[354] Frend, *Severus*, *op. cit*., p.263.

[355] *Ibid*., p.274.

[356] Mansi, *Collectio* VI. 1021ff. Nicolas Zernov, *Eastern Christendom* (London: Weidenfield and Nicolson, 1963), p.78, states that the Christological disputes caused by the Chalcedonian Council split Eastern monasticism in two, but he certainly cannot be arguing that the split was into equal or nearly equal factions.

[357] Zacharias Rhetor, *Hist. Eccl*. IV. 1.

[358] *Ibid*., IV. 3.

[359] Frend, *Severus*, *op. cit*., p.264.

[360] *Ibid*., pp.202–203. Both are published (with French translation) by M.-A. Kugener, *Vie de Sévère, par Zacharie le Scholastique* and *Vie de Sévère, par Jean du monastère de Beith-Aphthonia*, in *Patrol. Orient*. 2.1 and 3.

[361] Frend, *Monophysite*, *op. cit*., pp.201f.

[362] *Ibid*., p.202. See Severus, *Select Letters*, V.2, for Severus' account of the influence Peter had on his acceptance of the monophysite theology.

[363] *Ibid*., pp.207–213.

[364] Mansi, *Collectio* VIII.1039.

[365] Severus, *Select Letters* V. 2.

[366] Frend, *Severus*, *op. cit*., p.271.

[367] Severus, *Select Letters* V. 15.

[368] Frend, *Severus*, *op. cit*., pp.272ff. Severus held a council in exile in Alexandria (p. 270), from which he gave instructions to his own followers in Syria. His continued presence in Egypt tacitly argues for sympathy and support from Egyptian monophysites, and in 530, Severus' ordination of many to clerical offices provided the basis for a Severan monophysite church through much of the eastern Empire.

[369] Jones, *op. cit*., I, 270. Credit is given the Empress Theodora for Justinian's softened attitude toward the Monophysites, for she was a strong adherent of that theological position.

[370] Frend, *Severus*, *op. cit*., p.274.

[371] Baus, *Hist. op. cit*., II, p.472.

EPILOGUE

Egyptian Christianity did not begin as a national religious movement, nor was the motive of separation from Catholicism and the
founding of a national Church behind the actions of the Egyptian
participants at the Council of Chalcedon. Formal separation from
Catholicism was accomplished with reluctance, indicating that the
expression of religious nationalism followed Chalcedon, for the most
part, rather than preceded it. A number of factors arising in Egypt
during the four centuries between the introduction of Christianity
into Egypt and that Council in 451 nevertheless made the emergence
of an Egyptian Coptic Church during the succeeding century the
natural, if not inevitable, result.

Christianity was introduced into Egypt during the first century, as
is well attested by the first century Biblical and non-Biblical Christian
manuscripts discovered in that country. Egyptian Christianity in the
first two centuries can be characterized in its organization as consisting of autonomous groups throughout the country presided over by
local presbyters rather than by the bishop of Alexandria. Doctrinally,
these groups accepted a much broader scope of texts and traditions
than was accepted in nascent Catholicism. The imposition of Catholic
ecclesiasticism upon Egyptian Christianity occurred near the end of
the second century, and brought with it a more stringent canonical
and doctrinal tradition than typified the local Egyptian Christian
groups. This imposition resulted in tension between the Alexandrian
bishops and leading spokesmen for Egyptian Christians (such as
teachers in the Catechetical School and local leaders in Egypt) which
continued down to the episcopacy of Athanasius in the fourth century. An attempt to overcome the tension can be seen in the third
century in the gradual absorption of the Catechetical School of Alexandria into the regulated province of the Alexandrian bishop. This
move decreased the influential expression of Christians in a non-
Catholic tradition, but a new manner of Egyptian Christian expression originated about the same time. Monasticism, at first an Egyptian
Christian phenomenon before being spread abroad, grew apace during the third century, and the rise of monasticism can be seen as a
Christian movement independent of Catholicism as well as an at-

tempt to move away from the world. From the later writings of monastic leaders and of Alexandrian bishops to the monks, one sees that monasticism maintained some degree of doctrinal independence and freedom from ecclesiasticism in its later as well as early stages.

Athanasius entered the scene in the fourth century as the most effective representative of Catholicism in establishing a bond between Alexandria and monasticism. Although the problems associated with the Melitian and Arian controversies may have contributed to Athanasius' desire to obtain an allegiance with the leading monks, the patriarch's own admiration for asceticism was sufficient to pursue that goal. The strength of the allegiance was dramatically increased through the founding of monastic communities under the leadership of Pachomius, who was generally on friendly terms with Athanasius, and the resultant organization became susceptible to greater ecclesiastical influence and limitations on doctrinal positions than was the case with anchorite monks. The relationship between Catholicism and monasticism in Egypt remained rather tenuous, however, until further developments took place.

The increasing importance of the see of Constantinople (at the expense of the prestige previously enjoyed by the Alexandrian bishop) and long standing disputes with Antioch were external stimuli which urged the Alexandrian patriarch to strengthen his position in late fourth-century Egyptian Christianity, and Theophilus' overthrow of Origenist theology in favor of the anti-Origenist position taken by the majority of the monastic communities further alienated Alexandria from other Eastern sees. Battles with Antiochenes appointed to the bishop's throne in Constantinople plagued Theophilus and his successors, and they were driven by politics as much as by religion to an inescapable position of alienation and separation from the Catholic Church. Meanwhile, within Egypt monasticism was organized more authoritatively than before under an autocratic and violent leader, Shenoute. Well beyond the entreaties of Athanasius to the monks in his Festal letters to hold fast to the Catholic canon and doctrines were the activities of Shenoute, who aggressively attacked the heterodox and pagan elements yet remaining within Egyptian monasticism, and Christianity in general. The friendship of Shenoute with the equally autocratic bishop of Alexandria, Cyril, further cemented the bond of the monastic movement, which was intensely loyal to Shenoute, to the ecclesiastical Church.

The Nestorian controversy in the fifth century brought into focus all the tensions building between Alexandria and the sees of Constantinople and Antioch. The intransigence of Cyril and his immediate successor, Dioscorus, forced the major confrontation where strong personalities were faced with political and religious differences at the Council of Chalcedon in 451. By that time the Alexandrian bishop had exchanged his unity with Catholicism for unity with monasticism, and an unwillingness to compromise or to become subservient to Constantinople made the reality of an Egyptian Christian Church only a matter of time, for the separation itself had already taken place.

BIBLIOGRAPHY

Ackroyd, P. R. and C. F. Evans. *The Cambridge History of the Bible, Vol. I: From the Beginnings to Jerome.* Cambridge: Cambridge Univ. Press, 1970.

Aland, Kurt, et al., eds. *The Greek New Testament,* third edition. New York: American Bible Society, 1975.

————. "The Relation Between Church and State in Early Times: A Reinterpretation." *JThS,* 19 (1968), 115–127.

Allberry, C. R. C., ed. *A Manichaean Psalm-Book.* Stuttgart: W. Kohlhammer, 1938.

Altheim, Franz, and Ruth Stiehl. *Christentum am Roten Meer, Zweiter Band.* Berlin: Walter de Gruyter & Co., 1973.

Amelineau, Emile. *Histoire de St. Pakhôme et de ses communautés, Documents coptes et arabes inédits.* Paris: Annales du Museé Guimet, Vol. 17, 1889.

Athanassakis, Apostolos N. *The Life of Pachomius.* Missoula: Scholars Press, 1975.

Atiya, Aziz S. *History of Eastern Christianity.* Notre Dame: Univ. of Notre Dame Press, 1968.

Bacht, Heinrich. *Das Vermächtnis des Ursprungs I: Studien zum frühen Mönchtum.* Würzburg: Echter Verlag, 1972 (1984).

————. *Das Vermächtnis des Ursprungs II: Pachomius—Der Mann und sein Werk.* Würzburg: Echter Verlag, 1983.

Barnard, L. W. "The Date of S. Athanasius' *Vita Antonii,*" *Vigiliae Christianae* 29 (1974), pp. 169–175.

Barnes, T. *Constantine and Eusebius.* Cambridge: Harvard Univ. Press, 1981.

Barns, J. W. B. "Greek and Coptic Papyri from the Covers of the Nag Hammadi Codices," *Essays on the Nag Hammadi Texts, NHS VI.* Leiden: E. J. Brill, 1975, pp. 9–18.

Barns, J. W. B., G. M. Browne, and J. C. Shelton, eds. *Nag Hammadi Codices: Greek and Coptic Papyri from the Cartonnage of the Covers, NHS* 16. Leiden: E. J. Brill, 1981.

234 BIBLIOGRAPHY

Bartelink, G. J. M. "Die literarische Gattung der *Vita Antonii,* Struktur und Motive," *Vigiliae Christianae* 36 (1982), pp. 38–62.

Bauer, Walter. (transl. by Arndt and Gingrich). *A Greek-English Lexicon of the New Testament and Other Early Christian Literature.* Chicago: Univ. of Chicago Press, 1954.

―――― . *Orthodoxy and Heresy in Earliest Christianity.* Philadelphia: Fortress Press, 1971.

Baus, Karl. *From the Apostolic Community to Constantine.* London: Burns and Oates, 1965.

Baus, Karl., et al. *The Imperial Church from Constantine to the Early Middle Ages. History of the Church,* Vol. II (Eng. transl. by A. Biggs). New York: Seabury Press, 1980.

Baynes, Norman H. "Alexandria and Constantinople: A study in Ecclesiastical Diplomacy." *JEA,* 12 (1926), 145–156.

―――― . "Athanasiana," *JEA,* 11 (1925), pp. 58–69.

―――― . *Constantine the Great and the Christian Church.* Raleigh Lecture on History, 12 March 1930. London: British Academy, 1932.

―――― . "Sozomen Ecclesiastica Historia, I.15." *JThS,* 49 (1948), pp. 165–168.

Beckwith, John. *Coptic Sculpture, 300–1300.* London: Alec Tivanti, 1963.

Bell, H. I., *Cults and Creeds in Graeco-Roman Egypt.* New York: Philosophical Library, 1953.

―――― . *Egypt from Alexander the Great to the Arab Conquest.* Oxford: Clarendon Press, 1948.

―――― . "Evidences of Christianity in Egypt During the Roman Period." *HThR,* 37 (1944), 185–208.

―――― . *Jews and Christians in Egypt.* London: Oxford Univ. Press, 1924.

―――― . "Popular Religion in Graeco-Roman Egypt: I. The Pagan Period." *JEA,* 34 (1948), 82–97.

―――― . *Recent Discoveries of Biblical Papyri.* Oxford: Clarendon Press, 1937.

Bell, H. I., and T. C. Skeat. *Fragments of an Unknown Gospel and Other Early Christian Papyri*. London: British Museum Pub., 1935.

Bell, H. I., and W. Thompson. "A Greek-Coptic Glossary on Hosea and Amos," *JEA*, 11 (1925), pp. 341–346.

Bigg, Charles. *The Christian Platonists of Alexandria*. Oxford: Clarendon Press, 1968. (Reprint of 1913 edition).

Böhlig, Alexander, ed. *Kephalaia*, Vol. 1, Part 2. Stuttgart, 1966.

Böhlig, Alexander, and Frederik Wisse. *Nag Hammadi Codices*. III, 2 and IV, 2. *The Gospel of the Egyptians*, NHS IV. Leiden: E. J. Brill, 1975.

Brennan, B. R. "Dating Athanasius' *Vita Antonii*," *Vigiliae Christianae* 30 (1976), pp. 52–54.

Brinkmann, A. *Alexandri Lycopolitani contra Manichaei opiniones disputatio*. Leipzig, 1895.

Brown, P. R. L. *The Making of Late Antiquity*. Cambridge: Harvard Univ. Press, 1978.

Brown, Raymond E. *The Birth of the Messiah*. New York: Doubleday, 1977.

––––––. *The Gospel According to John*. 2 vols. New York: Doubleday, 1966–1970.

––––––. *New Testament Essays*. New York: Bruce Publishing Co., 1965.

Bruce, F. F. *The Acts of the Apostles*. Grand Rapids: Wm. B. Eerdmans, 1968.

––––––. *The New International Commentary on the Bible: The Book of the Acts*. Grand Rapids: Wm. B. Eerdmans, 1954.

––––––. *New Testament History*. New York: Doubleday, 1972.

Buckler, F. W. "Regnum et Ecclesia." *Ch. Hist.*, 3 (1934), 16–40.

Budge, E. A. Wallis. *The Book of Paradise*. 2 vols. London: W. Drugulin, printer, 1904.

––––––. *Coptic Texts*. 5 vols. in 6 parts. 1910–1914; reprint. New York: AMS Press, 1977.

Bullard, Roger Aubrey. *The Hypostasis of the Archons*. Berlin: Walter de Gruyter & Co., 1970.

Burkitt, F. C. *The Religion of the Manichees*. Cambridge: Cambridge Univ. Press, 1925.

Burmester, O. H. E. "The Baptismal Rite of the Coptic Church," *Extrait du Bulletin de la Société d'Archéologie Copte*. T. XI (1945). Cairo: Imprimerie de L'Institut Français d'Archéologie Orientale, 1947.

_____ . "The Canonical Hours of the Coptic Church." *Orientalia, Christina Periodica*, II, No. 1–2. Rome: Pont. Institutum Orientalium Studiorum, 1936.

_____ . "Egyptian Mythology in the Coptic Apocrypha." *Orientalia*, n.s., VII, fasc. 4. Rome: Pontificium Institutum Biblicum, 1938.

Bury, J. B. *History of the Later Roman Empire*. New York: Dover, 1958 (Reprint), I.

Butcher, E. L. *The Story of the Church of Egypt*. 2 vols. London: Smith, Elder & Co., 1897.

Butler, Alfred J. *The Ancient Coptic Churches of Egypt*. 2 vols. Oxford: Clarendon Press, 1884.

Butler, Cuthbert. *The Lausiac History of Palladius*. 2 vols. Hildesheim: Georg Olms Verlagsbuchhandlung, 1967.

Butterworth, G. W. *Clement of Alexandria*. Cambridge: Harvard Univ. Press, 1968.

_____ ., ed. *Origen, On First Principles*. New York: Harper and Row, 1966.

Cadiou, M. *La Jeunesse d'Origene; Histoire de l'école d'Alexandrie au début du III* siecle*. Paris, 1935.

Cary, M., and H. H. Scullard. *A History of Rome*, 3rd ed. New York: St. Martin's Press, 1975.

Cassian, John. *Institutes of the Coenobia*.

_____ . *Conferences*.

Chadwick, Henry, ed. *Alexandrian Christianity*. Philadelphia: Westminster Press, 1954.

_____ . *The Early Church*. Baltimore: Penguin Books, 1973.

_____ . "Faith and Order at the Council of Nicea: A Note on the Background of the Sixth Canon." *HThR*, 53 (1960), pp. 171–195.

Chaine, M. *Le Manuscrit de la Version Copte en Dialecte Sahidique des 'Apophthegmata Patrum'.* Cairo: L'Institut Français d'Archéologie Orientale, 1960.

Charles, R. H. *Apocrypha and Pseudepigrapha of the Old Testament.* 2 vols. Oxford: Clarendon Press, 1913.

Charlesworth, J. H., ed. *The Old Testament Pseudepigrapha, Vol. 1: Aprocryphal Literature and Testaments.* New York: Doubleday, 1983.

Clarke, Somers. *Christian Antiquities in the Nile Valley.* Oxford: Clarendon Press, 1912.

Clementis Alexandrini Opera, 4 vols. (O. Stählin, ed.) Leipzig: J. C. Hinrichs, 1905–36.

Coleman-Norton, P. R. *Roman State & Christian Church.* 3 vols. London: SPCK Press, 1966.

Coxe, A. C. *Fathers of the Second Century.* Grand Rapids: Wm. B. Eerdmans, 1971.

Cramer, Maria. *Das Christlich-Koptische Ägypten Einst und Heute.* Wiesbaden: Otto Harrassowitz, 1959.

Cross, F. L. "The Council of Antioch in 325 A.D." *Catholic Quarterly Review* 128 (1939), pp. 49–76.

————. *The Oxford Dictionary of the Christian Church.* New York: Oxford Univ. Press, 1974.

Crum, W. E. *Der Papyruscodex Saec. VI-VII der Phillippsbibliothek in Cheltenham.* Strassburg, 1915.

Cumont, M. "La lettre de Claude aux Alexandrins," *Revue de l'histoire des religions 91* (1925), pp. 3–6.

Daniélou, Jean. (Translated by Walter Mitchell). *Origen.* New York: Sheed and Ward, 1955.

Daumas, F., A. Guillaumont, et al. *Kellia I, Kom 219.* Cairo: l'Institut Français d'Archéologie orientale du Caire, Vol. 28, 1969.

Davies, J. G. *The Early Christian Church.* New York: Holt, Rinehart, and Winston, 1965.

Deissmann, A. *Light From the Ancient East.* Grand Rapids: Baker Book House, 1965. (Reprint of earlier edition).

Dillon, John M. *The Middle Platonists.* Ithaca: Cornell Univ. Press, 1977.

Dodd, C. H. *Interpretation of the Fourth Gospel.* Cambridge: Harvard Univ. Press, 1953.

Doresse, Jean. *Apocryphon Johannis.* Copenhagen: Univ. of Copenhagen (diss.), 1963.

———. "Gnosticism." *Historia Religionum, Vol. I: Religions of the Past.* Leiden: E. J. Brill, 1969, pp. 533–579.

———. *The Secret Books of the Egyptian Gnostics.* New York: Viking Press, 1960.

Dörries, Hermann. "Die Vita Antonii als Geschichtsquelle," *Wort und Stunde* (Gesammelte, Studien zur Kirchengeschichte des vierten Jahrhunderts). Göttingen: Vandenhoeck & Ruprecht, 1966, Erster Band (Originally published: Nachrichten der Akad. der Wissenschaften Göttingen, Philosoph.-hist. Kl., Abh. 14, 1949).

DuBourguet, Pierre. *Coptic Art.* London: Methuen, 1971.

Duchesne, L. *Early History of the Christian Church.* London, 1910–11.

Ehrman, Bart. *Didymus the Blind and the Text of the Gospels,* Atlanta: Scholar's Press, 1986.

———. "The New Testament Canon of Didymus the Blind," *Vigiliae Christianae* 37 (1983), pp. 1–21.

Eusebius. *Historia Ecclesia.*

———. *Vita Constantini.*

Eutychius Alexandrinus. *Annales.*

The Facsimile Edition of the Nag Hammadi Codices. 10 vols. Leiden: E. J. Brill, 1972–1977.

Festugiére, A., ed. *Historia Monachorum in Egypt, Subsidia Hagiographica* 34. Brussels, 1961.

Finegan, Jack. *Encountering New Testament Manuscripts.* Grand Rapids: Wm. B. Eerdman's, 1974.

———. *Handbook of Biblical Chronology.* Princeton: Princeton Univ. Press, 1964.

_____ . *Light from the Ancient Past.* Princeton: Princeton Univ. Press, 1951.

Foerster, Werner. (Trans. by R. McL. Wilson). *Gnosis, A Selection of Gnostic Texts.* 2 vols. Oxford: Clarendon Press, 1974.

Frend, W. H. C. *The Early Church.* Philadelphia: Lippincott, 1965.

_____ . *Martyrdom and Persecution in the Early Church.* New York: New York Univ. Press, 1965.

_____ . *The Rise of Christianity.* Philadelphia: Fortress Press, 1984.

_____ . *The Rise of the Monophysite Movement; Chapters in the History of the Church in the Fifth and Sixth Centuries.* Cambridge: Cambridge Univ. Press, 1972.

_____ . "Severus of Antioch and the Origins of the Monophysite Hierarchy," *Orientalia Christiana Analecta 195* (Rome: Pont. Inst. Stud. Orient., 1973).

Frickel, Josef. *Hellenistiche Erlösung in Christlicher Deutung.* Leiden: E. J. Brill, 1984.

Garitte, G. *S. Antonii Vitae. Versio Sahidica.* Paris: *CSCO*, *Scriptores Coptici*, Ser. 4, 1., 1949.

Gibbon, Edward. (Introd., notes, and commentary by J. B. Bury). *The History of the Decline and Fall of the Roman Empire,* 7 vols. London, 1909–1914.

Goodenough, E. R. "The Perspective of Acts," *Studies in Luke-Acts* (ed. by Keck and Martyn). Nashville: Abingdon Press, 1966, pp. 551–59.

Goodspeed, Edgar J. (Rev. by R. M. Grant). *A History of Early Christian Literature.* Chicago: Univ. of Chicago Press, 1966.

_____ . *Paul.* New York: Abingdon Press, 1947.

Granfield, P., and J. Jungmann, eds. *Kyriakon, Festschrift Johannes Quasten.* 2 Vols. Münster: Verlag Aschendorff, 1970.

Grant, Frederick C. *Hellenistic Religions, The Age of Syncretism.* New York: The Liberal Arts Press, 1953.

Grant, Robert M. *Historical Introduction to the New Testament.* New York: Harper & Row, 1963.

———. "Manichees and Christians in the Third and Early Fourth Centuries," *Ex Orbe Religionum, Studia Geo Widengren Oblata.* Leiden: E. J. Brill, 1972, Vol. 1.

Gray, Patrick. *The Defense of Chalcedon in the East.* Leiden: E. J. Brill, 1979, pp. 10–16.

Greenlee, J. Harold. *Introduction to New Testament Textual Criticism.* Grand Rapids: Wm. B. Eerdmans, 1975.

Greenslade, S. L. *Church and State from Constantine to Theodosius.* Westport: Greenwood Press, 1981 (Reprint of 1954 ed.)

Gregg, Robert C., and Dennis E. Groh. *Early Arianism: A View of Salvation.* Philadelphia: Fortress Press, 1981.

Grenfell, B. P., and A. S. Hunt. *New Sayings of Jesus and Fragment of a Lost Gospel from Oxyrhynchus.* New York: Oxford Univ. Press, American Branch, 1904, (published for the Egyptian Exploration Fund).

———. *Oxyrhynchus Papyri,* Part IV. London: Egyptian Exploration Fund, 1904.

Griffith, F. Ll. "The Old Coptic Horoscope of the Stobart Collection," *ZÄS* 38 (1900), pp. 71–85.

Griggs, C. Wilfred. "The Origin and Formation of the Corpus of Apocryphal Literature," *Apocryphal Writings and the Latter-day Saints.* Provo: Brigham Young University Religious Studies Center, 1986, pp. 35–52.

Grosheide, F. W. *Some Early Lists of the Books of the New Testament, Textus Minores, Vol. I.* Leiden, 1948.

Guerrier, Louis. *Le Testament en Galilée. Patrol. Orient IX.* Paris, 1913.

Guillaumont, A., et al. *The Gospel According to Thomas.* New York: Harper and Row, 1959.

Guthrie, Donald. *New Testament Introduction, Vol. 3: Hebrews to Revelation,* 2nd ed. Chicago: Inter-Varsity Press, 1964.

Gwatkin, H. M. *The Arian Controversy.* London: Longman's, Green and Co., 1891.

———. *Studies of Arianism.* Cambridge: Cambridge Univ. Press, 1900.

Haenchen, Ernst. *The Acts of the Apostles.* Philadelphia: Westminster Press, 1971.

_____ . "The Book of Acts as Source Material for the History of Early Christianity," *Studies in Luke-Acts* (ed. by Keck and Martyn). Nashville: Abingdon Press, 1966; pp. 258–278.

Halkin, F., ed. *Sancti Pachomii Vitae Graecae*. Brussels, 1932.

Hallock, Frank H. "Christianity and the Old Egyptian Religion." *Eg. Rel.*, II (1934), 6–17.

_____ . "Coptic Apocrypha." *JBL*, LII, parts 2 and 3 (1933), 163–174.

Hardy, Edward Roche. *Christian Egypt: Church and People*. New York: Oxford Univ. Press, 1952.

Harnack, Adolf. *Die Briefsammlung des Apostels Paulus*. Leipzig: J. C. Hinrichs, 1926.

_____ . (trans. by Neil Buchanan). *History of Dogma*. 7 vols. bound as 4. New York: Dover Publications, 1961.

_____ . (trans. by James Moffatt). *The Mission and Expansion of Christianity in the First Three Centuries*. 2 vols. New York: G. P. Putnam's Sons, 1908.

Haugaard, William P. "Arius: Twice a Heretic?" *Ch. Hist.* 29 (1960), pp. 251–263.

Hefele, C. J. (trans. by H. Oxenham). *History of the Councils of the Church*. Edinburgh: T & T Clark, 1896.

Helmbold, Andrew K. *The Nag Hammadi Gnostic Texts and The Bible*. Grand Rapids: Baker Book House, 1967.

Hennecke, Edgar, and Wilhelm Schneemelcher. (trans. by R. McL. Wilson). *New Testament Apocrypha*. 2 vols. Philadelphia: Westminster Press, 1963.

Henrichs, A., "Mani and the Babylonian Baptists: A Historical Confrontation," *HSCP* 77 (1973), pp. 23–59.

_____ . "The Cologne Mani Codex Reconsidered," *HSCP* 83 (1979), pp. 339–367.

Henrichs, A., and L. Koenen. "Ein griechischer Mani-Codex," *ZPE 5* (1970), pp. 97–214, and *ZPE* 19 (1975), pp. 1–85.

Hohl, Ernst. H., ed. *Scriptores Historiae Augustae.* 2 vols. Leipzig: B. G. Teubneri, 1927.

Hohl, Ernst. H., ed. *Scriptores Historiae Augustae.* 2 vols. Leipzig: B. G. Teubneri, 1927.

Honigmann, E. "The Original List of the Members of the Council of Nicea, the Robber Synod and the Council of Chalcedon." *Byzantion,* 16 (1942), 20–80.

Hornschuh, Manfred. "Das Leben des Origenes und die Entstehung der alexandrinischen Schule," *Zeitschrift für Kirchengeschichte* 71 (1960), pp. 1–25, 193–214.

————. *Studien zur Epistula Apostolorum.* Berlin: Walter de Gruyter & Co., 1965.

Hunt, A. S., and C. C. Edgar. *Select papyri.* 2 vols. Cambridge: Harvard Univ. Press, 1959, 1963, (Loeb Classical Library).

Irenaeus. *Adversus omnes Haereses.*

Jackson, A. V. W. *Researches in Manichaeism.* New York: AMS Press, Inc., 1932.

Jülicher, A. "Ammonias," in Pauly-Wissowa, *Real-Encyclopaedie.* Stuttgart, 1894, Vol. 1, part 2, col. 1867.

————. "Clemens Alexandrinus," in Pauly-Wissowa, *Real-Encyclopaedie.* Stuttgart, 1901, vol. 4, col. 13.

Jonas, Hans. *The Gnostic Religion.* Boston: Beacon Press, 1958.

Jones, A. H. M. "Were Ancient Heresies National or Social Movements in Disguise?" *JThS,* n.s. 10 (1959), 280–298.

————. *The Later Roman Empire.* 2 vols. Norman: Univ. of Oklahoma Press, 1964.

Josephus, Flavius. *Opera Omnia.*

Kahle, Paul. *Bala'izah; Coptic Texts from Deir el-Bala'izah in Upper Egypt.* 2 vols. Oxford Univ. Press, 1954.

Kammerer, W. *A Coptic Bibliography.* Ann Arbor: Univ. of Michigan Press, 1950.

Kannengiesser, Charles. *Athanase d'Alexandria, Évêque et Écrivain.* Paris: *Beauchesne Éditeur,* 1983.

————. *Holy Scripture and Hellenistic Hermeneutics in Alexandrian Christology: The Arian Crisis.* Berkeley: The Center for Hermeneutical Studies, Colloquy 41, 1981.

Käsemann, Ernst. "Die Johannesjunger von Ephesus." *Zeitschrift für Theologie und Kirche* (1952), pp. 144–154.

Kasser, Rodolphe. *Papyrus Bodmer III, Evangile de Jean et Genese I-IV,* 2. Louvain: *CSCO, Scriptores Coptici,* Vols. 25–26, 1960.

————. et al., eds. *Tractatus Tripartitus.* pars I. *De Supernis* Bern: Francke Verlag, 1973.

————. *Tractatus Tripartitus,* pars II. *De Creatione Hominis.* pars III. *De Generibus Tribus.* Bern: Francke Verlag, 1975.

Keizer, Lewis S. *The Eighth Reveals the Ninth: New Hermetic Initiation Disclosure.* (Nag Hammadi, Codex VI, No. 6). Seaside: Academy of Arts and Humanities, 1974.

Kelly, J. N. D. *Early Christian Doctrines.* London: Adam and Charles Black, 1968.

————. *Jerome, His Life, Writings, and Controversies.* London: G. Duckworth & Co., 1975.

Kemp, Eric Waldram. "Bishops and Presbyters at Alexandria." *JEH* 6 (1955), pp. 125–142.

Kenyon, F. G. (revised and augmented by A. W. Adams). *The Text of the Greek Bible,* 3rd ed. London: Buckworth and Co. Ltd., 1975.

Kidd, B. J. *A History of the Church to A.D. 461.* 3 vols. Oxford: Clarendon Press, 1922.

Knipfing, R. "The Libelli of the Decian Persecution," *HThR* 16 (1923), pp. 345–390.

Knowles, David. *Christian Monasticism.* New York: McGraw-Hill, 1969.

Koenen, L. "Zur Herkunft des Kölner Mani-Codex," *Zeitschrift für Papyrologie und Epigraphik* 11 (1973), pp. 240–241.

Koschorke, Klaus. *Die Polemik der Gnostiker gegen das kirchliche Christentum.* Leiden: E. J. Brill, *NHS* XII, 1978.

Krause, Martin. *Die Gnosis.* 2 vols. Zurich: Artemis Verlag, 1975.

————. *Essays on the Nag Hammadi Texts.* NHS VI. Leiden: E. J. Brill, 1975.

Kugener, M.-A. (ed. and transl.). *Vie de Sévère, par Zacharie de Scholastique,* and *Vie de Sévère, par Jean du monastère de Beith-Aphthonia,* in *Patrol. Orientalis* 2.1 and 3.

Kuhn, K. H. *Letters and Sermons of Besa.* Louvain: *CSCO, Scriptores Coptici,* Tomus 17, 1956.

————. *A Panegyric on Apollo:* Louvain: *CSCO, Scriptores Coptici,* Tomus 39, 1978.

Kümmel, W. G. *Introduction to the New Testament.* London: SCM Press, 1970.

Latourette, Kenneth S. *A History of Christianity.* New York: Harper and Row, 1953.

Lawlor, H. J., and J. E. L. Oulton. *Eusebius, Ecclesiastical History and Martyrs.* 2 vols. London: SPCK Press, 1954.

Layton, Bentley. *The Gnostic Scriptures.* New York: Doubleday, 1987.

————., ed. *The Rediscovery of Gnosticism, Proceedings of the Conference at Yale,* 2 Vols. (I: *The School of Valentinus;* II: *Sethian Gnosticism*). Leiden: E. J. Brill, 1980, 1981.

Lebreton, J., and J. Zeiller. *The History of the Primitive Church.* New York: MacMillan, 1949.

Lefort, L. Th. *Les Pères Apostoliques en Copte.* Louvain: *CSCO, Scriptores Coptici,* Tomus 17, 1952.

————. *S. Athanese, Lettres Festales et Pastorales en Copte.* Louvain: *CSCO, Scriptores Coptici,* Tomus 19, 1965.

————. *S. Pachomii Vita Bohairice Scripta.* Louvain: *CSCO, Scriptores Coptici,* Vols. 7, 9, 10, 1965.

————. *S. Pachomii vitae Sahidice Scriptae.* Paris: *CSCO, Scriptores Coptici,* ser. 3, 8, pts. 1–2, 1933.

————. *Sinuthi Archimandritae Vita.* Paris: *CSCO, Scriptores Coptici.* ser. 2, 2–5, 1906–1913.

Lexa, Frantisek. "La Légende gnostique sur Pistis Sophia et Le Mythe ancien Égyptian sur L' oeil de Re." *Eg. Rel.,* I (1933), 106–116.

Lietzmann, Hans. *A History of the Early Church.* 4 Vols. London: Lutterworth Press, 1951.

Lieu, Samuel N. C. *Manichaeism in the Later Roman Empire and Medieval China, a Historical Survey.* Manchester: Manchester Univ. Press, 1985.

Lipsius, R. A., ed. *Acta Apostolorum Apocrypha.* 3 Vols. Darmstadt: Wissenschaftliche Buchgesellschaft, 1959.

Loofs, F. *Nestorius and His Place in the History of Christian Doctrine.* Cambridge: Cambridge Univ. Press, 1914.

MacLennan, Hugh. *Oxyrhynchus.* Amsterdam: AM Hakkert, 1968.

Mallon, Alexis, S. J. (rev. by M. Malinine). *Grammaire Copte.* (with Bibliography). Beyrouth: Imprimerie Catholique, 1956.

Malinine, M., et al., eds. *De Resurrectione.* Zürich und Stuttgart: Rascher Verlag, 1963.

_____. *Epistula Iacobi Apocrypha.* Zürich and Stuttgart: Rascher Verlag, 1963.

_____. *Evangelium Veritatis.* Zürich and Stuttgart: Rascher Verlag, 1961.

Mansi, J. D., ed. *Sacrorum Conciliorum nova et amplissima Collectio.* Paris, 1901–1927.

Menard, Jacques. *L'Évangile selon Philippe.* Paris: Letovzey & Ané, 1967.

Metzger, Bruce M. *A Textual Commentary on the Greek New Testament.* New York: United Bible Societies, 1971.

Meyer, Robert T. *St. Athanasius, the Life of Saint Antony* (Ancient Christian Writers, Vol. 10). New York: Newman Press, 1950.

Migne, J. P., ed. *Patrologiae Graecae.*

_____. *Patrologiae Latinae.*

Milne, Joseph G. *A History of Egypt.* 6 vols. London: Methuen, 1898.

Momigliano, A., ed. *The Conflict Between Paganism and Christianity in the Fourth Century.* Oxford: Clarendon Press, 1963.

Morris, Leon. *Commentary on the Gospel of John.* Grand Rapids: Wm. B. Eerdmans, 1971.

Munck, Johannes. *Acts of the Apostles*. New York: Doubleday, 1967.

Nibley, H. *When the Lights Went Out, Three Studies on the Ancient Apostasy*. Salt Lake City: Deseret Book, 1970.

Nock, Arthur Darby. *Early Gentile Christianity and its Hellenistic Background*. New York: Harper & Row, 1964.

Origen. *Opera Omnia*. (Kötschau et al, eds.) Leipzig: J. C. Hinrichs, 1899–1955.

Parrott, Douglas. "The Nag Hammadi Library and the Pachomian Monasteries," unpublished paper in the possession of the author of this study.

Pearson, Birger. "Anti-Heretical Warnings from Codex IX from Nag Hammadi," *Essays on the Nag Hammadi Texts, NHS VI*. Leiden: E. J. Brill, 1975, pp. 145–154.

Peel, Malcolm Lee. *The Epistle to Rheginos*. Philadelphia: Westminster Press, 1969.

Percival, Henry R., ed. *Cyril's Third Letter, The Seven Ecumenical Councils of the Undivided Church*. Grand Rapids: Wm. B. Eerdmans, 1971 (Reprint).

Philo. *Opera Omnia*.

Pietersma, Albert. *The Acts of Phileas, Bishop of Thmuis*. Geneva, 1984.

Plummer, Alfred. *A Critical and Exegetical Commentary on the Second Epistle of St. Paul to the Corinthians*. Edinburgh: T. & T. Clark, 1975.

Pollard, T. E. "The Origins of Arianism." *JThS*, n.s. 9 (1959), pp. 103–111.

Polotsky, H. J., ed. *Manichäische Homilien*. Stuttgart, 1934.

Polotsky, H. J., and A. Böhlig, eds. *Kephalaia*, Vol. 1, Part 1. Stuttgart, 1940.

Quasten, Johannes. *Patrology*. 3 vols. Utrecht: Spectrum Publishing, 1950–1960.

―――. *Patrology IV*. Westminster, Maryland: Christian Classics, 1986.

Queffeléc, Henri. *Saint Anthony of the Desert*. New York: E. P. Dutton, 1954.

Quispel, Gilles. "Origen and the Valentinian Gnosis," *Vigiliae Christianae* 28 (1974), 29–42.

Ramsay, W. M. *The Bearing of Recent Discoveries on the Trustworthiness of the New Testament*, 4th ed. London, 1920.

Rees, B. R. "Popular Religion in Graeco-Roman Egypt: II. The Transition to Christianity." *JEA*, 36 (1950), 86–100.

Reinach, Salomon. "La première allusion au Christianisme dans l'histoire." *Revue de l'histoire des religions* 90 (1924), pp. 108–122.

Reynolds, L. D., and N. E. Wilson. *Scribes and Scholars, A Guide to the Transmission of Greek and Latin Literature*, 2nd ed. revised and enlarged. Oxford: Clarendon Press, 1975.

Roberts, C. H. "The Christian Book and the Greek Papyri." *JThS*, 50 (1949), 155–168.

———. "Early Christianity in Egypt: Three Notes." *JEA* 40 (1954), 92–96.

———. *Manuscript, Society, and Belief in Early Christian Egypt*. London: Oxford Univ. Press for the British Academy, 1979.

———. *An Unpublished Fragment of the Fourth Gospel*. Manchester: The Manchester Univ. Press, 1935.

Robinson, J. Armitage, ed. *Texts and Studies*, Vol. IV, No. 2. *Coptic Apocryphal Gospels*. Cambridge: Cambridge Univ. Press, 1896.

Robinson, James M., ed. *The Facsimile Edition of the Nag Hammadi Codices, Introduction*. Leiden: E. J. Brill, 1984.

———. *The Nag Hammadi Codices*. Claremont: The Ink spot, 1977.

———. *The Nag Hammadi Library in English*. New York: Harper & Row, 1977.

Robinson, James M., and H. Koester, eds. *Trajectories Through Early Christianity*. Philadelphia: Fortress Press, 1971.

Routh, M. J., ed. "Epistle of Peter of Alexandria to the Church," *Reliquiae Sacrae*. Oxford: Oxford Press, 1815.

Rudolph, Kurt. *Gnosis und Gnostizismus*. Darmstadt: Wissenschaftliche Buchgesellschaft, 1975.

Ruinart, R. P. D. Thierry. *Les véritables Actes des Martyrs*. Paris: A Besançon, 1818 (reprint).

Salmond, S. D. "Theonas of Alexandria," *The Ante-Nicene Fathers VI.* Grand Rapids: Wm. B. Eerdmans, 1971 (reprint).

Säve-Söderbergh, Torgny. *Studies in the Coptic Manichaean Psalm-Book.* Uppsala: Almquist and Wiksells Boktryckeri AB, 1949.

Schmidt, Carl. *Gespräche Jesu mit seinen Jüngern nach der Auferstehung* (TU 43). Leipzig, 1919.

Schmidt, Carl, et. al. *Kephalaia.* Stuttgart, 1940.

Schmithals, Walter. (Trans. by John E. Steeley). *Gnosticism in Corinth.* New York: Abingdon Press, 1971.

———. *Paul and the Gnostics.* New York: Abingdon Press, 1972.

Schwartz, Eduard, ed. *Acta Conciliorum Oecumenicorum.* Berlin: Walter de Gruyter, 1922–1929. Tome 1, vols. 1–5.

Sealey, Raphael. *A History of the Greek City States, 700–338 B.C.,* Berkeley: Univ. of Calif. Press, 1976.

Sellers, R. V. *The Council of Chalcedon.* London: SPCK Press, 1953.

———. *Two Ancient Christologies.* London: SPCK Press, 1954.

Severus Ibn Al-Mukaffa. (Arabic text edited and translated by B. Evetts). *History of the Patriarchs of the Coptic Church of Alexandria.* Patrol. Orientalis I. 101–214 and 381–518.

Smith, Morton. *Clement of Alexandria and a Secret Gospel of Mark.* Cambridge: Harvard Univ. Press, 1973.

———. "Clement of Alexandria and Secret Mark: The Score at the End of the First Decade," *HThR* 75:4 (1982), pp. 449–461.

Smith, William. *A Dictionary of Greek and Roman Geography.* 2 vols. London: John Murray, 1873, (reprinted by AMS Press in New York, 1966).

Socrates. *Historia Ecclesia.*

Sozomenus. *Historia Ecclesia.*

Stead, G. C. "In Search of Valentinus," *Rediscovery of Gnosticism, Vol. 1: The School of Valentinus,* ed. by B. Layton. Leiden: E. J. Brill, 1980, pp. 75–102.

———. "The Platonism of Arius." *JThS,* n.s. 15 (1964), pp. 16–31.

Stevenson, J. *Creeds, Councils, and Controversies.* London: SPCK Press, 1966.

Telfer, W. "Episcopal Succession in Egypt." *JEH* 3 (1952), 1–13.

————. "When Did the Arian Controversy Begin?" *JThS* 47 (1946), pp. 129–142.

————. "Sozomen I. 15, A Reply." *JThS* 50 (1949), pp. 187–191.

Tetz, Martin. "Athanasius und die Vita Antonii," *Zeitschrift für die neutestamentliche Wissenschaft* 73 (1982), pp. 1–30.

Theodoret. *Historia Ecclesia.*

Thompson, Sir Herbert. *The Gospel of John According to the Earliest Coptic Manuscript.* London: The British School of Archaeology in Egypt, 1924.

Thomsom, Robert W. *Athanasius, Contra Gentes and De Incarnatione.* Oxford: Clarendon Press, 1971.

Till, W. C. "Coptic and Its Value." *Bulletin of the John Rylands Library* 40 (1957–58), pp. 229–232.

————. *Die Gnostischen Schriften des Koptischen Papyrus Berolinensis 8502.* Berlin: Akademie Verlag. 1955.

————. "Schenutes Werke," *Koptische Grammatik.* Leipzig: VEB Verlag, 1966.

Tischendorf, K., ed. *Evangelia Apocrypha.* Hildesheim: Georg Olms, 1966.

Van der Horst, P. W., and Mansfield, J. *An Alexandrian Platonist Against Dualism.* Leiden: E. J. Brill, 1974.

Veilleux, Armand. *Pachomian Koinonia I: The Life of Saint Pachomius and His Disciples.* Kalamazoo: Cistercian Publications, 1980.

————. *Pachomian Koinonia II: Pachomian Chronicles and Rules.* Kalamazoo: Cistercian Publications, 1981.

————. *Pachomian Koinonia III: Instructions, Letters, and Other Writings of Saint Pachomius and His Disiples,* 1982.

Von Campenhausen, H. "Augustine and the Fall of Rome." *Tradition and Life in the Church.* Philadelphia: Fortress Press, 1968, pp. 201–216.

Von Campenhausen, H. "Christians and Military Service in the Early Church." *Tradition and Life in the Church.* Philadelphia: Fortress Press, 1968, pp. 160–170.

Waddell, Helen. *The Desert Fathers.* Ann Arbor: Univ. of Michigan Press, 1957.

Walters, C. C. *Monastic Archaeology in Egypt.* Warminster: Aris and Phillips, 1974.

Ward, Benedicta. *The Sayings of the Desert Fathers.* London: Mowbrays, 1975.

Wessel, Klaus. *Coptic Art.* New York: McGraw-Hill, 1965.

Widengren, Geo. (Trans. by Birger A. Pearson). *The Gnostic Attitude.* Santa Barbara: Institute of Religious Studies, 1973.

Wiles, Maurice. "In Defence of Arius." *JThS,* n.s. 13 (1962), pp. 330–347.

⸻. "ΟΜΟΟΓΣΙΟΣ ΗΜΙΝ" *JThS,* n.s. 16 (1965), pp. 454–461.

Williams, Frank, ed. and transl. *The Panarion of Epiphanius of Salamis, Book I, NHS* 35. Leiden: E. J. Brill, 1987.

Wilson, R. McL. *Gnosis and the New Testament.* Philadelphia: Fortress Press, 1968.

Winkelmann, F., ed. *Philostorgius, Hist. Eccl.,* Berlin, Akademie Verlag (*GCS*), 1981.

Wisse, Frederik. "The Nag Hammadi Library and the Heresiologists," *Vigiliae Christianae* 25 (1971), 205–223.

Workman, Herbert B. *The Evolution of the Monastic Ideal.* Boston: Beacon Press, 1962.

Worrell, William H. *A Short Account of the Copts.* Ann Arbor: Univ. of Michigan Press, 1945.

Wright, F. A., ed. *Jerome, Select Letters.* Cambridge: Harvard Univ. Press, 1963.

Yamauchi, Edwin M. *Pre-Christian Gnosticism.* Grand Rapids: Wm. B. Eerdmans, 1973.

Young, Frances M. *From Nicaea to Chalcedon, A guide to the Literature and its Background.* Philadelphia: Fortress Press, 1983.

Zernov, Nicolas. *Eastern Christendom.* London: Weidenfield and Nicolson, 1963.

INDEX—PLACE NAMES

Achaea   4
Adrianople   182
Africa   99
Ailat   95
Akhmim   7, 25
Alexandria   1, 5, 14–18, 20, 23, 25, 26, 28, 31–33, 35–37, 49, 50, 53,
        57, 58, 60–62, 65–70, 79, 80, 82, 83, 86, 88, 90–95, 97 98, 99,
        100, 102, 105, 106, 117–125, 127–133, 135–137, 139, 140,
        141–145, 150, 152–154, 157, 159–163, 165, 166, 168, 170, 171,
        173, 175, 179–187, 189–193, 195, 199, 201–203, 205, 207, 208,
        210–215
Antaradus of Phoenicia   203
Antioch   8, 58, 68, 79, 90, 93, 103, 133, 135, 137, 143, 146, 186, 188,
        192, 193, 197, 203, 207, 212, 214
Antinoe   213
Aquileia   144
Arabia   3, 61
Armenia   215
Arsinoe   83, 87, 91
Asia   4, 5, 7, 27, 29, 47, 150
Asia Minor   4, 5, 7, 29
Athens   56, 57
Athribis   82, 83
Babylon   17, 18, 36
Baucalis   135
Berenice   95
Beroea (in Syria)   194
Berytus   214
Bethlehem   13
Bithynia   136
Bosporus   188
Caesarea   65, 91, 94, 126, 127, 133, 139
Cairo   17, 35, 96, 177
Cana   101
Canopus   211
Cappadocia   144
Carthage   131

Castle-on-the-Beach 95
Cephro in Libya 86
Cephro Oasis 86
Chalcedon 90, 173, 205, 206, 208, 209, 215
Chenoboskia 178
Chenoboskion 152, 177
Coele-Syria 57
Coma, Village of 103
Constantinople 141, 150, 180, 183–189, 192, 197, 200, 203, 205,
    206, 208, 211, 214, 215
Cordova 136
Corinth 5
Cyprus 16, 54, 184, 187, 195
Cyrene 16
Cyrrhus 134
Cyzicus 208
Damascus 3, 4, 147
Deir Anba Antonios 104
Delta 23, 122, 150
Dio-Caesarea in Galilee 182
Diospolis Parva 152
Edessa 204
Egypt 1, 2, 4, 5, 7, 13–30, 32–38, 45–48, 50, 51, 53–58, 62, 67–70,
    79, 81–89, 91–106, 117, 119, 121–125, 127, 128, 130, 131, 132,
    135–141, 143–146, 148–150, 152–154, 156–165, 170, 171,
    172–177, 181, 182, 184–190, 192–194, 197, 199–202, 206, 207,
    208–215
Egyptian Babylon 18
El-Ushmunain 90
Elephantine 15
Ephesus 17, 25, 35, 47, 159, 186, 187, 192, 196, 197, 199, 203–205,
    208, 209, 214
Esneh 152
Ethiopia 8, 14, 35, 149, 193, 215
Faw Qibli 129
Fayum 14, 24, 25, 83, 95, 96
Galatia 4, 149
Gangra 208, 211
Gaul 141, 154

Great Oasis in Egypt   197
Greece   7, 57, 119
Hathor   126, 127
Heliopolis   182
Heraclea   208
Heracleopolis Magna   129
Heracleopolite   127
Hermopolis   13, 186, 188
Hermopolis Parva   147, 186
Hipponon   127
Hypseles   95
Iberia   210
India   8, 95, 147, 149
Inner Mountain   104
Jabal al-Tarif   176
Jerusalem   3, 4, 14–16, 35, 58, 79, 101, 141, 158, 184, 187, 191, 206, 207
Jordan River   26
Judea   3, 19
Kellia   150
Laodicaea   94, 123
Letopolis   122, 128
Libya   14, 93, 131, 136
Lower Egypt   98, 170
Luxor   96
Lycopolis   95, 96, 99, 118, 121
Lyons   33
Macedonia   4
Magna Graccia   57
Mareotis   141
Medinet Medi   96
Mediterranean   28
Memphis   104, 122, 126
Mesopotamian Babylon   18
Middle Egypt   24, 25, 122
Mount of Olives   149
Nag Hammadi   52, 96, 129, 176, 198
New Rome   202
Nicaea   121–123, 131, 134, 136, 137, 140, 142, 143, 145, 172, 206

Nicomedia   124, 141
Nile   1, 5, 13, 14, 16, 17, 23, 34, 36, 37, 80–82, 86, 95, 104, 118, 149, 171, 179, 186, 198, 200, 211, 213
Nile Delta   17
Nile Valley   14, 23, 80, 95, 179
Nitria   150, 186–188, 191
Nitrian Desert   81, 186
Nubia   215
Outer Mountain   104
Oxyrhynchus   24, 27, 29, 89, 96
Palace of the Oak   188
Palestine   3–5, 16, 19, 24, 29, 57, 61, 62, 101, 118, 164, 166, 184, 186
Palestinian Syria   127
Panopolis   25
Pboou   177
Pbow   129
Pentapolis   93, 131
Perrha   203
Persia   94
Pharbaithus   82
Phoenicia   203
Pisidia   214
Pispir   104
Prosopitis   82, 83
Red Sea   104
Rhone   55
Roman   4, 7, 28, 36, 37, 57, 69, 89, 93, 94, 103, 133, 143, 144, 152, 155, 156, 159, 160, 162, 182, 184, 185, 189–192, 194, 196, 204, 205, 212, 215
Rome   1, 4, 5, 7, 18, 20, 34, 35, 37, 48, 53–55, 63, 68–70, 79, 87, 89, 93, 131, 136, 142–144, 146, 152, 153, 157, 159, 160, 162, 174, 181–185, 188, 190, 193, 194, 202, 205, 206, 208, 212
Sais   82
Salamis   135
Samaria   3
Sardica   93, 143, 144
Sasima   183
Scetis   150, 188
Scythia   8

Sicily 57
Sotinen 13
Syria 5, 7, 19, 34, 57, 94, 127, 134, 149, 190, 193, 194, 212, 214, 215
Syrian Antioch 16
Tabennesis 152, 155
Taposiris 18
Tarsus 3
Tentyra 153
The Nile 1, 5, 13, 14, 16, 17, 23, 34, 36, 37, 80–82, 86, 95, 104, 118,
     149, 171, 179, 186, 198, 200, 211, 213
The Sudan 18
Thebaid 80, 88, 95, 97, 98, 103, 121, 122, 126, 128, 152, 153
Thebes 83, 123, 136
Theonas 144
Therapeutae 20, 29
Thessalonica 205
Thmuis 98
Trier 141
Tyre 126, 128, 141, 143
Upper Cynopolite nome 126
Upper Egypt 7, 24, 25, 79, 81, 82, 84, 96, 98, 104, 122, 154, 157,
     161, 165, 176
Wadi Habib 129
White Monastery 196

INDEX—PROPER NAMES

Abilius   91
Acacius of Constantinople   211, 212
Acacius, bishop of Beroea   194
Achillas   97, 119, 120
Adda   95
Aetius   139
Alexander, bishop of Alexandria   93, 118, 119, 120, 122, 123, 124,
     132, 133, 135–137, 138
Alexander, bishop of Jerusalem   58
Alexander of Lykopolis   95
Alexander of Phoenicia   203
Altheim   18
Alypius   202
Ambrose   64
Ammianus Marcellinus   145
Ammonius   63, 142, 186, 191
Amos   81
Amun   146
Anastasius   205
Anastasius, Emperor   214
Anatolius   94, 205–207
Andrew   8
Andrew of Samosata   195
Anicetus   54
Anthony   102–105, 122, 138, 139, 150, 151, 171, 200
Antoninus Pius   81
Apa Paieous   126
Apa Panai   96
Apollinaris   123, 184
Appollo   129
Apollos   16, 17, 22, 55
Aquila   17
Archelaus   128
Aretas   4
Aristotle   50
Arius   118–122, 125, 130, 133–137, 139–141, 145, 146
Arsenius   126

Athanasius   93,   103–105,   117,   121–128,   130–132,   135–147,
    150–155, 170, 172, 174, 175, 180–182, 184, 190, 197, 202, 203
Athanasius II   213
Atiya   81, 154
Augustine   7
Augustus   145
Aurelius Pageus   127
Avilius   91
Bacht   155
Bahram I of Persia   94
Barnabas   4, 5, 16, 59
Barnard   103
Barnes   134, 137
Barns   176
Baronius, C.   8
Bartholomew   21
Basil   184
Basilides   47, 49–51, 55, 60, 82
Basiliscus   211
Bauer   17, 21, 22, 32, 45
Baus   89, 121, 192, 194, 196, 201, 215
Beatty   80, 81
Bell   18, 23, 25, 27, 33, 80, 90, 99, 118, 122, 124–128
Besa   198, 199, 201
Bigg   62
Brennan, B. R.   103
Brown   105
Browne   176
Bruce   3, 14, 17
Budge   80, 81
Bury   208
Butterworth   62, 66
Cadiou   62
Callistus   128
Caracalla   58
Carpocrates   47, 48, 50, 51, 55
Celadion   91
Celestine   194, 196, 197
Cerinthus   47

Cestius   14

Chadwick   48, 50, 51, 58, 60, 62, 63, 121, 137, 184, 186, 212

Charles   7

Christ   6, 7, 47–49, 53, 84, 120, 134, 136, 193, 195, 200, 207, 208,
        211

Chrysaphius   203

Chrysostom, John   185, 187, 188, 189, 192, 193, 203

Claudius   18, 19

Clement of Alexandria   20, 21, 28, 31, 48–50, 56–61, 64, 65, 67, 70,
        79, 81, 82, 100

Constans   144

Constantine, Emperor   123–125, 127, 134, 136, 139, 140–142

Constantine II   142, 143

Constantius   144, 145

Cross   55, 58, 62

Crum   126, 155

Cumont   19

Cyprian   68

Cyril   146, 156, 190–199, 201–203, 205, 207–210, 212

Damasus of Rome   146, 182, 183

Damian, Patriarch   129

Danielou   62, 66

David the King   200

Davies   184

Decius   89, 92, 98

DeFaye   63, 66

Demetrius   26, 28, 33, 45, 56, 57, 61, 62, 66, 67, 70, 79, 82, 91, 92, 97,
        102, 130, 131, 143

Demophilus   180

Didymus the Blind   153, 175, 182

Dillon   63

Diocletian   97, 117

Dionysius of Alexandria   61, 67–70, 79, 82, 86–93, 98, 100, 102,
        123, 184

Dionysius of Rome   69, 70, 93

Dioscorus   154, 186, 188, 201–210

Domnus of Antioch   201, 204

Donatists   99

Dracontius   147

Duchesne   105
Ehrman   175
Elijah   6, 101, 200
Elisha   200
Ephraim, Patriarch of Antioch   8
Epicureans   66
Epiphanes   48, 50
Epiphanius   49, 51, 53, 54, 56, 82, 83, 95, 117, 118, 120, 122,
    123–125, 132, 135, 141, 186
Eudoxia, Empress   189, 194, 203
Eudoxius   180
Eunomius   139
Eusebius of Caesarea   5, 7, 8, 19–22, 28, 29, 33, 46, 55, 57, 59,
    61–64, 67, 69, 70, 87–89, 91–94, 97, 98, 100, 101, 124–126,
    133, 134, 140, 145, 186
Eusebius of Dorylaeum   204
Eusebius of Nicomedia   126, 130, 173
Eustace   186
Eustathius   146
Euthymius   186
Eutyches   203–205, 209, 212
Eutychius   90–92, 130
Euzoius   181
Evagrius of Pontus   103, 150, 187
Ezekiel   200
Fabius   63, 68, 90
Flavius   205
Foerster   59
Frend   98, 121, 137, 139, 143, 146, 151–154, 171, 190, 202, 204,
    205, 209, 210, 213, 214
Frontonius   81
Galerius   118
George of Cappadocia   144, 145
Germanus   68, 86, 90
Goodspeed   5
Grant, R. M.   95
Gratian   183
Gray   212
Greenslade   134

Gregory   143, 144, 183
Gregory Thaumaturgos   66
Grenfell   23, 24, 29, 33
Hadrian   22, 47
Hannon   131
Hardy   89, 210
Harnack   5, 22, 83
Hatres   126
Henrichs   96
Heraclas   67, 69, 79, 87, 92, 121
Heracleon   66
Hermas   7
Herod   13
Hieracas   83
Hierax   70, 191
Hilary   7
Hippolytus   45, 47–49, 54
Homer   103
Hornschuh   58, 63
Horsiesios   149, 155, 156
Hosea   81
Hosius   136
Hunt   23, 29, 33
Hyginus   54
Hypatia   191
Ibas of Edessa   204
Ignatius of Antioch   5
Irenaeus   33, 34, 45–49, 51, 53–55, 60
Isaac   128, 129
Isidore   142, 186, 187
James   4, 59
Jeremiah   200
Jerome   7, 61, 92, 98, 102, 135, 142, 149, 154, 182, 187, 189
Jesus   3, 4, 6, 13, 15, 17, 23, 26, 27, 29, 30, 32, 47, 55, 84, 94, 101,
      180, 195, 200
Jmmoute   96
John   4, 6, 17, 26, 27, 47, 59, 66, 67, 122, 186, 188, 189, 196
John Arkaph   142
John Cassian   154, 194

John of Antioch   195–197
John of Beith-Aphthonia   214
John of Jerusalem   187
John the Baptist   3, 200
Jones   90, 99
Joseph   13
Josephus   14
Jude   4, 7
Julian   21, 91, 145, 155
Julian of Cos   205
Julius   143, 144
Justin, Emperor   51, 214, 215
Justinian   215
Juvenal   206, 207
Kannengiesser   139
Käsemann   17
Kelly   187, 193, 195
Kemp   92
Kidd   131
Knipfing   89
Koschorke   85
Lawlor   86
Leipoldt   22
Leo, Emperor   210
Leo, Bishop of Rome   202–204, 206–208, 213
Leonides   61
Liberatus   132
Licinius   152
Lietzmann   122, 150
Lieu   95
Lucianus   97
Lucius   146, 180–182
Luke   4–6, 14
Marcarius   128, 150, 182
Magnentius of Gaul   144
Mani
        Manichaean   95, 96
        Manichaica   96
        Manichaios   94
        Manichees   95

Marcellina   48
Marcian, Emperor   206–208, 210
Marcosians   55
Marcus   55
Mark   6, 17–21, 28, 48
Mary   13, 193, 195
Matthew   6, 13
Matthias   8
Maximin   97, 105, 118
Maximinus   152
Maximus   93, 94, 97, 144, 183, 185
Maximus of Antioch   207
Melchizedek   83
Melitius   98, 99, 117–123, 129, 130, 137
Memmon, bishop of Ephesus   196
Mongus, Peter   212, 213
Miltiades   51
Moses   6, 13, 27
Muhammed Ali   175
Narcissus   101
Nectarius   185
Nepos   70, 87
Nero   4, 14
Nestorius   192–197, 199, 203, 212
Novatian   68
O'Callaghan   18
Odysseus   103
Orestes   190, 191
Origen   28, 57, 58, 60–67, 69, 79, 83, 88, 100, 101, 120, 133, 135,
   153
Origen the Christian   63
Ouiton   86
Pachomius   122, 138, 148–150, 152–156, 170, 174, 178, 197, 200,
   201
Pageus   127
Pahome   178
Palamon   152
Palladius   149–151, 154, 181, 188
Pantaenus   21, 22, 56–58, 61, 70, 79

Papias 20
Papnoute 178
Pappos 95
Parrott 179
Paschasinus 207
Paul 4–6, 17, 19, 81, 85, 93, 148, 200
Paul of Samosata 93, 94
Paul of Thebes 150
Paulinus 102
Pearson 85
Peisistratus 119
Percival 131
Peter, Apostle 4, 17, 18, 20, 59, 84, 97, 99, 143
Peter, Bishop of Alexandria 117–120, 135, 146
Peter of Alexandria 181–183, 185
Peter Mongus 211, 215
Petronius 155
Philaster 49
Phileas 98, 99
Philemon 69
Philip 89
Philo 14, 20
Philostorgius 123, 135, 140
Photius 8, 58, 59
Pius 54, 81
Pjol 197, 200
Plato 31, 66
Plotinus 63
Polycarp 5
Porphyry 63
Poseidonius 202
Priscilla 17
Proculus 51
Proterius 209–211, 213
Psammetichus 14
Pseudo-Tertullian 49
Pshai 96
Ptolemaeus 51
Pulcheria 194, 205, 206, 208

Pythagoras 52
Quasten 58, 60
Queffélec, H. 103
Quispel 64
Reinach 19
Roberts 23–25, 33
Robinson 198
Rufinus 61, 140, 141, 149, 150, 182, 189
Sabellian 69
Samaritans 3
Sansnos 178
Saul 3, 4
Schäferdiek 8
Schmidt 47, 96
Schmithals 5
Schneemelcher 29
Scythianus 95
Sellers 193, 202, 205, 208
Serapion, bishop of Tentyra 153
Sergius of Cyrrhus 214
Servianus 22
Severus of Antioch 213–215
Severus, son of El-Mukaffa 90–92
Shelton 177, 178
Shenoute 148, 156, 196–199, 201, 209
Simon (Magus) 47
Simon of Cyrene 49
Sisinnius, bishop of Constantinople 192
Skeat 27
Smith 20, 21, 48, 60
Socrates 94, 119, 120, 134, 136, 140, 181, 185, 186, 190, 191, 193
Sophia 53
Sozomen 119, 120, 123, 125, 126, 134, 135, 140, 185
Stiehl 18
Sylvester, Pope 136
Syrianus 144
Tall Brothers 186, 187
Telfer 25, 26, 28, 32, 33, 131, 132
Tertullian 45, 51–54

Theodore, and Clement   20, 42
Theodore, the monk   148, 149, 153, 155, 156, 175, 179
Theodore of Antinoe   213
Theodoret   47, 121, 125, 134, 140, 201, 202, 207
Theodoret of Cyprus   195
Theodoret, Bishop of Cyrrhus   201, 204
Theodosius   183, 184, 191, 194, 201, 203–205, 208
Theodosius II   191, 192, 194, 196, 206
Theon   191
Theonas, bishop of Alexandria   97
Theopemptos   190
Theophilus   83, 120, 185–190, 192, 197
Theophilus of Alexandria   150
Theophilus, bishop of Alexandria   83
Theophoros   195
Theotecnus of Caesarea   94
Thomas   8
Thompson   140, 145
Timothy   184, 190, 210, 211
Timothy nicknamed Wobble-cap   211
Timothy the Cat   211, 212
Turner   177
Valens, Emperor   146, 180, 182
Valentinian I   180
Valentinus   47, 51, 53–55, 60, 64, 66, 82, 83, 143, 203
Valerian   86
Walters   154
Workman   105
Xystus III   197
Xystus, bishop of Rome,   69, 87
Young   145
Zacharias Scholasticus   214
Zeno   211, 212

INDEX—GENERAL

Adoptionism   193
Akephaloi   212, 213
Alexandrian
    archbishop   173
    bishop   172, 185, 186, 189, 192, 196, 206
    bishopric   210
    bishops   171, 204, 215
    Christology   205
    church   191, 192, 198
    diocese   189
    diptychs   193
    episcopate   202, 204, 213
    metropolitan   188
    patriarch   171, 188, 201, 207
    patriarchate   188
    patriarchs   215
    population   190
    prelates   187, 189
    scholars   175
    school   57, 63, 138, 193
    see   211
    successes   205
    theologians   184, 195
    theology   184
Alexandrinus   175
Anthropomorphites   187
Anti-Alexandrian bishops   204
Anti-Arian sources   135, 139, 143, 180
Anti-Chalcedonian   209, 212, 213, 214
    forces   213
    monks   212
    movement   209, 213
    organization   214
Anti-Origenism   83, 135, 136, 187
Anti-Origenist monks   186
Antiochene   184, 189, 193, 208
    bishops   196

Antiochene *continued*
  Christology 193
  doctrinal structure 193
  school 205
Apocalyptic 96, 200
  Apocalypticism 5, 153
  Christian 6
  literature 153
  tradition 151, 152
Apocrypha 174
  Apocryphal 148
  books 173, 174
  manuscripts 176
  teachings 174
  works 173, 174
Apollinarianism 184, 195, 203
Apostles
  Twelve Apostles 200
Archimandrite 198, 199, 200, 201, 203, 204, 214
Arian
  Arianism 125, 130, 133–136, 138, 140, 181, 182
  Arians 105, 119–121, 123–125, 130, 132, 135, 137–142, 144–146, 171, 173, 174,180–183
  cause 134, 141
  church 181
  controversy 125, 133, 134, 137
  doctrine 121
  heresy 120, 136, 137
  point of view 135
Aristotelian school 94, 137
Athanasius
  Athanasian party 145
  Athanasian-Arian 145
  Golden Decade of 144
  Pro-Athanasian mob 181
  See also Proper Names
Babylonian Baptist 94
Basilidians 49, 50, 52, 55

Bishop
    Alexandria   190
    Constantinople   197
    Egyptian   207
    Ephesus   196
    Illyricum   207
Byzantium   208
Canon   175
Canonical   174, 176
Carpocratians   48–50, 52, 55, 60, 100
Catechetical School   23, 57, 58, 67, 70, 79, 102, 153, 175, 182
Catholic
    Catholicism   84, 121, 125, 130, 148, 151, 183, 197, 215
    Catholics   118, 120, 123–125, 150
    Christianity   143, 215
    church   84, 125, 130, 171, 180, 185, 204
    heterodoxy   180
    non-Catholic Christianity   172
    see   208
Cenobitic movement   213
Chalcedonians   213–215
    Pre-Chalcedonian theology   212
    Pro- and anti-Chalcedonian   209, 213, 214
Christology   136, 137, 184, 194, 203
    Cyril   195
    one nature   205
    Word-flesh Christology   196
    Word-man Christology   184
Coenobitic, or communal, monasticism   148
    monasteries   175
Constantinople   192, 215
Convent   198
Coptic   176, 215
    Egyptian Church   209
    Gnostic documents   173
    Gnostic library   176
    language   172
    letter   178
    Monophysites   207

Council   122–124, 134, 137, 141, 143, 184
    in Rome   143
    of   449 205
    of Antioch   134
    of Chalcedon   106, 171, 194, 208–210, 215
    of Ephesus in   431 196, 199, 204, 209, 214
    of Nicaea   120, 121, 123, 124, 130, 131
    of Sardica   144
    of Tyre   99, 128, 141, 143
    of Constantinople in   381 215
    Third General Council   197
    see also Synod
Creed   146
Cyril
    Christology   195
    Twelve anathemas of   212
Cyrillians   209
De-Hellenization   215
Deacons   182
Docetic theology   49
Donatists   99
Egyptian monastic movement   138
Ephesian
    church   196
    Council of   449 206, 208
Ephesus
    Latrocinium, or Robber council of   204, 209
    Robber Council in   449 205
    Synod of   205
Epicureans   66
Eusebian party   141
Eutychian   211
Gentiles   3
Gnosis   53, 59
    Christian Gnosticism   59, 60
    Christian Gnostics   64
    Gnostic   6, 23, 34, 48, 51, 54, 55, 56, 59, 60, 64, 66, 67, 84, 85, 96, 171, 198
    Gnosticism   23, 33, 50, 59, 60, 64, 66, 179

Gnosis *continued*
 Monadic 48
 Valentianian gnosticism 64, 203
Goths 182
Grand Chamberlain 203
Greeks 181, 198, 214
Home Synod 204, 207
Jews 181, 190
 expulsion in 415 190
 Jewish 191
 Judaism 190
Latin 214
Libellus 89
Manichaean 8, 95, 96, 171, 187
 Manichaeism 94, 95, 97
 Manichaica . . . are 96
 Manichees 95
Melchite 90
 (Imperial) church 212
 Melchites 207
Melitian
 bishops 122, 128
 brethren 128
 controversy 124
 groups 118
 hierarchy 122
 issue 133
 monasteries 122
 monastic community 126
 monasticism 129
 monks 125, 127, 128, 150
 movement 131
 problem 125, 130, 131, 136
 schism 99, 120–122, 125, 127, 133
 Melitianish 133
 Melitians 99, 117, 119–126, 128–130, 132, 135, 138, 140, 141,
  146, 171, 173
Monadism 48

Monastic   3, 64, 102–104, 122, 174, 177, 189, 197, 200, 209, 214
   celibacy   146
   communities   129, 197
   ideal   103, 149
   life   155
   monasteries   122, 129, 139, 175, 178, 198, 199, 209
   monastery   173, 177, 198, 200
   movement   120, 142, 148, 149, 150, 176, 182, 189, 197
   Monasticism   100–102, 105, 130, 146–149, 150–154, 171,
      173, 176, 177, 179, 180, 188, 209
   Monasticism, Antonian and Pachomian   150
   monk   81, 101, 102, 104, 105, 128, 129, 146, 147, 149–155,
      175, 178, 179, 186, 194, 198–202, 205, 210
   monks   2, 38, 64, 65, 83, 101–105, 117, 120, 125–127,
      138–140, 142, 144, 146, 147, 149–156, 167, 171–176,
      178–182, 186–191, 194, 196–205, 207–213, 215
   monks of Egypt   172
   rule   149, 153, 154
Monophysite   90, 129, 208, 210, 211, 213–215
Nag Hammadi Library   29, 64, 84, 176, 179, 180, 198
Neoplatonist   63
Nestorian   193, 194, 208
   theology   207
   Nestorianism   199, 202
   Nestorianizers   203
New Rome   202
Nicaea   131
   Nicaean Council   119
   Nicene   121, 122, 124, 145
   Nicene bishops   185
   Nicene canons   133
   Nicene Council   88, 121, 123, 124, 130, 131, 134
   Nicene Creed   143, 145, 146
   Nicene supporters   182
Novatian
   Novatianist bishop   190
   Novatianists   184
   Novatians   190

Origen
  Non-Origenist monks   120
  Origenism   83
  Origenist bishops   144
  Origenist controversy   186
  Origenist monks   120, 186–188, 190
  Origenistic   133, 134, 136, 137, 187
  Origenists   83, 101, 120, 135, 137, 142, 187
  Theology of   186
Pachomius
  Pachomian   156, 177, 179
  Pachomian monasteries   177, 178, 189
  Pachomian monasticism   179
  Pachomian monks   176, 179, 210, 213
  Pachomian rule   154, 155
  Pachomian system of monasteries   197
  rule of monastic life   149
  the rule   154, 155
Palestinian bishops   207
Patriarch
  of Alexandria   201, 212
  of Constantinople   206
Pelagian heretics   194
Persecution
  Decian   67, 68
  Diocletianic   126
Persians   192
Platonic   63, 137
Pleroma   52
Post-Nicene   122
Praetorian Prefects   188
Presbyters   136, 178, 182, 186
Ptolemaic dynasty   23
Roman Empire   94
Roman legates   204
Sabellian
  Sabellian schism   69
  Sabellianism   69
  Sabellians   69

Samaritans   3
St. Mark, See of   202
Sinaiticus   175
Stoicism   21
Synod   93, 189, 199
    of Antioch   93
    of Caesarea   126
    of Tyre   126
Syrian monks   204, 209
Tall Brothers   83
Theotokos   193, 195, 212
Therapeutae   20, 29
Valentinian   52, 53, 55, 64, 66, 95
    Valentinian gnosticism   64, 203
    Valentinianism   51, 55
    Valentinians   51–53, 60, 64, 83, 100

MAP 275

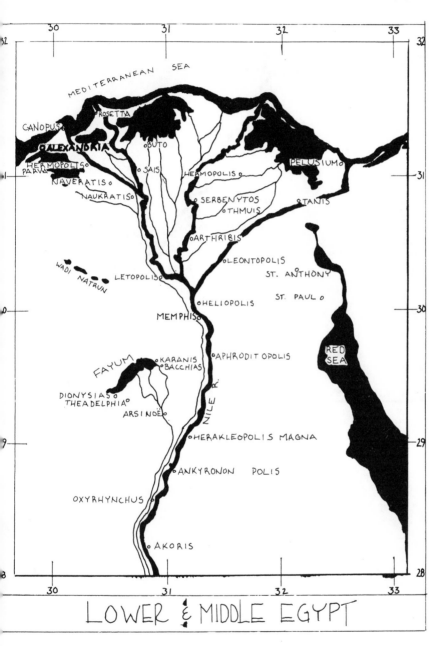

LOWER & MIDDLE EGYPT

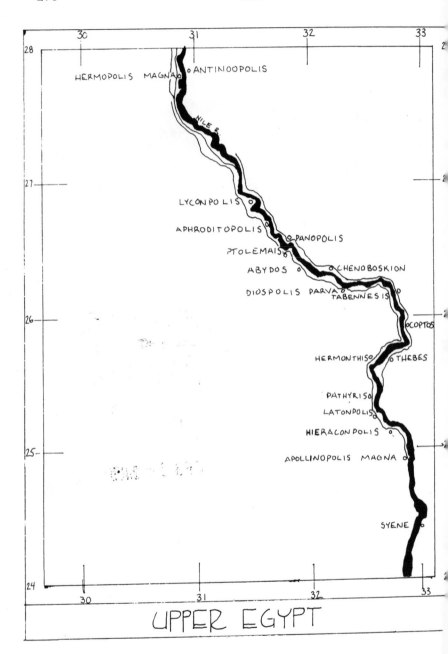

UPPER EGYPT